PHILLIP KELLER
THE INSPIRATIONAL WRITINGS

# PHILLIP KELLER

# THE
# INSPIRATIONAL
# WRITINGS

*Inspirational Press*
*New York*

Published in 1993 by

Inspirational Press
A division of Budget Book Service, Inc.
386 Park Avenue South
New York, NY 10016

Inspirational Press is a registered trademark of
Budget Book Service, Inc.
Published by arrangement with Word, Inc.

Library of Congress Catalog Card Number: 93-78585
ISBN: 0-88486-086-8

Designed by Hannah Lerner

Printed in the United States of America.

# CONTENTS

*A Shepherd
Looks at Psalm 23*
*1*

*A Layman
Looks at
the Lord's Prayer*
*123*

*A Shepherd
Looks at
the Good Shepherd
and His Sheep*
*263*

*A Gardener
Looks at
the Fruits
of the Spirit*
*421*

# A SHEPHERD

# LOOKS AT PSALM 23

*In tribute to "Chic"*
*who*
*during many years of adventure*
*was*
*my beloved mate and companion*

# Contents

Introduction     7

1   The Lord Is My Shepherd     10

2   I Shall Not Want     20

3   He Maketh Me to Lie Down in Green Pastures     28

4   He Leadeth Me Beside the Still Waters     40

5   He Restoreth My Soul     48

6   He Leadeth Me in the Paths of Righteousness
    for His Name's Sake     58

7   Yea, Though I Walk Through the Valley. . .     68

8   Thy Rod and Thy Staff They Comfort Me     78

9   Thou Preparest a Table Before Me. . .     88

10   Thou Anointest My Head With Oil. . .     98

11   Surely Goodness and Mercy Shall Follow Me. . .     110

12   I Will Dwell in the House of the Lord For Ever     118

# Introduction

TO A GREAT extent the Bible is a collection of books written by
men of humble origin, who penned under the guidance of God's
Spirit. Much of its terminology and teaching is couched in rural
language, dealing with outdoor subjects and natural phenomena.
The audience to whom these writings were originally addressed
were for the most part themselves simple, nomadic folk familiar
with nature and the outdoor life of the countryside about them.

Today this is not the case. Many who either read or study the
Scriptures in the twentieth century come from an urban, man-
made environment. City people, especially, are often unfamiliar
with such subjects as livestock, crops, land, fruit, or wildlife. They
miss much of the truth taught in God's Word because they are not
familiar with such things as sheep, wheat, soil or grapes.

Yet divine revelation is irrevocably bound up with the basic
subjects of the natural world. Our Lord Himself, when He was
amongst us, continually used natural phenomena to explain supernatural truth in His parables. It is a sound, indisputable method,
both scientifically and spiritually valid.

All this is understandable and meaningful when we recognize
the fact that God is author and originator of both the natural and
supernatural (spiritual). The same basic laws, principles and pro-
cedures function in these two contiguous realms. Therefore it follows that to understand one is to grasp the parallel principle in
the other.

It must be stated here that it is through this type of scriptural
interpretation that my own understanding of the Bible has become
meaningful. It explains in part, too, why truths which I shared with
various audiences have been long remembered by them with great
clarity.

Accordingly I make no apologies for presenting this collection
of "shepherd insights" into the well-known and loved—but often
misunderstood—23rd Psalm.

This book has been developed against a rather unique background which has perhaps given me a deeper appreciation than most men of what David had in mind when he wrote his beautiful poem. First of all I grew up and lived in East Africa, surrounded by simple native herders whose customs closely resembled those of their counterparts in the Middle East. So I am intimately acquainted with the romance, the pathos, the picturesque life of an Eastern shepherd. Secondly, as a young man, I actually made my own livelihood for about eight years as a sheep owner and sheep rancher. Consequently I write as one who has had firsthand experience with every phase of sheep management. Later, as the lay pastor of a community church, I shared the truths of this Psalm, as a shepherd, with my "flock," every Sunday for several months.

It is, therefore, out of the variety of these firsthand experiences with sheep that the following chapters have emerged. To my knowledge this is the first time that a down-to-earth, hard-handed sheep man has ever written at length about the Shepherd's Psalm.

There is one difficulty that arises when writing a book based on a familiar portion of the Scriptures. One disillusions or disenchants the reader with some of his former notions about the Psalm. Like much spiritual teaching the 23rd Psalm has had a certain amount of sentimental imagery wrapped around it with no sound basis in actual life. Some ideas advanced about it have, in fact, been almost ludicrous.

I would ask, then, that the reader approach the pages that follow with an open mind and an unbiased spirit. If he does, fresh truth and exciting glimpses of God's care and concern for him will flood over his being. Then he will be brought into a bold, new appreciation of the endless effort put forth by our Saviour, for His sheep. Out of this there will then emerge a growing admiration and affection for The Great Shepherd of his soul.

# 1
# The Lord
# Is My Shepherd

THE LORD! BUT who is the Lord? What is His character? Does He have adequate credentials to be my Shepherd—my manager—my owner?

And if He does—how do I come under His control? In what way do I become the object of His concern and diligent care?

These are penetrating, searching questions and they deserve honest and basic examination.

One of the calamities of Christianity is our tendency to talk in ambiguous generalities.

David, the author of the poem, himself a shepherd, and the son of a shepherd, later to be known as the "Shepherd King" of Israel, stated explicitly, "The Lord is my Shepherd." To whom did he refer?

He referred to Jehovah, the Lord God of Israel.

His statement was confirmed by Jesus the Christ.

When He was God incarnate amongst men, He declared emphatically, "I am the good Shepherd."

But who was this Christ?

Our view of Him is often too small—too cramped—too provincial—too human. And because it is we feel unwilling to allow Him to have authority or control—much less outright ownership of our lives.

He it was who was directly responsible for the creation of all things both natural and supernatural (see Colossians 1:15–20).

If we pause to reflect on the person of Christ—on His power and upon His achievements—suddenly like David we will be glad to state proudly, "The Lord—*He* is my Shepherd!"

But before we do this it helps to hold clearly in mind the particular part played upon our history by God the Father, God the Son, and God the Holy Spirit.

God the Father is God the author—the originator of all that exists. It was in His mind, first, that all took shape.

God the Son, our Saviour, is God the artisan—the artist, the Creator of all that exists. He brought into being all that had been originally formulated in His Father's mind.

God the Holy Spirit is God the agent who presents these facts to both my mind and my spiritual understanding so that they become both real and relative to me as an individual.

Now the beautiful relationships given to us repeatedly in Scripture between God and man are those of a father to his children and a shepherd to his sheep. These concepts were first conceived in the mind of God our Father. They were made possible and practical through the work of Christ. They are confirmed and made real in me through the agency of the gracious Holy Spirit.

So when the simple—though sublime—statement is made by a man or woman that "The Lord is my Shepherd," it immediately implies a profound yet practical working relationship between a human being and his Maker.

It links a lump of common clay to divine destiny—it means a mere mortal becomes the cherished object of divine diligence.

This thought alone should stir my spirit, quicken my own sense of awareness, and lend enormous dignity to myself as an individual. To think that God in Christ is deeply concerned about me as a particular person immediately gives great purpose and enormous meaning to my short sojourn upon this planet.

And the greater, the wider, the more majestic my concept is of the Christ—the more vital will be my relationship to Him. Obviously, David, in this Psalm, is speaking not as the shepherd, though he was one, but as a sheep; one of the flock. He spoke with a strong sense of pride and devotion and admiration. It was as though he literally boasted aloud, "Look at who my shepherd is— my owner—my manager!" The Lord is!

After all, he knew from firsthand experience that the lot in life of any particular sheep depended on the type of man who owned it. Some men were gentle, kind, intelligent, brave and selfless in their devotion to their stock. Under one man sheep would struggle, starve and suffer endless hardship. In another's care they would flourish and thrive contentedly.

So if the Lord is my Shepherd I should know something of His character and understand something of His ability.

To meditate on this I frequently go out at night to walk alone under the stars and remind myself of His majesty and might. Looking up at the star-studded sky I remember that at least 250,000,000 x 250,000,000 such bodies—each larger than our sun, one of the smallest of the stars, have been scattered across the vast spaces of the universe by His hand. I recall that the planet earth, which is my temporary home for a few short years, is so minute a speck of matter in space that if it were possible to transport our most powerful telescope to our nearest neighbor star, Alpha Centauri, and look back this way, the earth could not be seen, even with the aid of that powerful instrument.

All this is a bit humbling. It drains the "ego" from a man and puts things in proper perspective. It makes me see myself as a mere mite of material in an enormous universe. Yet the staggering fact remains that Christ the Creator of such an enormous universe of overwhelming magnitude, deigns to call Himself my Shepherd and invites me to consider myself His sheep—His special object of affection and attention. Who better could care for me?

By the same sort of process I stoop down and pick up a handful of soil from the backyard or roadside. Placing it under an electron microscope I am astounded to discover it teems with billions upon billions of micro-organisms. Many of them are so complex in their own peculiar cellular structure that even a fraction of their functions in the earth are not yet properly understood.

Yes, He the Christ—the Son of God brought all of this into being. From the most gigantic galaxy to the most minute microbe all function flawlessly in accordance with definite laws of order and unity which are utterly beyond the mind of finite man to master.

It is in this sense, first of all, that I am basically bound to admit that His ownership of me as a human being is legitimate—simply because it is He who brought me into being and no one is better able to understand or care for me.

I belong to Him simply because He deliberately chose to create me as the object of His own affection.

It is patently clear that most men and women refuse to acknowledge this fact. Their deliberate attempts to deny that such a relationship even exists or could exist between a man and his Maker demonstrate their abhorrence for admitting that anyone really can claim ownership or authority over them by virtue of bringing them into being.

This was of course the enormous "risk" or "calculated chance," if we may use the term, which God took in making man initially.

But in His usual magnanimous manner He took the second step in attempting to restore this relationship which is repeatedly breached by men who turn their backs upon Him.

Again in Christ He demonstrated at Calvary the deep desire of His heart to have men come under His benevolent care. He Himself absorbed the penalty for their perverseness, stating clearly that "all we like sheep have gone astray, we have turned every one to his own way, and the Lord hath laid on Him the iniquity of us all" (Isaiah 53:6).

Thus, in a second very real and vital sense I truly belong to Him simply because He has bought me again at the incredible price of His own laid-down life and shed blood.

Therefore He was entitled to say, "I am the Good Shepherd, the Good Shepherd giveth his life for the sheep."

So there remains the moving realization that we have been bought with a price, that we are really not our own and He is well within His rights to lay claim upon our lives.

I recall quite clearly how in my first venture with sheep, the question of paying a price for my ewes was so terribly important. They belonged to me only by virtue of the fact that I paid hard cash for them. It was money earned by the blood and sweat and tears drawn from my own body during the desperate grinding years of the depression. And when I bought that first small flock I was buying them literally with my own body which had been laid down with this day in mind.

Because of this I felt in a special way that they were in very truth a part of me and I a part of them. There was an intimate identity involved which though not apparent on the surface to the casual observer, nonetheless made those thirty ewes exceedingly precious to me.

But the day I bought them I also realized that this was but the first stage in a long, lasting endeavor in which from then on, I would, as their owner, have to continually lay down my life for them, if they were to flourish and prosper. Sheep do not "just take care of themselves" as some might suppose. They require, more than any other class of livestock, endless attention and meticulous care.

It is no accident that God has chosen to call us sheep. The behavior of sheep and human beings is similar in many ways as will be seen in further chapters. Our mass mind (or mob instincts), our fears and timidity, our stubbornness and stupidity, our perverse habits are all parallels of profound importance.

Yet despite these adverse characteristics Christ chooses us, buys us, calls us by name, makes us His own and delights in caring for us.

It is this last aspect which is really the third reason why we are under obligation to recognize His ownership of us. He literally lays Himself out for us continually. He is ever interceding for us; He is ever guiding us by His gracious Spirit; He is ever working on our behalf to ensure that we will benefit from His care.

In fact, Psalm 23 might well be called "David's Hymn of Praise to Divine Diligence." For the entire poem goes on to recount the manner in which the Good Shepherd spares no pains for the welfare of His sheep.

Little wonder that the poet took pride in belonging to the Good Shepherd. Why shouldn't he?

In memory I can still see one of the sheep ranches in our district which was operated by a tenant sheepman. He ought never to have been allowed to keep sheep. His stock were always thin, weak and riddled with disease or parasites. Again and again they would come and stand at the fence staring blankly through the woven wire at the green lush pastures which my flock enjoyed. Had they been able to speak I am sure they would have said, "Oh, to be set free from this awful owner!"

This is a picture which has never left my memory. It is a picture of pathetic people the world over who have not known what it is to belong to the Good Shepherd . . . who suffer instead under sin and Satan.

How amazing it is that individual men and women vehemently refuse and reject the claims of Christ on their lives. They fear that to acknowledge His ownership is to come under the rule of a tyrant.

This is difficult to comprehend when one pauses to consider the character of Christ. Admittedly there have been many false caricatures of this Person, but an unbiased look at His life quickly reveals an individual of enormous compassion and incredible integrity.

He was the most balanced and perhaps the most beloved being ever to enter the society of men. Though born amid most disgusting surroundings, the member of a modest working family, He bore Himself always with great dignity and assurance. Though He enjoyed no special advantages as a child, either in education or employment, His entire philosophy and outlook on life were the highest standards of human conduct ever set before mankind. Though He had no vast economic assets, political power or military might, no other person ever made such an enormous impact on the world's history. Because of Him millions of people across almost twenty centuries of time have come into a life of decency and honor and noble conduct.

Not only was He gentle and tender and true but also righteous, stern as steel, and terribly tough on phony people.

He was magnificent in His magnanimous spirit of forgiveness for fallen folk but a terror to those who indulged in double talk or false pretenses.

He came to set men free from their own sins, their own selves, their own fears. Those so liberated loved Him with fierce loyalty.

It is this One who insists that He was the Good Shepherd, the understanding Shepherd, the concerned Shepherd who cares enough to seek out and save and restore lost men and women.

He never hesitated to make it quite clear that when an individual once came under His management and control there would be a certain new and unique relationship between Him and them. There would be something very special about belonging to this particular Shepherd. There would be a distinct mark upon the man or woman that differentiated them from the rest of the crowd.

The day I bought my first thirty ewes, my neighbor and I sat on the dusty corral rails that enclosed the sheep pens and admired the choice, strong, well-bred ewes that had become mine. Turning to me he handed me a large, sharp, killing knife and remarked tersely, "Well, Phillip, they're yours. Now you'll have to put your mark on them."

I knew exactly what he meant. Each sheep-man has his own distinctive earmark which he cuts into one or other of the ears of his sheep. In this way, even at a distance, it is easy to determine to whom the sheep belongs.

It was not the most pleasant procedure to catch each ewe in turn and lay her ear on a wooden block then notch it deeply with the razor-sharp edge of the knife. There was pain for both of us. But from our mutual suffering an indelible lifelong mark of ownership was made that could never be erased. And from then on every sheep that came into my possession would bear my mark.

There is an exciting parallel to this in the Old Testament. When a slave in any Hebrew household chose, of his own freewill, to become a lifetime member of that home, he was subjected to a certain ritual. His master and owner would take him to his door, put his ear lobe against the door post and with an awl puncture a hole through the ear. From then on he was a man marked for life as belonging to that house.

For the man or woman who recognizes the claim of Christ and gives allegiance to His absolute ownership, there comes the question of bearing His mark. The mark of the cross is that which should identify us with Himself for all time. The question is—does it?

Jesus made it clear when He stated emphatically, "If any man would be my disciple [follower] let him deny himself and take up his cross daily and follow me."

Basically what it amounts to is this: A person exchanges the fickle fortunes of living life by sheer whimsy for the more productive and satisfying adventure of being guided by God.

It is a tragic truth that many people who really have never come under His direction or management claim that "The Lord is my Shepherd." They seem to hope that by merely admitting that He is their Shepherd somehow they will enjoy the benefits of His care and management without paying the price of forfeiting their own fickle and foolish way of life.

One cannot have it both ways. Either we belong or we don't. Jesus Himself warned us that there would come a day when many would say, "Lord, in Your name we did many wonderful things," but He will retort that He never knew us as His own.

It is a most serious and sobering thought which should make us search our own hearts and motives and personal relationship to Himself.

Do I really belong to Him?

Do I really recognize His right to me?

Do I respond to His authority and acknowledge His ownership?

Do I find freedom and complete fulfillment in this arrangement?

Do I sense a purpose and deep contentment because I am under His direction?

Do I know rest and repose, besides a definite sense of exciting adventure, in belonging to Him?

If so, then with genuine gratitude and exaltation I can exclaim proudly, just as David did, "The Lord is my Shepherd!" and I'm thrilled to belong to Him, for it is thus that I shall flourish and thrive no matter what life may bring to me.

# 2
# I Shall
# Not Want

WHAT A PROUD, positive, bold statement to make! Obviously, this is the sentiment of a sheep utterly satisfied with its owner, perfectly content with its lot in life.

Since the Lord is my Shepherd, then I shall not want. Actually the word "want" as used here, has a broader meaning than might at first be imagined. No doubt the main concept is that of not lacking—not deficient—in proper care, management or husbandry.

But a second emphasis is the idea of being utterly contented in the Good Shepherd's care and consequently not craving or desiring anything more.

This may seem a strange statement for a man like David to have made if we think in terms only of physical or material needs. After all he had been hounded and harried repeatedly by the forces of his enemy Saul as well as those of his own estranged son Absalom. He was obviously a man who had known intense privation: deep personal poverty, acute hardship, and anguish of spirit.

Therefore it is absurd to assert on the basis of this statement that the child of God, the sheep in the Shepherd's care, will never experience lack or need.

It is imperative to keep a balanced view of the Christian life. To do this it is well to consider the careers of men like Elijah, John the Baptist, our Lord Himself—and even modern men of faith such as Livingstone—to realize that all of them experienced great personal privation and adversity.

When He was among us, the Great Shepherd Himself warned His disciples before His departure for glory, that—"In this world ye *shall* have tribulation—but be of good cheer—I have overcome the world."

One of the fallacies that is common among Christians today is the assertion that if a man or woman is prospering materially it is a significant mark of the blessing of God upon their lives. This simply is not so.

Rather, in bold contrast we read in Revelation 3:17, "Because thou sayest, I am rich, and increased with goods, and have need of nothing; and knowest not that thou art wretched, and miserable, and poor, and blind, and naked . . ."

Or, in an equally pointed way, Jesus made clear to the rich young ruler who wished to become His follower. "One thing thou *lackest:* go thy way, sell whatsoever thou hast, and give to the poor . . . and come . . . follow me" (Mark 10:21).

Based on the teachings of the Bible we can only conclude that David was not referring to material or physical poverty when he made the statement, "I shall not want."

For this very reason the Christian has to take a long, hard look at life. He has to recognize that as with many of God's choice people before him, he may be called on to experience lack of wealth or material benefits. He has to see his sojourn upon the planet as a brief interlude during which there may well be some privation in a physical sense. Yet amid such hardship he can still boast, "*I shall not want . . . I shall not lack* the expert care and management of my Master."

To grasp the inner significance of this simple statement it is necessary to understand the difference between belonging to one master or another—to the Good Shepherd or to an imposter. Jesus Himself took great pains to point out to anyone who contemplated following Him that it was quite impossible to serve two masters. One belonged either to Him or to another.

When all is said and done the welfare of any flock is entirely dependent upon the management afforded them by their owner.

The tenant sheepman on the farm next to my first ranch was the most indifferent manager I had ever met. He was not concerned about the condition of his sheep. His land was neglected. He gave little or no time to his flock, letting them pretty well forage for themselves as best they could, both summer and winter. They fell prey to dogs, cougars and rustlers.

Every year these poor creatures were forced to gnaw away at bare brown fields and impoverished pastures. Every winter there was a shortage of nourishing hay and wholesome grain to feed the hungry ewes. Shelter to safeguard and protect the suffering sheep from storms and blizzards was scanty and inadequate.

They had only polluted, muddy water to drink. There had been a lack of salt and other trace minerals needed to offset their sickly pastures. In their thin, weak and diseased condition these poor sheep were a pathetic sight.

In my mind's eye I can still see them standing at the fence, huddled sadly in little knots, staring wistfully through the wires at the rich pastures on the other side.

To all their distress, the heartless, selfish owner seemed utterly callous and indifferent. He simply did not care. What if his sheep did *want* green grass; fresh water; shade; safety or shelter from the storms? What if they did *want* relief from wounds, bruises, disease and parasites?

He ignored their needs—he couldn't care less. Why should he— they were just sheep—fit only for the slaughterhouse.

I never looked at those poor sheep without an acute awareness that this was a precise picture of those wretched old taskmasters, Sin and Satan, on their derelict ranch—scoffing at the plight of those within their power.

As I have moved among men and women from all strata of society as both a lay pastor and as a scientist I have become increasingly aware of one thing. It is the boss—the manager—the Master in people's lives who makes the difference in their destiny.

I have known some of the wealthiest men on this continent intimately—also some of the leading scientists and professional people. Despite their dazzling outward show of success, despite their affluence and their prestige, they remained poor in spirit, shrivelled in soul, and unhappy in life. They were joyless people held in the iron grip and heartless ownership of the wrong master.

By way of contrast, I have numerous friends among relatively poor people—people who have known hardship, disaster and the struggle to stay afloat financially. But because they belong to Christ and have recognized Him as Lord and Master of their lives, their owner and manager, they are permeated by a deep, quiet, settled peace that is beautiful to behold.

It is indeed a delight to visit some of these humble homes where men and women are rich in spirit, generous in heart, and large of soul. They radiate a serene confidence and quiet joy that surmounts all the tragedies of their time.

They are under God's care and they know it. They have entrusted themselves to Christ's control and found contentment.

Contentment should be the hallmark of the man or woman who has put his or her affairs in the hands of God. This especially applies in our affluent age. But the outstanding paradox is the intense fever of discontent among people who are ever speaking of security.

Despite an unparalleled wealth in material assets we are outstandingly insecure and unsure of ourselves and well nigh bankrupt in spiritual values.

Always men are searching for safety beyond themselves. They are restless, unsettled, covetous, greedy for more—wanting this and that, yet never really satisfied in spirit.

By contrast the simple Christian, the humble person, the Shepherd's sheep can stand up proudly and boast.

"The Lord is my Shepherd—I shall not want."

I am completely satisfied with His management of my life. Why? Because He is the sheepman to whom no trouble is too great as He cares for His flock. He is the rancher who is outstanding because of His fondness for sheep—who loves them for their own sake as well as His personal pleasure in them. He will, if necessary, be on the job twenty-four hours a day to see that they are properly provided for in every detail. Above all, He is very jealous of His name and high reputation as "The Good Shepherd."

He is the owner who delights in His flock. For Him there is no greater reward, no deeper satisfaction, than that of seeing His sheep contented, well fed, safe and flourishing under His care. This is indeed His very "life." He gives all He has to it. He literally lays Himself out for those who are His.

He will go to no end of trouble and labor to supply them with the finest grazing, the richest pasturage, ample winter feed, and clean water. He will spare Himself no pains to provide shelter from storms, protection from ruthless enemies and the diseases and parasites to which sheep are so susceptible.

No wonder Jesus said, "I am the Good Shepherd—the Good Shepherd giveth his life for the sheep." And again "I am come that ye might have life and that ye might have it more abundantly."

From early dawn until late at night this utterly self-less Shepherd is alert to the welfare of His flock. For the diligent sheepman rises early and goes out first thing every morning without fail to look over his flock. It is the initial, intimate contact of the day. With a practiced, searching, sympathetic eye he examines the sheep to see that they are fit and content and able to be on their feet. In an instant he can tell if they have been molested during the night—whether any are ill or if there are some which require special attention.

Repeatedly throughout the day he casts his eye over the flock to make sure that all is well.

Nor even at night is he oblivious to their needs. He sleeps as it were "with one eye and both ears open" ready at the least sign of trouble to leap up and protect his own.

This is a sublime picture of the care given to those whose lives are under Christ's control. He knows all about their lives from morning to night.

"Blessed be the Lord, who daily loadeth us with benefits—even the God of our salvation."

"He that keepeth thee will not slumber or sleep."

In spite of having such a master and owner, the fact remains that some Christians are still not content with His control. They are somewhat dissatisfied, always feeling that somehow the grass beyond the fence must be a little greener. These are carnal Christians—one might almost call them "fence crawlers" or "half Christians" who want the best of both worlds.

I once owned an ewe whose conduct exactly typified this sort of person. She was one of the most attractive sheep that ever belonged to me. Her body was beautifully proportioned. She had a strong constitution and an excellent coat of wool. Her head was clean, alert, well-set with bright eyes. She bore sturdy lambs that matured rapidly.

But in spite of all these attractive attributes she had one pronounced fault. She was restless—discontented—a fence crawler.

So much so that I came to call her "Mrs. Gad-about."

This one ewe produced more problems for me than almost all the rest of the flock combined.

No matter what field or pasture the sheep were in, she would search all along the fences or shoreline (we lived by the sea) looking for a loophole she could crawl through and start to feed on the other side.

It was not that she lacked pasturage. My fields were my joy and delight. No sheep in the district had better grazing.

With "Mrs. Gad-about" it was an ingrained habit. She was simply never contented with things as they were. Often when she had forced her way through some such spot in a fence or found a way around the end of the wire at low tide on the beaches, she would end up feeding on bare, brown, burned-up pasturage of a most inferior sort.

But she never learned her lesson and continued to fence crawl time after time.

Now it would have been bad enough if she was the only one who did this. It was a sufficient problem to find her and bring her back. But the further point was that she taught her lambs the same tricks. They simply followed her example and soon were as skilled at escaping as their mother.

Even worse, however, was the example she set the other sheep. In a short time she began to lead others through the same holes and over the same dangerous paths down by the sea.

After putting up with her perverseness for a summer I finally came to the conclusion that to save the rest of the flock from becoming unsettled, she would have to go. I could not allow one obstinate, discontented ewe to ruin the whole ranch operation.

It was a difficult decision to make, for I loved her in the same way I loved the rest. Her strength and beauty and alertness were a delight to the eye.

But one morning I took the killing knife in hand and butchered her. Her career of fence crawling was cut short. It was the only solution to the dilemma.

She was a sheep, who in spite of all that I had done to give her the very best care—still wanted something else.

She was not like the one who said, "The Lord is my Shepherd— I shall not want."

It is a solemn warning to the carnal Christian—backslider—the half-Christian—the one who wants the best of both worlds.

Sometimes in short order they can be cut down.

# 3
# He Maketh Me
# to Lie Down
# in Green Pastures

THE STRANGE THING about sheep is that because of their very make-up it is almost impossible for them to be made to lie down unless four requirements are met.

Owing to their timidity they refuse to lie down unless they are free of all fear.

Because of the social behavior within a flock sheep will not lie down unless they are free from friction with others of their kind.

If tormented by flies or parasites, sheep will not lie down. Only when free of these pests can they relax.

Lastly, sheep will not lie down as long as they feel in need of finding food. They must be free from hunger.

It is significant that to be at rest there must be a definite sense of freedom from fear, tension, aggravations and hunger. The unique aspect of the picture is that it is only the sheepman himself who can provide release from these anxieties. It all depends upon the diligence of the owner whether or not his flock is free of disturbing influences.

When we examine each of these four factors that affect sheep so severely we will understand why the part the owner plays in their management is so tremendously important. It is actually he who makes it possible for them to lie down, to rest, to relax, to be content and quiet and flourishing.

A flock that is restless, discontented, always agitated and disturbed never does well.

And the same is true of people.

It is not generally known that sheep are so timid and easily panicked that even a stray jackrabbit suddenly bounding from behind a bush can stampede a whole flock. When one startled sheep runs in fright a dozen others will bolt with it in blind fear, not waiting to see what frightened them.

One day a friend came to call on us from the city. She had a tiny Pekingese pup along. As she opened the car door the pup jumped out on the grass. Just one glimpse of the unexpected little dog was enough. In sheer terror over 200 of my sheep which were resting nearby leaped up and rushed off across the pasture.

As long as there is even the slightest suspicion of danger from dogs, coyotes, cougars, bears or other enemies the sheep stand up ready to flee for their lives. They have little or no means of self-defense. They are helpless, timid, feeble creatures whose only recourse is to run.

When I invited friends to visit us, after the Pekingese episode, I always made it clear their dogs were to be left at home. I also had to drive off or shoot other stray dogs that came to molest or disturb the sheep. Two dogs have been known to kill as many as 292 sheep in a single night of unbridled slaughter.

Ewes, heavy in lamb, when chased by dogs or other predators will slip their unborn lambs and lose them in abortions. A shepherd's loss from such forays can be appalling. One morning at dawn I found nine of my choicest ewes, all soon to lamb, lying dead in the field where a cougar had harried the flock during the night.

It was a terrible shock to a young man like myself just new to the business and unfamiliar with such attacks. From then on I slept with a .303 rifle and flashlight by my bed. At the least sound of the flock being disturbed I would leap from bed and calling my faithful collie, dash out into the night, rifle in hand, ready to protect my sheep.

In the course of time I came to realize that nothing so quieted and reassured the sheep as to see me in the field. The presence of their master and owner and protector put them at ease as nothing else could do, and this applied day and night.

There was one summer when sheep rustling was a common occurrence in our district. Night after night the dog and I were out under the stars, keeping watch over the flock by night, ready to defend them from the raids of any rustlers. The news of my diligence spread along the grapevine of our back country roads and the rustlers quickly decided to leave us alone and try their tactics elsewhere.

"He maketh me to lie down."

In the Christian's life there is no substitute for the keen awareness that my Shepherd is nearby. There is nothing like Christ's presence to dispel the fear, the panic, the terror of the unknown.

We live a most uncertain life. Any hour can bring disaster, danger and distress from unknown quarters. Life is full of hazards. No one can tell what a day will produce in new trouble. We live either in a sense of anxiety, fear and foreboding, or in a sense of quiet rest. Which is it?

Generally it is the "unknown," the "unexpected," that produces the greatest panic. It is in the grip of fear that most of us are unable to cope with the cruel circumstances and harsh complexities of life. We feel they are foes which endanger our tranquility. Often our first impulse is simply to get up and run from them.

Then in the midst of our misfortunes there suddenly comes the awareness that He, the Christ, the Good Shepherd is there. It makes all the difference. His presence in the picture throws a different light on the whole scene. Suddenly things are not half so black nor nearly so terrifying. The outlook changes and there is hope. I find myself delivered from fear. Rest returns and I can relax.

This has come to me again and again as I grow older. It is the knowledge that my Master, my Friend, my Owner has things under control even when they may appear calamitous. This gives me great consolation, repose, and rest. "Now I lay me down in peace and sleep, for Thou God keepest me."

It is the special office work of God's gracious Spirit to convey this sense of the Christ to our fearful hearts. He comes quietly to reassure us that Christ Himself is aware of our dilemma and deeply involved in it with us.

And it is in fact in this assurance that we rest and relax.

"For God hath not given us the spirit of fear; but of power, and of love, and of a sound [disciplined] mind" (2 Timothy 1:7).

The idea of a sound mind is that of a mind at ease—at peace—not perturbed or harassed or obsessed with fear and foreboding for the future.

"I will both lay me down in peace and sleep: for thou, Lord, only makest me dwell in safety."

The second source of fear from which the sheepman delivers his sheep is that of tension, rivalry, and cruel competition within the flock itself.

In every animal society there is established an order of dominance or status within the group. In a penful of chickens it is referred to as the "pecking order." With cattle it is called the "horning order." Among sheep we speak of the "butting order."

Generally an arrogant, cunning and domineering old ewe will be boss of any bunch of sheep. She maintains her position of prestige by butting and driving other ewes or lambs away from the best grazing or favorite bedgrounds. Succeeding her in precise order the other sheep all establish and maintain their exact position in the flock by using the same tactics of butting and thrusting at those below and around them.

A vivid and accurate word picture of this process is given to us in Ezekiel 34:15–16 and 20–22. This is a startling example, in fact, of the scientific accuracy of the Scriptures in describing a natural phenomenon.

Because of this rivalry, tension, and competition for status and self-assertion, there is friction in a flock. The sheep cannot lie down and rest in contentment. Always they must stand up and defend their rights and contest the challenge of the intruder.

Hundreds and hundreds of times I have watched an austere old ewe walk up to a younger one which might have been feeding contentedly or resting quietly in some sheltered spot. She would arch her neck, tilt her head, dilate her eyes and approach the other with a stiff-legged gait. All of this was saying in unmistakable terms, "Move over! Out of my way! Give ground or else!" And if the other ewe did not immediately leap to her feet in self-defense she would be butted unmercifully. Or if she did rise to accept the challenge one or two strong thrusts would soon send her scurrying for safety.

This continuous conflict and jealousy within the flock can be a most detrimental thing. The sheep become edgy, tense, discontented and restless. They lose weight and become irritable.

But one point that always interested me very much was that whenever I came into view and my presence attracted their attention, the sheep quickly forgot their foolish rivalries and stopped their fighting. The shepherd's presence made all the difference in their behavior.

This, to me, has always been a graphic picture of the struggle for status in human society. There is the eternal competition "to keep up with the Joneses" or, as it is now—"to keep up with the Joneses' kids."

In any business firm, any office, any family, any community, any church, any human organization or group, be it large or small, the struggle for self-assertion and self-recognition goes on. Most of us fight to be "top sheep." We butt and quarrel and compete to "get ahead." And in the process people are hurt.

It is here that much jealousy arises. This is where petty peeves grow into horrible hate. It is where ill-will and contempt come into being, the place where heated rivalry and deep discontent is born. It is here that discontent gradually grows into a covetous way of life where one has to be forever "standing up" for himself, for his rights, "standing up" just to get ahead of the crowd.

In contrast to this, the picture in the Psalm shows us God's people lying down in quiet contentment.

One of the outstanding marks of a Christian should be a serene sense of gentle contentment.

"Godliness with contentment is great gain."

Paul put it this way, "I have learned in whatsoever state I am, therewith to be content," and certainly this applies to my status in society.

The endless unrest generated in the individual who is always trying to "get ahead" of the crowd, who is attempting always to be top man or woman on the totem pole, is pretty formidable to observe.

In His own unique way, Jesus Christ, the Great Shepherd, in His earthly life pointed out that the last would be first and the first last. In a sense I am sure He meant first in the area of His own intimate affection. For any shepherd has great compassion for the poor, weak sheep that get butted about by the more domineering ones.

More than once I have strongly trounced a belligerent ewe for abusing a weaker one. Or when they butted lambs not their own I found it necessary to discipline them severely, and certainly they were not first in my esteem for their aggressiveness.

Another point that impressed me, too, was that the less aggressive sheep were often far more contented, quiet and restful. So that there were definite advantages in being "bottom sheep."

But more important was the fact that it was the Shepherd's presence that put an end to all rivalry. And in our human relationships when we become acutely aware of being in the presence of Christ, our foolish, selfish snobbery and rivalry will end. It is the humble heart walking quietly and contentedly in the close and intimate companionship of Christ that is at rest, that can relax, simply glad to lie down and let the world go by.

When my eyes are on my Master they are not on those around me. This is the place of peace.

And it is good and proper to remind ourselves that in the end it is He who will decide and judge what my status really is. After all, it is His estimation of me that is of consequence. Any human measurement at best is bound to be pretty unpredictable, unreliable, and far from final.

To be thus, close to Him, conscious of His abiding Presence, made real in my mind, emotions and will by the indwelling gracious Spirit, is to be set free from fear of my fellow man and whatever he might think of me.

I would much rather have the affection of the Good Shepherd than occupy a place of prominence in society. . . especially if I had attained it by fighting, quarreling and bitter rivalry with my fellow human beings. "Blessed [happy, to be envied] are the merciful: for they shall obtain mercy" (Matthew 5:7).

As is the case with freedom from fear of predators or friction within the flock, the freedom of fear from the torment of parasites and insects is essential to the contentment of sheep. This aspect of their behavior will be dealt with in greater detail later in the Psalm. But it is nevertheless important to mention it here.

Sheep, especially in the summer, can be driven to absolute distraction by nasal flies, bot flies, warble flies and ticks. When tormented by these pests it is literally impossible for them to lie down and rest. Instead they are up and on their feet, stamping their legs, shaking their heads, ready to rush off into the bush for relief from the pests.

Only the diligent care of the owner who keeps a constant lookout for these insects will prevent them from annoying his flock. A good shepherd will apply various types of insect repellents to his sheep. He will see that they are dipped to clear their fleeces of ticks. And he will see that there are shelter belts of trees and bush available where they can find refuge and release from their tormentors.

This all entails considerable extra care. It takes time and labor and expensive chemicals to do the job thoroughly. It means, too, that the sheepman must be amongst his charges daily, keeping a close watch on their behavior. As soon as there is the least evidence that they are being disturbed he must take steps to provide them with relief. Always uppermost in his mind is the aim of keeping his flock quiet, contented and at peace.

Similarly in the Christian life there are bound to be many small irritations. There are the annoyances of petty frustrations and ever-recurring disagreeable experiences. In modern terminology we refer to these upsetting circumstances or people as "being bugged."

Is there an antidote for them?

Can one come to the place of quiet contentment despite them?

The answer, for the one in Christ's care, is definitely "Yes!"

This is one of the main functions of the gracious Holy Spirit. In Scripture He is often symbolized by oil—by that which brings healing and comfort and relief from the harsh and abrasive aspects of life.

The gracious Holy Spirit makes real in me the very presence of the Christ. He brings quietness, serenity, strength, and calmness in the face of frustrations and futility.

When I turn to Him and expose the problem to Him, allowing

Him to see that I have a dilemma, a difficulty, a disagreeable experience beyond my control, He comes to assist. Often a helpful approach is simply to say aloud, "O Master, this is beyond me—I can't cope with it—it's bugging me—I can't rest—please take over!"

Then it is He does take over in His own wondrous way. He applies the healing, soothing, effective antidote of His own person and presence to my particular problem. There immediately comes into my consciousness the awareness of His dealing with the difficulty in a way I had not anticipated. And because of the assurance that He has become active on my behalf, there steals over me a sense of quiet contentment. I am then able to lie down in peace and rest. All because of what He does.

Finally, to produce the conditions necessary for a sheep to lie down there must be freedom from the fear of hunger. This of course is clearly implied in the statement, "He maketh me to lie down in green pastures."

It is not generally recognized that many of the great sheep countries of the world are dry, semi-arid areas. Most breeds of sheep flourish best in this sort of terrain. They are susceptible to fewer hazards of health or parasites where the climate is dry. But in those same regions it is neither natural nor common to find green pastures. For example, Palestine where David wrote this Psalm and kept his father's flocks, especially near Bethlehem, is a dry, brown, sun-burned wasteland.

Green pastures did not just happen by chance. Green pastures were the product of tremendous labor, time, and skill in land use. Green pastures were the result of clearing rough, rocky land; of tearing out brush and roots and stumps; of deep plowing and careful soil preparation; of seeding and planting special grains and legumes; of irrigating with water and husbanding with care the crops of forage that would feed the flocks.

All of this represented tremendous toil and skill and time for the careful shepherd. If his sheep were to enjoy green pastures amid the brown, barren hills it meant he had a tremendous job to do.

But green pastures are essential to success with sheep. When lambs are maturing and the ewes need green, succulent feed for a heavy milk flow, there is no substitute for good pasturage. No sight so satisfies the sheep owner as to see his flock well and quietly fed to repletion on rich green forage, able to lie down to rest, ruminate and gain.

In my own ranching operations one of the keys to the entire enterprise lay in developing rich, lush pastures for my flock. On at least two ranches there were old, worn out, impoverished fields that were either bare or infested with inferior forage plants. By skillful management and scientific land use these were soon converted into flourishing fields knee deep in rich green grass and legumes. On such forage it was common to have lambs reach 100 pounds in weight within 100 days from birth.

The secret to this was that the flock could fill up quickly, then lie down quietly to rest and ruminate.

A hungry, ill-fed sheep is ever on its feet, on the move, searching for another scanty mouthful of forage to try and satisfy its gnawing hunger. Such sheep are not contented, they do not thrive, they are no use to themselves nor to their owners. They languish and lack vigor and vitality.

In the Scriptures the picture portrayed of the Promised Land, to which God tried so hard to lead Israel from Egypt, was that of a "land flowing with milk and honey." Not only is this figurative language but also essentially scientific terminology. In agricultural terms we speak of a "milk flow" and "honey flow." By this we mean the peak season of spring and summer when pastures are at their most productive stages. The livestock that feed on the forage and the bees that visit the blossoms are said to be producing a corresponding "flow" of milk or honey. So a land flowing with milk and honey is a land of rich, green, luxuriant pastures.

And when God spoke of such a land for Israel He also foresaw such an abundant life of joy and victory and contentment for His people.

For the child of God, the Old Testament account of Israel moving from Egypt into the Promised Land, is a picture of us moving from sin into the life of overcoming victory. We are promised such a life. It has been provided for us and is made possible by the unrelenting effort of Christ on our behalf.

How He works to clear the life of rocks of stoney unbelief. How He tries to tear out the roots of bitterness. He attempts to break up the hard, proud human heart that is set like sun-dried clay. He then sows the seed of His own precious Word, which, if given half a chance to grow will produce rich crops of contentment and peace. He waters this with the dews and rain of His own presence by the Holy Spirit. He tends and cares and cultivates the life, longing to see it become rich and green and productive.

It is all indicative of the unrelenting energy and industry of an owner who wishes to see his sheep satisfied and well fed. It all denotes my Shepherd's desire to see my best interests served. His concern for my care is beyond my comprehension, really. At best all I can do is to enjoy and revel in what He has brought into effect.

This life of quiet overcoming; of happy repose; of rest in His presence, of confidence in His management is something few Christians ever fully enjoy.

Because of our own perverseness we often prefer to feed on the barren ground of the world around us. I used to marvel how some of my sheep actually chose inferior forage at times.

But the Good Shepherd has supplied green pastures for those who care to move in onto them and there find peace and plenty.

# 4
# He Leadeth Me
# Beside the
# Still Waters

ALTHOUGH SHEEP THRIVE in dry, semi-arid country, they still require water. They are not like some of the African gazelles which can survive fairly well on the modest amount of moisture found in natural forage.

It will be noticed that here again the key or the clue to where water can be obtained lies with the shepherd. It is he who knows where the best drinking places are. In fact very often he is the one who with much effort and industry has provided the watering places. And it is to these spots that he leads the flock.

But before thinking about the water sources themselves, we do well to understand the role of water in the animal body and why it is so essential for its well-being. The body of an animal such as a sheep is composed of about 70 percent water on an average. This fluid is used to maintain normal body metabolism; it is a portion of every cell, contributing to its turgidity and normal life functions. Water determines the vitality, strength and vigor of the sheep and is essential to its health and general well-being.

If the supply of water for an animal drops off, bodily desiccation sets in. This dehydration of the tissues can result in serious damage to them. It can also mean that the animal becomes weak and impoverished.

Any animal is made aware of water lack by thirst. Thirst indicates the need of the body to have its water supply replenished from a source outside itself.

Now, just as the physical body has a capacity and need for water, so Scripture points out to us clearly that the human personality, the human soul has a capacity and need for the water of the Spirit of the eternal God.

When sheep are thirsty they become restless and set out in search of water to satisfy their thirst. If not led to the good water supplies of clean, pure water, they will often end up drinking from the polluted pot holes where they pick up such internal parasites as nematodes, liver flukes or other disease germs.

And in precisely the same manner Christ, our Good Shepherd, made it clear that thirsty souls of men and women can only be fully satisfied when their capacity and thirst for spiritual life is fully quenched by drawing on Himself.

In Matthew 5:6 He said, "Blessed are they which do hunger and thirst after righteousness: for they shall be filled [satisfied]."

At the great feast in Jerusalem He declared boldly, "If any man thirst, let him come unto me and drink."

"To drink" in spiritual terminology simply means "take in"—or "to accept"—or "to believe." That is to say it implies that a person accepts and assimilates the very life of God in Christ to the point where it becomes a part of him.

The difficulty in all of this is that men and women who are "thirsty" for God (who do have a deep inner sense of searching and seeking; who are in quest of that which will completely satisfy) often are unsure of where to look or really what they are looking for. Their inner spiritual capacity for God and divine life is desiccated and in their dilemma they will drink from any dirty pool to try and satisfy their thirst for fulfillment.

Saint Augustine of Africa summed it up so well when he wrote, "O God! Thou hast made us for Thyself and our souls are restless, searching, 'til they find their rest in Thee."

All the long and complex history of earth's religions, pagan worship and human philosophy is bound up with this insatiable thirst for God.

David, when he composed Psalm 23, knew this. Looking at life from the standpoint of a sheep he wrote, "He [the Good Shepherd] leadeth me beside the still waters." In other words, He alone knows where the still, quiet, deep, clean, pure water is to be found that alone can satisfy His sheep and keep them fit and strong.

Generally speaking, water for the sheep came from three main sources . . . dew on the grass . . . deep wells . . . or springs and streams.

Most people are not aware that sheep can go for months on end, especially if the weather is not too hot, without actually drinking, if there is heavy dew on the grass each morning. Sheep, by habit, rise just before dawn and start to feed. Or if there is bright moonlight they will graze at night. The early hours are when the vegetation is drenched with dew, and sheep can keep fit on the amount of water taken in with their forage when they graze just before and after dawn.

Of course, dew is a clear, clean, pure source of water. And there is no more resplendent picture of still waters than the silver droplets of the dew hanging heavy on leaves and grass at break of day.

The good shepherd, the diligent manager, makes sure that his sheep can be out and grazing on this dew drenched vegetation. If necessary it will mean he himself has to rise early to be out with his flock. On the home ranch or afield he will see to it that his sheep benefit from this early grazing.

In the Christian life it is of more than passing significance to observe that those who are often the most serene, most confident and able to cope with life's complexities are those who rise early each day to feed on God's Word. It is in the quiet, early hours of the morning that they are led beside the quiet, still waters where they imbibe the very life of Christ for the day. This is much more than mere figure of speech. It is practical reality. The biographies of the great men and women of God repeatedly point out how the secret of the success in their spiritual life was attributed to the "quiet time" of each morning. There, alone, still, waiting for the Master's voice one is led gently to the place where as the old hymn puts it, "The still dews of His Spirit can be dropped into my life and soul."

One comes away from these hours of meditation, reflection and communion with Christ refreshed in mind and spirit. The thirst is slaked and the heart is quietly satisfied.

In my mind's eye I can see my flock again. The gentleness, stillness and softness of early morning always found my sheep knee

deep in dew drenched grass. There they fed heavily and contentedly. As the sun rose and its heat burned the dewdrops from the
leaves, the flock would retire to find shade. There, fully satisfied
and happily refreshed, they would lie down to rest and ruminate
through the day. Nothing pleased me more.

I am confident this is precisely the same reaction in My Master's
heart and mind when I meet the day in the same way. He loves
to see me contented, quiet, at rest and relaxed. He delights to know
my soul and spirit have been refreshed and satisfied.

But the irony of life, and tragic truth for most Christians, is that
this is not so. It is often the case that they try, instead, to satisfy
their thirst by pursuing almost every other sort of substitute.

For their minds and intellects they will pursue knowledge, science, academic careers, vociferous reading or off-beat companions.
But somehow they are always left panting and dissatisfied.

Some of my friends have been among the most learned and
highly respected scientists and professors in the country. Yet, often,
about them there is a strange yearning, an unsatisfied thirst which
all their learning, all their knowledge, all their achievements have
not satisfied.

To appease the craving of their souls and emotions men and
women will turn to the arts, to culture, to music, to literary forms,
trying to find fulfillment. And again, so often, these are amongst
the most jaded and dejected of people.

Amongst my acquaintances are some outstanding authors and
artists. Yet it is significant that to many of them life is a mockery.
They have tried drinking deeply from the wells of the world only
to turn away unsatisfied—unquenched in their soul's thirst.

There are those who, to quench this thirst in their parched lives,
have attempted to find refreshment in all sorts of physical pursuits
and activities.

They try travel. Or they participate feverishly in sports. They
attempt adventures of all sorts, or indulge in social activities. They
take up hobbies or engage in community efforts. But when all is
said and everything has been done they find themselves facing the
same haunting, hollow, empty, unfilled thirst within.

The ancient prophet Jeremiah put it very bluntly when he

declared, "My people . . . they have forsaken me the fountain of living waters, and hewed them out cisterns, broken cisterns that can hold no water" (Jeremiah 2:13).

It is a compelling picture. It is an accurate portrayal of broken lives—of shattered hopes—of barren souls that are dried up and parched and full of the dust of despair.

Among young people, especially the "beat" generation, the recourse to drugs, to alcohol, to sexual adventure in a mad desire to assuage their thirst is classic proof that such sordid indulgences are no substitute for the Spirit of the living God. These poor people are broken cisterns. Their lives are a misery. I have yet to talk to a truly happy "hippie." Their faces show the desperation within.

And amid all this chaos of a confused, sick society, Christ comes quietly as of old, and invites us to come to Him. He invites us to follow Him. He invites us to put our confidence in Him. For He it is who best knows how we can be satisfied. He knows the human heart, the human personality, the human soul with its amazing capacity for God can never be satisfied with a substitute. Only the Spirit and life of Christ Himself will satisfy the thirsting soul.

Now, strange as it may appear on the surface, the deep wells of God from which we may drink are not always necessarily the delightful experiences we may imagine them to be.

I recall so clearly standing under the blazing equatorial sun of Africa and watching the native herds being led to their owner's water wells. Some of these were enormous, hand-hewn caverns cut from the sandstone formation along the sandy rivers. They were like great rooms chiselled out of the rocks with ramps running down to the water trough at the bottom. The herds and flocks were led down into these deep cisterns where cool, clear, clean water awaited them.

But down in the well, stripped naked, was the owner bailing water to satisfy the flock. It was hard, heavy, hot work. Perspiration poured off the body of the bailer whose skin glistened under the strain and heat of his labor.

As I stood there watching the animals quench their thirst at the still waters I was again immensely impressed by the fact that everything hinged and depended upon the diligence of the owner, the shepherd. Only through his energy, his efforts, his sweat, his strength could the sheep be satisfied.

In the Christian life exactly the same applies. Many of the places we may be led into will appear to us as dark, deep, dangerous and somewhat disagreeable. But it simply must be remembered that He is there with us in it. He is very much at work in the situation. It is His energy, effort and strength expended on my behalf that even in this deep, dark place is bound to produce a benefit for me.

It is there that I will discover He only can really satisfy me. It is He who makes sense and purpose and meaning come out of situations which otherwise would be but a mockery to me. Suddenly life starts to have significance. I discover I am the object of His special care and attention. Dignity and direction come into the events of my life and I see them sorting themselves out into a definite pattern of usefulness. All of this is refreshing, stimulating, invigorating. My thirst for reality in life is assuaged and I discover that I have found that satisfaction in my Master.

Of course there is always a percentage of perverse people who will refuse to allow God to lead them. They insist on running their own lives and following the dictates of their own wills. They insist they can be masters of their own destinies even if ultimately such destinies are destructive. They don't want to be directed by the Spirit of God—they don't want to be led by Him—they want to walk in their own ways and drink from any old source that they fancy might satisfy their whims.

They remind me very much of a bunch of sheep I watched one day which were being led down to a magnificent mountain stream. The snow-fed waters were flowing pure and clear and crystal clean between lovely banks of trees. But on the way several stubborn ewes and their lambs stopped, instead, to drink from small, dirty, muddy pools beside the trail. The water was filthy and polluted not only with the churned up mud from the passing sheep but even with the manure and urine of previous flocks that had passed that way. Still these stubborn sheep were quite sure it was the best drink obtainable.

The water itself was filthy and unfit for them. Much more, it was obviously contaminated with nematodes and liver fluke eggs that would eventually riddle them with internal parasites and disease of destructive impact.

People often try this pursuit or that with the casual comment, "So, what? I can't see that it's going to do any harm!" Little do they appreciate that often there is a delayed reaction and that considerable time may elapse before the full impact of their misjudgment strikes home. Then suddenly they are in deep trouble and wonder why.

To offset these dangers and guard against them God invites us to allow ourselves to be led and guided by His own gracious Spirit. Much of the emphasis and teaching of the Pauline Epistles in the New Testament is that the child of God should not end up in difficulty. Galatians 5 and Romans 8 bring this out very clearly.

Jesus' own teaching to His twelve disciples just before His death, given to us in John 14 through 17, points out that the gracious Holy Spirit was to be given to lead us into truth. He would come as a guide and counselor. Always He would lead us into the things of Christ. He would make us see that the life in Christ was the only truly satisfying life. We would discover the delight of having our souls satisfied with His presence. It would be He who would become to us very meat and drink—that as His resurrection, overcoming life was imparted to me by His Spirit each day I would be refreshed and satisfied.

# 5

# He Restoreth
# My Soul

IN STUDYING THIS Psalm it must always be remembered that it is a sheep in the Good Shepherd's care who is speaking. It is essentially a Christian's claim of belonging in the family of God. As such he boasts of the benefits of such a relationship.

This being the case, one might well ask, "Why then this statement . . . 'He restoreth my soul'?" Surely it would be assumed that anyone in the Good Shepherd's care could never become so distressed in soul as to need restoration.

But the fact remains that this does happen.

Even David, the author of the Psalm, who was much loved of God, knew what it was to be cast down and dejected. He had tasted defeat in his life and felt the frustration of having fallen under temptation. David was acquainted with the bitterness of feeling hopeless and without strength in himself.

In Psalm 42:11 he cries out, "Why art thou cast down, O my soul? And why art thou disquieted within me? Hope thou in God. . . ."

Now there is an exact parallel to this in caring for sheep. Only those intimately acquainted with sheep and their habits understand the significance of a "cast" sheep or a "cast down" sheep.

This is an old English shepherd's term for a sheep that has turned over on its back and cannot get up again by itself.

A "cast" sheep is a very pathetic sight. Lying on its back, its feet in the air, it flays away frantically struggling to stand up, without success. Sometimes it will bleat a little for help, but generally it lies there lashing about in frightened frustration.

If the owner does not arrive on the scene within a reasonably short time, the sheep will die. This is but another reason why it is so essential for a careful sheepman to look over his flock every day, counting them to see that all are able to be up and on their feet. If one or two are missing, often the first thought to flash into his mind is, *One of my sheep is cast somewhere. I must go in search and set it on its feet again.*

One particular ewe that I owned in a flock of Cheviots was notorious for being a cast sheep. Every spring when she became heavy in lamb it was not uncommon for her to become cast every second or third day. Only my diligence made it possible for her to survive from one season to the next. One year I had to be away from the ranch for a few days just when she was having her problems. So I called my young son aside and told him he would be responsible for her well-being while I was absent. If he managed to keep her on her feet until I came home he would be well paid for his efforts. Every evening after school he went out to the fields faithfully and set up the old ewe so she could survive. It was quite a task but she rewarded us with a fine pair of twin lambs that spring.

It is not only the shepherd who keeps a sharp eye for cast sheep, but also the predators. Buzzards, vultures, dogs, coyotes and cougars all know that a cast sheep is easy prey and death is not far off.

This knowledge that any "cast" sheep is helpless, close to death and vulnerable to attack, makes the whole problem of cast sheep serious for the manager.

Nothing seems to so arouse his constant care and diligent attention to the flock as the fact that even the largest, fattest, strongest and sometimes healthiest sheep can become cast and be a casualty. Actually it is often the fat sheep that are the most easily cast.

The way it happens is this. A heavy, fat, or long fleeced sheep will lie down comfortably in some little hollow or depression in the ground. It may roll on its side slightly to stretch out or relax. Suddenly the center of gravity in the body shifts so that it turns on its back far enough that the feet no longer touch the ground.

It may feel a sense of panic and start to paw frantically. Frequently this only makes things worse. It rolls over even further. Now it is quite impossible for it to regain its feet.

As it lies there struggling, gases begin to build up in the rumen. As these expand they tend to retard and cut off blood circulation to extremities of the body, especially the legs. If the weather is very hot and sunny a cast sheep can die in a few hours. If it is cool and cloudy and rainy it may survive in this position for several days.

If the cast sheep is an ewe with lambs, of course, it is a multiple loss to the owner. If the lambs are unborn they, too, perish with her. If they are young and suckling they become orphans. All of which adds to the seriousness of the situation.

So it will be seen why a sheepman's attention is always alert for this problem.

During my own years as a keeper of sheep, perhaps some of the most poignant memories are wrapped around the commingled anxiety of keeping a count of my flock and repeatedly saving and restoring cast sheep. It is not easy to convey on paper the sense of this ever present danger. Often I would go out early and merely cast my eye across the sky. If I saw the black-winged buzzards circling overhead in their long slow spirals anxiety would grip me. Leaving everything else I would immediately go out into the rough wild pastures and count the flock to make sure every one was well and fit and able to be on its feet.

This is part of the pageantry and drama depicted for us in the magnificent story of the ninety and nine sheep with one astray. There is the Shepherd's deep concern; his agonizing search; his longing to find the missing one; his delight in restoring it not only to its feet but also to the flock as well as to himself.

Again and again I would spend hours searching for a single sheep that was missing. Then more often than not I would see it at a distance, down on its back, lying helpless. At once I would start to run toward it—hurrying as fast as I could—for every minute was critical. Within me there was a mingled sense of fear and joy: fear it might be too late; joy that it was found at all.

As soon as I reached the cast ewe my very first impulse was to pick it up. Tenderly I would roll the sheep over on its side. This would relieve the pressure of gases in the rumen. If she had been down for long I would have to lift her onto her feet. Then straddling the sheep with my legs I would hold her erect, rubbing her limbs to restore the circulation to her legs. This often took quite a little time. When the sheep started to walk again she often just stumbled, staggered and collapsed in a heap once more.

All the time I worked on the cast sheep I would talk to it gently, "When are you going to learn to stand on your own feet?"—"I'm so glad I found you in time—you rascal!"

And so the conversation would go. Always couched in language that combined tenderness and rebuke, compassion and correction.

Little by little the sheep would regain its equilibrium. It would start to walk steadily and surely. By and by it would dash away to rejoin the others, set free from its fears and frustrations, given another chance to live a little longer.

All of this pageantry is conveyed to my heart and mind when I repeat the simple statement, "He restoreth my soul!"

There is something intensely personal, intensely tender, intensely endearing, yet intensely fraught with danger in the picture. On the one hand there is the sheep so helpless, so utterly immobilized though otherwise strong, healthy and flourishing; while on the other hand there is the attentive owner quick and ready to come to its rescue—ever patient and tender and helpful.

At this point it is important to point out that similarly in the Christian life there is an exciting and comforting parallel here.

Many people have the idea that when a child of God falls, when he is frustrated and helpless in a spiritual dilemma, God becomes disgusted, fed-up and even furious with him.

This simply is not so.

One of the great revelations of the heart of God given to us by Christ is that of Himself as our Shepherd. He has the same identical sensations of anxiety, concern and compassion for cast men and women as I had for cast sheep. This is precisely why He looked on people with such pathos and compassion. It explains His magnanimous dealing with down-and-out individuals for whom even human society had no use. It reveals why He wept over those who spurned His affection. It discloses the depth of His understanding of undone people to whom He came eagerly and quickly, ready to help, to save, to restore.

When I read the life story of Jesus Christ and examine carefully His conduct in coping with human need, I see Him again and again as the Good Shepherd picking up "cast" sheep. The tenderness, the love, the patience that He used to restore Peter's soul after the terrible tragedy of his temptations is a classic picture of the Christ coming to restore one of His own.

And so He comes quietly, gently, reassuringly to me no matter when or where or how I may be cast down.

In Psalm 56:13 we are given an accurate commentary on this aspect of the Christian's life in these words, ". . . thou has delivered my soul from death: wilt not thou deliver my feet from falling, that I may walk before God in the light of the living."

We have to be realistic about the life of the child of God and face facts as they really are. Most of us, though we belong to Christ and desire to be under His control and endeavor to allow ourselves to be led by Him, do on occasion find ourselves cast down.

We discover that often when we are most sure of ourselves we stumble and fall. Sometimes when we appear to be flourishing in our faith we find ourselves in a situation of utter frustration and futility.

Paul in writing to the Christians at Corinth warned them of this danger. "Wherefore let him that thinketh he standeth take heed lest he fall" (I Corinthians 10:12).

Admittedly this may appear as one of the paradoxes and enigmas of our spiritual lives. When we examine it carefully, however, we will not find it too difficult to understand.

As with sheep, so with Christians, some basic principles and parallels apply which will help us to grasp the way in which a man or woman can be "cast."

There is, first of all, the idea of looking for a soft spot. The sheep that choose the comfortable, soft, rounded hollows in the ground in which to lie down very often become cast. In such a situation it is so easy to roll over on their backs.

In the Christian life there is great danger in always looking for the easy place, the cozy corner, the comfortable position where there is no hardship, no need for endurance, no demand upon self-discipline.

The time when we think "we have it made," so to speak, is actually when we are in mortal danger. There is such a thing as the discipline of poverty and privation which can be self-imposed to do us worlds of good. Jesus suggested this to the rich young man who mistakenly assumed he was in a safe position when in truth he was on the verge of being cast down.

Sometimes if, through self-indulgence, I am unwilling to forfeit or forego the soft life, the easy way, the cozy corner, then the Good Shepherd may well move me to a pasture where things aren't quite so comfortable—not only for my own good but also His benefit as well.

There is the aspect, too, of a sheep simply having too much wool. Often when the fleece becomes very long, and heavily matted with mud, manure, burrs and other debris, it is much easier for a sheep to become cast, literally weighed down with its own wool.

Wool in Scripture depicts the old self-life in the Christian. It is the outward expression of an inner attitude, the assertion of my own desire and hopes and aspirations. It is the area of my life in which and through which I am continually in contact with the world around me. Here is where I find the clinging accumulation of things, of possessions, of worldly ideas beginning to weigh me down, drag me down, hold me down.

It is significant that no high priest was ever allowed to wear wool when he entered the Holy of Holies. This spoke of self, of pride, of personal preference—and God could not tolerate it.

If I wish to go on walking with God and not be forever cast down, this is an aspect of my life which He must deal with drastically.

Whenever I found that a sheep was being cast because it had too long and heavy a fleece, I soon took swift steps to remedy the situation. In short order I would shear it clean and so forestall the danger of having the ewe lose her life. This was not always a pleasant process. Sheep do not really enjoy being sheared and it represents some hard work for the shepherd, but it must be done.

Actually when it is all over both sheep and owner are relieved. There is no longer the threat of being cast down, while for the sheep there is the pleasure of being set free from a hot, heavy coat. Often the fleece is clogged with filthy manure, mud, burrs, sticks and ticks. What a relief to be rid of it all!

And similarly in dealing with our old self-life, there will come a day when the Master must take us in hand and apply the keen cutting edge of His Word to our lives. It may be an unpleasant business for a time. No doubt we'll struggle and kick about it. We may get a few cuts and wounds. But what a relief when it is all over. Oh, the pleasure of being set free from ourselves! What a restoration!

The third chief cause of cast sheep is simply that they are too fat. It is a well-known fact that over-fat sheep are neither the most healthy nor the most productive. And certainly it is the fattest that most often are cast. Their weight simply makes it that much harder for them to be agile and nimble on their feet.

Of course once a sheepman even suspects that his sheep are becoming cast for this reason he will take long-range steps to correct the problem. He will put the ewes on a more rigorous ration; they will get less grain and the general condition of the flock will be watched very closely. It is his aim to see that the sheep are strong, sturdy and energetic, not fat, flabby and weak.

Turning to the Christian life we are confronted with the same sort of problem. There is the man or woman, who because they may have done well in business or their careers or their homes, feel that they are flourishing and have "arrived." They may have a sense of well-being and self-assurance which in itself is dangerous. Often when we are most sure of ourselves we are the most prone to fall flat.

In His warning to the church in Revelation 3:17 God points out that though some considered themselves rich and affluent, they were actually in desperate danger. The same point was made by Jesus in His account of the wealthy farmer who intended to build more and bigger barns, but who, in fact, faced utter ruin.

Material success is no measure of spiritual health. Nor is apparent affluence any criteria of real godliness. And it is well for us that the Shepherd of our souls sees through this exterior and takes steps to set things right.

He may well impose on us some sort of "diet" or "discipline" which we may find a bit rough and unpalatable at first. But again we need to reassure ourselves that it is for our own good, because He is fond of us, and for His own reputation as the Good Shepherd.

In Hebrews 12 we read how God chooses to discipline those He loves. At the time it may prove a tough routine. But the deeper truth is that afterward it produces a life of repose and tranquility free from the fret and frustration of being cast down like a helpless sheep.

The toughness it takes to face life and the formidable reverses which it brings to us can come only through the discipline of endurance and hardship. In His mercy and love our Master makes this a part of our program. It is part of the price of belonging to Him.

We may rest assured that He will never expect us or ask us to face more than we can stand (I Corinthians 10:13). But what He does expose us to will strengthen and fortify our faith and confidence in His control. If He is the Good Shepherd we can rest assured that He knows what He is doing. This in and of itself should be sufficient to continually refresh and restore my soul. I know of nothing which so quiets and enlivens my own spiritual life as the knowledge that—"God knows what He is doing with me!"

6
# He Leadeth Me
# in the Paths of
# Righteousness
# for His Name's Sake

SHEEP ARE NOTORIOUS creatures of habit. If left to themselves they will follow the same trails until they become ruts; graze the same hills until they turn to desert wastes; pollute their own ground until it is corrupt with disease and parasites. Many of the world's finest sheep ranges have been ruined beyond repair by over-grazing, poor management and indifferent or ignorant sheep owners.

One need only travel through countries like Spain, Greece, Mesopotamia, North Africa and even parts of the western United States and New Zealand or Australia to see the havoc wrought by sheep on the land. Some areas in these countries which were formerly productive grasslands have gradually been reduced to ravaged wastelands. Too many sheep over too many years under poor management have brought nothing but poverty and disaster in their wake.

A commonly held, but serious misconception about sheep is that they can just "get along anywhere." The truth is quite the reverse. No other class of livestock requires more careful handling, more detailed direction, than do sheep. No doubt David, as a shepherd himself, had learned this firsthand from tough experience. He knew beyond dispute that if the flock was to flourish and the owner's reputation was to be held in high esteem as a good manager, the sheep had to be constantly under his meticulous control and guidance.

The first sheep farm I purchased as a young man was a piece of derelict land that had been "sheeped to death." An absentee owner had rented the place to a tenant. The latter simply loaded the ranch with sheep, then left them pretty much to their own ways. The result was utter desolation. Fields became so overgrazed and impoverished they would grow little but poverty grass. Little sheep trails had deteriorated into great gullies. Erosion on the slopes was rampant and the whole place was ravaged almost beyond repair.

All of this happened simply because the sheep, instead of being managed and handled with intelligent care, had been left to struggle for themselves—left to go their own way, left to the whims of their own destructive habits.

The consequence of such indifference is that the sheep gnaw the grass to the very ground until even the roots are damaged. I have seen places in Africa where grass roots were pawed out of the soil, leaving utter barrenness behind. Such abuse means loss of fertility and the exposure of the land to all the ravages of erosion.

Because of the behavior of sheep and their preference for certain favored spots, these well-worn areas become quickly infested with parasites of all kinds. In a short time a whole flock can thus become infected with worms, nematodes, and scab. The final upshot is that both land and owner are ruined while the sheep become thin, wasted, and sickly.

The intelligent shepherd is aware of all this. Not only just for the welfare of his sheep and the health of his land, but also for his own sake and reputation as a rancher, he must take the necessary precautions to safeguard against these adverse animal traits. Such habits, in themselves, comprise very serious hazards.

The greatest single safeguard which a shepherd has in handling his flock is to keep them on the move. That is to say, they dare not be left on the same ground too long. They must be shifted from pasture to pasture periodically. This prevents over-grazing of the forage. It also avoids the rutting of trails and erosion of land from over-use. It forestalls the reinfestation of the sheep with internal parasites or disease, since the sheep move off the infested ground before these organisms complete their life cycles.

In a word—there must be a pre-determined plan of action, a deliberate, planned rotation from one grazing ground to another in line with right and proper principles of sound management. This is precisely the sort of action and the idea David had in mind when he spoke of being led in paths of righteousness.

In this following of a precise plan of operation lies the secret for healthy flocks and healthy land. Here is the key to successful sheep husbandry. The owner's entire name and reputation depends on how effectively and efficiently he keeps his charges moving onto wholesome, new, fresh forage. The one who directs his flock along this course is sure of success.

Casting my mind's eye back over the years that I kept sheep, no other single aspect of the ranch operations commanded more of my careful attention than this moving of the sheep. It literally dominated all my decisions. Not a day went by but what I would walk over the pasture in which the sheep were feeding to observe the balance between its growth and the grazing pressure upon it. As soon as the point was reached where I felt the maximum benefit for both sheep and land was not being met, the sheep were moved to a fresh field. On the average this meant they were put onto new ground almost every week. In very large measure the success I enjoyed in sheep ranching must be attributed to this care in managing my flock.

A similar procedure applies to flocks of sheep taken out on summer range in the hills by itinerant herders. They deliberately lead or drive their sheep onto fresh range almost every day. A pattern of grazing is worked out carefully in advance so that the sheep do not feed over the same ground too long or too frequently. Some shepherds set up a base camp and fan out from it in wide circles, like the lobes of a clover leaf, covering new pasturage each day, returning to camp at night.

Coupled with this entire concept of management, there is of course the owner's intimate knowledge of his pastures. He has been all over this ground again and again. He knows its every advantage and every drawback. He knows where his flock will thrive and he is aware of where the feed is poor. So he acts accordingly.

A point worthy of mention here is that whenever the shepherd opens a gate into a fresh pasture the sheep are filled with excitement. As they go through the gate even the staid old ewes will often kick up their heels and leap with delight at the prospect of finding fresh feed. How they enjoy being led onto new ground.

Now as we turn to the human aspect of this theme we will be astonished at some of the parallels. As mentioned earlier it is no mere whim on God's part to call us sheep. Our behavior patterns and life habits are so much like that of sheep it is well nigh embarrassing.

First of all Scripture points out that most of us are a stiff-necked and stubborn lot. We prefer to follow our own fancies and turn to our own ways. "All we like sheep have gone astray; we have turned every one to his own way" (Isaiah 53:6). And this we do deliberately, repeatedly even to our own disadvantage. There is something almost terrifying about the destructive self-determination of a human being. It is inexorably interlocked with personal pride and self-assertion. We insist we know what is best for us even though the disastrous results may be self-evident.

Just as sheep will blindly, habitually, stupidly follow one another along the same little trails until they become ruts that erode into gigantic gullies, so we humans cling to the same habits that we have seen ruin other lives. Turning to "my own way" simply means doing what I want. It implies that I feel free to assert my own wishes and carry out my own ideas. And this I do in spite of every warning.

We read in Proverbs 14:12 and 16:25, "There is a way which seemeth right unto a man, *but* the end thereof are the ways of death."

In contrast to which Christ the Good Shepherd comes gently and says, "I am the way, the truth, and the life: no man cometh unto the Father, but by me" (John 14:6). "I am come that they might have life, and that they might have it more abundantly" (John 10:10).

The difficult point is that most of us don't want to come. We don't want to follow. We don't want to be led in the paths of righteousness. Somehow it goes against our grain. We actually prefer to turn to our own way even though it may take us straight into trouble.

The stubborn, self-willed, proud, self-sufficient sheep that per-

sists in pursuing its old paths and grazing on its old polluted ground
will end up a bag of bones on ruined land. The world we live in
is full of such folk. Broken homes, broken hearts, derelict lives and
twisted personalities remind us everywhere of men and women
who have gone their own way. We have a sick society struggling
to survive on beleaguered land. The greed and selfishness of mankind leaves behind a legacy of ruin and remorse.

Amid all this chaos and confusion Christ the Good Shepherd
comes and says, If any man will follow me, let him deny himself
daily and take up his cross and follow me (Mark 8:34). But most
of us, even as Christians, simply don't want to do this. We don't
want to deny ourselves, give up our right to make our own decisions—we don't want to follow; we don't want to be led.

Of course, most of us, if confronted with this charge, would deny
it. We would assert vehemently that we are "led of the Lord." We
would insist that we would follow wherever He leads. We sing
songs to this effect and give mental assent to the idea. But as far
as actually being led in paths of righteousness is concerned, precious few of us follow that path.

Actually this is the pivot point on which a Christian either "goes
on" with God or at which point he "goes back" from following on.

There are many willful, wayward, indifferent, self-interested
Christians who cannot really be classified as followers of Christ.
There are relatively few diligent disciples who forsake all to fol-
low the Master.

Jesus never made light of the cost involved in following Him.
In fact He made it painfully clear that it was a rugged life of rigid
self-denial. It entailed a whole new set of attitudes. It was not the
natural, normal way a person would ordinarily live and this is
what made the price so prohibitive to most people.

In brief, seven fresh attitudes have to be acquired. They are the
equivalent of progressive forward movements onto new ground
with God. If one follows them they will discover fresh pasturage;
new, abundant life; and increased health, wholesomeness and
holiness, in their walk with God. Nothing will please Him more
and most certainly no other activity on our part will or can result
in as great benefit to other lives around us.

1. Instead of loving myself most I am willing to love Christ best and others more than myself.

Now love in a scriptural sense is not a soft, sentimental emotion. It is a deliberate act of my will. It means that I am willing to lay down my life, lay myself out, put myself out on behalf of another. This is precisely what God did for us in Christ. "Hereby perceive [understand] we the love of God, because he laid down his life for us" (I John 3:16).

The moment I deliberately do something definite either for God or others that costs me something, I am expressing love. Love is "self-lessness" or "self-sacrifice" in contradistinction to "selfishness." Most of us know little of living like this or being "led" in this right way. But once a person discovers the delight of doing something for others, he has started through the gate being led into one of God's green pastures.

2. Instead of being one of the crowd I am willing to be singled out, set apart from the gang.

Most of us, like sheep, are pretty gregarious. We want to belong. We don't want to be different in a deep, distinctive way, though we may wish to be different in minor details that appeal to our selfish egos.

But Christ pointed out that only a few would find His way acceptable. And to be marked as one of His would mean a certain amount of criticism and sarcasm from a cynical society. Many of us don't want this. Just as He was a man of sorrows and acquainted with grief, so we may be. Instead of adding to the sorrows and sadness of society we may be called on to help bear some of the burdens of others, to enter into the suffering of others. Are we ready to do this?

3. Instead of insisting on my rights I am willing to forego them in favor of others.

Basically this is what the Master meant by denying one's self. It is not easy, nor normal, nor natural to do this. Even in the loving atmosphere of the home, self-assertion is pretty evident and the powerful exercise of individual rights is always apparent.

But the person who is willing to pocket his pride, to take a back seat, to play second fiddle without a feeling of being abused or put upon has gone a long way onto new ground with God.

There is a tremendous emancipation from "self" in this attitude. One is set free from the shackles of personal pride. It's pretty hard to hurt such a person. He who has no sense of self-importance cannot be offended or deflated. Somehow such people enjoy a wholesome outlook of carefree abandon that makes their Christian lives contagious with contentment and gaiety.

4. Instead of being "boss" I am willing to be at the bottom of the heap. Or to use sheep terminology, instead of being "Top Ram" I'm willing to be a "tailender."

When the desire for self-assertion, self-aggrandizement, self-pleasing gives way to the desire for simply pleasing God and others, much of the fret and strain is drained away from daily living.

A hallmark of the serene soul is the absence of "drive," at least, "drive" for self-determination. The person who is prepared to put his personal life and personal affairs in the Master's hands for His management and direction has found the place of rest in fresh fields each day. These are the ones who find time and energy to please others.

5. Instead of finding fault with life and always asking "Why?" I am willing to accept every circumstance of life in an attitude of gratitude.

Human beings, being what they are, somehow feel entitled to question the reasons for everything that happens to them. In many instances life itself becomes a continuous criticism and dissection of one's circumstances and acquaintances. We look for someone or something on which to pin the blame for our misfortunes. We are often quick to forget our blessings, slow to forget our misfortunes.

But if one really believes his affairs are in God's hands, every event, no matter whether joyous or tragic, will be taken as part of God's plan. To know beyond doubt that He does all for our welfare is to be led into a wide area of peace and quietness and strength for every situation.

6. Instead of exercising and asserting my will, I learn to cooperate with His wishes and comply with His will.

It must be noted that all the steps outlined here involve the will. The saints from earliest times have repeatedly pointed out that nine-tenths of religion, of Christianity, of becoming a true follower, a dedicated disciple, lies in the will.

When a man or woman allows his will to be crossed out, canceling the great I in their decisions, then indeed the Cross has been applied to that life. This is the meaning of taking up one's cross daily—to go to one's own death—no longer my will in the matter but His will be done.

7. Instead of choosing my own way I am willing to choose to follow in Christ's way: simply to do what He asks me to do.

This basically is simple, straightforward obedience. It means I just do what He asks me to do. I go where He invites me to go. I say what He instructs me to say. I act and re-act in the manner He maintains is in my own best interest as well as for His reputation (if I'm His follower).

Most of us possess a formidable amount of factual information on what the Master expects of us. Precious few have either the will, intention or determination to act on it and comply with His instructions. But the person who decides to do what God asks him has moved onto fresh ground which will do both him and others a world of good. Besides, it will please the Good Shepherd no end.

God wants us all to move on with Him. He wants us to walk with Him. He wants it not only for our welfare but for the benefit of others as well as His own dear reputation.

Perhaps there are those who think He expects too much of us. Maybe they feel the demands are too drastic. Some may even consider His call impossible to carry out.

It would be if we had to depend on self-determination, or self-discipline to succeed. But if we are in earnest about wanting to do His will, and to be led, *He makes this possible* by His own gracious Spirit who is given to those who *obey* (Acts 5:32). For it is He who works in us *both* to *will* and *to do* of His good pleasure (Philippians 2:13).

# 7
# Yea,
# Though I Walk
# Through the Valley . . .

FROM A SHEPHERD'S point of view this statement marks the halfway stage in the Psalm. It is as though up to this point the sheep has been boasting to its unfortunate neighbor across the fence about the excellent care it received from its owner on the "home" ranch throughout the winter and spring.

Now it turns to address the shepherd directly. The personal pronouns *I* and *Thou* enter the conversation. It becomes a most intimate discourse of deep affection.

This is natural and normal. The long treks into the high country with their summer range begin here. Left behind are the neglected sheep on the other side of the fence. Their owner knows nothing of the hill country—the mountain meadows to which these sheep will be led. Their summer will be spent in the close companionship and solitary care of the good shepherd.

Both in Palestine and on our western sheep ranches, this division of the year is common practice. Most of the efficient sheepmen endeavor to take their flocks onto distant summer ranges during summer. This often entails long "drives." The sheep move along slowly, feeding as they go, gradually working their way up the mountains behind the receding snow. By late summer they are well up on the remote alpine meadows above timberline.

With the approach of autumn, early snow settles on the highest ridges, relentlessly forcing the flock to withdraw back down to lower elevations. Finally, toward the end of the year as fall passes, the sheep are driven home to the ranch headquarters where they will spend the winter. It is this segment of the yearly operations that is described in the last half of the poem.

During this time the flock is entirely alone with the shepherd. They are in intimate contact with him and under his most personal attention day and night. That is why these last verses are couched in such intimate first-person language. And it is well to remember that all of this is done against a dramatic background of wild mountains, rushing rivers, alpine meadows and high rangelands.

David, the psalmist, of course knew this type of terrain first hand. When Samuel was sent of God to anoint him king over Israel, he was not at home with his brothers on the "home" ranch. Instead he was high up on the hills tending his father's flock. They had to send for him to come home. It is no wonder he could write so clearly and concisely of the relationship between a sheep and its owner.

He knew from firsthand experience about all the difficulties and dangers, as well as the delights, of the treks into high country. Again and again he had gone up into the summer range with his sheep. He knew this wild but wonderful country like the palm of his own strong hand. Never did he take his flock where he had not already been before. Always he had gone ahead to look over the country with care.

All the dangers of rampaging rivers in flood; avalanches; rock slides; poisonous plants; the ravages of predators that raid the flock or the awesome storms of sleet and hail and snow were familiar to him. He had handled his sheep and managed them with care under all these adverse conditions. Nothing took him by surprise. He was fully prepared to safeguard his flock and tend them with skill under every circumstance.

All of this is brought out in the beautiful simplicity of the last verses. Here is a grandeur, a quietness, an assurance that sets the soul at rest. "I will not fear, for thou art with me . . ."—with me in every situation, in every dark trial, in every dismal disappointment, in every distressing dilemma.

In the Christian life we often speak of wanting "to move onto higher ground with God." How we long to live above the lowlands of life. We want to get beyond the common crowd, to enter a more intimate walk with God. We speak of mountaintop experiences and we envy those who have ascended the heights and entered into this more sublime sort of life.

Often we get an erroneous idea about how this takes place. It is as though we imagined we could be "air lifted" onto higher ground. On the rough trail of the Christian life this is not so. As with ordinary sheep management, so with God's people, one only gains higher ground by climbing up through the valleys.

Every mountain has its valleys. Its sides are scarred by deep ravines and gulches and draws. And the best route to the top is always along these valleys.

Any sheepman familiar with the high country knows this. He leads his flock gently, but persistently up the paths that wind through the dark valleys. It should be noticed that the verse states, "Yea, though I *walk through* the valley of the shadow of death." It does not say I die there, or stop there—but rather "I walk through."

It is customary to use this verse as a consolation to those who are passing through the dark valley of death. But even here, for the child of God, death is not an end but merely the door into a higher and more exalted life of intimate contact with Christ. Death is but the dark valley opening out into an eternity of delight with God. It is not something to fear, but an experience through which one passes on the path to a more perfect life.

The Good Shepherd knows this. It is one reason why He has told us, "Lo, I am with you always"—yes, even in the valley of death. What a comfort and what a cheer.

I was keenly aware of this consolation when my wife went to "higher ground." For two years we had walked through the dark valley of death watching her beautiful body being destroyed by cancer. As death approached I sat by her bed, her hand in mine. Gently we "passed" through the valley of death. Both of us were quietly aware of Christ's presence. There was no fear—*just a going on to higher ground.*

For those of us who remain on earth, there is still a life to live here and now. There are still valleys to walk through during our remaining days. These need not be "dead end" streets. The disappointments, the frustrations, the discouragements, the dilemmas, the dark, difficult days, though they be shadowed valleys, need not be disasters. They can be the road to higher ground in our walk with God.

After all, when we pause to think about it a moment, we must realize that even our modern mountain highways follow the valleys to reach the summit of the passes they traverse. Similarly the ways of God lead upward through the valleys of our lives.

Again and again I remind myself, "O God, this seems terribly tough, but I know for a fact that in the end it will prove to be the easiest and gentlest way to get me onto higher ground." Then when I thank Him for the difficult things, the dark days, I discover that He is there with me in my distress. At that point my panic, my fear, my misgivings give way to calm and quiet confidence in His care. Somehow, in a serene quiet way I am assured all will turn out well for my best because He is with me in the valley and things are under His control.

To come to this conviction in the Christian life is to have entered into an attitude of quiet acceptance of every adversity. It is to have moved onto higher ground with God. Knowing Him in this new and intimate manner makes life much more bearable than before.

There is a second reason why sheep are taken to the mountain tops by way of the valleys. Not only is this the way of the gentlest grades, but also it is the well watered route. Here one finds refreshing water all along the way. There are rivers, streams, springs and quiet pools in the deep defiles.

During the summer months long drives can be hot and tiresome. The flocks experience intense thirst. How glad they are for the frequent watering places along the valley route where they can be refreshed.

I recall one year when an enormous flock of over 10,000 sheep was being taken through our country en route to their summer range. The owners came asking permission to water their sheep at the river that flowed by our ranch. Their thirsty flocks literally ran to the water's edge to quench their burning thirst under the blazing summer sun. Only in our valley was there water for their parched flesh. How glad we were to share the water with them.

As Christians we will sooner or later discover that it is in the valleys of our lives that we find refreshment from God Himself. It is not until we have walked with Him through some very deep troubles that we discover He can lead us to find our refreshment in Him right there in the midst of our difficulty. We are thrilled beyond words when there comes restoration to our souls and spirits from His own gracious Spirit.

During my wife's illness and after her death I could not get over the strength, solace and serene outlook imparted to me virtually hour after hour by the presence of God's gracious Spirit Himself.

It was as if I was being repeatedly refreshed and restored despite the most desperate circumstances all around me. Unless one has actually gone through such an experience it may seem difficult to believe. In fact there are those who claim they could not face such a situation. But for the man or woman who walks with God through these valleys, such real and actual refreshment is available.

The corollary to this is that only those who have been through such dark valleys can console, comfort or encourage others in similar situations. Often we pray or sing the hymn requesting God to make us an inspiration to someone else. We want, instinctively, to be a channel of blessing to other lives. The simple fact is that just as water can only flow in a ditch or channel or valley—so in the Christian's career, the life of God can only flow in blessing through the valleys that have been carved and cut into our own lives by excruciating experiences.

For example, the one best able to comfort another in bereavement is the person who himself has lost a loved one. The one who can best minister to a broken heart is one who has known a broken heart.

Most of us do not want valleys in our lives. We shrink from them with a sense of fear and foreboding. Yet in spite of our worst misgivings God can bring great benefit and lasting benediction to others through those valleys. Let us not always try to avoid the dark things, the distressing days. They may well prove to be the way of greatest refreshment to ourselves and those around us.

A third reason why the rancher chooses to take his flock into the high country by way of the valleys is that this is generally where the richest feed and best forage is to be found along the route.

The flock is moved along gently—they are not hurried. There are lambs along which have never been this way before. The shepherd wants to be sure there will not only be water but also the best grazing available for the ewes and their lambs. Generally the choicest meadows are in these valleys along the stream banks. Here the sheep can feed as they move toward the high country.

Naturally these grassy glades are often on the floor of steep-walled canyons and gulches. There may be towering cliffs above them on either side. The valley floor itself may be in dark shadow with the sun seldom reaching the bottom except for a few hours around noon.

The shepherd knows from past experience that predators like coyotes, bears, wolves or cougars can take cover in these broken cliffs and from their vantage point prey on his flock. He knows these valleys can be subject to sudden storms and flash floods that send walls of water rampaging down the slopes. There could be rock slides, mud or snow avalanches and a dozen other natural disasters that would destroy or injure his sheep. But in spite of such hazards he also knows that this is still the best way to take his flock to the high country. He spares himself no pains or trouble or time to keep an eye out for any danger that might develop.

One of the most terrible threats is the sudden chilling storms of sleet, rain and snow that can sweep down through the valleys from the mountain peaks. If sheep become soaked and chilled with a freezing rain, the exposure can kill them in a very short time. They are thin-skinned creatures, easily susceptible to colds, pneumonia and other respiratory complications. I recall one storm I went through in the foothills of the Rockies in early summer. The morning had been bright and clear. Suddenly around noon enormous dark, black, forbidding clouds began to sweep down over the hills from the north. A chilling wind accompanied the approaching storm. The sky grew blacker by the hour. Suddenly in mid afternoon long streamers of rain and sleet began to sweep across the valley. I ran to take shelter in a clump of stunted, wind-blown spruce. The rain soaked me through. As it fell it cooled the whole country. The rain turned to sleet, then to commingled snow and hail. In a short time the whole mountain slope (in mid July!) was white and frozen. Ominous darkness shrouded the whole scene. The sheep sensed the storm approaching. Perhaps the flock would have perished if they had not raced away to find shelter in the steep cliffs at the edge of the canyon.

But in these valleys was where the grass grew best and it was the route to the high country.

Our Shepherd knows all of this when He leads us through the valleys with Himself. He knows where we can find strength, and sustenance and gentle grazing despite every threat of disaster about us.

It is a most reassuring and reenforcing experience to the child of God to discover that there is, even in the dark valley, a source of strength and courage to be found in God. It is when he can look back over life and see how the Shepherd's hand has guided and sustained him in the darkest hours that renewed faith is engendered.

I know of nothing which so stimulates my faith in my Heavenly Father as to look back and reflect on His faithfulness to me in every crisis and every chilling circumstance of life. Over and over He has proved His care and concern for my welfare. Again and again I have been conscious of the Good Shepherd's guidance through dark days and deep valleys.

All of this multiplies my confidence in Christ. It is this spiritual, as well as emotional and mental exposure to the storms and adversities of life that puts stamina into my very being. Because He has led me through without fear before, He can do it again, and again, and again. In this knowledge fear fades and tranquility of heart and mind takes its place.

Let come what may. Storms may break about me, predators may attack, the rivers of reverses may threaten to inundate me. But because He is in the situation with me, I shall not fear.

To live thus is to have taken some very long treks toward the high country of holy, calm, healthy living with God.

Only the Christian who learns to live this way is able to encourage and inspire the weaker ones around him. Too many of us are shaken up, frightened and panicked by the storms of life. We claim to have confidence in Christ but when the first dark shadows sweep over us and the path we tread looks gloomy we go into a deep slump of despair. Sometimes we just feel like lying down to die. This is not as it should be.

The person with a powerful confidence in Christ; the one who has proved by past experience that God is with him in adversity; the one who walks through life's dark valleys without fear, his head held high, is the one who in turn is a tower of strength and a source of inspiration to his companions.

There are going to be some valleys in life for all of us. The Good Shepherd Himself assured us that "in this world ye shall have tribulation: but be of good cheer; I have overcome the world" (John 16:33).

The basic question is not whether we have many or few valleys. It is not whether those valleys are dark or merely dim with shadows. The question is how do I react to them? How do I go through them? How do I cope with the calamities that come my way?

With Christ I face them calmly.

With His gracious Spirit to guide me I face them fearlessly.

I know of a surety that only through them can I possibly travel on to higher ground with God. In this way not only shall I be blessed but in turn I will become a benediction to others around me who may live in fear.

# 8
# Thy Rod
# and Thy Staff
# They Comfort Me

WHEN THE SHEPHERD is afield with his flock in the high country, it is customary for him to carry a minimum of equipment. This was especially true in olden times where the sheepman did not have the benefit of mechanized equipment to transport camp supplies across the rough country. Even today the so-called "shepherd shacks" or "cabooses" in which the herder spends his lonely summers with the sheep are equipped with only the barest essentials.

But during the hours that he is actually in the field the sheepman carries only a rifle slung over his shoulder and a long slender staff in his hand. There will be a small knapsack in which are packed his lunch, a bottle of water and perhaps a few simple first aid remedies for his flock.

In the Middle East the shepherd carries only a rod and staff. Some of my most vivid boyhood recollections are those of watching the African herdsmen shepherding their stock with only a long slender stick and a rough *knob-kerrie* in their hands. These are the common and universal equipment of the primitive sheepman.

Each shepherd boy, from the time he first starts to tend his father's flock, takes special pride in the selection of a rod and staff exactly suited to his own size and strength. He goes into the bush and selects a young sapling which is dug from the ground. This is carved and whittled down with great care and patience. The enlarged base of the sapling where its trunk joins the roots is shaped into a smooth, rounded head of hard wood. The sapling itself is shaped to exactly fit the owner's hand. After he completes it, the shepherd boy spends hours practicing with this club, learning how to throw it with amazing speed and accuracy. It becomes his main weapon of defense for both himself and his sheep.

I used to watch the native lads having competitions to see who could throw his rod with the greatest accuracy across the greatest distance. The effectiveness of these crude clubs in the hands of skilled shepherds was a thrill to watch. The rod was, in fact, an extension of the owner's own right arm. It stood as a symbol of his strength, his power, his authority in any serious situation. The rod was what he relied on to safeguard both himself and his flock in danger. And it was, furthermore, the instrument he used to discipline and correct any wayward sheep that insisted on wandering away.

There is an interesting sidelight on the word, "rod," which has crept into the colloquial language of the West. Here the slang term "rod" has been applied to hand-guns such as pistols and revolvers which were carried by cowboys, and other western rangemen. The connotation is exactly the same as that used in this Psalm.

The sheep asserts that the owner's rod, his weapon of power, authority and defense, is a continuous comfort to him. For with it the manager is able to carry out effective control of his flock in every situation.

It will be recalled how when God called Moses, the desert shepherd, and sent him to deliver Israel out of Egypt from under Pharaoh's bondage, it was his rod that was to demonstrate the power vested in him. It was always through Moses' rod that miracles were made manifest not only to convince Pharaoh of Moses' divine commission, but also to reassure the people of Israel.

The rod speaks, therefore, of the spoken Word, the expressed intent, the extended activity of God's mind and will in dealing with men. It implies the authority of divinity. It carries with it the convicting power and irrefutable impact of *"Thus saith the Lord."*

Just as for the sheep of David's day, there was comfort and consolation in seeing the rod in the shepherd's skillful hands, so in our day there is great assurance in our own hearts as we contemplate the power, veracity and potent authority vested in God's Word. For, in fact, the Scriptures are His rod. They are the extension of His mind and will and intentions to mortal man.

Living as we do in an era when numerous confused voices and strange philosophies are presented to people, it is reassuring to the child of God to turn to the Word of God and know it to be His Shepherd's hand of authority. What a comfort to have this authoritative, clear-cut, powerful instrument under which to conduct ourselves. By it we are kept from confusion amid chaos. This in itself brings into our lives a great sense of quiet serenity which is precisely what the psalmist meant when he said, ". . . thy rod . . . comfort[s] me."

There is a second dimension in which the rod is used by the shepherd for the welfare of his sheep—namely that of discipline. If anything, the club is used for this purpose perhaps more than any other.

I could never get over how often, and with what accuracy, the African herders would hurl their knob-kerries at some recalcitrant beast that misbehaved. If the shepherd saw a sheep wandering away on its own, or approaching poisonous weeds, or getting too close to danger of one sort or another, the club would go whistling through the air to send the wayward animal scurrying back to the bunch.

As has been said of the Scripture so often, "This Book will keep you from sin!" It is the Word of God that comes swiftly to our hearts, that comes with surprising suddenness to correct and reprove us when we go astray. It is the Spirit of the Living God, using the living Word, that convicts our conscience of right conduct. In this way we are kept under control by Christ who wants us to walk in the ways of righteousness.

Another interesting use of the rod in the Shepherd's hand was to examine and count the sheep. In the terminology of the Old Testament this was referred to as passing "under the rod" (Ezekiel 20:37). This meant not only coming under the owner's control and authority, but also to be subject to his most careful, intimate and firsthand examination. A sheep that passed "under the rod" was one which had been counted and looked over with great care to make sure all was well with it.

Because of their long wool it is not always easy to detect disease, wounds, or defects in sheep. For example at a sheep show an inferior animal can be clipped and shaped and shown so as to appear a perfect specimen. But the skilled judge will take his rod and part the sheep's wool to determine the condition of the skin, the cleanliness of the fleece and the conformation of the body. In plain language, "One just does not pull the wool over his eyes."

In caring for his sheep, the good shepherd, the careful manager, will from time to time make a careful examination of each individual sheep. The picture is a very poignant one. As each animal comes out of the corral and through the gate, it is stopped by the shepherd's outstretched rod. He opens the fleece with the rod; he runs his skillful hands over the body; he feels for any sign of trouble; he examines the sheep with care to see that all is well. This is a most searching process entailing every intimate detail. It is, too, a comfort to the sheep for only in this way can its hidden problems be laid bare before the shepherd.

This is what was meant in Psalm 139:23, 24 when the psalmist wrote, "Search me, O God, and know my heart: try me, and know my thoughts: and see if there be any wicked way in me, and lead me in the way everlasting."

If we will allow it, if we will submit to it, God by His Word will search us. There will be no "pulling the wool over His eyes." He will get below the surface, behind the front of our old self-life and expose things that need to be made right.

This is a process from which we need not shrink. It is not something to avoid. It is done in concern and compassion for our welfare. The Great Shepherd of our souls has our own best interests at heart when He so searches us. What a comfort this should be to the child of God, who can trust in God's care.

Wool in Scripture speaks of the self-life, self-will, self-assertion, self-pride. God has to get below this and do a deep work in our wills to right the wrongs which are often bothering us beneath the surface. So often we put on a fine front and brave, bold exterior when really deep down below there needs to be some remedy applied.

Finally the shepherd's rod is an instrument of protection both for himself and his sheep when they are in danger. It is used both as a defense and a deterrent against anything that would attack.

The skilled shepherd uses his rod to drive off predators like coyotes, wolves, cougars or stray dogs. Often it is used to beat the brush discouraging snakes and other creatures from disturbing the flock. In extreme cases, such as David recounted to Saul, the psalmist no doubt used his rod to attack the lion and the bear that came to raid his flocks.

Once in Kenya photographing elephants, I was being accompanied by a young Masai herder who carried a club in his hand. We came to the crest of a hill from which we could see a herd of elephants in the thick bush below us. To drive them out into the open we decided to dislodge a boulder and roll it down the slope. As we heaved and pushed against the great rock, a cobra, coiled beneath it, suddenly came into view ready to strike. In a split second the alert shepherd boy lashed out with his club killing the snake on the spot. The weapon had never left his hand even while we worked on the rock.

"Thy rod . . . comfort[s] me." In that instant I saw the meaning of this phrase in a new light. It was the rod ever ready in the shepherd's hand that had saved the day for us.

It was the rod of God's Word that Christ, our Good Shepherd, used in His own encounter with that serpent—Satan—during His desert temptation. It is the same Word of God which we can count on again and again to counter the assaults and attacks of Satan. And it matters not whether the guise He assumes is that of a subtle serpent or a roaring lion that desires to destroy us.

There is no substitute for the Scriptures in coping with the complexities of our social order. We live in an evermore involved and difficult milieu. We are part of a world of men and women whose code of conduct is contrary to all that Christ has advocated. To live with such people is to be ever exposed to enormous temptations of all sorts. Some people are very subtle, very smooth, very sophisticated. Others are capable of outright, violent, vituperative attacks against the children of God.

In every situation and under every circumstance there is comfort in the knowledge that God's Word can meet and master the difficulty if we will rely on it.

We turn now to discuss and consider the shepherd's staff. In a sense the staff, more than any other item of his personal equipment, identifies the shepherd as a shepherd. No one in any other profession carries a shepherd's staff. It is uniquely an instrument used for the care and management of sheep—and only sheep. It will not do for cattle, horses or hogs. It is designed, shaped and adapted especially to the needs of sheep. And it is used only for their benefit.

The staff is essentially a symbol of the concern, the compassion that a shepherd has for his charges. No other single word can better describe its function on behalf of the flock than that it is for their *comfort.*

Whereas the rod conveys the concept of authority, of power, of discipline, of defense against danger, the word "staff" speaks of all that is longsuffering and kind.

The shepherd's staff is normally a long, slender stick, often with a crook or hook on one end. It is selected with care by the owner; it is shaped, smoothed, and cut to best suit his own personal use.

Some of the most moving memories I carry with me from Africa and the Middle East are of seeing elderly shepherds in the twilight of life, standing silently at sunset, leaning on their staves, watching their flocks with contented spirits. Somehow the staff is of special comfort to the shepherd himself. In the tough tramps and during the long weary watches with his sheep he leans on it for support and strength. It becomes to him a most precious comfort and help in his duties.

Just as the rod of God is emblematic of the Word of God, so the staff of God is symbolic of the Spirit of God. In Christ's dealings with us as individuals there is the essence of the sweetness, the comfort and consolation, the gentle correction brought about by the work of His gracious Spirit.

There are three areas of sheep management in which the staff plays a most significant role. The first of these lies in drawing sheep together into an intimate relationship. The shepherd will use his staff to gently lift a newborn lamb and bring it to its mother if they become separated. He does this because he does not wish to have the ewe reject her offspring if it bears the odor of his hands upon it. I have watched skilled shepherds moving swiftly with their staffs amongst thousands of ewes that were lambing simultaneously. With deft but gentle strokes the newborn lambs are lifted with the staff and placed side by side with their dams. It is a touching sight that can hold one spellbound for hours.

But in precisely the same way, the staff is used by the shepherd to reach out and catch individual sheep, young or old, and draw them close to himself for intimate examination. The staff is very useful this way for the shy and timid sheep that normally tend to keep at a distance from the shepherd.

Similarly in the Christian life we find the gracious Holy Spirit, "The Comforter," drawing folks together into a warm, personal fellowship with one another. It is also He who draws us to Christ, for as we are told in Revelation, "The Spirit and the bride say, Come."

The staff is also used for guiding sheep. Again and again I have seen a shepherd use his staff to guide his sheep gently into a new path or through some gate or along dangerous, difficult routes. He does not use it actually to beat the beast. Rather, the tip of the long slender stick is laid gently against the animal's side and the pressure applied guides the sheep in the way the owner wants it to go. Thus the sheep is reassured of its proper path.

Sometimes I have been fascinated to see how a shepherd will actually hold his staff against the side of some sheep that is a special pet or favorite, simply so that they "are in touch." They will walk along this way almost as though it were "hand-in-hand." The sheep obviously enjoys this special attention from the shepherd and revels in the close, personal, intimate contact between them. To be treated in this special way by the shepherd is to know comfort in a deep dimension. It is a delightful and moving picture.

In our walk with God we are told explicitly by Christ Himself that it would be His Spirit who would be sent to guide us and to lead us into all truth (John 16:13). This same gracious Spirit takes the truth of God, the Word of God, and makes it plain to our hearts and minds and spiritual understanding. It is He who gently, tenderly, but persistently says to us, "This is the way—walk in it." And as we comply and cooperate with His gentle promptings a sense of safety, comfort and well-being envelops us.

It is He, too, who comes quietly but emphatically to make the life of Christ, my Shepherd, real and personal and intimate to me. Through Him I am "in touch" with Christ. There steals over me the keen awareness that I am His and He is mine. The gracious Spirit continually brings home to me the acute consciousness that I am God's child and He is my Father. In all of this there is enormous comfort and a sublime sense of "oneness," of "belonging," of "being in His care," and hence the object of His special affection.

The Christian life is not just one of subscribing to certain doctrines or believing certain facts. Essential as all of this confidence in the Scriptures may be, there is, as well, the actual reality of experiencing and knowing firsthand the feel of His touch—the sense of His Spirit upon my spirit. There is for the true child of God that intimate, subtle, yet magnificent experience of sensing the Comforter at his side. This is not imagination—it is the genuine, bona-fide reality of everyday life. There is a calm, quiet repose in the knowledge that He is there to direct even in the most minute details of daily living. He can be relied on to assist us in every decision, and in this there lies tremendous comfort for the Christian.

Over and over I have turned to Him and in audible, open language asked for His opinion on a problem. I have asked, "What would you do in this case?" or I have said, "You are here now. You know all the complexities; tell me precisely what is the best procedure at this point." And the thrilling thing is He does just that. He actually conveys the mind of Christ in the matter to my mind. Then the right decisions are made with confidence.

It is when I do not do this that I end up in difficulty. It is then that I find myself in a jam of some sort. And here again the gracious Spirit comes to my rescue just as the shepherd rescues his sheep out of the situations into which their own stupidity leads them.

Being stubborn creatures sheep often get into the most ridiculous and preposterous dilemmas. I have seen my own sheep, greedy for one more mouthful of green grass, climb down steep cliffs where they slipped and fell into the sea. Only my long shepherd's staff could lift them out of the water back onto solid ground again. One winter day I spent several hours rescuing a ewe that had done this very thing several times before. Her stubbornness was her undoing.

Another common occurrence was to find sheep stuck fast in labyrinths of wild roses or brambles where they had pushed in to find a few stray mouthfuls of green grass. Soon the thorns were so hooked in their wool they could not possibly pull free, tug as they might. Only the use of a staff could free them from their entanglement.

Likewise with us. Many of our jams and impasses are of our own making. In stubborn, self-willed, self-assertion we keep pushing ourselves into a situation where we cannot extricate ourselves. Then in tenderness, compassion and care our Shepherd comes to us. He draws near and in tenderness lifts us by His Spirit out of the difficulty and dilemma. What patience God has with us! What longsuffering and compassion! What forgiveness!

Thy staff comforts me! Your Spirit, O Christ, is my consolation!

# 9
# Thou Preparest
# a Table Before Me . . .

In thinking about this statement it is well to bear in mind that the sheep are approaching the high mountain country of the summer ranges. These are known as alplands or tablelands so much sought after by sheepmen.

In some of the finest sheep country of the world, especially in the Western United States and Southern Europe, the high plateaux of the sheep ranges are always referred to as "mesas"—the Spanish word for "tables."

Oddly enough the Kiswahili (African) word for a table is also "mesa." Presumably this had its origin with the first Portuguese explorers to touch the East African coast. In fact the use of this word is not uncommon in referring to the high, flat-topped plateaux of the continent. The classic example, of course, is Table Mountain, near Cape Town, which is world renowned.

So it may be seen that what David referred to as a table was actually the entire high summer range. Though these "mesas" may have been remote and hard to reach, the energetic and aggressive sheep owner takes the time and trouble to ready them for the arrival of his flocks.

Early in the season, even before all the snow has been melted by spring sunshine, he will go ahead and make preliminary survey trips into this rough, wild country. He will look it over with great care, keeping ever in mind its best use for his flock during the coming season.

Then just before the sheep arrive he will make another expedition or two to prepare the tableland for them. He takes along a supply of salt and minerals to be distributed over the range at strategic spots for the benefit of the sheep during the summer. The intelligent, careful manager will also decide well ahead of time where his camps will be located so the sheep have the best bed grounds. He goes over the range carefully to determine how vigorous the grass and upland vegetation is. At this time he decides whether some glades and basins can be used only lightly whereas other slopes and meadows may be grazed more heavily.

He will check to see if there are poisonous weeds appearing, and if so, he will plan his grazing program to avoid them, or take drastic steps to eradicate them.

Unknown to me the first sheep ranch I owned had a rather prolific native stand of both blue and white cammas. The blue cammas were a delightful sight in the spring when they bloomed along the beaches. The white cammas, though a much less conspicuous flower, were also quite attractive but a deadly menace to sheep. If lambs, in particular, ate or even just nibbled a few of the lily-like leaves as they emerged in the grass sward during spring, it would spell certain death. The lambs would become paralyzed, stiffen up like blocks of wood and simply succumb to the toxic poisons from the plants.

My youngsters and I spent days and days going over the ground plucking out these poisonous plants. It was a recurring task that was done every spring before the sheep went on these pastures. Though tedious and tiring with all of the bending, it was a case of "preparing the table in the presence of mine enemies." And if my sheep were to survive it simply had to be done.

A humorous sidelight on this chore was the way I hit on the idea of making up animal stories to occupy the children's minds as we worked together this way for long hours, often down on our hands and knees. They would become so engrossed in my wild fantasies about bears and skunks and raccoons that the hours passed quite quickly. Sometimes both of them would roll in the grass with laughter as I added realistic action to enliven my tales. It was one way to accomplish an otherwise terribly routine task.

All of this sort of thing was in the back of David's mind as he penned these lines. I can picture him walking slowly over the summer range ahead of his flock. His eagle eye is sharp for any signs of poisonous weeds which he would pluck before his sheep got to them. No doubt he had armfuls to get rid of for the safety of his flock.

The parallel in the Christian life is clear. Like sheep, and especially lambs, we somehow feel that we have to try everything that comes our way. We have to taste this thing and that, sampling everything just to see what it's like. And we may very well know that some things are deadly. They can do us no good. They can be most destructive. Still somehow we give them a whirl anyway.

To forestall our getting into grief of this sort, we need to remember our Master has been there ahead of us coping with every situation which would otherwise undo us.

A classic example of this was the incident when Jesus warned Peter that Satan desired to tempt him and sift him like wheat. But Christ pointed out that He had prayed that Peter's faith might not fail during the desperate difficulty he would encounter. And so it is even today. Our great Good Shepherd is going ahead of us in every situation, anticipating what danger we may encounter, and praying for us that in it we might not succumb.

Another task the attentive shepherd takes on in the summer is to keep an eye out for predators. He will look for signs and spoor of wolves, coyotes, cougars and bears. If these raid or molest the sheep he will have to hunt them down or go to great pains to trap them so that his flock can rest in peace.

Often what actually happens is that these crafty ones are up on the rimrock watching every movement the sheep make, hoping for a chance to make a swift, sneaking attack that will stampede the sheep. Then one or other of the flock is bound to fall easy prey to the attacker's fierce teeth and claws.

The picture here is full of drama, action, suspense—and possible death. Only the alertness of the sheepman who tends his flock on the tableland in full view of possible enemies can prevent them from falling prey to attack. It is only his preparation for such an eventuality that can possibly save the sheep from being slaughtered and panicked by their predators.

And again we are given a sublime picture of our Saviour who knows every wile, every trick, every treachery of our enemy Satan and his companions. Always we are in danger of attack. Scripture sometimes refers to him as "a roaring lion" who goes about seeking whom he may devour.

It is rather fashionable in some contemporary Christian circles to discredit Satan. There is a tendency to try and write him off, or laugh him off, as though he was just a joke. Some deny that such a being as Satan even exists. Yet we see evidence of his merciless attacks and carnage in a society where men and women fall prey to his cunning tactics almost every day. We see lives torn and marred and seared by his assaults though we may never see him personally.

It reminds me of my encounters with cougars. On several occasions these cunning creatures came in among my sheep at night working terrible havoc in the flock. Some ewes were killed outright, their blood drained and livers eaten. Others were torn open and badly clawed. In these cases the great cats seemed to chase and play with them in their panic like a housecat would chase a mouse. Some had huge patches of wool torn from their fleeces. In their frightened stampede some had stumbled and broken bones or rushed over rough ground injuring legs and bodies.

Yet despite the damage, despite the dead sheep, despite the injuries and fear instilled in the flock, I never once actually saw a cougar on my range. So cunning and so skillful were their raids they defy description.

At all times we would be wise to walk a little closer to Christ. This is one sure place of safety. It was always the distant sheep, the roamers, the wanderers, which were picked off by the predators in an unsuspecting moment. Generally the attackers are gone before the shepherd is alerted by their cry for help. Some sheep, of course, are utterly dumb with fear under attack; they will not even give a plaintive bleat before their blood is spilled.

The same is true of Christians. Many of us get into deep difficulty beyond ourselves; we are stricken dumb with apprehension, unable even to call or cry out for help; we just crumple under our adversary's attack.

But Christ is too concerned about us to allow this to happen. Our Shepherd wants to forestall such a calamity. He wants our summer sojourn to be in peace. Our Lord wants our mountaintop times to be tranquil interludes. And they will be if we just have the common sense to stay near Him where He can protect us. Read His Word each day. Spend some time talking to Him. We should give Him opportunity to converse with us by His Spirit as we contemplate His life and work for us as our Shepherd.

There is another chore which the sheepman takes care of on the tableland. He clears out the water holes, springs and drinking places for his stock. He has to clean out the accumulated debris of leaves, twigs, stones and soil which may have fallen into the water source during the autumn and winter. He may need to repair small earth dams he has made to hold water. And he will open the springs that may have become overgrown with grass and brush and weeds. It is all his work, his preparation of the table for his own sheep in summer.

The parallel in the Christian life is that Christ, our great Good Shepherd, has Himself already gone before us into every situation and every extremity that we might encounter. We are told emphatically that He was tempted in all points like as we are. We know He entered fully and completely and very intimately into the life of men upon our planet. He has known our sufferings, experienced our sorrows and endured our struggles in this life; He was a man of sorrows and acquainted with grief.

Because of this He *understands* us, He has totally *identified* Himself with humanity. He has, therefore, a care and compassion for us beyond our ability to grasp. No wonder He makes every possible provision to insure that when we have to cope with Satan, sin or self, the contest will not be one-sided. Rather, we can be sure He has been in that situation before; He is in it now again with us and because of this the prospects of our preservation are excellent.

It is this attitude of rest in Him, of confidence in His care, of relaxation as we realize His presence in the picture that can make the Christian's life one of calm and quiet confidence. The Christian walk can thus become a mountaintop experience—a tableland trip—simply because we are in the care and control of Christ who has been over all this territory before us and prepared the "table" for us in plain view of our enemies who would demoralize and destroy us if they could.

It is encouraging to know that just as in any other aspect of life where there are lights and shadows, so in the Christian life there are valleys and mountaintops. Too many people assume that once one becomes a Christian, automatically life becomes one glorious garden of delight. This is simply not the case. It may well become a garden of sorrow just as our Saviour went through the garden of Gethsemane. As was pointed out previously, you do not have mountains without valleys, and even on the mountaintop there can be some tough experiences.

Just because the shepherd has gone ahead and made every possible provision for the safety and welfare of his sheep while they are on the summer range does not mean they will not have problems there. Predators can still attack; poisonous weeds can still grow; storms and gales can still come swirling up over the peaks; and a dozen other hazards can haunt the high country.

Yet, in His care and concern for us Christ still insures that we shall have some gladness with our sadness; some delightful days as well as dark days; some sunshine as well as shadow.

It is not always apparent to us what tremendous personal cost it has been for Christ to prepare the table for His own. Just as the lonely, personal privation of the sheepman who prepares the summer range for his stock entails a sacrifice, so the lonely agony of Gethsemane, of Pilate's hall, of Calvary, have cost my Master much.

When I come to the Lord's Table and partake of the communion service which is a feast of thanksgiving for His love and care, do I fully appreciate what it has cost Him to prepare this table for me?

Here we commemorate the greatest and deepest demonstration of *true love* the world has ever known. For God looked down upon sorrowing, struggling, sinning humanity and was moved with compassion for the contrary, sheep-like creatures He had made. In spite of the tremendous personal cost it would entail to Himself to deliver them from their dilemma He chose deliberately to descend and live amongst them that He might deliver them.

This meant laying aside His splendor, His position, His prerogatives as the perfect and faultless One. He knew He would be exposed to terrible privation, to ridicule, to false accusations, to rumor, gossip and malicious charges that branded Him as a glutton, drunkard, friend of sinners and even an imposter. It entailed losing His reputation. It would involve physical suffering, mental anguish and spiritual agony.

In short, His coming to earth as the Christ, as Jesus of Nazareth, was a straightforward case of utter self-sacrifice that culminated in the cross of Calvary. The laid-down life, the poured-out blood were the supreme symbols of total selflessness. This was *love*. This was *God*. This was *divinity* in action, delivering men from their own utter selfishness, their own stupidity, their own suicidal instincts as lost sheep unable to help themselves.

In all of this there is an amazing mystery. No man will ever be able fully to fathom its implications. It is bound up inexorably with the concept of God's divine love of self-sacrifice which is so foreign to most of us who are so self-centered. At best we can only grasp feebly the incredible concept of a perfect person, a sinless one being willing actually to be made sin that we who are so full of faults, selfish self-assertion and suspicion might be set free from sin and self to live a new, free, fresh, abundant life of righteousness.

Jesus told us Himself, that He had come that we might have life and have it more abundantly. Just as the sheepman is thrilled beyond words to see his sheep thriving on the high, rich summer range (it is one of the highlights of his whole year), so my Shepherd is immensely pleased when He sees me flourish on the tablelands of a noble, lofty life that He has made possible for me.

Part of the mystery and wonder of Calvary, of God's love to us in Christ, is bound up too with the deep desire of His heart to have me live on a higher plane. He longs to see me living above the mundane level of common humanity. He is so pleased when I walk in the ways of holiness, of selflessness, of serene contentment in

His care, aware of His presence and enjoying the intimacy of His companionship.

To live thus is to live richly.

To walk here is to walk with quiet assurance.

To feed here is to be replete with good things.

To find this tableland is to have found something of my Shepherd's love for me.

# 10
## Thou Anointest
## My Head With Oil . . .

As ONE MEDITATES on this magnificent poem it is helpful to keep in mind that the poet is recounting the salient events of the full year in a sheep's life. He takes us with him from the home ranch where every need is so carefully supplied by the owner, out into the green pastures, along the still waters, up through the mountain valleys to the high tablelands of summer.

Here, now, where it would appear the sheep are in a sublime setting on the high meadows; where there are clear running springs; where the forage is fresh and tender; where there is the intimate close contact with the shepherd; suddenly we find "a fly in the ointment," so to speak.

For in the terminology of the sheepman, "summer time is fly time." By this, reference is made to the hordes of insects that emerge with the advent of warm weather. Only those people who have kept livestock or studied wildlife habits are aware of the serious problems for animals presented by insects in the summer.

To name just a few parasites that trouble stock and make their lives a misery: there are warble flies, bot flies, heel flies, nose (nasal) flies, deer flies, black flies, mosquitos, gnats and other minute, winged parasites that proliferate at this time of year. Their attacks on animals can readily turn the golden summer months into a time of torture for sheep and drive them almost to distraction.

Sheep are especially troubled by the nose fly, or nasal fly, as it is sometimes called. These little flies buzz about the sheep's head, attempting to deposit their eggs on the damp, mucous membranes of the sheep's nose. If they are successful the eggs will hatch in a few days to form small, slender, worm-like larvae. They work their way up the nasal passages into the sheep's head; they burrow into the flesh and there set up an intense irritation accompanied by severe inflammation.

For relief from this agonizing annoyance sheep will deliberately beat their heads against trees, rocks, posts, or brush. They will rub them in the soil and thrash around against woody growth. In extreme cases of intense infestation a sheep may even kill itself in a frenzied endeavor to gain respite from the aggravation. Often advanced stages of infection from these flies will lead to blindness.

Because of all this, when the nose flies hover around the flock, some of the sheep become frantic with fear and panic in their attempt to escape their tormentors. They will stamp their feet erratically and race from place to place in the pasture trying desperately to elude the flies. Some may run so much they will drop from sheer exhaustion. Others may toss their heads up and down for hours. They will hide in any bush or woodland that offers shelter. On some occasions they may refuse to graze in the open at all.

All this excitement and distraction has a devastating effect on the entire flock. Ewes and lambs rapidly lose condition and begin to drop in weight. The ewes will go off milking and their lambs will stop growing gainfully. Some sheep will be injured in their headlong rushes of panic; others may be blinded and some even killed outright.

Only the strictest attention to the behavior of the sheep by the shepherd can forestall the difficulties of "fly time." At the very first sign of flies among the flock he will apply an antidote to their heads. I always preferred to use a homemade remedy composed of linseed oil, sulphur and tar which was smeared over the sheep's nose and head as a protection against nose flies.

What an incredible transformation this would make among the sheep. Once the oil had been applied to the sheep's head there was an immediate change in behavior. Gone was the aggravation; gone the frenzy; gone the irritability and the restlessness. Instead, the sheep would start to feed quietly again, then soon lie down in peaceful contentment.

This, to me is the exact picture of irritations in my own life. How easy it is for there to be a fly in the ointment of even my most lofty spiritual experience! So often it is the small, petty annoyances that ruin my repose. It is the niggling distractions that become burning issues that can well nigh drive me round the bend or up the wall. At times some tiny, tantalizing thing torments me to the point where I feel I am just beating my brains out. And so my behavior as a child of God degenerates to a most disgraceful sort of frustrated tirade.

Just as with the sheep there must be continuous and renewed application of oil to forestall the "flies" in my life, there must be a continuous anointing of God's gracious Spirit to counteract the ever-present aggravations of personality conflicts. Only one application of oil, sulphur and tar was not enough for the entire summer. It was a process that had to be repeated. The fresh application was the effective antidote.

There are those who contend that in the Christian life one need only have a single, initial anointing of God's Spirit. Yet the frustrations of daily dilemmas demonstrate that one must have Him come continuously to the troubled mind and heart to counteract the attacks of one's tormentors.

This is a practical and intimate matter between myself and my Master. In Luke 11:13 Christ Himself, our Shepherd, urges us to ask for the Holy Spirit to be given to us by the Father.

It is both a logical and legitimate desire for us to have the daily anointing of God's gracious Spirit upon our minds. God alone can form in us the mind of Christ. The Holy Spirit alone can give to us the attitudes of Christ. He alone makes it possible for us to react to aggravations and annoyances with quietness and calmness.

When people or circumstances or events beyond our control tend to "bug" us, it is possible to be content and serene when these "outside" forces are counteracted by the presence of God's Spirit. In Romans 8:1-2, we are told plainly it is the law of the Spirit of life in Christ Jesus that makes us free from the law of sin and death.

It is this daily anointing of God's gracious Spirit upon my mind which produces in my life such personality traits as joy, contentment, love, patience, gentleness and peace. What a contrast this is to the tempers, frustration and irritableness which mars the daily conduct of so many of God's children.

What I do in any given situation is to expose it to my Master, my Owner, Christ Jesus, and say simply, "O Lord, I can't cope with these petty, annoying, peevish problems. Please apply the oil of Your Spirit to my mind. Both at the conscious and sub-conscious levels of my thought-life enable me to act and react just as You would." And He will. It will surprise you how promptly He complies with such a request made in deadly earnest.

But summertime for the sheep is more than just flytime. It is also "scab-time." Scab is an irritating and highly contagious disease common among sheep the world over. Caused by a minute, microscopic parasite that proliferates in warm weather, "scab" spreads throughout a flock by direct contact between infected and non-infected animals.

Sheep love to rub heads in an affectionate and friendly manner. Scab is often found most commonly around the head. When two sheep rub together the infection spreads readily from one to the other.

In the Old Testament when it was declared that the sacrificial lambs should be without blemish, the thought uppermost in the writer's mind was that the animal should be free of scab. In a very real and direct sense scab is significant of contamination, of sin, of evil.

Again as with flies, the only effective antidote is to apply linseed oil, sulphur and other chemicals that can control this disease. In many sheep-rearing countries dips are built and the entire flock is put through the dip. Each animal is completely submerged in the solution until its entire body is soaked. The most difficult part to do is the head. The head has to be plunged under repeatedly to insure that scab there will be controlled. Some sheepmen take great care to treat the head by hand.

Only once did my sheep become infected by scab. I had purchased a few extra ewes from another rancher to increase the flock. It so happened they had, unknown to me, a slight infection of scab which quickly began to spread through the entire healthy flock. It meant I had to purchase a huge dipping tank and install it in my corrals. At great expense, to say nothing of the time and heavy labor involved, I had to put the entire flock, one by one through the dipping solution to clear them of the disease. It was a tremendous task and one which entailed special attention to their heads. So I know precisely what David meant when he wrote, "Thou anointest my head with oil." Again it was the only antidote for scab.

Perhaps it should be mentioned that in Palestine the old remedy for this disease was olive oil mixed with sulphur and spices. This home remedy served equally well in the case of flies that came to annoy the flocks.

In the Christian life, most of our contamination by the world, by sin, by that which would defile and disease us spiritually comes through our minds. It is a case of mind meeting mind to transmit ideas, concepts and attitudes which may be damaging.

Often it is when we "get our heads together" with someone else who may not necessarily have the mind of Christ, that we come away imbued with concepts that are not Christian.

Our thoughts, our ideas, our emotions, our choices, our impulses, drives and desires are all shaped and molded through the exposure of our minds to other people's minds. In our modern era of mass communication, the danger of the "mass mind" grows increasingly grave. Young people in particular, whose minds are so malleable find themselves being molded under the subtle pressures and impacts made on them by television, radio, magazines, newspapers, and fellow classmates, to say nothing of their parents and teachers.

Often the mass media which are largely responsible for shaping our minds are in the control of men whose characters are not Christlike: who in some cases are actually anti-Christian.

One cannot be exposed to such contacts without coming away contaminated. The thought patterns of people are becoming increasingly abhorrent. Today we find more tendency to violence, hatred, prejudice, greed, cynicism, and increasing disrespect for that which is noble, fine, pure or beautiful.

This is precisely the opposite of what Scripture teaches us. In Philippians 4:8 we are instructed emphatically in this matter,

". . . whatsoever things are true, whatsoever things are honest, whatsoever things are just, whatsoever things are pure, whatsoever things are lovely, whatsoever things are of good report; if there be any virtue, and if there be any praise, think on these things"! Here again, the only possible, practical path to attaining such a mind free of the world's contamination is to be conscious daily, hourly of the purging presence of God's Holy Spirit, applying Himself to my mind.

There are those who seem unable to realize His control of their minds and thoughts. It is a simple matter of faith and acceptance. Just as one asks Christ to come into the life initially to assure complete control of one's conduct, so one invites the Holy Spirit to come into one's conscious and subconscious mind to monitor one's thought-life. Just as by faith we believe and know and accept and thank Christ for coming into our lives, so by simple faith and confidence in the same Christ, we believe and know and accept with thanks the coming (or anointing) of His gracious Spirit upon our minds. Then having done this, we simply proceed to live and act and think as He directs us.

The difficulty is that some of us are not in dead earnest about it. Like a stubborn sheep we will struggle, kick and protest when the Master puts His hand upon us for this purpose. Even if it is for our own good, we still rebel and refuse to have Him help us when we need it so desperately.

In a sense we are a stiff-necked lot and were it not for Christ's continuing compassion and concern for us, most of us would be beyond hope or help. Sometimes I am quite sure Christ comes to us and applies the oil of His own Spirit to our minds in spite of our own objections. Were this not so, where would most of us be? Surely every gracious thought that enters my mind had its origin in Him.

Now as summer, in the high country, moves gradually into autumn, subtle changes occur both in the countryside and in the sheep. The nights become cooler; there are the first touches of frost; the insects begin to disappear and are less a pest; the foliage on the hills turns to crimson, gold and bronze; mist and rain begin to fall and the earth prepares for winter.

In the flock there are also subtle changes. This is the season of the rut, of mating, of great battles between the rams for possession of the ewes. The necks of the monarchs swell and grow strong. They strut proudly across the pastures and fight furiously for the favors of the ewes. The crash of heads and thud of colliding bodies can be heard through the hours of day and night.

The shepherd knows all about this. He knows that some of the sheep will and can actually kill, injure and maim each other in these deadly combats. So he decides on a very simple remedy. At this season of the year he will catch his rams and smear their heads with grease. I used to apply generous quantities of axle grease to the head and nose of each ram. Then when they collided in their great crashing battles the lubricant would make them glance off each other in such a ludicrous way they stood there feeling rather stupid and frustrated. In this way much of the heat and tension was dissipated and little damage done.

Among God's people there is a considerable amount of knocking each other. Somehow if we don't see eye to eye with the other person, we persist in trying to assert ourselves and become "top sheep." A good many become badly bruised and hurt this way.

In fact I found as a pastor that much of the grief, the wounds, the hurts, the ill will, the unforgiven things in people's lives could usually be traced back to old rivalries or jealousies or battles that had broken out between believers. Scores of skeptical souls will never enter a church simply because away back in their experience someone had battered them badly.

To forestall and prevent this sort of thing from happening among His people our Shepherd loves to apply the precious ointment of the presence of His gracious Spirit to our lives. It will be recalled that just before His crucifixion, our Lord in dealing with His twelve disciples, who, even then, were caught up in jealous bickering and rivalry for prestige, told of the coming of the Comforter—the Spirit of Truth. Because of His being sent to them, He said, they would know peace. He went on to say that His people would be known everywhere for their love for one another.

But too often this simply is not true among God's own people. They hammer and knock each other, stiff-necked with pride and self-assertion. They are intolerant, dogmatic and uncharitable with other Christians.

Yet when the gracious Holy Spirit invades a man or woman, when He enters that life and is in control of the personality, the attributes of peace, joy, long-suffering and generosity become apparent. It is then that suddenly one becomes aware of how ridiculous are all the petty jealousies, rivalries and animosities which formerly motivated their absurd assertions. This is to come to a place of great contentment in the Shepherd's care. And it is then the cup of contentment becomes real in the life. As the children of God, the sheep in the Divine Shepherd's care, we should be known as the most contented people on earth. A quiet, restful contentment should be the hallmark of those who call Christ their Master.

If He is the One who has all knowledge and wisdom and understanding of my affairs and management; if He is able to cope with every situation, good or bad, that I encounter, then surely I should be satisfied with His care. In a wonderful way my cup, or my lot in life, is a happy one that overflows with benefits of all sorts.

The trouble is most of us just don't see it this way. Especially when troubles or disappointments come along, we are apt to feel forgotten by our Shepherd. We act as though He had fallen down on the job.

Actually He is never asleep. He is never lax or careless. He is never indifferent to our well-being. Our Shepherd always has our best interests in mind.

Because of this we are actually under obligation to be a thankful, grateful, appreciative people. The New Testament instructs us clearly to grasp the idea that the cup of our life is full and overflowing with good, with the life of Christ Himself and with the presence of His gracious Spirit. And because of this we should be joyous, grateful and serene.

This is the overcoming Christian life. It is the life in which a Christian can be content with whatever comes his way—*even trouble* (Hebrews 13:5). Most of us are glad when things go well. How many of us can give thanks and praise when things go wrong?

Looking again at the round of the year through which the sheep pass in the shepherd's care, we see summer moving into autumn. Storms of sleet and hail and early snow begin to sweep over the high country. Soon the flocks will be driven from the alplands and tablelands. They will turn again toward the home ranch for the long, quiet winter season.

These autumn days can be golden under Indian summer weather. The sheep have respite now from flies and insects and scab. No other season finds them so fit and well and strong. No wonder David wrote, "My cup runneth over."

But at the same time, unexpected blizzards can blow up or sleet storms suddenly shroud the hills. The flock and their owner can pass through appalling suffering together.

It is here that I grasp another aspect altogether of the meaning of a cup that overflows. There is in every life a cup of suffering. Jesus Christ referred to His agony in the Garden of Gethsemane and at Calvary as His cup. And had it not overflowed with His life poured out for men, we would have perished.

In tending my sheep I carried a bottle in my pocket containing a mixture of brandy and water. Whenever a ewe or lamb was chilled from undue exposure to wet, cold weather I would pour a few spoonfuls down its throat. In a matter of minutes the chilled creature would be on its feet and full of renewed energy. It was especially cute the way the lambs would wiggle their tails with joyous excitement as the warmth from the brandy spread through their bodies.

The important thing was for me to be there on time, to find the frozen, chilled sheep before it was too late. I had to be in the storm with them, alert to every one that was in distress. Some of the most vivid memories of my sheep ranching days are wrapped around the awful storms my flock and I went through together. I can see again the gray-black banks of storm clouds sweeping in off the sea; I can see the sleet and hail and snow sweeping across the hills; I can see the sheep racing for shelter in the tall timber; I can see them standing there soaked, chilled, and dejected. Especially the young lambs went through appalling misery without the benefit of a full, heavy fleece to protect them. Some would succumb and lie down in distress only to become more cramped and chilled.

Then it was that my mixture of brandy and water came to their rescue. I'm sure the Palestinian shepherds must have likewise shared their wine with their chilled and frozen sheep.

What a picture of my Master, sharing the wine, the very life blood of His own suffering from His overflowing cup, poured out at Calvary for me. He is there with me in every storm. My Shepherd is alert to every approaching disaster that threatens His people. He has been through the storms of sufferings before. He bore our sorrows and was acquainted with our grief.

And now no matter what storms I face, His very life and strength and vitality is poured into mine. It overflows so the cup of my life runs over with His life . . . often with great blessing and benefit to others who see me stand up so well in the midst of trials and suffering.

# 11
# Surely
# Goodness and Mercy
# Shall Follow Me . . .

THROUGHOUT THE STUDY of this Psalm continuous emphasis has been put upon the care exercised by the attentive sheepman. It has been stressed how essential to the welfare of the sheep is the rancher's diligent effort and labor. All the benefits enjoyed by a flock under skilled and loving management have been drawn in bold lines.

Now all of this is summed up here by the Psalmist in one brave but simple statement: "Surely goodness and mercy shall follow me all the days of my life"!

The sheep with such a shepherd knows of a surety that his is a privileged position. No matter what comes, at least and always he can be perfectly sure that goodness and mercy will be in the picture. He reassures himself that he is ever under sound, sympathetic, intelligent ownership. What more need he care about? Goodness and mercy will be the treatment he receives from his master's expert, loving hands.

Not only is this a bold statement, but it is somewhat of a boast, an exclamation of implicit confidence in the One who controls his career and destiny.

How many Christians actually feel this way about Christ? How many of us are truly concerned that no matter what occurs in our lives we are being followed by goodness and mercy? Of course it is very simple to speak this way when things are going well. If my health is excellent; my income is flourishing; my family is well; and my friends are fond of me it is not hard to say "Surely goodness and mercy shall follow me all the days of my life."

But what about when one's body breaks down? What do I say

when I stand by helpless, as I have had to do, and watch a life partner die by degrees under appalling pain? What is my reaction when my job folds up and there is no money to meet bills? What happens if my children can't make their grades in school or get caught running with the wrong gang? What do I say when suddenly, without good grounds, friends prove false and turn against me?

These are the sort of times that test a person's confidence in the care of Christ. These are the occasions during which the chips are down and life is more than a list of pious platitudes. When my little world is falling apart and the dream castles of my ambitions and hopes crumble into ruins can I honestly declare "Surely—yes—surely—goodness and mercy shall follow me all the days of my life"? Or is this sheer humbug and a maddening mockery?

In looking back over my own life, in the light of my own love and care for my sheep, I can see again and again a similar compassion and concern for me in my Master's management of my affairs. There were events which at the time seemed like utter calamities; there were paths down which He led me that appeared like blind allies; there were days He took me through which were well nigh black as night itself. But all in the end turned out for my benefit and my well-being.

With my limited understanding as a finite human being I could not always comprehend His management executed in infinite wisdom. With my natural tendencies to fear, worry and ask "why," it was not always simple to assume that He really did know what He was doing with me. There were times I was tempted to panic, to bolt and to leave His care. Somehow I had the strange, stupid notion I could survive better on my own. Most men and women do.

But despite this perverse behavior I am so glad He did not give me up. I am so grateful He did follow me in goodness and mercy. The only possible motivation was His own love, His care and concern for me as one of His sheep. And despite my doubts, despite my misgivings about His management of my affairs, He has picked me up and borne me back again in great tenderness.

As I see all of this in retrospect I realize that for the one who is truly in Christ's care, no difficulty can arise, no dilemma emerge, no seeming disaster descend on the life without eventual good coming out of the chaos. This is to see the goodness and mercy of my Master in my life. It has become the great foundation of my faith and confidence in Him.

I love Him because He first loved me.

His goodness and mercy and compassion to me are new every day. And my assurance is lodged in these aspects of His character. My trust is in His love for me as His own. My serenity has as its basis an implicit, unshakable reliance on His ability to do the right thing, the best thing in any given situation.

This to me is the *supreme* portrait of my Shepherd. Continually there flows out to me His goodness and His mercy, which, even though I do not deserve them, come unremittingly from their source of supply—His own great heart of love.

Herein is the essence of all that has gone before in this Psalm.

All the care, all the work, all the alert watchfulness, all the skill, all the concern, all the self-sacrifice are born of His love—the love of One who loves His sheep, loves His work, loves His role as a Shepherd.

"I am the good shepherd: the good shepherd giveth his life for the sheep."

"Hereby perceive we the love of God, because he laid down his life for us" (I John 3:16).

With all this in view it is then proper to ask myself, "Is this outflow of goodness and mercy for me to stop and stagnate in my life? Is there no way in which it can pass on through me to benefit others?"

Yes, there is a way.

And this aspect is one which eludes many of us.

There is a positive, practical aspect in which my life in turn should be one whereby goodness and mercy follow in my footsteps for the well-being of others.

Just as God's goodness and mercy flow to me all the days of my life, so goodness and mercy should follow me, should be left behind me, as a legacy to others, wherever I may go.

It is worth reiterating at this point that sheep can, under mismanagement, be the most destructive livestock. In short order they can ruin and ravage land almost beyond remedy. But in bold contrast they can, on the other hand, be the most beneficial of all livestock if properly managed.

Their manure is the best balanced of any produced by domestic stock. When scattered efficiently over the pastures it proves of enormous benefit to the soil. The sheep's habit of seeking the highest rise of ground on which to rest insures that the fertility from the rich low land is re-deposited on the less productive higher ground. No other livestock will consume as wide a variety of herbage. Sheep eat all sorts of weeds and other undesirable plants which might otherwise invade a field. For example, they love the buds and tender tips of Canada thistle which, if not controlled, can quickly become a most noxious weed. In a few years a flock of well-managed sheep will clean up and restore a piece of ravaged land as no other creature can do.

In ancient literature sheep were referred to as "those of the golden hooves"—simply because they were regarded and esteemed so highly for their beneficial effect on the land.

In my own experience as a sheep rancher I have, in just a few years, seen two derelict ranches restored to high productivity and usefulness. More than this, what before appeared as depressing eyesores became beautiful, park-like properties of immense worth. Where previously there had been only poverty and pathetic waste, there now followed flourishing fields and rich abundance.

In other words, goodness and mercy had followed my flocks. They left behind them something worthwhile, productive, beautiful and beneficial to both themselves, others and me. Where they had walked there followed fertility and weed-free land. Where they had lived there remained beauty and abundance.

The question now comes to me pointedly, is this true of my life?

Do I leave a blessing and benediction behind me?

Sir Alfred Tennyson wrote in one of his great classic poems, "The good men do lives after them."

On one occasion two friends spent a few days in our home while passing through en route to some engagements in the East. They invited me to go along. After several days on the road one of the men missed his hat. He was sure it had been left in our home. He asked me to write my wife to find it and kindly send it on to him.

Her letter of reply was one I shall never forget. One sentence in particular made an enormous impact on me. "I have combed the house from top to bottom and can find no trace of the hat. The only thing those men left behind was a great blessing!"

Is this the way people feel about me?

Do I leave a trail of sadness or of gladness behind?

Is my memory, in other people's minds, entwined with mercy and goodness, or would they rather forget me altogether?

Do I deposit a blessing behind me or am I a bane to others? Is my life a pleasure to people or a pain?

In Isaiah 52:7 we read, "How beautiful upon the mountains are the feet of [them] that bringeth good tidings, that publisheth peace. . . ."

Sometimes it is profitable to ask ourselves such simple questions as—

"Do I leave behind peace in lives—or turmoil?"

"Do I leave behind forgiveness—or bitterness?"

"Do I leave behind contentment—or conflict?"

"Do I leave behind flowers of joy—or frustration?"

"Do I leave behind love—or rancor?"

Some people leave such a sorry mess behind them wherever they go that they prefer to cover their tracks.

For the true child of God, the one under the Shepherd's care, there should never be any sense of shame or fear in going back to where they have lived or been before. Why? Because there they have left a legacy of uplift, encouragement and inspiration to others.

In Africa, where I spent so many years, one of the greatest marks left by any man was that of David Livingstone. No matter where his footsteps took him through the bush and plains of the great continent there remained the impact of his love. Natives, whose language he never learned, long years after, remembered him as the kindly, tender doctor whom goodness and mercy had followed all the days of his life.

There remains in my own mind boyhood recollections of the

first stories I was told about Jesus Christ as a man amongst us. His life was summed up in the simple, terse, but deeply profound statement, "He went about, doing good!" It was as though this was the loftiest, noblest, most important thing on which He could possibly spend His few short years.

But I also was deeply impressed by the fact that His good and kindly acts were always commingled with mercy. Where so often other human beings were rude and harsh and vindictive of one another, His compassion and tenderness was always apparent. Even the most flagrant sinners found forgiveness with Him, whereas at the hands of their fellow men they knew only condemnation, censure and cruel criticism.

And again I have to ask myself is this my attitude to other people? Do I sit up on my pedestal of self-pride and look with contempt upon my contemporaries, or do I get down and identify myself with them in their dilemma and there extend a small measure of the goodness and mercy given to me by my Master?

Do I see sinners with the compassion of Christ or with the critical eye of censure?

Am I willing to overlook faults and weaknesses in others and extend forgiveness as God has forgiven me my failings?

The only real, practical measure of my appreciation for the goodness and mercy of God to me is the extent to which I am, in turn, prepared to show goodness and mercy to others.

If I am unable to forgive and extend friendship to fallen men and women, then it is quite certain I know little or nothing in a practical sense of Christ's forgiveness and mercy to me.

It is this lack of love among Christians which today makes the church an insipid, lukewarm institution. People come to find affection and are turned off by our tepidity.

But the man or woman who knows firsthand about the goodness and mercy of God in his own life, will be warm and affectionate with goodness and mercy to others. This is to be a benefit to them, but equally important, it is to be a blessing to God.

Yes, a blessing to God!

Most of us think only God can bring a blessing to us. The Christian life is a two-way proposition.

Nothing pleased me more than to see my flock flourish and prosper. It delighted me personally, no end, to feel compensated for the care I had given them. To see them content was wonderful. To see the land benefiting was beautiful. And the two together made me a happy man. It enriched my own life; it was a reward for my efforts and energy. In this experience I received full compensation for all that I had poured into the endeavor.

Most of us forget that our Shepherd is looking for some satisfaction as well. We are told that He looked upon the travail of His soul and was satisfied.

This is the benefit we can bring to Him.

He looks on my life in tenderness for He loves me deeply. He sees the long years during which His goodness and mercy have followed me without slackening. He longs to see some measure of that same goodness and mercy not only passed on to others by me but also passed back to Him with joy.

He longs for love—my love.

And I love Him—only and because He first loved me.

Then He is satisfied.

# 12
# I Will Dwell
# in the House of
# the Lord For Ever

THIS PSALM OPENED with the proud, joyous statement, "The Lord is my Shepherd."

Now it closes with the equally positive, buoyant affirmation, "And I will dwell in the house of the Lord forever."

Here is a sheep so utterly satisfied with its lot in life, so fully contented with the care it receives, so much "at home" with the shepherd that there is not a shred of desire for a change.

Stated in simple, direct, rather rough ranch language it would be put like this, "Nothing will ever make me leave this outfit—it's great!"

Conversely on the shepherd's side there has developed a great affection and devotion to his flock. He would never think of parting with such a sheep. Healthy, contented, productive sheep are his delight and profit. So strong, now, are the bonds between them that it is in very truth—forever.

The word "house" used here in the poem has wider meaning than most people could attach to it. Normally we speak of the house of the Lord as the sanctuary or church or meeting place of God's people. In one sense David may have had this in mind. And, of course, it is pleasant to think that one would always delight to be found in the Lord's house.

But it must be kept in mind always, that the Psalmist, writing from the standpoint of a sheep, is reflecting on and recounting the full round of the year's activities for the flock.

He has taken us from the green pastures and still waters of the home ranch, up through the mountain passes onto the high tablelands of the summer range. Fall has come with its storms and rain and sleet that drives the sheep down the foothills and back to the home ranch for the long, quiet winter. In a sense this is coming home. It is a return to the fields and corrals and barns and shelters of the owner's home. During all seasons of the year, with their hazards, dangers and disturbances, it is the rancher's alertness, care and energetic management that has brought the sheep through satisfactorily.

It is with a sublime feeling of both composure and contentment that this statement, "I will dwell in the house of the Lord for ever," is made.

Actually what is referred to by "house" is the family or household or flock of the Good Shepherd. The sheep is so deeply satisfied with the flock to which it belongs, with the ownership of this particular shepherd that it has no wish to change whatever.

It is as if it had finally come home again and was now standing at the fence, bragging to its less fortunate neighbors on the other side. It boasts about the wonderful year it has had and its complete confidence in its owner.

Sometimes I feel we Christians should be much more like this. We should be proud to belong to Christ. Why shouldn't we feel free to boast to others of how good our Shepherd is? How glad we should be to look back and recall all the amazing ways in which He has provided for our welfare. We should delight to describe, in detail, the hard experiences through which He has brought us. And we should be eager and quick to tell of our confidence in Christ. We should be bold to state fearlessly that we are so glad we are His. By the contentment and serenity of our lives we should show what a distinct advantage it is to be a member of His "household," of His flock.

I can never meditate on this last phrase in the Psalm without there welling up in my memory vivid scenes from some of the early days on my first sheep ranch.

As winter, with its cold rains and chilling winds came on, my neighbor's sickly sheep would stand huddled at the fence, their tails to the storm, facing the rich fields in which my flock flourished. Those poor, abused, neglected creatures under the ownership of a heartless rancher had known nothing but suffering most of the year. With them there had been gnawing hunger all summer. They were thin and sickly with disease and scab and parasites. Tormented by flies and attacked by predators, some were so weak and thin and wretched that their thin legs could scarcely bear their scanty frames.

Always there seemed to lurk in their eyes the slender, faint hope that perhaps with a bit of luck they could break through the fence or crawl through some hole to free themselves. Occasionally this used to happen, especially around Christmas. This was the time of extreme tides when the sea retreated far out beyond the end of the fence lines which ran down to it. The neighbor's emaciated, dissatisfied, hungry sheep would wait for this to happen. Then at the first chance they would go down on the tidal flats; slip around the end of the fence and come sneaking in to gorge themselves on our rich green grass.

So pitiful and pathetic was their condition that the sudden feast of lush feed, to which they were unaccustomed, often proved disastrous. Their digestive systems would begin to scour and sometimes this led to death. I recall clearly coming across three of my neighbor's ewes lying helpless under a fir tree near the fence one drizzly day. They were like three old, limp, gray, sodden sacks collapsed in a heap. Even their bony legs would no longer support them.

I loaded them into a wheelbarrow and wheeled them back to their heartless owner. He simply pulled out a sharp killing knife and slit all three of their throats. He couldn't care less.

What a picture of Satan who holds ownership over so many.

Right there the graphic account of Jesus portrayed of Himself as being the door and entrance by which sheep were to enter His fold flashed across my mind.

Those poor sheep had not come into my ranch through the proper gate. I had never let them in. They had never really become mine. They had not come under my ownership or control. If they had, they would not have suffered so. Even starting out under my management they would have been given very special care. First they would have been put on dry, limited rations, then they would gradually have been allowed green feed until they were adjusted to the new diet and mode of life.

In short, they tried to get in on their own. It simply spelled disaster. What made it doubly sad was that they were doomed anyway. On the old impoverished ranch they would have starved to death that winter.

Likewise with those apart from Christ. The old world is a pretty wretched ranch and Satan is a heartless owner. He cares not a wit for men's souls or welfare. Under his tyranny there are hundreds of hungry, discontented hearts who long to enter into the household of God—who ache for His care and concern.

Yet there is only one way into this fold. That way is through the owner, Christ Himself—the Good Shepherd. He boldly declared, "I am the door: by me if any man enter in, he shall be saved, and shall go in and out, and find pasture" (John 10:9).

Almost every day I am literally rubbing shoulders with men and women "on the other side of the fence." What is my impact upon them? Is my life so serene, so satisfying, so radiant because I walk and talk and live with God, that they become envious? Do they see in me the benefits of being under Christ's control? Do they see something of Himself reflected in my conduct and character? Does my life and conversation lead them to Him—and thus into life everlasting?

If so, then I may be sure some of them will also long to dwell in the house of the Lord forever. And there is no reason why this cannot happen if they come under His proper ownership.

There is one other beautiful and final sense in which the psalmist was speaking as a sheep. It is brought out in the Amplified Old Testament where the meaning of this last phrase is, "I will dwell in the 'presence' of the Lord forever."

My personal conviction is that this is the most significant sentiment that David had in his heart as he ended this hymn of praise to divine diligence.

Not only do we get the idea of an ever-present Shepherd on the scene, but also the concept that the sheep wants to be in full view of his owner at all times.

This theme has run all through our studies. It is the alertness, the awareness, the diligence of a never-tiring master which alone assures the sheep of excellent care. And from the sheep's standpoint it is knowing that the shepherd is there; it is the constant awareness of his presence nearby that automatically eliminates most of the difficulties and dangers while at the same time providing a sense of security and serenity.

It is the sheep owner's presence that guarantees there will be no lack of any sort; that there will be abundant green pastures; that there will be still, clean waters; that there will be new paths into fresh fields; that there will be safe summers on the high tablelands; that there will be freedom from fear; that there will be antidotes for flies and disease and parasites; that there will be quietness and contentment.

In our Christian lives and experience precisely the same idea and principle applies. For when all is said and done on the subject of a successful Christian walk, it can be summed up in one sentence. "Live ever aware of God's presence."

There is the "inner" consciousness, which can be very distinct and very real, of Christ's presence in my life, made evident by His gracious Holy Spirit within. It is He who speaks to us in distinct and definite ways about our behavior. For our part it is a case of being sensitive and responsive to that inner voice.

There can be an habitual awareness of Christ within me, empowering me to live a noble and richly rewarding life in cooperation with Himself. As I respond to Him and move in harmony with His wishes I discover life becomes satisfying and worthwhile. It acquires great serenity and is made an exciting adventure of fulfillment as I progress in it. This is made possible as I allow His gracious Spirit to control, manage and direct my daily decisions. In fact, I should deliberately ask for His direction even in minute details.

Then there is the wider but equally thrilling awareness of God all around me. I live surrounded by His presence. I am an open person, an open individual, living life open to His scrutiny. He is conscious of every circumstance I encounter. He attends me with care and concern because I belong to Him. And this will continue through eternity. What an assurance!

I shall dwell in the presence (in the care of) the Lord forever. Bless His Name.

# A LAYMAN

# LOOKS AT

# THE LORD'S PRAYER

*In honor of my father,*
*a*
*humble layman*
*who*
*walked with God.*

# Acknowledgments

A word of gratitude is due those many men and women who, across the years, have sat in my Bible studies, absorbing truths contained in this work. Had it not been for those willing to study God's Word with me, there would not have been the delightful incentive to search deeply for the great meanings implied in the Lord's Prayer.

Also, my genuine appreciation is extended to my wife, who, with great care and affection, typed and prepared the final manuscript for publication. Often we have prayed together that this book be used widely by God our Father to inspire and encourage His children the world over.

# Contents

Preface    133

  1   Our Father    136

  2   Which Art in Heaven    148

  3   Hallowed Be Thy Name    166

  4   Thy Kingdom Come    178

  5   Thy Will Be Done    188

  6   In Earth, as It Is in Heaven    200

  7   Give Us This Day Our Daily Bread    212

  8   And Forgive Us Our Debts    222

  9   As We Forgive Our Debtors    230

10   And Lead Us Not into Temptation    238

11   But Deliver Us from Evil    248

12   For Thine Is the Kingdom, and the Power, and the Glory, for Ever. Amen    256

# The Lord's Prayer

9 *Our Father which art in heaven, Hallowed be thy name.*

10 *Thy kingdom come. Thy will be done in earth, as it is in heaven.*

11 *Give us this day our daily bread.*

12 *And forgive us our debts, as we forgive our debtors.*

13 *And lead us not into temptation, but deliver us from evil: For thine is the kingdom, and the power, and the glory, for ever. Amen.*

MATTHEW 6: 9–13

# Preface

NEXT TO PSALM 23, perhaps the most beloved and certainly the best-known passage in Scripture is the Lord's Prayer. It has been repeated millions upon millions of times by countless numbers of human beings for nearly twenty centuries. Yet, in spite of so much use, in spite of so much repetition, in spite of so much worldwide familiarity, it has never lost its luster.

The profound, eternal concepts compressed into its few, concise phrases shine with enduring brilliance. These truths radiated from the very heart of our Lord as He moved among men. They embrace the deepest secrets of God, quietly stated in human language of disarming simplicity. Some of the petitions included in this prayer by Christ were utterly revolutionary. If fully grasped by us, they can overturn much of our own wrong thinking about God.

The Lord's Prayer, in the King James version, contains only sixty-six words. It can be repeated in less than a minute. Despite its brevity, it has been an enormous benefit to multitudes of men and women. Many of them knew little or nothing else about the Scriptures. Yet there is inherent in this prayer all the strength and compassion of our Father in heaven. There moves through it a beauty and serenity which no mortal man can fully explain. It reassures our hearts, strengthens our resolve, and leads us into personal contact with God, our Father.

Much that is deep and profound has already been written about this prayer. Still, that does not dissuade me from writing about it as a layman. To me it is a most precious passage. And here, as in my previous book, *A Shepherd Looks at Psalm 23*, I dare to share with the reader what these Scriptures mean to me—an ordinary man and a child of God.

# 1
# Our Father

# "OUR FATHER."

What an intimate, personal, family-like approach to God. What a reassuring, comfortable way in which to address the Almighty, Creator of heaven and earth. Can it be that He, who is from everlasting to everlasting, the infinite One, really regards me as His child? Does He care enough to consider me His own son?

This is a startling concept.

It is unique. It stands as a brand new revelation of God, given to us with repeated emphasis and clarity by Christ.

Prior to the time of Jesus, God was regarded as someone remote and august in His demeanor. He sat in the high and holy place, a stern Judge behind the hard, harsh bar of the Law. Only with fear and foreboding did any man dare to address himself to such a powerful potentate.

All through the Old Testament account of God's dealing with His people He is referred to as YAHWEH, the name which dared not be spoken for fear of offense. Fewer than seven times is He even referred to as a father, except indirectly and rather remotely.

Yet in the first four gospels, Jesus, the Christ, casting aside all restraint, speaks of God as Father more than seventy times. It is a radical, new, and very exciting disclosure that God is our Father. Suddenly it puts man's relationship to Him into an entirely new light. He moves from behind the bar of justice to come knocking on the door of our human hearts. He enters our lives to become a "Father to the fatherless."

The whole concept is replete with wonder and incredible love. It hardly seems possible that He who has been from everlasting to everlasting, the eternal, infinite God, should delight to have us call Him, "Our Father."

But not all of us can do this either easily or in sincerity. It is a frightening fact that for many people, the word father does not denote a dear one. It does not conjure up the thought of a happy home. Rather, to them it may well be a repulsive and abhorrent title.

Many people have known only harsh, hard fathers. Their human father may have been a selfish, self-centered person who cared little for their well-being. He may have been a derelict, a drunkard, a dope addict, or some other distorted person who wrought havoc with their personalities in early childhood.

Or the human father may have been a weak-willed person who could command no respect from his children. He may have neglected his duties to his home and family, so that he earned only contempt and scorn from his offspring. Even at his very best, he may have at times fluctuated in his moods and temper, one day lenient in dealing with his children, the next tough and terrifying. So how could one so inconsistent, so unpredictable, be trusted?

Little do many fathers know the importance of their role in shaping the characters of their children at an early age. Long before boys and girls are even off to school, the cast of their characters and the pattern of their personalities have been shaped under the parents' hands in the home. More often than we would admit, this is a period of pain to the child. Deep doubts and miserable misgivings arise in the malleable minds of youngsters. They wonder if they are really wanted. They long to know if they are really loved. They search for someone who can really be trusted, someone who really understands them.

Because of all this the name *father*, instead of being rich with warm and happy memories, is frequently associated with fear and repulsion, anger and hostility, sometimes even hate and scorn.

And the tragedy is that in ascribing the title to God as our Father, we sometimes unconsciously transfer to Him all those debasing attributes associated in our minds with our human fathers.

Of course this is not done deliberately. Still, it is done. The consequences for both us and God can be devastating. We do Him an enormous injustice by superimposing upon His character the facsimile of a human father. At very best it can be no more than a caricature, a distortion of His true being.

If our human fathers have been fair, honest, decent individuals, then our mental picture of God is bound to be more favorable. If they have been generous, loving, gentle men, endowed with more than the usual degree of human understanding and compassion, this will enhance our concept of what God may be like. And it is inevitable that, in our minds, we will take a more magnanimous view of God.

But the fact remains that, to a large degree, our thoughts and ideas of God as our Father are conditioned by our childhood impressions and recollections of our rather frail and fallible human fathers. Far, far too often we ascribe to God in heaven all the weaknesses, idiosyncrasies, failings, and inconsistencies of our very unpredictable human fathers.

None of this was in the mind of Christ when He spoke so sincerely and so simply of God as His Father. His view of God was not conditioned by His childhood relationship to Joseph, the carpenter of Nazareth, but by His own personal identity with God the Father throughout the eons of eternity.

He alone knew fully the true essence of God's character. He alone comprehended the beauty and integrity and wonder of God's personality. And He spared no pains to portray to us the caliber of this One.

If we are to appreciate fully the kind of person God is, if we are to grasp His essential love and goodness, if we are to understand even a little of the wonder of His winsomeness, if we are to know the strength of His integrity and reliability, then we must see Him as Christ saw Him.

Obviously God the Father completely dominated Christ's thinking. He influenced all of the Son's conduct. He occupied the prior place in all His affections. He was ever in His mind and on His lips.

One of the half-truths which plagues Christians is the old saying, "What you are speaks so loud, I cannot hear what you say." It is true, one's actions should correspond with one's words. But we can really only comprehend what a person's inner thoughts and life are like by what he says. "For out of the abundance of the heart the mouth speaketh" (Mt 12:34).

So if we are to fully grasp Christ's innermost thoughts and concepts of God as Father, we must, of necessity, pay careful attention to what He said about Him, as well as observe how Christ conducted Himself before His Father.

Jesus stated emphatically, "He that hath seen me hath seen the Father" (Jn 14:9). And we are most grateful for this personal, open revelation of God to us mortal men. In addition to His impeccable life, lived out before us on the stage of human affairs, we have as well His precepts and parables given to us for illumination. They are an endeavor to have us fully appreciate what God our Father is like.

There is no doubt that when Christ addressed God as His Father, it was in the full and splendid relationship of perfect Sonship. There was complete understanding. There was absolute agreement. There was total unity and harmony. There was deep delight.

But for us there is not always this open and unclouded approach to our Father.

We are haunted by our own misgivings. We are sometimes uneasy because of our own misconduct. We come rather gingerly because of our guilt. We wonder if we really will be understood because we are not sure we even understand ourselves. And often we question secretly if we will even be accepted.

Because of all this, it is essential to a reassuring and satisfying relationship with God that we study what His character is like. Unless we do begin to grasp what kind of person God is, we shall never fully develop a simple, strong confidence in Him. Yet, this is what He wants from us more than anything else, our trust and affection as His children.

The most outstanding attribute of our Father God is His love. There is a quality of selflessness and altruism to His character which is almost foreign to our finite human concept of love. So much of our love is self-centered. Often we are loving only when such conduct serves our own ends or satisfies our own selfish impulses.

With God, however, there is a love of magnificent and unchanging proportions. His care and concern and affection for us are not dependent upon His moods or our good behavior or our response to His overtures. Rather, it flows out to us in a clear, pure, powerful stream that has as its source and strength His own great heart of love. It is constant and unconditional.

Evidence of this lies in the fact that He Himself was willing to pay the penalty for our misdeeds. For God was in Christ reconciling the wayward world to Himself, not charging men's transgressions to their account (2 Co 5:19). And this He did for us through the death of His own dear Son while we were still alienated from Him.

Such a magnanimous gesture is almost beyond the bounds of our finite human comprehension. Nonetheless, it is an attested fact, which in itself undergirds our confidence in Him. It enables us to come to Him quietly, confidently, and without fear as, "Our Father." We can do this, not because of any merit on our part but rather because of His own generous attitude of concern and affection for us. We come freely because He has invited us to come, with an openhanded, greathearted welcome. But we can come and receive that welcome only through true repentance toward God and faith in His Son, the Lord Jesus Christ, as our Saviour. Only in this way can the Father-son relationship be established.

All too often God is viewed as a stern, austere Judge standing over us in an attitude of disdain and deprecation. We seem to see Him holding in His hands a giant set of scales. In it our bad deeds are weighed against our good conduct. And often we are filled with dismay at how our sins outweigh our good.

But this is a caricature of God our Father. It is a most distorted view of the One who loves us deeply and is able to enter fully and completely into our human dilemma. This is so because having made us, He understands our limitations and is sympathetic to our earthly struggles. He remembers that we are born and shaped in iniquity, that our brief sojourn upon the planet is a fleeting interval in which we struggle to cope with the assaults of sin and Satan upon our souls.

No, God our Father is not some distant deity who stands apart and aloof from the trials of men. He is not one to sit sternly in condemnation of His children. Rather, because He did identify

Himself completely with us through the birth, life, and death of His Son our Saviour, He is touched with the feelings of our infirmities (Heb 2:16–18). He looks upon us in compassion and deep concern. He is moved by the least inclination on our part to resist evil and do good. And at every opportunity, He extends His helping hand to us by His gracious Spirit, eager to lift us up above the downward pull of evil.

Moreover, when we approach God, our Father, we are drawing close to Him who completely understands us. This is a concept which should give us enormous comfort and consolation.

It is an unfortunate fact that the great majority of human difficulties arise because we do not understand each other. At our very best, we humans are unpredictable. We can never fully understand why we do or say the things we do. No wonder we have so much conflict and chaos in interpersonal relations.

Besides our inability to understand others, no man or woman fully understands even himself or herself. We cannot possibly unravel all the peculiar characteristics we may have acquired through complex hereditary processes from our parents. What makes one child in a family docile and agreeable while a brother or sister may be a self-willed young rebel?

Nor, likewise, can any person possibly determine the impact made upon his character by his parents or siblings during his formative years. At this critical time of life, all sorts of forces, unknown to him, have shaped the pattern of his future conduct. The influences of home, school, friends, teachers, parents, and casual acquaintances throughout one's life, condition his behavior, reactions, and outlook. Who can possibly understand all this? Certainly we cannot. At best we do not understand ourselves, let alone others. This is why so often we are so hard on ourselves and so harsh in our judgment and censure of others.

But this is not the case with the infinite, all-knowing God our Father. For He does know our makeup. He does understand why we are as we are. He does, in His all embracing tenderness, appreciate our particular problems. And because He does, He has a much more magnanimous attitude toward us than most of us have to ourselves or to each other (Ps 103:13–14).

It is for this reason that we can come to Him as our Father with the assurance that we will be given an understanding hearing. Unlike dealing with human beings, we will not be given short shrift. We will not be held in contempt. We will not be cut off or cut down with a critical attitude or cruel condemnation. Christ Himself reassured us of this when He emphasized that He had not come into the world to condemn men but to deliver them from their dilemma.

When we fully appreciate that the thoughts and inner attitudes of God toward us are good and gentle and understanding, what a difference it can make in our approach to Him. We come now, knowing full well that we shall be met with compassion and kindness, understanding and affection.

This reassures our hearts. It sets our minds at ease. It frees our spirits and releases us into a deep dimension of delight in our dealings with our heavenly Father. How good to know, here is someone who really understands; who knows all about us and who, even though He knows the worst, still loves us.

This explains why we can come to Him in any situation and find a warm welcome. It explains why we can count on a sympathetic hearing. Nothing else is so sure to dispel our fears and allay our anxiety as to know that in dealing with our Father, we are indeed dealing with a consistent character.

In human relations, all of us know that many of our problems arise because of the unpredictable nature of people. If a parent wakes up in the morning with a sick headache or upset stomach, it is more than likely the rest of the family will feel the brunt of the malady. We tend to vent our suffering and stresses on those around us. When a man is in a good mood and cheerful frame of mind, he will probably treat his children with great forbearance and leniency. But if, on the other hand, things are going wrong and he is in a bad mood, it is probable he will be harsh and hard with his family.

But there is none of this about God our Father. He is not fickle. He is not changeable. He is not subject to unpredictable fluctuations of temperament. He is always the same (Heb 13:8). Because of this, our relationship with Him can be a most beautiful thing.

There is nothing else to compare with it in the whole realm of human relationships.

Only those who do truly know Him as Father are aware of how wonderful it is to be acquainted with such a being. For the rest, there lurks in the background of their minds the suspicion that somehow all of this is just too good to be true. They feel unsure of Him and unsure of others.

In order to convey this reliable aspect of God His Father's character to us, Jesus told the moving story of a father and his two sons (Lk 15:11–32). It is perhaps the most poignant parable in the gospels. The father's attitude toward both boys never altered, never changed. The young rascal subjected his father to appalling anxiety and awful anguish of heart. His dear old dad died a thousand deaths for that lad while he was away living it up. His father was no fool. He knew what the boy was doing in the distant land. Even the older brother knew that much. Not only was the father's fortune being squandered, but also his good name was being dragged in the dust. And on top of this, the old man's heart was being crushed relentlessly with sorrow.

Yet, despite all that the profligate son did to dismay his father, the parent's attitude toward him never deviated. In spite of all the shame, suffering, scandal, and loss, the father's love never diminished. Instead there went out from him forgiveness, compassion, love, and concern. At no time did he reject or repudiate his child. Despite all the boy had done, he was forgiven. He was never disowned or disinherited. And the day that broken, battered boy stumbled up the road toward home, he was met with the father's open arms and open heart that had never been shut against him.

The picture is replete with pathos and power. The essence of the character of God our Father comes through to us here with no textual difficulty. The language is too clear, too simple, too potent for us to explain it away. This boy, despite all his misdeeds, had always been forgiven. All he had to do was come to his father and accept the forgiveness which was always there. The day he did this, he knew and felt fully accepted by his father. His misconduct was forgiven. The price and penalty for all his perverseness had been paid for in the suffering of his father.

This is what sets the forgiveness of God our Father on a plane far above that of us human beings. Not only has He forgiven us our misdemeanors, not only does He forget them, but He Himself bears the penalty of suffering which attends our misconduct.

The best of human beings, even when they find it within themselves to forgive another, seldom if ever can forget the wrong done to them. And, what is more, they expect that the one who committed the offense shall somehow, in due course, be made to pay the penalty for his misbehavior.

Even if we look at the relationship between the older of the two sons and his father, we find Christ conveying the same principle to our hearts. The elder brother, in his attitude of self-righteousness and self-pity had built a wall between himself and his father. All of his father's attempts to reach across that barrier had apparently been of no avail. He reassured the boy that everything he owned was his. In fact, according to tradition, he was entitled to twice as much as his younger brother because he was the first-born son. His father's love and affection and interest in him were ever the same. But the poor fellow's pride and self-esteem prevented him from enjoying all the benefits at his disposal. This was simply because he did not believe what his father said. He was trying so hard to earn and merit by diligent service what was already rightfully his as the elder son.

His plight is almost the more pathetic of the two. It shows us a man who really never got to know his father. The picture painted for us is that of a person who sees God his Father, as someone harsh and hard and very demanding. He has never sensed His love, compassion, generosity, and fantastic forgiveness. And because he keeps his father at arm's length there has never been that wondrous sensation of feeling those open arms flung about him. He has never felt accepted. He has never felt wanted.

But just because the older boy took this attitude toward his father, it did not change the father's love and concern. For, after all, this lad too was still his son, his heir. He still yearned for him. He still reached out to him in tenderness. He still reassured him that everything he had was at his disposal if he would just come and accept it.

In the light of this account, we can see God our Father in a new and wondrous way, if we so choose. We can come to Him without reservations, no matter what our background may be. We can count on being accepted with warmth and wondrous delight.

Wrapped up in this little expression, "Our Father," lies a whole dimension of intimate companionship between father and child, between God and me. It reduces all the complications of life to a very simple, though very special relationship.

I sense that I am a child of God. I know assuredly that God is my Father and I am the object of His constant love and attention. There steals over my soul the realization that His concern and care for me are never ending, that His patience and compassion and mercy and understanding are always extended to me. In every situation of life, no matter how unusual or adverse, there comes the quiet assurance to my heart that I am His and He is mine.

What a consolation! What an encouragement! What a stabilizing influence in my affairs!

It is little wonder that among the most favored phrases to fall from our Lord's lips, those of "Our Father," "My Father," "Father in heaven" held prior place. This concept and this relationship was the most precious He held in His heart. It provided the central meaning and direction to all of His life and ministry.

Throughout His earthly sojourn it is moving to note how often Christ referred to His Father. He saw Himself as here on earth completing His Father's will, carrying on His Father's work, complying with His Father's wishes, conversing quietly with His Father, while all the time making His way gently toward His Father's home.

This was the ever enduring hope and joy held before Him. It was the central relationship about which all the rest of His life and work revolved. And when the day dawns that we too see and know God truly as our Father, our walk and life with Him will have become one of great serenity and enormous import.

It is on this basis and against this sort of background that we can address God as our Father with confidence. We can come with the quiet assurance that He will be receptive of our petitions and appreciative of our gratitude.

There is no more beautiful nor meaningful manner in which to present our prayers, be they pleas for help or expressions of praise. Simply because He is our Father, we can expect that we shall be heard and our heart's communion will be reciprocated.

If Christ chose to preface His prayers in this intimate manner, then we may be quite sure we can do no better. It is fitting and appropriate that we come to God in an attitude that combines both respect and gentle endearment. No doubt this delights His heart. It is one of the honors we can bestow upon Him in return for the great honor He confers upon us by calling us His children (1 Jn 3:1–3).

There are times when we tend to take for granted the enormous privileges extended to us by being brought into the family of God. This is no small honor. There devolves upon us the responsibility to bear this family name with dignity and high esteem. This theme is developed in the prayer. Emphasis is placed upon the paramount prestige of God, as our Father, and the desire for us to comply with His desires and wishes in our conduct.

*Our Father*—just two short words. Yet they have a whole world of meaning wrapped up in them. They set the tone of this entire prayer. They embrace all the beauty to be found in a unified family. They convey to our hearts and minds the strength and serenity of the Almighty. They speak to our souls and spirits of the love that comes from an understanding Father's heart.

No other religion in all the world carries such a happy, contented concept of communion between God and man. No other philosophy or teaching so intimately touches the heart of our human needs. Where else can one turn to find words more tender, more meaningful, more mighty in their simplicity than *Our Father*.

Do we really know Him this way? We can!

# 2
# Which
# Art in Heaven

"WHO IS IN heaven."

The title of this chapter has been repeated deliberately in modern terminology. It has always seemed an enigma to me that the impersonal pronoun *which* should ever have been used for someone as personal and precious as "Our Father."

Unusual terminology is but one of many difficulties that have dogged the footsteps of those who, across the years, have endeavored to know God. Men and women of great sincerity and simple faith have had to struggle with the complexities and limitations of human language in their endeavor to understand divine truth. The marvel is that our grasp of our Father's mind and intentions toward us has been as broad and clear as it is despite the difficulties of human speech in its expression of abstract ideas.

If, for instance, the average person on the street, who had never been exposed to scriptural teaching, were to read the phrase, "Our Father which art in heaven," it would mean almost nothing to him. And even among those of us who have been accustomed to reading the Word of God in the more archaic form of English, there are those who are bewildered a bit by a simple statement of this sort. The stark fact is that it is a phrase repeated glibly by millions of men and women who have never stopped to ask, what does it really mean? If pressed on the point they would scarcely know what to say.

Where is heaven? What is heaven? Is it a place? Is it a condition of life? Is it a different dimension of living? Is it far away or close at hand? These are all legitimate questions which deserve open and honest answers.

Too many of us are far too vague in our ideas about spiritual realities. If God is in heaven, then we ought to know something about heaven. If He is our Father and heaven is His natural environment, we should understand what that realm is really like.

The word *heaven* is derived from the old Anglo-Saxon word *heave-on*, meaning to be lifted up or uplifted.

So it implies the thought of a place or a state which is above that of the commonplace condition on earth.

Actually in the Scriptures, *heaven* is used to describe three rather distinct and different realms. First, we find it used over and over with reference to the earth's atmosphere. It is used to describe the envelope of air that surrounds the planet, conditions our climate, and sustains life. The formation of clouds, the precipitation of rain or hail or snow, the water vapor that provides mist and dew and frost, all are regarded as coming from heaven.

In other words, all that we normally associate with the atmosphere which enables life to flourish on the planet is said to be heaven. "For as the rain cometh down, and the snow from heaven, and returneth not thither, but watereth the earth, and maketh it bring forth and bud, that it may give seed to the sower, and bread to the eater" (Is 55:10).

Second, there is a very much broader sense in which the word *heaven* or *heavens* is used to describe outer space. It specifically refers to the sun, moon, stars, and sky. It denotes the unmeasured immensity of numberless galaxies flung across infinite expanses. It is used for the unending realm of stellar constellations that circle through the night in majestic movements. "The heavens declare the glory of God, and the firmament sheweth his handiwork. Day unto day uttereth speech, and night unto night sheweth knowledge. His going forth is from the end of the heaven, and his circuit unto the ends of it" (Ps 19:1–2, 6).

Finally there is a third heaven referred to throughout the New Testament as the realm of God. It is sometimes described as a definite place, a heavenly country, a New Jerusalem, a home prepared especially for God's children.

Paul wrote of a man who had been lifted up, or uplifted, into this third heaven and who declined to speak of it or even describe it. On the other hand, John, the grand old apostle and much loved prophet of God, went to great pains to recount all he had been shown of heaven in his Revelation.

Because of all this, it is not entirely surprising that there has been real bewilderment in the minds of many people about heaven.

We need to ask ourselves some very ordinary questions, to which we can give very honest answers. The Word of God says our Father is in heaven. Does this then mean He can be in the earth's atmosphere? Yes. Does it imply that He can occupy outer space? Yes. Does He inhabit the realm of the righteous? Yes. For God is a Spirit, able to be present anywhere and everywhere.

Is not the love of my Father, His concern and compassion for me, expressed in the gentle rain that falls upon the fields and forests, the meadows and the mountains? The air I breathe, charged with oxygen to energize my body, the water I drink to maintain my body metabolism, the food I eat to sustain my strength—where do they all originate? Are they not gifts from God, my Father? "Every good gift and every perfect gift is from above, and cometh down from the Father of lights, with whom is no variableness, neither shadow of turning" (Ja 1:17).

The sunrises and sunsets that flood the world in glory are deeply moving hours, hushed with the presence of our Father. The splendor of snow scenes, the incredible beauty of individual snowflakes or frost formations speak softly but surely of the One who has designed all of this with magnificent precision. The coming and going of cloud patterns with ethereal beauty and endless variety are but a reminder that *He is here.*

If we cannot see and sense and know the presence of our Father in the simple splendor of the earth's atmosphere around us, then how can we hope to know Him in some more mystical or super-spiritual way?

He is everywhere present! He makes Himself apparent to us in a dozen different dimensions of daily contacts. The trouble is that most of us are too busy, too preoccupied with our own pursuits, too distracted by the gross materialism of our man-made world to pause and feel His hand upon us in the everyday environment of our lives.

When was the last time you went out alone to walk in the rain, your face uplifted, to let its freshness fall upon your cheeks? And, as you walked, did it dawn on your dull heart that this was a gentle reminder that all good gifts come from your Father? Or when was the last time that in breathless wonder you paused to humbly thank your Father for sharing some of His splendor with you in a glorious sunrise or glowing sunset?

It has been well said that the true measure of any man's spirituality is the degree to which he can detect God in the most simple events around him. It is no mere spiritual phraseology when Scripture declares, "They should seek the Lord, if haply they might feel after him, and find him, though he is not far from every one of us; For in him we live, and move, and have our being" (Ac 17:27–28).

There is such a thing as moving quietly and humbly through life, keenly aware and conscious of the fact that we are walking with God our Father. We sense that we are surrounded with His presence in the very air we breathe, the water we drink, the food we eat. We sense our souls being inspired and uplifted by the beauty and wonder of the environment which surrounds us. We sense our spirits quickened by that very intimate communion with our Father as He lifts us up and impresses our hearts with the beauty of sunshine and cloud, of the interplay of light and shadow on leaves, rocks, bark, sea, and sky. This is to know something of our Father in heaven, the heaven of the very natural but wondrous world around us.

What is true in sensing the presence of our Father in the immediate environment around us, applies equally to the vast reaches of outer space. The moon, planets, sun, stars, galaxies, and remote immensity of space are, despite their enormous distance from us, still very much a vital and moving part of our lives.

Who of us has not responded happily and eagerly to the warmth and brightness of sunlight. How it stirs us in spring after the long, drab, cold days of winter. Even animals and plants, trees and birds respond to its touch and turn themselves toward its life-giving rays. All the world seems a brighter and better place to live when it is bathed in the beauty of sunlight. This is one of our Father's kind gifts to all His earthborn creatures. Without it, life on the planet would end abruptly. This golden, light-energy transmitted across millions of miles of subzero space enables photosynthesis to proceed on the earth. And this is the basis of all life.

We accept such a phenomenon as a matter of course, but in fact it is of such complexity that even the most erudite scientists cannot fully comprehend it. For those of us who are the children of God, we look up, lift up our hearts and give thanks for so great a gift. It is to us another demonstration of our Father's care and provision for us as His people.

Our Saviour made some very startling remarks on this subject when He said, "Love your enemies, bless them that curse you, do good to them that hate you, and pray for them which despitefully use you, and persecute you; That ye may be the children of your Father, which is in heaven; for he maketh his sun to rise on the evil and on the good, and sendeth rain on the just and on the unjust" (Mt 5:44–45).

What has been said of the sun holds equally true of clear blue skies, whose splendor and brightness are a tremendous uplift to the human spirit. How our hopes soar and our hearts sing under clear skies. Again a gift from above.

In contemplating the glory and wonder of the night sky, most of us would admit freely that we have been moved by the magic of moonlight. The gentle touch of silver light that can soften the landscape and turn lakes, rivers, or ocean to quicksilver is one of the most serene sensations. Under the stars, in quiet night hours, the human heart can be very open to and very aware of the presence of our Father who is in heaven.

Our Father is very much in the heaven of outer space. He draws near to us in His own inimitable way and there speaks peace and comfort to our questing souls. The enormity and immensity of space may, it is true, tend to dwarf our spirits and humble our hearts before Him. But at the same time, we are reassured that He who could conceive and create such a unified and splendid universe deserves all of our devotion and adoration as His children.

How good to know our Father is in His heaven and that He does in fact hold the whole world in His hands (Job 41:11).

Up to this point we have been dealing with two realms of heaven which are familiar to all of us, the earth's atmosphere and outer space. Now in order to understand something of that third realm, referred to in Scripture, as the third heaven (see 2 Co 12: 1–7), we must turn our attention to a spiritual dimension of life.

Strange to say, we are not told as much about this heaven as we might wish. No doubt there is a very good and simple reason. I suggest sincerely it is because of our lifelong conditioning to an earthly existence, wherein our capacity to grasp or understand heavenly things is exceedingly limited.

It is akin to someone like myself, who loves the high, alpine country above the timberline in the Rockies, attempting to describe its delights to a group of little children from the slums of a great city. Never having been exposed to anything as beautiful as an alpine lake of exquisite blue or the fragile perfection of a mountain meadow carpeted in wild flowers, how could they imagine what I was describing? After the first few minutes, they would be lost and bewildered. So, to a degree, it is with us in considering the heaven of spiritual realities. We are so engulfed and surrounded by the sordid conditions of our own existence on earth, we can scarcely imagine being set free into a fresh, dynamic dimension of living, totally divorced from all that we know here.

Still our spirits do at times seek to comprehend a little of that realm. And so we set out to search the Scriptures and find out for ourselves what we can discover. What little I have been able to gather across the years is here shared with the reader. In doing so, no attempt is being made to be dogmatic. I am aware others may have quite divergent views to which they are fully entitled.

It was roughly seven years ago that my first, beloved wife, my companion of more than twenty years, was admitted to a cancer clinic. After her initial operation, the specialists called me in privately. They informed me she was stricken with the most virulent form of cancer known to science. In a few months her beautiful body and perhaps also her fine mind would be completely destroyed. There was no known way to counteract the awful ravages of the dread disease. The best I could do was to take her home and endeavor to make her final days as comfortable and easy as possible.

In such circumstances and at such an hour a man and woman, if they know God, are in deadly earnest to discover what heaven is all about. So, with death camping on our doorstep, we set out to search the Scriptures to see for ourselves what this third heaven was really like. After all, she would soon step through death's door to be home with the Lord. With a sense of anticipation and adventure upon us, we studied the Word of our God, and what we found gave enormous consolation and encouragement to our hearts.

Perhaps our most important discovery was that this third heaven is more than just merely a place; it also provides an entirely new dimension of living. It is a state in which God's children are set free from the cloying constrictions and limitations of their earthly life.

It includes being released from the crippling conditions common to our struggles here, into the enormous emancipation of a region and realm governed by God. It is to enjoy incredible freedom. In a word it means to be *free*.

The most astonishing aspect we found was that some fourteen (2 X 7) devastating difficulties which we contend with on earth are absent from heaven. Similarly there were seven delightful conditions present in heaven which are virtually unknown to men on earth. Quite briefly here are the twenty-one (3 X 7) aspects of heaven, deserving our careful consideration. As we examine them, it is well to remind ourselves that this is our Father's native environment. This is His natural abode. This is His home which He wants to share with us. And it is because He is in heaven that it is this way at all. It is His presence and His person which governs the conditions extant there.

1. We are set free from the assaults of our archenemy, Satan. In heaven the child of God no longer contends with the subtle insinuations and dark deceptions which the devil devises. His temptations and deceitful tactics are no more. What a glorious relief! Our doubting days are done. Our temptations are past.

2. The second aspect of our freedom is release from the strain

of separation. We live in a world where the parting of ways and leave-taking of loved ones always wrenches the heart and strains our emotions. But in heaven, this no longer poses a problem. Instead we are in an atmosphere of quiet contentment. We are finally at home. Our restless spirits are at rest because they have found their abode in God.

3. In heaven, we shall be free from tears of anguish, despair, and frustration. As C. S. Lewis points out in his book, *The Problem of Pain*, life carries with it more pain than pleasure. For many of God's children, the most bitter tears are those shed inwardly or alone where no one else sees the agony of our spirits. What a delightful deliverance to be free of such anguished moments!

4. In heaven there is no more death. Because of the power of our Father's eternal presence, and because of what Christ accomplished at Calvary, death cannot exist. For us who know God as our Father, death is but the doorway into His home. Still death hovers on the horizon of many lives. In our natural human condition we are still bound to ask, How will it come? Where? When? Most of us would prefer to pass on quietly into Christ's presence in our sleep. Most of us shrink from the dread thought of painful accidents or long and lingering disease prior to death. But in heaven, we will be free from this foreboding.

5. We shall enjoy total deliverance from the sorrow that is occasioned by regrets and remorse. At our best, we are bound to have made some grievous errors. We have entertained wrong attitudes, spoken unkind words, harbored selfish motives, and indulged in wrongful acts. Out of all this, there flows a muddied stream of remorse and sorrow. Yet, in heaven what a joy to know that we are fully forgiven, that we are free of folly and sorrow of spirit. Instead we shall be in a dimension of deep delight, free from the guilt and regret of our life's misdeeds.

6. John, the beloved apostle of Christ, also assures us that there is no crying in this wondrous realm—crying in the sense of a soul in search of truth, crying in the way that our hearts cry out for God. All of this will be gone. For in heaven the questing soul has at last come home to find our Father there waiting to welcome us, as always, with open arms.

7. The last of the first seven freedoms is our deliverance from pain. Surely it is wondrous enough to anticipate freedom from bodily, physical suffering. But how much more is the boundless pleasure of release from mental anguish and spiritual agony? Those conditions which plague our days and make of our nights a nightmare will have no place there. It scarcely seems possible, especially for those of us who, down through the long years of life's journey, have endured suffering of all sorts, including the agony of watching others, whom we love, grapple with the tyranny of pain.

All of this leaves us a bit breathless and amazed. Humanly, we cannot possibly imagine such a state of blessed relief. But we are given our Father's quiet assurance that this is what heaven is like. We scarce can take it in. Yet at this point we are still only one-third way through its wonders.

8. When God's new heaven, new earth, and New Jerusalem are unveiled, we will discover that in our new, eternal abode, there is no temple, no church, no sanctuary, no formal edifice or structure of any sort. *Structure* no doubt implies much more than a mere building. There will be a delightful, relaxed freedom between all God's people. Gone are the formal barriers and doctrinal divisions which divide us down here. Among our Father's children will flow the warmth and love and understanding which only His divine presence can produce.

9. We are told too that there will be no sun or moon there. That is to say, no moon which we now know as the earth's satellite in the night sky. Nor will the sun, of which the planet earth is a satellite, be the dominant light of life. For in that realm, set free from our ties to this terrestrial sphere, time will be no more. No longer will we be limited by the time-space concept which conditions life on the planet earth.

This is almost beyond our imagination. From birth we are accustomed to think in terms of day and night, summer and winter, spring and fall. We grow up tied to time. We are always meeting deadlines and keeping appointments according to time. We set schedules, plan programs, and organize all of our lives around the clock and calendar. As the years go by, we sense our time, as sand in an hourglass, is running out. We feel a certain sense of helplessness as the years march on, inexorably taking their toll of our strength and stamina.

Over there, all of this will alter. Gone will be the sense of desperate urgency, of being crowded by the calendar, of being threatened by the tyranny of time. In its place will be the serene peace of a quiet and unhurried life, free from the fret and strain of earth's on-rushing pace. What a wondrous release!

10. Nor is there any night there. No doubt, in part, this implies physical darkness as we know it here. With new spiritual bodies, the need for night and sleep and restoration, so essential for our limited physical bodies, will no longer be a factor.

11. But over and beyond this, the night or darkness of misunderstanding will be banished. Perhaps of all the magnificent deliverances promised to God's children, this is one of the most glorious. To think that at long last the misunderstandings, the darkness and clouds which so readily come between human beings, will be dispersed forever, is utterly beyond our grasp.

About eighty percent of the problems and perplexities that plague the human race are caused by misunderstandings which cloud our relationships. Most of us do not understand each other. We do not understand our Father in His dealings with us. We do not understand our own complex selves. Yet all of this will change. We shall enter an era of total and complete enlightenment. We shall know as we are known. There will vanish forever all the fears, doubts, misjudgments, animosities, and despair spawned in our present darkness of misunderstanding.

12. John also tells us that there is no defilement in that realm; nothing to contaminate our thoughts nor mar our moral life. It scarcely seems possible does it?

In our earthly society, at almost every turn we take, we are confronted with those influences which would besmirch our lives. We hear things which distort our minds and weaken our wills. We read about, see, handle those things which draw us away from our devotion to God. But in heaven these influences are no longer at play. They will cease to exert their influence on our lives.

Almost the same may be said for the perversion and corruption of the whole world system to which we are conditioned. We become so enmeshed in the affairs of life; we are so preoccupied with the never-ending struggle to earn a living, to provide for our families, that we forget how completely the world and its ways have dominated our thinking. But in our new home there is total deliverance from all the strain and stresses of our unpredictable earthly sojourn.

In his first epistle, John tells us, "Love not the world, neither the things that are in the world" (1 Jn 2:15). In heaven the attractions of the world system will no longer be present to defile us and drag us down. Their impact will be nil. What a deliverance!

13. Then, too, we are given to see that there will no longer be any deceit, falsehood, lies, or dishonesty there. To a large degree, all of us on earth have become accustomed to the deception, duplicity, and scheming which make up a part of our false fronts. We tend to live behind masks. We would have others believe that we are making a success of things. It is all one with the idea that we must not be seen in our true colors. We must not appear as failures. To do so is to lose face. And so even the best of us tend to say one thing yet mean another.

All of this will be at an end.

We shall be in the presence of the One who sees right through us. We can let down the front, take off the mask, and just be ourselves, both before God and before one another. What a relief! What a relaxation! The tension and suspense of all duplicity, contriving, and playacting will be past. What a rest for God's dear people.

14. Finally the fourteenth influence which will not be at work in our eternal home is sin. If all that has gone before us is a bit overwhelming, how much more this! Just think, the old, wearisome, never-ending downward pull of evil will have finally come to an end. It is a bit like suddenly finding ourselves set free from the pull of gravity.

It will be as though great lead weights have been unstrapped from our feet. We can walk freely, yes, even run, in the paths of righteousness. Imagine being no longer burdened down with the contamination of sin that clogs our feet, no longer loaded with the evil that stains our souls and starts our tears. Instead we will exult with lighthearted abandon. We will revel in the ecstasy of a new glory given us by our lovely Lord!

We have now examined the fourteen undesirable aspects of earth life not found in the home Christ has prepared for us. In the same way, there are seven beneficial aspects of that home which are not fully known to us in our earthly condition. This makes a total of three times seven, representing the ultimate in divine perfection.

Let us briefly examine these seven glorious concepts. Because they are so totally foreign to us, we can scarcely take them into our finite and very limited human understanding, but let us at least try.

1. There is a dimension of satisfaction and tranquility not known here. It is epitomized by the pure water of life, clear as crystal that flows from the throne of God. A quality of life exists there, seldom if ever experienced by us here. It has to do with complete and enduring contentment and repose.

In our earthbound life, our best efforts, our finest endeavors, our loftiest achievements, still leave us a bit disappointed and disenchanted. No situation or circumstance, no matter how sublime, lasts long or remains free from some outside, corroding influence which tends to mar its brief bliss. The net result is that a sense of uncertainty hovers in the background of our best moments. We tell ourselves, "This is just too good to last." Not so in heaven. There, the very nature and unchanging character of our Father insures that our satisfaction shall be complete and continuous.

2. The second amazing attribute of heaven is its abounding life. Life there has such an abundant quality that we really have nothing on earth with which to compare it. It is true that in our very best moments we may have a slight foretaste of it. But to imagine that such will be the norm there is enough to overwhelm us. To think that such things as absolute love, honesty, goodwill, and righteousness make up the warp and woof of life in heaven is incredible. The more so after long years of coping with bitterness, hate, lies, deceit, and ill will in our human relationships.

There the ever present healing influence of God's own presence will be the balm that mends our broken spirits and heals our injured hearts.

3. The third thrilling aspect of heaven will be absolute justice and fairness which will characterize it. This obviously is so because God's throne is there. And where He rules, justice and righteousness reign.

Complete justice and fair treatment are seldom experienced in this world. On every side, we are dismayed by the injustices perpetrated between men and nations. Human beings are quick to exploit each other. We do not hesitate to take undue advantage of others whenever the opportunity arises. We are skilled and cunning in the way we use or abuse others for our own ends. But, in heaven, all that will end. Where God our Father reigns, so does righteousness and justice.

Gone will be discrimination, unfairness, scheming, conniving, and the smooth tactics and fast talk which take innocent people unawares. What a relief!

4. Surprising as it may seem, the fourth feature of heaven will be our service to God Himself. Put in ordinary layman's language, all the work we do there will have special significance and deep meaning, for it will be divine.

Just what form it will take we are not told exactly. It really does not matter that much, for, whatever its nature, it will be good. From experience, we know that much of our work here is pretty pointless. In fact, millions of men and women live lives "of quiet desperation." Life is one, long, tedious bore. All their efforts, energy, time, intelligence, and attention are directed to work which they find empty and meaningless.

In eternity, our service will be different. Life there takes a new turn. It assumes a new direction. The smallest action will be linked to a divine destiny. And from that linking, there will emerge a series of delightful enterprises in which men and God are active co-workers.

5. The fifth aspect is exquisite fellowship. This is perhaps the best known and most commonly accepted attribute of heaven. We here live life by faith. There we shall see our heavenly Father face to face. The joy of such an encounter will be tremendous.

Because all of us shall be exposed to such an intimate contact there is no question but that it will bind us together in a common fraternity and family atmosphere. Our Father will preside over His adoring children, and we, in turn, will be doubly attracted and drawn together in the presence and power of His own gracious person. His character and love will draw us all close together, making us one with Himself.

6. By virtue of this very full and complete revelation and disclosure of Himself, it is natural that there will be a full and complete illumination of every aspect of life. No longer will or could there be doubts, misgivings, or apprehension of any sort.

Because we are beleaguered by so much doubt and misunderstanding here, it is almost impossible to project our thoughts or imagination to a realm where all will be bright and right. To live and move and have our being in such a dimension is beyond our most optimistic hopes. We will be set free from all the fears and forebodings which attend our days here. And this is simply because God our Father is in heaven.

7. The last and seventh positive aspect of heaven is, in a way, its most comforting to the child of God. It is the realm of victory. It is the place of rest at last. It is the dimension of life where the battles, struggles, and contest with sin and Satan and self are all over, and the warrior of the Lord has come into His inheritance. We are told we shall reign for ever and ever with Christ. It seems almost too good to be true, but like all the other promises of God our Father, we can count on it.

Looking back over this long list of heaven's attributes, it is important to remind ourselves again that this is our Father's native realm. It is His natural environment. It is His home and habitat. Heaven is what it is by virtue of the fact that His presence, power, conduct, and character make it such.

We have been taught very clearly in Scripture that Christ is pleased to come into any life where He is invited (see Jn 14:23 and Rev 3:20). He takes up residence there and makes real in that life His very nature and person.

This is a very crucial concept in the Christian life. It can make all the difference between a victorious Christian and a very indifferent Christian.

If Christ resides within my heart, by His Spirit, then there should be a foretaste, at least, of heaven in my life down here. Some of us have known blessed days in our experience, when, from dawn to dusk, we appeared to behave, think, and speak exactly as Christ would have us to do. At the end of the day, we could look back and know assuredly that to have so lived was in fact to have had a brief preview of heaven.

When, in teaching the disciples this magnificent prayer, Jesus said, "Our Father, who is in heaven," He was not thinking of a distant being in some remote heaven. He was referring to One whose existence was a vital part of His own life.

What was true of Christ as He lived in Palestine twenty centuries ago, can and may be equally true of us today.

"Our Father, who is in heaven," is also in my heart. To know this is to know a new dimension to life. To sense the presence and person of God our Father within is to have set our feet on the highway to heaven. But, even more than that, we will see our lives now as the residence and habitation of the Most High. We will know ourselves to be host to our heavenly Father. And in such knowing there will steal over us a quiet awe and deep respect for our Father who deigns to have His Son come and share Himself with us as Lord and King.

In Luke 17:20–21, Jesus was asked where was the Kingdom of God. His forthright reply was, "It is within you."

Once God's sovereignty has been established in any human heart, the establishment of an environment that resembles heaven itself follows within that life.

Unless we have experienced something of this sort and feel somewhat at home with God down here, it is less than likely that we would ever feel comfortable over there. Some people hold the preposterous notion that they can do pretty well as they please in this life, then still have hope of feeling at ease in heaven. Not likely!

Unless a man or woman has accepted Jesus as Saviour and thus knows God as Father in this world, he would not feel at home in heaven. This is a most solemn and serious consideration. And, I am sure, it was one of the thoughts in our Master's mind when

He taught His disciples to pray, "Our Father, who is in heaven [here and now]."

In layman's language, what He was implying was this: "Seek to know God as your Father here. Let heaven begin now in this life."

And this can be so if we wish it to happen.

# 3
# Hallowed
# Be Thy Name

"HALLOWED BE THY name."

A very positive, potent statement. What does it mean? What is implied in this affirmation? It is not just a petition. Nor is it just a pious hope, as if to say in passing, "May Your name be honored."

The concepts in Christ's mind, when He inserted this declaration into His prayer, were tremendously important to Him. It was not a casual bit of religiosity for Him to insist that God's name be hallowed. Rather, there was inherent in this four-word phrase, a whole world of respect, reverence, awe, and appreciation for the person of God His Father.

The word name, as used here by Christ, is not restricted to being a title. It means much more than just a surname, or given name, such as *George Macdonald*, might be used as a means of identifying a single human being. In Scripture, the name of God implies a very much greater concept.

"Thy name"—God's name—implies the title, person, power, authority, character, and the very reputation of God.

So enormous was the respect of the ancient Hebrew people for the name of God that they dared not even formulate it with their lips nor attempt to put it into human language. It was represented in writing by the letters Y H W H. Later these were expanded to Y A H W E H, which became the name *Jehovah*, and in our English translations, it is represented by the expression "the LORD" (e.g., KJV and NASB).

Obviously the eternal God, the One who is from everlasting to everlasting, could scarcely be identified by any simple human title.

Again and again when asked who He was, the simple reply that came back was, "I AM THAT I AM." Even Jesus, when pressed on this point replied, "Before Abraham was, I am" (Jn 8:58). By this it was intended to make clear that God is the eternal, enduring, everlasting Lord of all the universe, both heaven and earth. Because He, our Father, is from everlasting to everlasting the same, He deserves our utmost respect and reverence.

Yet, as pointed out in the first chapter, the amazing disclosure of His person, given to us by Christ, was not that of some distant, remote, unapproachable deity. Rather the revelation of Jesus regarding God that dispels our fears and warms our hearts is that He is in fact our Father, all compassionate, understanding, and totally approachable.

It is in the light of this revelation that the name of God our Father takes on a whole new dimension of devotion for us. We are not so much concerned here with the mere formality of His title, as we are with the quality of His person, character, and reputation.

Putting it into plain language, what Jesus is saying in this prayer is, "Father, may Your person, Your identity, Your character, Your reputation, Your very being always be honored."

The significance of such a statement may not have any special meaning for us unless we understand something of the caliber of God's character. I say this because, unless we do, the idea of keeping His name hallowed will have little or no importance.

God our Father is the most balanced being. He cannot in any way be compared to nor equated with human beings, who, at best are far from being balanced. In fact we are so twisted and distorted in our characters that we have difficulty trying to comprehend the beautiful character of our Father.

Actually it is our heavenly Father's character which is His great glory. Or, conversely, we may say that His glory is His character.

To help grasp this, I sometimes think of His character in the form of a perfectly symmetrical six-sided cube. On one side, He is utterly holy, pure, and flawless. But this is counterbalanced on the opposite side by His absolute love, compassion, and concern. Only because of this is it possible for us to approach such a sublime being. On a third side, He is completely righteous, just, impeccable. Yet again this is counterbalanced on the fourth side by His boundless mercy, kindness, and long-suffering. If it were not so, how could we ever stand in His presence? He is also, on the fifth side, utterly, honest, true, and reliable, again, counterbalanced on the sixth side by His infinite faithfulness, understanding, and interest in us as His children.

Such a character and such a person, if we even catch the faintest glimpse of His goodness, is bound to elicit our fondest affection and deepest gratitude. No wonder we are bound to exclaim, "We love him, because he first loved us!" (1 Jn 4:19). And it was this thought in Christ's mind which prompted Him to say, "Hallowed be thy name," or, "May Your very being be revered."

It will be recalled that this concept was the very heart and impulse of the early Church. Everything that small band of believers set out to do was always "In the name of Christ" or "In the name of Jesus of Nazareth." For in that name, there was vested all the power, dynamic, authority, prestige, and import of the character of the living Lord.

To help us get a grip on this idea, let us compare it to our modern concept of what can be implied by a name in business. Take, for example, the name *Rolls Royce*. When we see that name stamped on an automobile or an aircraft engine, we immediately have a special regard and respect for it. In that name resides the reputation of one of the world's most renowned engineering firms. That name stands for the finest in mechanical engineering. It represents the most advanced research. It bears the stamp of meticulous care and precision. It symbolizes the ultimate in reliability and dependability. It denotes the highest degree of craftsmanship and design.

Now if this be true in the case of a human enterprise that has earned an enviable reputation, how much more so must the same principle apply to our Father in heaven, Creator of the whole, wondrous universe.

All of this was in our Saviour's mind and heart as He formulated this simple yet profound prayer.

The word *hallowed* has been used in most of our English translations to convey the idea Christ was teaching here. Unfortunately *hallow* is not in common use today. It is associated with the word *holy*, which again seems to be grossly misunderstood by most modern readers. For us to say, "Father in heaven, may Your name be kept holy," sounds very trite. It smacks of musty, dim churches. It conjures up before our minds sad, mournful, almost morbid music. We associate it with cloistered halls, long robes, dismal chants, halos, and all the other tired traditions that somehow have been unfortunately identified with this idea of God being holy.

The word *holy* is derived from the old Anglo-Saxon words *halig* or *hale*. And these were used to denote that which was either set apart, very special, sound, healthy, or whole.

For instance, it is not uncommon to hear people say, "Oh, I'm hale and hearty," meaning that the person is in excellent health, wholesome, and fit.

So that basically when something is said to be holy, the first idea is that of being completely sound, solid, whole, healthy and wholesome, without blemish, weakness, soft spots, and without in any way being defiled or contaminated.

Following on this naturally comes the thought that anything or anyone holy was unique and unusual, set apart, free from defilement of any sort. So it may be seen that to speak of keeping God's name holy really embraces a very broad and sweeping appreciation of who He is and what He does.

What we would say in modern idiom is something like this: "May You be honored, revered, and respected because of who You are. May Your reputation, name, person, and character be kept untarnished, uncontaminated, unsullied. May nothing be done to debase or defame Your record."

In Isaiah 6, we are given a very dramatic and moving description of the prophet's impressions of the holy God. "I saw also the Lord sitting upon a throne, high and lifted up, and his train filled the temple. Above it stood the seraphim: each one had six wings; with twain he covered his face, and with twain he covered his feet, and with twain he did fly. And one cried unto another, and said, Holy, holy, holy, is the LORD of hosts; the whole earth is full of his glory. And the posts of the door moved at the voice of him that cried, and the house was filled with smoke. Then said I, Woe is me! For I am undone, because I am a man of unclean lips, and I dwell in the midst of a people of unclean lips; for mine eyes have seen the King, the LORD of hosts" (Is 6:1–5).

In the presence of the Almighty God, Isaiah became keenly aware of his own blemishes. The person and power and purity of the Holy One made him acutely conscious of his own contamination. It is in the intense and glowing wholesomeness of God's person that our own weakness and defilements appear their worst. The nearer we draw to Him, the more acutely we sense our own sinfulness. And this is as it should be, for only then do we discover our real need of cleansing from our own uncleanness.

Our society today is no different, basically, than that of Isaiah's day, nor of our Lord's day, when He taught His disciples this prayer. No matter what generation we are a part of, men and women in general do not revere nor respect the name and person of the Most High. That is partially why it was important for Jesus to put this phrase into the prayer.

Irrespective of what strata of society we move among, it is very common for men and women to degrade and defile God's name. His name is used in blasphemy. It is used in obscene jests; His character is lampooned and ridiculed; His person is heaped with insults and abuse equal to anything hurled at Christ during His mock trial and cruel crucifixion. From very small children to white-headed old men and women there races a continuing stream of scorn, sarcasm, sneering, and cursing against the Holy One.

Why this should be has always baffled me. The only adequate explanation I can find is that it is the very beauty, loveliness, wholesomeness, and purity of His wondrous character that makes human beings uncomfortable. His sublime attributes and person and name, instead of eliciting reverence and awe, draw out hostility, anger, and malice from men.

It is little marvel that among the first ten written commandments given by God to men there should have been included, "Thou shalt not take the name of the LORD thy God in vain" (Ex 20:7).

So in a sense, Jesus Christ, was reaffirming this thought when in His prayer He said, "Hallowed be thy name." This, of course especially applies to those of us who, not out of a sense of duty to the Law, but out of love and esteem for our Father in heaven, wish it that way. Not only do we wish it, but, much more, we see to it that His wondrous name is honored.

As in the case of Isaiah, so in ours. There are those great areas of life wherein it is essential that God's reputation and person be recognized and respected. These are, first, the world at large, for Isaiah records that the Seraphim's cry was, "Holy, holy, holy, is the LORD of hosts; *the whole earth is full of his glory.*" Or in other words, everywhere, all around us, there is made apparent the presence and power and character of God our Father.

Second, there is the whole area of the Church, the sanctuaries set apart for the Most High, the body of believers wherever they be and wherever they meet. Again Isaiah records "I saw also the Lord sitting upon a throne, high and lifted up, and his train filled the temple." His person and authority and honor were everywhere apparent in the sanctuary.

Third, there is the immediate area of our own lives and our innermost relationship to the Most High. Isaiah sensed that because of his own uncleanness, he was unworthy of the holy God with whom he communed. But after he had been cleansed, purified, and his iniquity removed, he knew he could have intimate fellowship with God. And it was with this awareness of having been accepted that he went out to deliver God's message to hard hearts.

When we consider the world at large, we face the fact that in general our Father's name is certainly not hallowed. In fact for many, even among those who do not openly blaspheme Him, He appears to be either dead or at best of little consequence at all. Especially is this true of our Western civilization. Here science and twentieth-century technology have usurped the throne of men's minds. Most of our people have been conditioned to believe that God really does not matter. Of so little importance is He that no time is even given in classrooms to consider His role in human history.

The common concept abroad today is that it is man, with his inquiring mind and huge research programs, who is discovering and inventing the intricate complexities of natural science. Technology is well nigh worshiped. Yet the naked truth is that all man really does is to uncover laws, principles, and concepts which were brought into existence eons ago. And for every door the scientist unlocks, he finds a half dozen more waiting to be opened. So really there is no end to the acquisition of knowledge. A moment's serious and honest reflection will reveal that this vast store of incredible information was first programmed, established, then set in motion by a superior intelligence, the divine mind and sublime power of our heavenly Father.

This is why whenever I am afield or outdoors, there steals over me the acute consciousness that I am confronted on every hand by the superb workmanship of my Father. It is as if every tree, rock, river, flower, mountain, bird, or blade of grass had stamped upon it the indelible label, "Made by God." Is it any wonder that in a simple yet sublime sense of devotion, respect, and reverence for all of life, Christ longed for His Father's name to be hallowed throughout the earth. After all it is His realm.

At least for me, as His child, there remains the quiet joy and pleasure of walking and living very humbly with Him whose superb and beautiful craftsmanship surrounds me on every side. This lends enormous dignity to my days here.

As I pen these lines, it is a sun-dappled day in the lovely lake country of British Columbia. The high hills across the lake lie in their own deep blue shadows. Cloud patterns drift across the wind-stirred waters. The call of wild Canadian geese is borne above the shore cliffs on the breeze. And all around, green grass springs from soil warmed by April's sunshine. Man and all his inventions have had no part in producing a single one of these glorious sensations. All of them have come directly from the creative hand of my Father in heaven. Little marvel I often bow my heart in quiet adoration and gratitude to whisper, "How great Thou art!"

When we come to consider the aspect of reverence and respect which should be given to God in the church, it would seem this should be natural. The reader may well ask, "Isn't that what the church is for, a place to worship God? Why bother even discussing it?"

The truth is that there are too many churches where His name is not hallowed. This is not written in an attitude of censure. It is merely to state the case as it exists. The concept that the sanctuary is a sacred place where men and women come to have a personal and profound encounter with the living God is rapidly passing from our modern approach to worship.

Very often the program, special music, latest social function, architecture of the building, or even the preacher's personality are considered of far more importance than the authority and person and presence of God Himself. His name is not honored in these places. His being and power are not revered. And in some cases, the people are scarcely even aware of His character.

It is not altogether surprising, therefore, that many churches are little more than another social organization in the community. For where our heavenly Father's name is not held high, the church loses its impact and power upon the lives of its people.

The late A. W. Tozer, who wrote at great length about the life of the modern church, maintained that its greatest loss today was the loss of reverence for God Himself. It was his firm conviction that God would honor any group of believers who honored Him. Whereas, wherever He was neglected or relegated to some mere religiosity, death and decadence were bound to follow.

Like the ancient prophet Isaiah, we would do well to have our spiritual eyes opened to see God's very presence pervading His temple. We would do well to worship reverently. And we would do well to remind ourselves always that God our Father deserves our sincere and honest respect, our deepest gratitude.

Finally, let us consider one last but perhaps most important aspect in which our Father's name needs to be hallowed and honored within our own personal lives. It follows, does it not, that if God is our Father, as Jesus expressed it in this prayer, then we are His children? And if we are His children, then naturally we ourselves bear His name. We may call ourselves "children of God," "Christians," "God's people," or any other such title. But the point remains that we carry His name. His name is vested in us. Therefore His name, reputation, person, and character are at stake in us.

It may very well be that a cynical and materialistic society will neither look for nor even expect to see God our Father in the natural world. Many of them are too cynical or totally indifferent to look for Him in the church. Yet, in a most surprising way, they will scrutinize anyone meticulously who claims to be a child of God.

The personal life and language of any person who says he is related to God comes in for close and continuous examination by an onlooking world. Not only do they expect much more of us, but, strangely enough, they almost demand perfection. This is one of those peculiar quirks in human nature so difficult to understand. Although almost anything goes for them, from God's children, they expect angelic conduct.

In large part, I am convinced this is simply because one dares to bear the name of our Father who is in heaven. So their attitude is, "If you claim to be a child of God, live like it!" No doubt Christ Himself was acutely aware of this attitude. That is why He urged His followers to live life on such a lofty and noble plane that men "may see your good works, and glorify [honor] your Father, which is in heaven" (Mt 5:16).

This is a very tall order indeed, for, human nature being what it is, people will find fault with even the best of men. It is impossible to please everyone. Anyone who tries to do so ends up pleasing no one. Jesus Himself pointed this out one day. Because of His own open, warmhearted and genial attitude to the social customs of His day, He was dubbed ''a glutton and winebibber, a friend of publicans and sinners." John the Baptist, on the other hand, whom Jesus declared "the greatest man ever born of a woman," was derided as "having a devil" by his detractors because of his own abstemious habits (Mt 11:17–19).

Still this does not excuse the people of God from living life in such a way that their Father's name shall be honored in their life and conduct. It is as if we were to pray each morning, "Father, Your reputation is at stake in me today. May I live in such a way as to do Your person great credit. Because of my behavior, may men see You in me, and so honor Your name because of it."

Throughout the Old Testament, and especially in the Psalms and Proverbs, great emphasis is placed upon reverence and respect for God our Father. It is pointed out repeatedly that to honor God and to accord Him prior place in our lives is the beginning of wisdom and the basis of all blessings from above. Over and over, the idea is impressed upon God's people that anyone who gave Him the esteem He so rightly deserved was bound to benefit to a degree beyond his wildest dreams.

Some of us forget this in our relationship to God our Father. Sometimes we may even be inclined to hold somewhat of a grudging attitude toward Him. We behave as though it is a bit of a burden and rather a bore to reverence and respect our heavenly Father. We are reluctant to honor Him.

Those of us who are human fathers know how very hurt we can be by such an attitude from our own children. Yet, on the other hand, when they act toward us in gratitude and appreciation, when they express their love and respect for us in consideration and affection, how our hearts are warmed! It is then our own love for them is multiplied and aroused to the point that we are willing and eager to do even more for them than ever before.

The same principle applies in our relationship to our Father in heaven. The least movement on our part, feeble as it may seem, to honor and uplift His great name, produces an immediate response of love in His great heart. We find ourselves engulfed by His sublime presence through His Spirit. We discover our lives enriched by boundless blessings beyond our fondest hopes. This is just the way it is with our Father when His name is honored.

# 4
## Thy
## Kingdom Come

"THY KINGDOM COME."

Like the phrase "Our Father," or, "My Father," which was so often on the Master's lips, so the phrases, "the Kingdom of God," or, "the Kingdom of heaven" were frequently uppermost in His thoughts and teaching. It is no wonder then, that He would introduce this theme into His prayer. It was such an important concept that He makes it a very pointed petition to God, His Father: "Thy kingdom come!"

A great deal of doctrinal discussion has surrounded the term *Kingdom of God* or *Kingdom of heaven*. It is not intended here to compound the difficulties concerning the subject. Rather an honest and sincere endeavor is made to explain the theme in laymen's language. Hopefully this will make its meaning clear and more helpful in our relationships to God as our Father.

Even in the time of Jesus, His most ardent followers had real difficulty in comprehending the Kingdom of God. Most of them were quite sure it referred to an earthly empire which He would establish. The people of Israel were weary with the burdens and angry at the abuse they bore under Rome's rigid rule. They were convinced Christ was their great, new, emerging monarch who, by supernatural force, would overthrow the oppressor. They were positive the might of the foreigners would be shattered, and they would be set free again.

Because of this implicit belief, the disciples especially were utterly baffled and beaten by the final bewildering sequence of events that led their Lord to a criminal's crucifixion at Calvary. It seemed strangely impossible to them that their Messiah, their Christ, their

Anointed One, should suddenly meet an ignominious end. After all, was not the "Kingdom of heaven" always on His mind and heart? Yet now it had suddenly come to nothing!

That they had misinterpreted His teachings was obvious, in spite of the fact that at one point Jesus went to the trouble to explain clearly that the Kingdom of God was more than an institution of physical composition, but was also a structure that could not be apprehended with one's ordinary finite faculties.

Being asked by the Pharisees when the Kingdom of God was coming, Jesus answered, "The kingdom of God does not come that you can watch closely for it. Nor shall they say, 'See here!' or 'See there!' for the kingdom of God is within you!" (Lk 17:20–21, Weymouth).

Even John the Baptist, despite his enormous spiritual insight, somehow failed to fully grasp what Christ meant by the Kingdom of God. From the depths of his despair in Herod's dungeon, he sent some of his disciples to discover whether Jesus was in fact the coming King whom he had heralded. Again and again, the rugged, fearless prophet had thundered in the wilderness, "Repent; for the kingdom of heaven is at hand" (Mt 3:2). And, what was more, the Messiah Himself had picked up exactly the same refrain and began His public ministry by declaring, "Repent; for the kingdom of heaven is at hand" (Mt 4:17).

Yet here, all of this emphasis on the coming kingdom had apparently come to nothing. All the teaching, parables, discourses dealing with the Kingdom of heaven, had, it seemed, only confused and confounded Christ's followers.

And, in some measure, it is true to say that the Kingdom of God, even to this day baffles people. For example, there are those who assert that "the Kingdom of heaven," referred to throughout Matthew's writing, is quite distinct from "the Kingdom of God" spoken of by Mark, Luke, and John.

Others contend that "the Kingdom of heaven" is some future, divine dynasty that is to be established on earth. They say it is of special significance only to the Jews, who, still awaiting their promised Messiah, will eventually see His righteous government in control of the world.

Other scholars assert that "the Kingdom of God" is the social activity and outreach of the Church during this era of human history.

When Jesus uttered the simple request to His Father, "Thy kingdom come," He was not only thinking of the Messianic kingdom, but also implied that He was inviting Him to establish His Kingship in the hearts and lives of men. In fact, when any human being utters this prayer, if it is done in sincerity, it conveys the request to have divine sovereignty, God's government, set up in a human life.

But, perhaps another way to express this thought clearly, is to say we are asking for God's Kingship to become paramount, His sovereignty to become supreme in our personal, private lives as well as in the ages to come.

The reader, unless he comes from a country where the king or queen are sovereign, may have some difficulty grasping this idea of a kingdom. But it should be understood that no king is a king without a kingdom to rule over. No sovereign is a sovereign without a state under his control. Even though the ruler may be deposed, dethroned or even exiled, he is still sovereign by right of rule over a state or territory or kingdom.

So what our Lord is saying in this prayer is, "Our Father . . . in heaven, hallowed be thy name; thy kingdom come," meaning, "You, oh God, our Father, who art Ruler of heaven and earth, whose authority is utterly paramount throughout the universe, come and establish Your sovereignty as well in the hearts of us men on earth, and eventually upon the earth itself."

Now this is a fairly simple statement that any human being can make rather glibly. It is made millions of times every year without any serious intention of having it happen. People pray it but do not mean it.

There is far too much at stake. The great majority are utterly unwilling to surrender the sovereignty of their lives to God. They have no intention whatever of abdicating the throne of their own inner wills and hearts to the King of Glory. They are no more prepared or willing to accept the rulership of Christ than were those who shouted at His crucifixion, "We have no king but Caesar!"

When all is said and done, most of us from our earliest childhood believe we are the king of our own castle. We determine our own destinies; we arrange our own affairs; we govern our own lives. We become supreme specialists in selfish, self-centered living where all of life revolves around the epicenter of *me, I, mine.*

So, if I sincerely, earnestly, and genuinely implore God to come into my life and experiences, there to establish His Kingdom, I can only expect that there is bound to be a most tremendous confrontation. It is inevitable that there will follow a formidable conflict between His divine sovereignty and my self-willed ego.

When I pray, "Thy kingdom come," I am willing to relinquish the rule of my own life, to give up governing my own affairs, to abstain from making my own decisions in order to allow God, by His indwelling Spirit, to decide for me what I shall do.

Paul emphasized this concept in 1 Corinthians 3:16: "Know ye not that ye are the temple of God, and that the Spirit of God dwelleth in you?"

Also, "Ye are the temple of the living God; as God hath said, I will dwell in them, and walk in them; and I will be their God, and they shall be my people. Wherefore, come out from among them, and be ye separate, saith the Lord, and touch not the unclean thing; and I will receive you, and will be a Father unto you, and ye shall be my sons and daughters, saith the Lord Almighty" (2 Co 6:16–18).

So when Christ uttered the simple yet profound petition, "Thy kingdom come," He envisaged His own future kingdom on earth and also the very Spirit of the living God coming into a human heart at regeneration to make it His holy habitation. He pictured the King of kings so permeating and invading a life that His authority would be established in that person's mind and will. He saw a human being as a temple, an abode, a residence of the Most High. But He knew that only when such an occupied heart is held and controlled by the indwelling Spirit could it be truly said that here indeed is a part of the spiritual Kingdom of God where His will was done on earth.

Of course, such a relationship conveys with it enormous benefits and privileges. It is no small thing to be a member of this select, spiritual community. It is a most lofty and noble honor to be counted among the citizens of God's heavenly Kingdom. It is even more amazing to think there is bestowed upon us the special distinction of being God's people.

It is probably true to say that most of us who have invited Christ to come into our lives by His Spirit are not sufficiently aware of *who* it is that has established residence within us. This one is *royalty*. This one is the *King of kings*. This one is the *Lord of lords*. He is the *Prince of peace*. For the gracious Spirit of God, who indwells our beings, is none other than the representative of the risen and living Christ.

An acute awareness of this fact can revolutionize our whole life. A keen sense of God's presence within can change our entire outlook, alter all our attitudes, redirect all our activities.

The basic difference between a defeated, dismal Christian and a victorious, vibrant Christian lies in whether or not God, by His Spirit, controls the life. If He has there taken up sovereignty as well as residence in the soul, establishing a bit of the Kingdom of God in this human heart, that person will know the presence of God which will transform his entire being. It will become to him a delight to do God's bidding. It will be to him an honor to be God's subject.

Perhaps an experience from my own boyhood will help the reader to grasp the greatness of this theme.

I was born in Kenya, when it was considered one of the remote, far-flung, frontier segments of the then mighty British Empire. In those days, it took weeks and weeks of tedious sea travel from Britain to reach this little-known country on the East Coast of Africa. The few white people in the colony were a rough-and-tumble band of frontiersmen with a rather casual allegiance to the distant British king in London.

Through force of circumstances, I was sent off to a distant boarding school, hundreds of miles from home. There, with a ragtag group of other frontier youngsters, I was given a rudimentary education. The school sat on a bleak, windswept hillside, looking out over the wild, wide African plains.

One day, the whole country was suddenly electrified with the startling news that the colony was to be visited by royalty from London. In fact King George V had, in response to our request, agreed to send his son, the Prince of Wales, to take up residence in Kenya. We were to receive royalty!

Never before had I seen such elaborate and painstaking preparations for anyone's arrival. We rough-and-ready youngsters were scrubbed and brushed until we shone. Our clothes were washed and ironed to perfection. Our rough boots were cleaned and polished until they glistened.

Finally the tremendous day for the prince to arrive had come. We were carefully instructed that, as his loyal subjects, we were to march down to the little dusty railway station where his royal train would stop. There we would stand at attention and present ourselves to him as his people. "The prince is coming! The prince is coming!" was the cry of excitement and elation on our lips.

Finally the royal train rolled into the little frontier station. We boys and men stood stiffly at attention. All the girls and ladies, erect and beautiful in gorgeous white gowns, were alert with eager anticipation. The prince stepped from the train. Graciously he walked up and down our little lines, greeting us personally and proudly. He had come to his people, his subjects. He had come among us to take up residence. He was establishing a bit of the British Empire, a bit of his father's kingdom, right there in that untamed, foreign soil of Africa.

It was explained to us that the keys to the city of Nairobi, the capital of Kenya, were to be handed over to him. We had thus, as his subjects, turned over the control of our country to him. He was to set up a bit of Britain on African soil. Since he was the king's son and his personal representative, it was exactly the same as if the king himself was in residence among us. The king had come!

It was a grand event in the life of the whole country. It bound us to the British crown and to our king as no other action could have done. We had received royalty!

And the test of our loyalty was soon to be made, when war broke out and most of us were glad to give ourselves freely for king and country. We were then faithful subjects, glad and willing to obey our king's commands.

This, without doubt, is the concept and picture held so clearly in our Lord's heart when He prayed to His Father: "Thy kingdom come. Thy will be done."

Bishop Taylor Smith, that great and godly bishop in the Church of England, put into one of his personal memos a moving statement of his own relationship to the Kingdom of God. He said, "As soon as I awake each morning I rise from bed at once. I dress promptly. I wash myself, shave and comb my hair. Then fully attired, wide awake and properly groomed I go quietly to my study. There, before God Almighty, and Christ my King, I humbly present myself as a loyal subject to my Sovereign, ready and eager to be of service to Him for the day."

To live thus is to know something of the Kingdom of God on earth. Is it any wonder this man's life made such an impact for God? How many of us conduct ourselves this way before our King?

When there steals over our spirits an acute awareness that God does in fact choose to reside within us, it is not nearly so difficult to vacate the throne of our own lives in His favor. We find it is a joy to pay deference to Him. As with David, we can say, "I would rather be a doorman of the temple of my God than live in palaces of wickedness" (Ps 84:10, TLB).

We see ourselves now in an entirely new light. We see our lives as the residence of divine royalty. We are the temple, the abode, the habitation of the Most High. We are no longer kings in our own castles nor bosses of our own houses. We are but the doormen, the doorkeepers, whose responsibility it is to see that these temples shall not be desecrated, damaged, nor defiled.

This is the role of the priest. Peter, in his first epistle, chapter two, points out clearly that as God's royal priesthood, we have this honor and responsibility before our King.

If indeed the Kingdom of God is within me, then I shall make it my business to see that nothing enters there to harm or offend my Sovereign, the Spirit of the living God.

What I eat, what I drink will be checked with care. I shall not be a glutton nor a drunkard. I will not permit narcotics, drugs, stimulants, sedatives, nor other harmful materials to enter my body unnecessarily and thus pollute the temple of the Most High.

The same applies to my mind and emotions. I shall carefully monitor the material I read and the television shows I watch, lest my soul be distorted by the impressions received through my eyes.

Likewise the conversations I listen to, the music I hear, the programs I tune into by radio will be carefully scrutinized to see that no subversive material intrudes on the Kingdom of God within my mind and emotions and will.

Even in the realm of my feelings and sensory perception, nothing shall be touched, handled, or fondled that would lead to damaging imaginations or activities which could jeopardize this inner sanctuary of my King, the Christ.

In the area of my innermost mind, will, and spirit, I shall see to it that no subversive ideas, suggestions, attitudes, or human philosophies contrary to Christ's teachings and commands will infiltrate my life. The Kingdom of God is within me. It follows therefore that no fifth column of any sort, no traitor of any kind can be tolerated, which might undermine my loyalty or subvert my allegiance to my God.

These are very practical but very important considerations for the earnest Christian to consider. It is no use whatever to pray, "Thy kingdom come," unless we fully intend to cooperate with the establishment of God's government in our lives. It is facetious to pray this prayer unless we intend fully to do our part in seeing that His Kingdom within us is kept inviolate and undefiled.

When that Kingdom does come, when it is established, what are its chief attributes and characteristics?

Paul tells us very plainly in his letter to the church at Rome, "For the kingdom of God is not meat and drink; but righteousness, and peace, and joy in the Holy Ghost" (Ro 14:17).

In other words, the government of God within my life establishes an inner state in which righteousness, peace, and joy in a spiritual dimension dominate my days.

The Kingdom spoken of here is no outward, external empire of erratic emotions. Instead, it is an inner condition of mind, will, and spirit in which God's will becomes my will!

The righteousness referred to here is that state of right living which embraces attitudes, conduct, and relationships with God, others, and myself.

In the same way, the peace which we enjoy in God's Kingdom surpasses any sort of mere outward tranquility. It is that deep, delightful serenity of soul characteristic of God's presence. It is based upon being at peace with God, at peace with others, and at peace with ourselves.

Finally, the joy which is a hallmark of God's Kingdom is not a state of happiness dependent on changing circumstances or on what is *happening* around us. It is, rather, a serene, stable spirit known only to those who enjoy the presence of God's person within their lives. They sense and *know* that the King is in residence. In this awareness, there lies enormous assurance and quiet joy. They can be confident that, under Christ's control and through the guidance of His Spirit, their relationships with others, as well as themselves, can be free from fear and joyous with the strength of God, no matter how tempestuous life may be.

All of this is bound up in the coming of God's Kingdom into a man's life. The benefits are beyond our fondest hopes. They can be ours if, in utter sincerity and earnestness, we mean what we say in addressing our Father and requesting, "Thy kingdom come."

# 5
# Thy
# Will Be Done

"THY WILL BE done."

God's will. What is it?

Our Father's will. Can it be known?

The eternal will of the eternal God. Will it be done? Can it be carried out and complied with by mortal men? Does or can the will of God become of paramount importance to strong-willed, self-willed men?

All of these are very searching, serious questions. And they deserve—yes, much more—they demand, sincere and satisfying answers.

It is traditionally true to say that uncounted millions of men and women have repeated these four words without having the faintest idea what God's will is. It is even more sobering to reflect that even more people have repeated them without any intention whatever of seeing to it that our Father's will is done; even if they did know it. So in a sense there is much vain and pointless repetition of a phrase which actually bears enormous import for the Christian.

It is well to remind ourselves that this is the very practice which Christ had warned His disciples not to indulge in, just before He taught them His prayer. He said very plainly, "But when ye pray, use not vain repetitions, as the heathen do: for they think that they shall be heard for their much speaking" (Mt 6:7).

What it amounts to is that most of us do not seriously consider what we are saying in repeating these words. We do not earnestly intend to have God's will done. It is a rather pleasant, pious sort of phrase that passes our lips too lightly.

Yet the tremendous truth is that the will of God and the doing of that will is the most important activity in all the world. The will of God is of such enormous magnitude and majesty that it completely overshadows all other concepts in the Christian life. Doing the Father's will is the one gigantic, central theme which should dominate the lives of all God's children.

That is why Jesus put it at the very heart and center of this prayer. It is the central theme about which all the others are grouped. It had been and was and ever would be the lodestar by which His own life was lived. What had He come down to earth for? To do the will of God. Why had He, the Son of God, set foot on the stage of human history? To do the will of God. Why did He condescend to be born among common men; to grow up among us as a man, a carpenter; to minister to us as a wandering prophet; to die deliberately for us, the sinless One for sinners; to be buried and rise again; to return to heaven? All of this was but to do the Father's will.

Again and again Jesus emphasized this fact during His earthly life. For example, in John 6:38, He states, "For I came down from heaven, not to do mine own will but the will of him that sent me."

In the garden of Gethsemane, where He faced the gigantic life-and-death decision of going to Calvary, the titanic struggle was resolved by the affirmation, "Not my will, but thine be done." And only because, from beginning to end, His life was lived fully in the context of this concept could He be acclaimed and confirmed as the Christ.

To make the subject of God, our Father's will, as simple as possible, it is helpful first to realize what it is. The will of God is simply God's intentions. It is what He purposes. It is what He plans and wants to be done.

Obviously if this be so, it is quite apparent that He has many wishes, intentions, desires, plans which He would like to see fulfilled. Because He is God and because His interests are universal, it follows that His wishes and His plans and His purposes run through and into every area of the universe. Far too many people assume rather naively that God's will is some spiritual intent confined to a few cut-and-dried commands that are found in Holy

Writ. That the will of God is so vast, so tremendous, so all-encompassing as to embrace all of the universe as well as to permeate every detail of that universe is beyond men's minds.

In order for us to fully appreciate the majesty and magnitude of God's will, we must bring it out from between the mere bindings of a book. We must see it flowing free, running strongly through every segment of heaven and earth. We must sense its power and impact made apparent everywhere, be it in the meticulous, mathematical accuracy of the great stellar systems of outer space; in the unbelievable forces within the nucleus of an atom; in the fall of a fledgling from its nest; in the response of a human will to the overtures of God's own gracious Spirit speaking the reassuring words, "[He is] not willing that any should perish, but that all should come to repentance" (2 Pe 3:9).

God's will penetrates every area of life. It is apparent in the orderly, physical laws and forces of the universe. It is made real in all the biological systems of the natural world. It is inherent in the vast complex chemical interactions that control the organic and inorganic world. This mighty will reveals itself in the beauty and wonder of nature. It can be seen and sensed in all the exciting environments of our planet. By far its most sublime and remarkable demonstration was in the life of our Lord. It carries on down through His family, the body of believers, the Church. It is found at work in any human heart and character when a sincere soul seeks to know and do the will of God. It is so all-pervading it even finds an outlet in the details of day-to-day decisions which Christ's followers make for His sake.

If we are to understand and appreciate the significance of this divine will, then we must, of necessity, know something of the Author and owner of that will. It is not possible to divorce or separate the will of God from God Himself. His will is not something detached from and external to the Person and character of our Father in heaven.

On the surface this may seem obvious. Yet, it is surprising how many of God's children speak of their Father's will as though it was something quite apart from Him. They often act as if the will of God was merely an abstract edict which could be acknowledged or ignored at a whim. The fact of the matter is that to recognize and acknowledge His will is to recognize and acknowledge Him. To ignore and repudiate His will is to ignore and repudiate Him.

This is so by virtue of the fact that God is not an abstract idea. He is not an influence or an ethic. He is a Person with all the attributes of personality which make up a total person. And of this complete person the most important part is His will.

God, our Father, has a mind. He reasons. He thinks. "Come now, and let us reason together," He invites us in Isaiah 1:18. "I know the thoughts which I think toward you" (Jer 29:11). "My thoughts are not your thoughts" (Is 55:8–9).

Our heavenly Father has emotions. He feels. He senses. "For God so loved the world" (Jn 3:16). He is "touched with the feelings of our infirmities" (Heb 4:15). "As a father pitieth his children, so the LORD pitieth them that fear him" (Ps 103:13).

And, likewise, He has a will. With it He decides. He chooses. He purposes and plans. "I have chosen thee, saith the LORD of hosts" (Hag 2:23). "He hath chosen us in him before the foundation of the world" (Eph 1:4).

It is the onward progress and movement of these various aspects of God's total Person which demonstrate and so convince us of His character. And as was shown in the chapter dealing with His name, it is His character which is His glory, and, conversely, His glory lies in His impeccable character. This character is of such a superb caliber that it invites our total trust and solicits our wholehearted cooperation. It is essentially what validates our faith. It confirms our confidence in Him. This is why no matter how feeble or frail or infinitesimal our kernel of faith in God may be, because it has as its object the Person and character of our Father in heaven, its potential is unlimited.

Therefore it should be apparent to us that, if our confidence is in the person and character of God, it must be likewise in His will. There should be no doubt in our innermost being that, if God is good, if He is reasonable, if He is compassionate, then His will too is of the same quality and character.

Still it is surprising—much more—it is astounding, how many people profess to love God but fear His will. They claim to trust

Him yet at the same time react against His will. One who does this finds himself in a hopeless impasse. It would be impossible to pray somewhat like this: "Our Father in heaven, hallowed be Your name; Your kingdom come; may Your will not be done."

It is an absurdity, but many endeavor to live this way.

Because of who God is, because of what He is like, because of the beauty of His behavior, because of the unique caliber of His character, His will is bound to be good and beneficial and acceptable, so that when we accept Him and sense our sonship, we also become clearly aware of His goodwill toward us in every aspect of life.

Fortunately for us, the will of God has found expression in both His work and in His words. It has been made clear to us not only in what He has done and still does, but also in what He said and still says. It is a most unfair charge to claim that God's will cannot be known. The truth is that most of us deliberately choose (with our wills) not to know. There is something very humbling about recognizing and acknowledging the magnitude of God's will. It tends to put the colossal conceit and intellectual pride of self-willed men into proper perspective, and, for this reason, most men reject it. They do not wish to acknowledge the will of God in the universe, much less accept the idea that it should be done at all in any area of their personal lives.

The will of God found its ultimate creative realization in producing the race of men. It was His intention to have beings resembling Himself, with an amazing capacity to accept and reciprocate His affection of their own free will. That such a relationship did not long endure without being shattered by man's self-will was and is no reflection on His good intentions toward us. That His very being yearned for objects of His love is evidence enough that His will for us from before the creation of the earth was of gracious and generous proportions.

The will of God, despite man's deceitful character, perverse personality, and strong-willed waywardness, continued to work for man's redemption, for his restoration to the family of God, for his rebirth and renewal as children of God. So much so was this the case, that, in accordance with His own will and His own wishes,

He had His Son take upon Himself the form of a man and came to live among us, clothed in the human personality of Jesus Christ.

Jesus Himself endorsed and affirmed this concept when He stated emphatically, "I must work the works of him that sent me" (Jn 9:4). He was fulfilling in human form the very activity and attitudes that comprised His Father's will. From His earliest boyhood to the moment of His triumphal return to His Father's right hand, His entire earthly sojourn was simply doing His Father's will.

Nor did the outworking of God's will on earth end with Christ's return to glory. It has continued on down through the long centuries since by the working of God's Holy Spirit in the Church and in men's hearts and lives. This is how it is being done.

The will of God for this planet, for its people, for all that is contained in the expression, "heaven and earth," is yet to be consummated. For instance, in Ephesians 1:9–10, we read this inspiring statement: "For God has allowed us to know the secret of His plan, and it is this: He purposes in His sovereign will that all human history shall be consummated in Christ, that everything that exists in Heaven or earth shall find its perfection and fulfillment in him" (Phillips).

Other passages make it clear that the ongoing of God's will, ultimately, will result in the millennial kingdom and the creation of a new heaven and a new earth of such a quality that nothing we now know can be compared to it. It will enjoy such perfection, peace, plenty, as to completely outdazzle even our most fantastic hopes.

Then there is that second great half of the will of God that has found expression in words. Our Father's will has been articulated for us in human language. It has been passed down to us in a unique and very wondrous disclosure of what His intentions are toward us and for us. Through His written word, we can obtain very clear and explicit concepts of what He wants. And, in large measure, it is from this source that we derive very definite instructions on what He expects of us as His own children. This applies to every area of our lives, be it physical, moral, spiritual, or even in our careers.

It is often mistakenly thought that the will of God, as expressed in the Ten Commandments of Exodus 20, constitute His entire code of conduct for our lives. This is not so. For example, there are numerous passages throughout the Bible which give us clear and explicit instructions about such everyday matters as what we should eat; what we should drink; how we should think; how we should exercise; how we should work; how we should handle our money; how we should treat our wives, husbands, children, and parents. We are even instructed on such subjects as law and order, paying taxes, borrowing and lending, debts, hospitality, talking too much, as well as beneficial and wholesome sex.

Naturally it follows, does it not, that if we are going to know the will of God in such everyday affairs, we are going to have to read the Book in which that will has been laid out. Many of us neglect to read God's Word. Little wonder then that we are often so very ignorant of what He expects of us and what He has in mind for our own best interests.

The last statement is so important it needs to be examined carefully. God, our Father, being our Father and our God who loves us with enormous compassion and concern, bears infinite goodwill toward us. Because of this, all those guidelines laid down for our conduct and which constitute His will for us, have our own best interests in mind. His laws, ordinances, instructions, commandments, teachings are not those of a despot or tyrant who is trying to make things tough or difficult for us. They are rather His formula for successful and satisfactory living. And when we see this, we are bound to agree with the beloved apostle when he wrote in his first epistle, 'For this is the love of God, that we keep [or carry out] his commandments: and his commandments are not grievous" (1 Jn 5:3).

It is in the light of the above that we can look at God's will, not with fear and dismay, but delight. This is what the psalmist means when he says, "I will delight myself in thy commandments, which I have loved" (Ps 119:47).

The will of God is not restricted to purely spiritual matters in Scripture. It covers the entire range of all our human activities. And this is what makes the Bible such a blessed, practical Book for God's children. It is the final authority to which they can turn in their difficult decisions as well as for the ordinary conduct of day-to-day living.

God's will is very much concerned that the human body be properly fed, clothed, exercised, regulated, rested, and kept clean. God's will is very much concerned with the simple fundamentals of wholesome houses, clean streets, well-kept farms, honest businesses, and the wise use of our natural resources. It permeates and penetrates every part of our physical world. And it is double-talk of the worst sort if we claim to be doing God's will in our spirits while we behave like beasts in our bodies.

Our Father's will is also very much concerned with our minds and emotions and our wills. There is a great mass of material in Scripture that deals with our moral conduct. As indicated earlier, this is by no means confined to the Ten Commandments. There is in the Old Testament alone an enormous fund of divine wisdom and instruction for any seeking soul. The Psalms pulse with divine light that can illuminate any person's path. The book of Proverbs is packed with more wisdom and common sense for successful living than any other piece of literature extant. In the four gospels of the New Testament, we find concentrated God's loftiest principles and most pungent teaching expressed in simple language by our Lord and Master, Jesus Christ. The Sermon on the Mount towers in glowing grandeur far above any other ethic ever propounded upon the planet. It is the will of God for the character and conduct of His people. Then on through the remainder of the New Testament, in a variety of histories, epistles, doctrinal treatises, and documents, we find the will of God for men's moral and spiritual life made very clear. Our business is to get into all this material and find out for ourselves what God says.

At this point it is well to pause a moment. It is not enough just to get in and study God's Word. It is not enough just to know what the will of God is. One then has to comply with it.

Jesus, at the very end of His Sermon on the Mount made this point with enormous emphasis. He said, "Not every one that saith unto me, Lord, Lord, shall enter into the kingdom of heaven, but he that doeth the will of my Father which is in heaven" (Mt 7:21).

It has been said, and rightly so, that no man or woman can

possibly live up to the lofty standards of moral character and moral conduct set by our Saviour. That is to say no one can meet these demands in his own strength by virtue of self-will, steel-like resolutions, or constant vigilance. But a way and a means of practical application to our lives has been supplied by our Father. He did not give expression to His will merely to mock us. He does not indulge in sadistic exercises. He finds no fun in our failure to fulfill His expectations of us.

In the person of Christ Jesus, He demonstrated that One so imbued and indwelt by His own Holy Spirit could indeed live such a faultless life. And now that Christ has ascended to sit at His right hand, having Himself fulfilled all the will of God, His same gracious Holy Spirit, who indwelt Him, indwells our bodies and energizes us to do God's will. But, this is only on the condition that we will cooperate with Him.

Paul, in his epistle to the Philippian church, makes this very clear. "Let this mind [attitude] be in you which was also in Christ Jesus. . . . For it is God [by His Spirit] who worketh in you both to will and to do of his good pleasure" (Phil 2:5, 13).

There lies the secret: complete cooperation between my will and God's will.

As we progress in our desire to do all of God's will, it comes as a real surprise for some of us to find that our Father's will concerns the common round of our careers. He is very interested in what courses I shall study at school, what major I shall follow in college, which young man or lady I shall marry, which company I shall work for, what kind of car I will buy, which city or town I shall live in, what church I shall attend, how many children I shall have in my family, what sort of house I shall purchase, how my home shall be furnished, what clubs or societies I shall join, what friends or strangers I shall have in my home, what service I shall undertake to assist His people and thus benefit my community, what endeavors I shall make to be an uplift and inspiration to my generation.

There will steal over me, as I mature in my Christian life and outlook, an acute awareness that all I have and own or acquire has only been entrusted to me by my Father for the few years that my life lasts on this planet. My mind, my personality, my peculiar abilities, my physical strength and energy, my unique talents are not of my own making or manufacture. The idea of "a self-made man" is utter nonsense and colossal conceit. It is simply that some have applied their God-given talents in such a way as to have prospered. So when we see that, in essence, everything we have or acquire really does originate with God our Father, a feeling of direct responsibility to Him for its use will develop in our thinking.

This concept of being those who hold in trust all that they possess can be a most powerful force in helping us to do God's will. We will consider it very essential to see that our time, our talents, our temperaments, our things (possessions of all kinds), our tireless energy, shall be used in accordance with His will and intentions for them. We are not entrusted with these benefits just to spend them on our own selfish interests. They have been entrusted to us to bless our generation.

It is one thing to become acutely conscious of all this. It is another thing to discover, day after day, just what God's will is in the particular issues or decisions that we must make concerning our careers. Many of God's children become very confused over deciding what is God's will in very practical issues. Here are seven sure guidelines to assist one in finding and doing God's will.

1. Is it definitely in agreement with God's will expressed and written in His Word? If so, fine. If not, don't do it.
2. Have you faced a similar situation before? If so what did God show you as His will then? If you made a mistake, don't repeat it.
3. If the decision is difficult and far beyond you, seek the wise and prayerful counsel of mature and godly persons who have the mind of Christ and know how to ascertain God's will.
4. Make the matter one of quiet but earnest prayer. Ask God, your Father, by His Spirit, to impress upon you distinctly by a deep inner conviction what the proper course of action is.
5. Our Father has endowed us with a fund of wholesome and practical knowledge which He expects us to use. We ignore it with risk.

6. Expect and wait to see events and circumstances surrounding this situation alter in such a manner as to influence your mind and will in determining God's will. Time takes care of many decisions. We are prone to be too impatient and hasty. God is seldom in a great rush about things.
7. Anticipate that as time goes on, the way will either open or the way will close for you to proceed along any given course. This should be accompanied by a sense of acceptance, gladness that you are being made aware of God's will, happiness in doing it, and peace about it.

When these points are followed precisely, and there is no great conflict between them, one can be assured of knowing and doing God's will.

There are times when one must, of absolute necessity, make an almost instant decision. If the mind is divided and no clear guidance is immediately available, there is a helpful way to arrive at a choice.

With an open mind, ask God to guide unmistakably in listing the pros and cons on a divided sheet of paper. Being utterly honest before the Lord, ascribe three points to each reason—pro or con—of major importance. Ascribe two points to each reason of moderate importance. And give only one point to each reason of only minor importance. Then total up the figures. It will sometimes astonish one how overwhelming the evidence is for or against a decision. If one is as honest and objective as possible before God in this, it is proper to feel at peace about the outcome.

In closing this important chapter, let it be emphasized that if any man or woman is really eager to know and willing to do God's will, he or she may be completely confident that he will not be mocked. God's distinct will most assuredly will be made known to him or her. And, equally wonderful, by His own indwelling Spirit, that person will be given the courage and ability to comply with that will in joyous and full-hearted cooperation.

"Father, Thy will be done. Amen. So be it!"

# 6
# In Earth,
# as It Is in Heaven

"IN EARTH, AS it is in heaven."

In the preceding chapter, we dealt primarily with what the will of God is. Its titanic proportions have been described. Emphasis has been placed on how this great will penetrates and permeates every part of the universe. It has been pointed out how tremendously important it is for us as God's people to see that His will is done.

But the basic question, and the one over which most of us mortals stumble is, "How?" How can the will of our Father really be done in earth as it is in heaven? How can His desires, His wishes, His intentions be realized on an earth dominated by evil; held under the tyranny of Satan; and populated by stubborn, self-willed men? Is it essentially possible? Can the divine desires and wishes of my heavenly Father really be fulfilled in me, at least, in this bit of human clay, in this small fragment of the earth?

Our Lord was not a deluded idealist. He did not indulge in idle speculation or empty dreaming. Nor did He pray impossible prayers. So when He said, "Thy will be done in earth, as it is in heaven," He did not envisage that the will of His Father would or could be done in the hearts and lives of those who rejected His authority. It would be absurd to ask or expect that the will of God be carried out by those who were in no way in harmony with God.

But this did not mean that God's overall purposes for the planet would not eventually be realized. They will. In spite of men and nations set against Him, the sovereign intentions of the Almighty are bound to be achieved.

"Why do the heathen rage, and the people imagine a vain thing? The kings of the earth set themselves, and the rulers take counsel together, against the Lord, and against his anointed, saying, Let us break their bands asunder, and cast away their cords from us. He that sitteth in the heavens shall laugh: the Lord shall have them in derision" (Ps 2:1–4).

Yet, here, in this simple request, the thought is, "Heavenly Father, may Your will be done in this bit of earth, in me here and now, just as it will be done someday on this earth."

This would be very simple, very straightforward, very feasible if we human beings did not have a will of our own. This is the single greatest deterrent to the accomplishment of God's will. We are not puppets who jump up and down, whirl our arms, or swing our legs by the pull of a string. Instead we deliberately make our own choices and reach our own decisions. We carry out our own ideas in response to our own wills.

Consequently we find ourselves faced by the fact that there are two wills moving separately, sometimes in harmony, sometimes in confrontation: God's will and my will. And the Christian's primary responsibility is to see to it that his human will responds to and complies with that of his heavenly Father. Well over 90% of all Christian growth and maturity and holiness lies in achieving this end.

In fact, we find that those great saints of God who have learned to know and love Him best, not only come to the place where they did the will of God but actually enjoyed the will of God. This is important to realize, because in heaven it is no hardship to do God's will, but a joy. Likewise in my heart, if God's kingdom on earth is there, doing the will of God should be a delight and not a drudgery.

The sooner a child of God discovers the great delight of moving in harmony with the will of God, the sooner he has set his feet on the threshold of heaven. For it is in doing the will of God and responding to it positively that heaven actually does descend to this fragment of earth and becomes a reality within. Because of our strong self-assertion and stubborn, unyielding wills, some of us deprive ourselves for years of the quiet joys and serene satisfaction that can be the heritage of those who adjust themselves to God's wishes.

The Scriptures use a number of very graphic illustrations to convey to us the manner in which God, by His Spirit, endeavors to manipulate and mold the minds and wills of men and women. Of these perhaps the most picturesque is that of the potter at work at his wheel. The picture of how an insignificant, unyielding, rigid lump of earth can, through the application of the master craftsman's skill and loving care, be formed into a beautiful, useful piece of china comes through clearly to us.

I watched a primitive potter at work in Pakistan. Nothing I had ever been told ever revealed to me half so clearly exactly what is meant by the phrase, "Thy will be done in earth as it is in heaven."

This aged craftsman, with deeply lined face, stooped shoulders and delicate, sensitive hands, welcomed my missionary companion and me to his little shabby shop on a back street of Peshwar. This trading town in the far northwest corner of West Pakistan stands in the foothills of the fabled Khyber Pass. It is a region as colorful as its notorious Phathan people. Up and down the dusty streets outside the potter's house roamed sharp-eyed, bearded, rifle-bearing tribesmen, bent on trade and barter.

Inside the shop the words from Jeremiah 18:2 came home to me clearly: "Arise, and go down to the potter's house, and there I will cause thee to hear my words."

In sincerity and earnestness I asked the old master craftsman to show me every step in the creation of a masterpiece. My request seemed to thrill him. As a small lad he had been apprenticed to a master potter in China who taught him every trick in the trade. Now he was happy to show me the skill and artistry that had been acquired through his long life working with clay. On his shelves stood gleaming goblets, lovely vases, and exquisite bowls of breathtaking beauty.

Then, crooking a bony finger toward me, he led the way to a small, dark, closed shed at the back of his shop. When he opened its rickety door, a repulsive, overpowering stench of decaying matter engulfed me. For a moment I stepped back from the edge of the gaping dark pit in the floor of the shed. "This is where the work begins!" he said, kneeling down beside the black, nauseating hole. With his long, thin arm, he reached down into the darkness. His slim, skilled fingers felt around amid the lumpy clay, searching for a fragment of material exactly suited to his task.

"I add special kinds of grass to the mud," he remarked. "As it rots and decays, its organic content increases the colloidal quality of the clay. Then it sticks together better." Finally his knowing hands brought up a lump of dark mud from the horrible pit where the clay had been tramped and mixed for hours by his hard, bony feet.

With tremendous impact the first verses from Psalm 40 came to my heart. In a new and suddenly illuminating way I saw what the psalmist meant when he wrote long ago, "I waited patiently for the LORD, and he inclined unto me, and heard my cry. He brought me up also out of an horrible pit, out of the miry clay." As carefully as the potter selected his clay, so God used special care in choosing me.

As the potter gently patted the ugly lump of mud in his hands into a round ball of earth, I knew God was dealing very plainly with my earthy heart. Gently the old man closed the door to the pit. He walked, clay in hand, over to where a huge, round slab of stone stood in the center of his shop. With meticulous precision, he placed the lump of earth exactly in the center of his wheel. The care he took in this apparently simple step astounded me. But it was necessary before he set the stone in motion with the clay whirling at its center.

Again the word of the Lord came through clearly to my heart from Psalm 40:2, "[He] set my feet upon a rock, and established my goings."

Just as the potter took special pains to center the clay on the stone wheel, so God exercises very particular care in centering my life in Christ. This was not a task that could be done down in the clay pit. I had to be literally lifted out of the horrible hole of my old, obnoxious life to be centered in Him who alone could set me going in a new direction. And the stone upon which I was placed was none other than Christ Himself, the Rock of God. I had never realized this before. Perhaps this was because of the darkness and despair of my former life. Yet now I saw it in amazing clarity. I too was a bit of earth in the Master's hands, and He was at work molding my life.

When the old potter settled himself on his wobbly little wooden stool before the stone, something impressed me enormously. It was the peculiar, fascinating look that crept across his lined face. A new light filled his eyes. Somehow I could sense that in the crude, shapeless fragment of earth between his hands, he already saw a vase or goblet of exquisite form and beauty. There was in this clod of crude clay enormous possibilities! The very thought seemed to thrill him. Out of this bit of mud would emerge a unique bit of beauty as his will was impressed upon it. His intentions, his wishes, his purposes for it were that it might become a handsome, useful article, like those other pieces of beautiful china that adorned his shelves.

And God's gentle Spirit spoke to me softly but surely in that dimly lit little shop, saying, "Don't you see how much anticipation and excitement fills your Father's heart as He looks on you and holds you in His hands? If only His will can be done in your life—in this bit of earth—a bit of heaven can be produced in your life."

The old gentleman began to whirl the wheel gently. In fact, almost everything I saw him do that day was done tenderly with a touch of compassion. The great slab of granite, carved from the rough rock of the high Hindu Kush mountains behind his home, whirled quietly. It was operated by a very crude, treadle-like device that was moved by his feet, very much like our antique sewing machines.

As the stone gathered momentum, I was taken in memory to Jeremiah 18:3. "Then I went down to the potter's house, and, behold, he wrought a work on the wheels."

But what stood out most before my mind at this point was the fact that beside the potter's stool, on either side of him, stood two basins of water. Not once did he touch the clay, now spinning swiftly at the center of the wheel, without first dipping his hands in the water. As he began to apply his delicate fingers and smooth palms to the mound of mud, it was always through the medium of the moisture of his hands. And it was fascinating to see how swiftly but surely the clay responded to the pressure applied to it through those moistened hands. Silently, smoothly, the form of a graceful goblet began to take shape beneath those hands. The water was the medium through which the master craftsman's will and wishes were being transmitted to the clay. His will actually was being done in earth.

For me this was a most moving demonstration of the simple, yet mysterious truth that my Father's will and wishes are expressed and transmitted to me through the water of His own Word. For though I may sense that He holds me in His own wondrous hands, and though I may be aware that those same strong, skilled hands are shaping my character and guiding my career, still His will and wishes are conveyed and transmitted to me always through the medium of His Word. It is the water of the Word—the expressed will of God—that finds fulfillment in fashioning me to His will.

Suddenly, as I watched, to my utter astonishment, I saw the stone stop. Why? I looked closely. The potter removed a small particle of grit from the goblet. His fingers had felt its resistance to his touch. He started the stone again. Quickly he smoothed the surface of the goblet. Then just as suddenly the stone stopped again. He removed another hard object—another tiny grain of sand—that left a scar in the side of the clay.

A look of anxiety and concern began to creep over the aged craftsman's face. His eyes began to hold a questioning look. Would the clay carry within it other particles of sand or grit or gravel that would resist his hands and wreck his work? Would all his finest intentions, highest hopes, and wonderful wishes come to nothing?

Suddenly he stopped the stone again. He pointed disconsolately to a deep, ragged gouge that cut and scarred the goblet's side. It was ruined beyond repair! In dismay he crushed it down beneath his hands, a formless mass of mud lying in a heap upon the stone.

"And the vessel that he made of clay was marred in the hand of the potter" (Jer 18:4). Seldom had any lesson come home to me with such tremendous clarity and force. Why was this rare and beautiful masterpiece ruined in the master's hands? Because he had run into resistance. It was like a thunderclap of truth bursting about me!

Why is my Father's will—His intention to turn out truly beautiful people—brought to nought again and again? Because of their resistance, because of their hardness. Why, despite His best efforts and endless patience with human beings, do they end up a disaster? Simply because they resist His will, they will not cooperate, they will not comply with His commands. His hands—those tender, gentle, gracious hands—are thwarted by our stubborn wills.

In dismay I turned to my missionary friend and asked him in a hoarse whisper, "What will the potter do now?" The question was passed on. Looking up at me through eyes now clouded and sad, he replied with a sorrowful shrug of his tired old shoulders, "Just make a crude finger bowl from the same lump."

The stone started to whirl again. Swiftly, deftly, and in short order a plain little finger bowl was shaped on the wheel. What might have been a rare and gorgeous goblet was now only a peasant's finger bowl. It was certainly second best. This was not the craftsman's first or finest intention, rather, just an afterthought. A bit of earth, a piece of clay that might have graced a nobleman's mansion was now destined to do menial service in some beggar's hovel.

And the word of God from Jeremiah came home to me like an arrow to its target: "So he [the potter—my God] made it again another vessel, as seemed good to the potter to make it" (Jer 18:4).

The sobering, searching, searing question I had to ask myself in the humble surroundings of that simple potter's shed was this: Am I going to be a piece of fine china or just a finger bowl? Is my life going to be a gorgeous goblet fit to hold the fine wine of God's very life from which others can drink and be refreshed? Or am I going to be just a crude finger bowl in which passersby will dabble their fingers briefly then pass on and forget all about it? It was one of the most solemn moments in all of my spiritual experiences.

"Father, thy will be done in earth [in clay], in me, as it is done in heaven."

Do I really mean this? Do I really want it? Do I really enjoy having it happen to me?

The old potter was not yet done with the little finger bowl. Reaching up beside him, he lifted a very fine thread, nearly as slender as a human hair, from a nail on the wall. He dipped it in the water beside him. Then, with it thoroughly soaked, he stretched it tight between his hands. With the bowl whirling rapidly on the stone, he drew the fine thread through the clay, cutting off the base of the bowl from the clay beneath. The separation was swift and smooth and sure.

"That is just like our lives," I mused to myself. We are separated, set aside unto good works. There comes a time when we must be cut off completely from the old ways, the old life, the old attitudes, the old habits. We are new creations in Christ, made and shaped by the will of God for special service.

Gently the craftsman stood up now and moved his stool away. Tenderly he lifted the new piece from the stone and carried it across the room to set it on a shelf. "It must rest there quite a while to cure," he explained. "Then after that it will be fired in my furnace to put the final touches to it." Slowly he crossed to the other side of his shed. Beckoning to me, he pointed through a small quartz window where I could see the fire glowing in his hot retort. "The fire gives the clay its gorgeous glaze that you see on my work here." He lifted a choice piece from its place of honor on the shelf. "It all takes time, much time, but it is worth it. My name and reputation as a master potter are at stake!"

Clearly now I could see why at times it was necessary for God to put me on the shelf. I could see why His will for me was to go through the fiery furnace of hardship. It all took time. It was all essential both for my beautification and for God's reputation. It was all part of having my Father's will done in this bit of earth.

From the foregoing illustration of the potter and the clay, it should be clear that the key to the success or failure of our fashioning under the Master's hands lies in how we respond to His touch.

Now if we look at this in a spiritual dimension we discover that the degree to which we respond to or resist God is the degree to which we are willing to obey Him. Unfortunately obedience is a most unpopular theme today. We live in a period of history when it is fashionable and popular to resist all restraints. It matters not whether it be in the home, at school, on campuses, in industry, toward government, or even against God. *Rebellion, resistance, confrontation* are the catchwords of our time. So it is not the least surprising to find many who are simply unwilling to submit to the will of God. It is considered stupid and demeaning to do what our Father in heaven wishes us to do.

To obey and to cooperate means to subject or submit myself to someone else. It means to give in to another. It means to put another's will first. It means, in essence, to just do what another wishes me to do.

Because of our personal, perverse, powerful pride this is extremely hard for us to accept. To be asked to obey raises our resistance. We feel sure we are debasing ourselves. This goes against our ego; our selfish self-centeredness.

Yet in spite of all this resistance, the Word of God comes through clearly and with enormous emphasis. "Obey and live! Disobey and die!" "Obey and be blessed; disobey and meet disaster!" "Comply with My commands and find life abundant; ignore them and be cut off!"

Strange as it may seem, many Christians associate the thought of obedience and obeying with rigid legalism. It need not be so. In fact in God's Word and in God's view, obedience and love are so intimately intertwined that we cannot separate them. For the proof, the ultimate demonstration that I love another is to put that one's wishes first, before my own. It follows, therefore, that if I love my mate, my parents, my school, my country, my heavenly Father, their wishes and their desires will be first, and it will be my joy and delight to do what they ask.

I say it will be a joy because the act of my cooperation and obedience is evidence of my love, affection, and respect for them. For my part the pleasure given to them by my obedience will be a rich compensation for any inconvenience it may have cost me.

The net result is that instead of having a confrontation, I find myself receiving generous cooperation. Instead of being cursed with ill will, hostility, and bitterness, I find my life blessed with peace and goodwill and beautiful comradeship. Instead of frustration, tensions, and turmoil filling my days, I find myself moving in a new dimension of freedom and joy.

It is no wonder the psalmist sang, "I delight to do thy will, O my God; yea, thy law is within my heart" (Ps 40:8).

To love the will of God, to love the intentions and purposes of God our Father is to comply with Him and His wishes.

Jesus Himself emphasized and reemphasized this point over and over. For example, "If ye keep [obey] my commandments, ye shall abide in my love" (Jn 15:10). "Ye are my friends if ye do whatever I command you" (Jn 15:14). "If a man love me, he will keep my words" (Jn 14:23).

To love Him is to obey Him. To obey Him is to do His will. To do His will is to have a bit of heaven on earth!

Who is the person who enjoys and feels wondrously free in his home, among family and friends? It is the one who obeys, cooperates, and complies with their wishes. Who is the person who revels and rejoices in the laws and liberty of his land? The one who obeys, loves, and cooperates with its constitution. Who is the person who enjoys the companionship and benefit of belonging to our Father in heaven and His family? It is the person who obeys and cooperates with His will.

God's will carries within it all that has been set in motion for our welfare and benefit. He has our best interests at heart. So to do His will is really to do ourselves as well as Him a great favor.

If a person sets himself against the will of God, the result is a catastrophic confrontation. This leads to hostility. The hostility produces ill will. Ill will in turn breeds bitterness and hate. These, like an awful cancer in the character, can utterly ruin us. They will distort our spirits, damage our emotions, endanger the well-being of our bodies, and alienate our family and friends.

It is perfectly valid to assert that no man or woman can violate and resist the gracious will of God without in the end being broken by that will. God's eternal love and concern for us has been expressed in His own unchangeable goodwill. And any person who proposes to ignore or—even worse—to deliberately revolt against or resist that will, can be sure he will be shattered by its irresistible intent.

Perhaps by this time the reader may well ask, "How does one become obedient? How does one reach the place where he really wants to do God's will and enjoy it?"

There are several definite steps we can take in this direction.

We must see and grasp the reasonableness of it all. If this has happened and a genuine desire has been born, then we must set the will to do it. With the help of God we determine definitely to cooperate with God's purposes.

Having made this very determined and definite decision, we then ask God, by His gracious Holy Spirit, to invade and permeate our minds, wills, and emotions, especially our wills.

As we set ourselves to obey God, as we decide and in practice actually do what God asks us to do, we discover God's Spirit is indeed given to us (Ac 5:32).

It is the Spirit of God, at work in our wills, minds and emotions, who produces there both an increasing desire to obey and an enlarged power to obey.

"For it is God [by His Spirit] who worketh in you both to will and to do of his good pleasure" (Phil 2:13).

As we deliberately respond to the directions and instructions that come to us from God's own Spirit, speaking through His Word, we will find the energy and strength and courage to do what He asks of us.

The final result is to find ourselves in complete accord and harmony with the will of our Father in heaven. This is to experience joy, serenity, usefulness, worth, and enormous adventure in our walk with God as we move in accord with His plans and purposes on this planet.

This in essence is precisely what Christ had in mind when He instructed His disciples to pray, "Thy will be done in earth [in me] as it is in heaven."

What a joyous experience!

# 7
# Give Us
# This Day
# Our Daily Bread

"GIVE US THIS day our daily bread."

Does it not seem strange that in the very center of this great prayer, our Lord should suddenly switch the emphasis from something as majestic as the will of God to a subject as earthy as bread?

But really this is just like Him.

You see, with Christ there really is nothing common. It is one of our human tendencies to tuck things away very tidily into little compartments. We call one thing sacred and another secular. We esteem some aspects of life very spiritual and very special, while others are considered quite simple and rather insignificant.

The fact of the matter is that anything touched by the presence of God has upon it sacred significance. This is why all through the Scriptures God's people are instructed to live their lives ever conscious of the abiding presence of Christ. When we do this, then even the most mundane objects or activities assume enormous import.

Brother Lawrence stated this idea very well when he wrote simply, "I can even pick up a straw from the ground and do it to the glory of God."

Therefore it should not surprise us unduly that Christ should include in this great prayer a request for food. It is, after all, the very basis of our existence. This applies whether we are dealing with the physical or spiritual aspects of our lives. The two realms are really contiguous. But, because of our traditional thought patterns, they are here referred to separately and will be dealt with in this chapter in that way. Still we should see that eating nourishing bread can be as significant to us as feeding on food from heaven.

The provision of food for the life of man is discussed all through the Word of God. Initially God gave man all that was needed to support and sustain his life without working for it. But after the first couple deliberately defied God's instructions and willfully refused to cooperate with His will, this entire arrangement altered. The categorical statement made to Adam after he sinned was, "In the sweat of thy face shalt thou eat bread, till thou return unto the ground" (Gen 3:19). Or, as another translation puts it, "Thou shalt earn thy bread with the sweat of thy brow, until thou goest back into the ground from which thou wast taken" (Gen 3:19, Knox).

As the carpenter craftsman, working in Joseph's woodworking shop in Nazareth, Jesus knew all about this. He later had to support His widowed mother and young siblings by the strength of His muscles, skill of His hands, and sweat of His brow. Hacking and chopping, sawing and planing, shaping and fitting the tough, twisted olive wood and hard, heavy acacia timber that grew in Galilee was no child's play. It was back-breaking toil that turned trees into cattle yokes, plows, tables, and candlesticks, that He could sell for a few shekels to buy bread.

Why then did He dare to ask now that He be given bread? Was it not God's decree that man must earn his bread? Was it not part and parcel of the whole plan for man on the planet that if a man did not work he should not eat? (see 2 Th 3:8–12.) Could anyone feel exempt from this principle? It must have been a revolutionary concept to Christ's disciples. A little later on in this same discourse with them, He elaborates on this concept of working and worrying in our constant struggle to survive. We must examine it to see what He meant.

The principles are fairly plain and straightforward. Basically He teaches us that the natural resources of the earth are supplied for us by God our Father. They are more than adequate to meet our basic needs. Just as He provides for the wild birds and the wild flowers, so He has provided enough for us. In the same way that birds must search for their food, and that flowers must extend their leaves to the sun for sunlight, and their roots into the soil for moisture and nutrients, so we must expend ourselves. God does not drop grubs down the gullets of young birds nor does He give handouts to indolent people who simply sit in the shade and do nothing.

Also, He would have us understand that all the many resources put at our disposal are really gifts from God. In James 1:17 we are told, "Every good gift and every perfect gift is from above, and cometh down from the Father of lights." So, be it soil or sunshine, rain or rare elements in the earth, air or ammonia, plants or animals, whatever is essential for the production of food has its origin with our heavenly Father. It is He who has bestowed this bounty upon the earth. It is through His generosity that the supply is sustained, even in the face of our extravagance, waste, and selfish exploitation of the planet.

In view of these concepts, Christ then instructs us in very plain and simple language to stop worrying and fretting over the provision of bread. He assures us that our Father knows it is essential to our survival. He has made the bread available if we but do our part. And what is even more remarkable, He assures us that if, unlike Adam and Eve who refused to acknowledge the primacy of God's will, we do just that, seeking first and foremost to cooperate with our Father's wishes, our bread will indeed be supplied.

"Seek ye first the kingdom of God, and his righteousness, and all these things [bread included] shall be added unto you" (Mt 6:33).

Putting all this into rather simple layman's language, we might state it this way: Any man or woman prepared to put God's wishes first in life is bound to have bread.

From the foregoing it should be apparent that the corollary to being given bread is that a person be right with God. Only the one who puts God first in his life, who above all else desires to see God's will done on earth as it is in heaven, is entitled to ask God to give them bread.

This is an important point that many miss. Millions of people pray this prayer who never put God first in their affairs, who have no thought of doing God's will or even complying with His commands. Yet glibly and gladly, they will ask God to give them bread.

It is a mark of the generosity of God our Father that in spite of all this He still sends rain on the just and unjust, still supplies sufficient for saint and sinner, still maintains the plant life of a planet, the majority of whose population ignores Him.

But those of us who know Him as our Father, who sense His love and concern for us, come daily, not only asking in humility for our bread but deeply grateful for the food already supplied.

Perhaps it is natural for us to take our daily food for granted. Especially is this true in our modern technological age with its affluence and welfare governments. But for those of us old enough to recall the dreadful hunger of the depression years, daily bread is still a significant aspect of life for which we are glad to pray and give thanks. While for those of us who have had to live abroad where poverty, starvation, famine, begging, and horrible hunger are a way of life, this petition is full of meaning. For uncounted millions of men and women, there is no assurance whatever that there will be bread today, much less bread tomorrow. They may not have had bread yesterday or the day before that.

So another concept which was clearly in our Lord's heart and mind was that, as God's people, we should pray that all His children everywhere might have bread today. Of course most of us are so busy with our own lives, we are so preoccupied with padding our own nests and feeding our own already overstuffed stomachs that we really do not take time to care much about the hungry elsewhere.

It will be noted Jesus said, "Give us this day our daily bread." He did not say, "Give me all I can consume on myself." When He was among us as a man, it is deeply moving and touching to see His concern for the hungry crowds. And He did not spare either Himself or His disciples in seeing to it that they were properly fed.

One of the very practical ways in which we can help to make this prayer much more than just a pious platitude is in helping to share and distribute the bounty given to us with others. This is part of feeding the hungry and giving water to the thirsty, which Jesus pointed out to be of such importance in God's estimation.

In addition to the foregoing, we must, of course, realize that Christ's primary concern was not with the bread used only to sustain our physical frames. His outlook and approach to all of men's problems embraced the whole of man, his body, his mind, his spirit. And there was just as much need for man's soul and his spirit to be nourished daily as there was for his body metabolism to be maintained. As has been reiterated in God's Word, "Man shall not live by bread [grain bread] alone, but by every word that proceedeth out of the mouth of God" (Deu 8:3; Mt 4:4; Lk 4:4).

The amazing thing is that this statement was first made by Moses to a nation whom God had supplied with manna day after day, during all their years of wilderness wanderings. He was emphasizing that this remarkable provision for their purely physical needs was not sufficient to sustain them in soul and spirit.

What kind of hard, belligerent, brutish human beings most of us would be were we divested of food for our souls and refreshment for our minds. Any person long deprived of the uplift and inspiration of all that is noble, lofty, sublime, and worthy quickly degenerates to the savage state. So if we are going to be honest and practical in this prayer, we need to take advantage of the gifts afforded us each day for the nourishment and stimulation of our souls.

As essential as all the foregoing may be for the welfare of men, there can be little doubt that the thought uppermost in our Master's mind when He asked for daily bread, was that of spiritual nourishment. Of course this may seem obvious. The trouble is, most of us do not really pause to reflect when we repeat the prayer.

Is it not surprising that Christ should request bread, when He Himself asserted that He was the bread from heaven? (see Jn 6:32–58). Is it that He here teaches us the great fundamental truth that we must daily draw upon the very life of God, as He did? For, just as God our Father is the Author and giver of all temporal benefits bestowed upon us, so He is likewise the giver of spiritual sustenance. Jesus made this clear when He stated, "My Father giveth you the true bread from heaven" (Jn 6:32).

In this discussion about bread, there are several salient points

which merit our attention if we are to understand why Christ included this petition in His prayer. First, like the manna of former
times, it was something that was collected each day. Second, it was
best when gathered early. Third, one day's supply could not be
carried over for the next, except before the Sabbath. And last, it
was a food that came from God.

Our Lord made it very clear that to come to Him was to eat
spiritual bread. As with manna so with Him, we have to come
regularly, daily, to derive nourishment afresh from God. To partake of His resurrection life is to feed on heavenly bread. In this
way the hungry heart can be satisfied and filled.

There is a bit of mystery to all of this. Yet it is not really surprising, for, even at our best, we humans can scarcely grasp the
unique and wondrous ways of God. In His mercy and generosity,
He has used temporal concepts to explain spiritual truth so that
our understanding of what is involved will be clear.

What is bread? It is the living kernels of grain, broken, crushed,
bruised, and ground into fine flour. This flour is mixed with salt,
water, and yeast. It is kneaded, shaped into loaves, then allowed
to rise. After that, it is baked to a beautiful brown. In this
new form as bread, the life of the grain provides life to those who
eat it.

The life of the wheat is thus transmitted to man through the
process of death and subsequent assimilation.

By a similar series of processes, the life of God in Christ has been
made available to us. Our Saviour became God's grain. It was He
who was broken and bruised at Calvary. He there took upon Himself our sins and ourselves. Out of that crushing, out of the grave,
out of death itself, emerged the risen and resurrected One. He thus
became God's bread for us.

Just as there is an enormous difference between bare kernels of
grain and a loaf of bread, so there is a remarkable difference between Jesus of Nazareth and the risen Lord. The life of the wheat
is limited to the kernel until it is crushed and milled. So the life
of God in Christ was confined to His single earthly body until
after His death and resurrection. Then He became available to all
men everywhere by His Spirit. In this way, any man who hun-

gers for bread from heaven, for life from God, for the vitality of Christ, may find Him available through His Spirit.

The special responsibility of the gracious Holy Spirit is to take the things of Christ, the life of Christ, the attributes of Christ, the character of Christ, and transmit them to us. This whole concept is made very clear to us in John's gospel, chapters 14–17. It is the actual resurrected life of Christ which is thus imparted to us. It is in this way that His life is made real in me and becomes part of my life. His life becomes my life.

With this then as a background, we can comprehend Christ as the bread from heaven. The prayer He taught us to pray becomes a most potent and powerful plea for the very life of God Himself. This is no mere, casual request for just ordinary food. It is a deep, desperate yearning to have the risen Christ made real in me each day. "Oh Father, give me this day my daily bread!" "Oh Father, let the very life of Your resurrected Son, my Lord the risen Christ, become my life today!"

Such a petition, such a prayer, such a desire could and does originate only with God Himself. It is not the sort of thing to spring from any self-centered, self-satisfied heart. Marvel of marvels, Christ Himself promised that anyone who so hungered would be filled (Mt 5–6).

If I, an ordinary mortal man, am nourished daily with the very life of Christ, what happens? Do I remain the same sort of person I was before I was given this bread from above? The answer is a very positive no.

There will gradually but surely steal over my life some amazing changes. My character will become like that of Christ Himself. My conduct will begin to resemble His conduct.

There will be formed in my mind the sort of thoughts that are in His mind—goodness, beauty, peace, and contentment. There will be born in me the same attitudes which He bears to others—compassion, acceptance, concern, and genuine forgiveness. There will be powerful and compelling motives produced within my being that have as their source the sort of love and understanding that He has in His heart.

The very life of the risen Lord will reach out through my hands in tenderness to actually touch the hands of those who suffer, to lift the load of the heavy laden, to mow a lawn for a friend, to dig a garden for a neighbor, to pen a letter to a lonely soul suffering awful boredom.

The life of Christ finding expression through my feet will take me to visit the sick, to carry some fruit or a bouquet of flowers to some stranger, to take time for a quiet walk with my mate or friends.

This life of Christ in me will find expression through my voice and lips and looks. It may be no more than a fleeting smile to a stranger, a gentle word of appreciation to someone who has served me in a store or restaurant, a few words of sincere endearment to those who are close to me. So, wherever I walk and wherever I live, there will be left behind a warm, uplifting legacy of goodwill.

This "daily bread" on which I feed will bring about subtle yet profound changes in my personal life-style. After all, it is Christ Himself who, by His Spirit, is permeating my whole being. Gradually I shall find myself less and less preoccupied with the sham and front, pretense and pretext of the secular scene. Pomp and pride and passion that command and demand so much of mortal men will no longer hold me in their grip. My foolish pride, my trivial vanity will be seen for the childish, self-centered characteristics that they are.

It has been said, "You are what you eat." If we feed our souls and spirits on God's bread from heaven, it follows that is what we shall become. This is a powerful principle. It explains why the Master included this apparently earthy petition in His noble prayer.

# 8
# And Forgive Us
# Our Debts

"AND FORGIVE US our debts."

The second petition in the Lord's Prayer which deals with our human dilemma is, "And forgive us our debts." The first three requests relate to the role of God as our Father. The last four focus on our very human needs as God's children. Of these seven, the matter of forgiveness assumes such enormous importance that it is the only one which our Lord later took the time to reemphasize and develop in depth.

The thoughts and concepts held in the Master's mind when He said, "Forgive us our debts," were much wider than this simple petition implies. Evidence of this can be found in the various ways this has been rendered in different translations. Here are some examples:

"Forgive us our trespasses" (Knox).
"Forgive us our shortcomings" (Weymouth).
"Forgive us what we owe to you" (Phillips).
"Forgive us our sins" (TLB).
"Forgive us our resentments" (Amplified).
"Forgive us the wrong we have done" (NEB).

Several salient points stand out sharply in this petition and command our attention. When we recognize them, then this prayer becomes a most poignant plea, the deep heart cry of a truly contrite soul.

If we sincerely pray, "Forgive us our debts," or, "Forgive us our trespasses," then we are openly and candidly admitting ourselves to be guilty of wrongdoing. Now this really does not come home to many of us who repeat these five simple words. Thousands of dear people who recite the Lord's Prayer do not see themselves really as debtors, trespassers, sinners, or offenders. They do not consider themselves actually guilty before God.

And, of course, it follows, does it not, that it is not until one feels convicted of wrongdoing that there is any sense of need for forgiveness? The irony of it all is that uncounted people do feel quite innocent. Consequently this petition, instead of being a genuine desire rising from a penitent heart, is often little more than an empty repetition of words by a self-satisfied soul.

All of which leads to the second very searching concept. Do I indeed come to my heavenly Father as one who feels indebted to Him? Do I sense in some deep instinctive way that I have trespassed on His love and generosity? Am I acutely conscious of wrongdoing, of wrong attitudes, of wrong motives? Unless I am, then obviously this prayer is not only pointless but absurd.

In saying this I am not advocating nor even suggesting that as God's children we are to indulge in morbid introspection. It is neither wholesome nor beneficial for us to become preoccupied with our particular faults and failings. Rather, the overwhelming emphasis placed upon God's people all through Scripture is that we are reborn, recreated as new creations in Christ Jesus. We are urged to forget those things which are behind us and to press on to new and abundant achievements through the indwelling power and presence of God's own gracious Spirit within us (Phil 2:13).

Yet none of this nullifies the fact that we should come to our Father keenly sensitive to sin and selfishness in our lives. The very recognition and admission that we are debtors, and trespassers produces within the human heart a genuine humility that opens our whole being to the presence and Person of God Himself.

"The LORD is nigh unto them that are of a broken heart; and saveth such as be of a contrite spirit" (Ps 34:18).

Perhaps the next point it is well to remind ourselves of is that our petitions are not likely to be answered if we come in an attitude of arrogance and pride. If we entertain the haughty idea that we are not debtors or trespassers at all, then the likelihood of knowing forgiveness is remote indeed. "God resisteth the proud, but giveth grace unto the humble" (Ja 4:6).

No doubt the thought held uppermost in Christ's mind when He taught this prayer was that of a human heart coming humbly to seek restoration from a forgiving Father. After all, He Himself made it abundantly clear to us that God's attitude toward anyone who sought forgiveness was one of immediate reconciliation. God our Father never holds anyone at arm's length who shows the slightest inclination to turn toward Him in honest and open need of forgiveness.

Now, it may very well be asked, "But what if I don't feel I have done wrong? What if I don't feel in need of forgiveness? What if I don't sense my indebtedness?"

The only possible answer which can be given is that such a soul has never yet had a personal encounter with the living Christ. That one has never yet sensed the overwhelming love and concern of God for him as a Father for His child.

It is when we stand alone, quietly, earnestly contemplating the cost to God of our forgiveness made possible by the cross, that there floods over us our deep debt of love to Him. The cross stands central in our Father's magnanimous scheme for the forgiveness of all men of all time. Someone, somewhere always must pay the penalty for misconduct. He Himself undertook, at Calvary, to bear that cost, to absorb the penalty, to pay the enormous price for our sin.

"For God caused Christ, who Himself knew nothing of sin, actually to be sin for our sakes, so that in Christ we might be made good, with the goodness of God" (2 Co 5:21, Phillips).

The majesty and the mystery of this titanic transaction that took place on the cross is beyond our ability to fully grasp. Any person who pauses, even for a few moments, in serious contemplation of Calvary must be overwhelmed by the generosity of our Father God. Imagine, if you can, His anguish at the sight of His sinless Son, bearing our burden of sin, paying the penalty for our perverseness and pride, broken, bruised, His blood outflowing, for our forgiveness! Little marvel great darkness covered the entire earth during that cataclysmic event. Little wonder that Christ, who already knew and foresaw all of this, should include in this prayer, "Forgive us our debts."

The outstanding, eternal debt which all men of all time owe their heavenly Father is a debt of gratitude and of love for the price paid for our forgiveness. The cost of that forgiveness was Calvary. No man, no woman who contemplates this expression of our Father's love and concern for us can help but feel a deep sense of unworthiness.

It is in the white light of such overwhelming generosity and graciousness that the best of our behavior appears pretty tawdry. It is in the presence of the sublime Person and selfless love of our Lord, the Christ, that the loftiest of our inner attitudes look selfish. It is in the awareness of the amazing mercy and goodness of our God that the best we have to offer is the simple admission that we are debtors to the grace and love of Him who loves us with an everlasting love.

Any transgressions we have committed, any offenses for which we are responsible, any misdeeds we admit, are wrongs against the compassion and concern of our Father. To see this is to feel a deep need of His forgiveness. To sense this is to seek reconciliation with Him now and always.

It is no wonder, then, that Christ should include this request for forgiveness in His prayer. It is the key which unlocks the door whereby we enter a rich and wondrous relationship to God our Father.

We live in a world where men and women often feel deep down inside that something is basically missing from life, a sense that somehow they are out of touch with eternity. There is a foreboding that they have failed to find fulfillment. A strange, restless void that no human or material achievement can satisfy occupies the center of their beings. Deep down they know something is wrong, something is missing, but what?

So when Christ taught His disciples this prayer, this petition was included to cover and deal with this deep need in the human heart. As long as we sense in any way that sin or wrongdoing stands between us and God or between us and others, we feel estranged and apart. It is only the acute awareness that forgiveness has been fully granted which draws us to Him and to other human beings and makes us feel true fulfillment.

Many of the world's leading religions teach and admonish men to try to make amends for their misconduct. They urge their followers to pay penance or to achieve some sort of compensating merit by dint of good works or self-discipline. None of these succeed in setting the soul at peace, but, rather, they only plunge it deeper into despair.

Christ, however, comes to us quietly and invites us to simply admit that we are wrong within and in need of forgiveness. He makes no greater demand upon us than that of sincerely pocketing our pride and seeking simple reconciliation with our Father, who is so very fond of us and so very eager to extend His forgiveness to us the moment we seek it.

"Forgive us our debts" may well be the four most important words that ever cross our lips, provided we really mean them. Any man, any woman who comes to our Father in heaven with a genuine, heartfelt attitude of contrition is bound to find forgiveness. There will fall from the shoulders the old burden of guilt, and, in its place, there will be wrapped around our hearts a radiant sense of warmth, affection, love, and acceptance. "You are forgiven. You are mine. You do belong. You are home!"

This is the reception which the father gave the prodigal son when he came home asking forgiveness. Little did he realize, all the time he was away from his home and his father, that he was a forgiven man. Little did he know that, despite his misconduct, his father's love and concern for him had never diminished. Little did he recognize the yearning outreach of his father's heart toward him, even when his behavior besmirched and shamed the family name.

This is perhaps the most poignant picture portrayed for us in all of Scripture depicting the loving forgiveness of our Father. The son's forgiveness was not contingent upon a change of conduct or his making a fresh resolution to behave better, or even upon his sense of remorse and contrition. His forgiveness was freely bestowed and gladly given simply because he had come, willing to admit his wrong and accept pardon. The very character of God our

Father can do no less than extend this sort of total and complete forgiveness to all who turn to Him for it.

Jesus knew all about this. He had been a resident of heaven for untold eons of time. Over and over again, He had shared in the ecstatic joy that swept through that celestial realm when even a single soul, searching for peace of heart and serenity of spirit, had simply turned to God and in sincerity prayed, "Forgive me my wrongdoing."

# 9
# As We Forgive
# Our Debtors

"As WE FORGIVE our debtors."

In all of our Lord's Prayer, by far the most difficult phrase is, "As we forgive our debtors." It is not easy for us either to understand or to apply in a practical way to our daily living.

There has been enormous confusion about this part of the prayer. It has produced a great deal of discussion and many differing views down through the long centuries that the prayer has occupied such an important place in our Christian heritage.

For this reason it calls for our special attention. It is significant that newer translations of the New Testament put this passage into the past tense rather than the present. In other words, what Christ said, was this:

> Forgive us our debts, as we also
> have forgiven our debtors (RSV).
> or
> Forgive us the wrong we have done,
> as we have forgiven those who have
> wronged us (NEB).

And, of course, the question which immediately confronts us is, *have* we forgiven others who have wronged us? Do we really have a clear conscience in our relationship with other human beings? Is the atmosphere between me and my fellowman open and unclouded by hostilities? Do I still harbor old hates in my heart? Am I inclined to indulge in ill will over some hurt? Do I allow resentments to rankle beneath the surface of my life? Is there a gnawing grudge against someone tucked away secretly in the back of my memory? Is there a bitter root of recrimination buried deep down in my subconscious that sends up its shoot of cynicism to my conscious mind whenever I am reminded of some abuse or injustice I have suffered? Do the wrongs I have endured from others eat away inside me like a consuming cancer?

These are very probing questions. They get below the surface of the superficial attitudes with which so many attempt to accommodate themselves to the teachings of Christ.

It is probably safe to say that the overwhelming majority of men and women who repeat this prayer have not forgiven others. They have not written off the old debts. They do not have a clear conscience. A backlog of lingering ill will, hostilities, resentments, and animosities beclouds their relationship with others. They are still demanding restitution. They still insist on getting their pound of flesh.

How then can we come and in good conscience ask our Father in heaven to forgive us, when we have failed to forgive others? It cannot be done except very hypocritically. God sees right through this sort of sham.

Our Lord was always emphasizing the fact that our inner attitudes were more important than our outward actions. It was His assertion that our Father in heaven knew our attitudes and rated them far above our outward appearance.

Most of us from early infancy are conditioned to put on a brave front. We become exceedingly skilled at pretense. We are good actors. We can say one thing but think quite another. We can smile sweetly at someone yet hold hidden resentment against him down below the surface. In all of this we may be able to bluff other human beings, but we simply cannot get away with it in dealing with the searching Spirit of God our Father.

Consequently if we are going to repeat this prayer and hope for it to have an impact either on God or ourselves, the phony pretense and playacting have to end. We must become deadly serious in our statements. What we say must be in a spirit of sincerity and truthfulness.

"God is a Spirit; and they that worship him must worship him in spirit and in truth" (Jn 4:24).

If we cannot honestly say we have forgiven others or are unwilling to forgive them, we should find out why. And having seen the cause, do something at once to put matters right.

Why do most of us have trouble forgiving those who have wronged us? Why is it so hard to give up old resentments and ill will? Why do we harbor hate and grudges? Why do we allow bitterness, hostility, and antagonism to cripple our characters, twist our personalities, and blight our relationship to others? All of this leads to enormous tension, stress, and darkness within.

Many of us do not even realize that this state of affairs exists in our lives. In some cases we have lived this way so long we are scarcely aware of the warfare within ourselves. Belligerence, spite, and ill will have been companions whom we almost accept as normal life partners.

Beneath all our difficulties in forgiving others lies the formidable foundational fact of human pride. The iron-like resistance of our egos, the great, central I, which stands like a huge, steel beam at the very core of our makeup refuses to budge, or bend, or be broken. We insist on our rights; we defend ourselves; we lay claim to our privileges; we hold fast to our positions. *Mine, me,* and *I* stand guard, jealously protecting our personal self-esteem and our proud reputation.

Picture an impregnable fortress, in which self sits upon the throne of the life. High walls of self-defense are built all around the personality. Anyone who dares to say or do anything which is provocative or threatening is considered a trespasser. Our immediate reaction is to lash out in retaliation or else quietly withdraw within the walls of self-defense. We pull up the drawbridge of open, friendly approach, holding others off at a cool arm's length.

All such self-esteem and self-preservation comes at a very high cost. It cuts us off from others. It turns us into self-centered, self-pitying introverts. It makes us hard, haughty, callous, quick to find fault, yet so very sensitive to our own hurts.

How can we get over this? What can change these inner attitudes that are so damaging, both to ourselves and others?

The answer lies again in coming to Christ and seeing something of what He endured for us at Calvary. Calvary stands eternally as God's demonstration to us of total selflessness. It towers above time as the supreme act of self-denial in a world that is largely selfish and self-indulgent.

It was no small thing that our Lord, who was God in human form, should be willing to humble Himself, make Himself of no reputation, take upon His innocent Person our wrongs, pride, and perverseness. All of this He did without murmuring or complaining.

This is the exact opposite of our usual behavior. It is the difference between God's conduct and man's conduct. It is love in action as opposed to selfishness in attitude.

If Christ had insisted upon His rights, if He had been interested in maintaining only His reputation, if He had taken umbrage at every unfounded charge against Him, as we generally behave, there would have been no cross, no self-sacrifice on our behalf, no forgiveness of our faults, no reconciliation to God our Father!

It is no wonder, then, that Paul should write to the Christians at Ephesus, "Be ye kind one to another, tenderhearted, forgiving one another, even as God, for Christ's sake hath forgiven you" (Eph 4:32).

Dr. Martyn Lloyd-Jones, the great minister of London, wrote, "Whenever I see myself before God and realize something of what my blessed Lord has done for me at Calvary, I am ready to forgive anybody anything. I cannot withhold it. I do not even want to withhold it."

A second view we can get of Calvary is a very practical one. While our Saviour lay stretched prone upon the cross, with the spikes being pounded through His palms and ankles, He cried out a most incredible petition, "Father, forgive them; for they know not what they do" (Lk 23:34).

With that deep spiritual perception which was so uniquely His, He knew the heartless soldiers with hammers in hand did not know what they were doing. He knew that those who had flogged Him, taunted Him, betrayed Him, were not fully aware of what they were doing, much less why they did it.

Nothing else can so completely shatter self and crush ego, leaving us undone, as a real look at our Lord at Calvary. In the presence of the Prince of peace dying upon the cross for me, my petty pride is pulverized. My self-esteem evaporates. The best I have appears as absolutely nothing. I see my sins and wrongs and misconduct for what they really are. I am then able to see myself in proper perspective, and, at that point, I am willing to forgive others.

The degree to which I am able and willing to forgive others is a clear indication of the extent to which I have personally experienced God my Father's forgiveness for me. The corollary to this is that anyone who is not willing to forgive another has certainly not known God's loving forgiveness.

A middle-aged rancher came to have coffee in our home one night. As the evening wore on, he unburdened his heart to us. For years and years, his life had been bleak and dark with a pent-up hostility against his harsh and overbearing father. In fact, at the last encounter they had had, the father, a huge, powerful man, had knocked him flat on his back. The younger man, though now a Christian, had never cleared the air between them.

When I pointed out to him all that Christ had suffered for his sake and how he in turn should be prepared to suffer humiliation in going to his father to put things right, it seemed a lot to ask. But that night he agreed he would do it.

Next morning early he went into the sagebrush hills alone and prayed for courage to go down and face his father. Then, swallowing his pride, he went to see the older gentleman. He told him of the deep hate and ill will that had accumulated in his heart against him. He told him how he regretted this. He told his father he was willing to forgive him all the abuse he had suffered at his hands, and in turn, asked to be forgiven for his own ill will.

The older man was completely overwhelmed. In a flood of joy, he flung his arms around his son and hugged him hard. It was the first time in thirty-four years the rancher could recall having felt his father's affection in this way.

A few weeks later this rancher and his father spent the whole day together, high in the hills, cutting special wood for the violins the father fashioned in his shop. I venture to say the quality of workmanship and the tone that comes from this old craftsman's instruments will, from now on, surpass anything he ever made before. There is a new music in his life. It is bound to be expressed in the violins he creates.

The beloved apostle, John, knew and fully understood this principle when he wrote to the early church, "If we confess our sins, he is faithful and just to forgive us our sins, and to cleanse us from all unrighteousness" (1 Jn 1:9).

Our Master put it like this: "If your brother wrongs you, go and have it out with him at once—just between the two of you. If he will listen to you, you have won him back as your brother" (Mt 18:15, Phillips).

It is the secret to contented relationships and goodwill between human beings. What is more, it brings a smile of approval to our heavenly Father's face. He looks on and is satisfied.

It is in the bright light of understanding something of God's kindness that we in turn are able to extend genuine forgiveness and kindness to others. We are made willing to accept others as they are just as we desire our Father in heaven to accept us with all our weaknesses. The marvelous thing is He does. And wonder of wonders, we begin to discover that we too can accept and forgive others with all their faults.

This is to find rest from our own restlessness. It is to be set free from our fault-finding. It is to know a quietness of spirit not readily aroused by those who trespass against us.

# 10
# And Lead Us
# Not into Temptation

"AND LEAD US not into temptation."

At first thought, "And lead us not into temptation" appears to be a very simple petition. But is it?

Would God lead anyone into temptation? Any person who truly loves his Father in heaven does not wish to be tempted. We don't want to displease Him. Who wants to be dragged down into evil? We have no desire to do wrong, do we?

Surely God, our Father, knows this. Why then should He ever lead anyone into temptation? Does He do this? Does He place us in situations where we can or will be tempted?

As we contemplate this request, we begin to see that it really is not as simple as it seems. The questions that come to mind demand answers. Do we really understand the part played by temptation in a Christian's life? Do we know how to cope with it when it does come? Can we fully understand why we should ask our Father to keep us from it?

It is well for us to remind ourselves that when Jesus Christ taught His disciples this prayer, He Himself had already been through very severe temptation. We are told that after His baptism in the Jordan, "Then was Jesus led up of the Spirit into the wilderness to be tempted of the devil" (Mt 4:1).

It had been an agonizing, exacting ordeal from which He emerged totally triumphant. Yet it was a test of such magnitude that we read, "Angels came and ministered unto him" (Mt 4:11). After this conquest of His archenemy, He well knew temptation was a strenuous trial for anyone to face.

No doubt, then, one of the reasons He included this petition in the prayer was a compassionate concern for His followers. Being touched with the feeling of our infirmities, He shrank from seeing us exposed to the sort of temptation He Himself had endured.

One of the wondrous aspects of our Lord's temptations is the absolute finality with which He completely routed His tempter, that ancient adversary, Satan. There was simply no question of giving in. True, He could not sin, but, much more glorious, He *would* not sin!

The first Adam gave ground to Satan when tempted. Because of his defeat, sin entered into our human heritage.

The last Adam (Christ) gave no ground to Satan when tempted. Because of His complete victory in every encounter, righteousness is made available to those who follow in His footsteps, to those made members of God's family.

In spite of this, there lies within us the tendency to give way under temptation. Even at our best we are often beaten in our battles with the wicked one. Jesus knew this. It grieves Him deeply to see His followers succumb to Satan's skilled and cunning tactics.

When He knew Peter would be severely tempted to deny Him just before His crucifixion, He said to Peter, "But I have prayed for you, that your faith might not fail." What solicitude!

He cautioned the eleven disciples who accompanied Him to the garden, with these words, "Watch and pray, that ye enter not into temptation; the spirit indeed is willing, but the flesh is weak" (Mt 26:41).

Basically, the above statement puts into very plain language the whole problem of temptation for God's children. If we are truly born into the family of God, we are bound to face not less but rather more temptation than before. The reason for this is that the enemy of our souls contests the control of our lives by God's gracious Spirit.

It is tremendously important to bear in mind that though temptation to evil is essentially a spiritual struggle that involves our wills, it is almost always fought in the realm of our personal passions (desires). This is why our Lord said that the spirit within us is willing to do what is in accordance with God's will, but it is our flesh, our personalities, our old natures, that buckle under in the battle for righteousness.

The temptations which assail God's children originate with Satan, called the great deceiver, and with our own lusts. Even the weakest Christian can sometimes rise to great heights of heroism in a cataclysmic hour of crisis. Instead Satan undertakes to get at us through our selfish, self-indulgent self-will. He tempts us to set our wills against our Father's will by appealing to one of three passionate points in our personalities.

These can be best understood and most easily set out in a diagram. It will be noted it was exactly along these lines Christ was tempted in the wilderness.

### SATAN'S SUBTLE POINTS OF APPROACH
### TO MY PERSON ARE THROUGH

1. MY EMOTIONS, i.e., self-pleasure, self-indulgence. Christ was tempted to make bread from stones.
2. MY MIND, my reason, i.e., self-preservation, self-reasoning. Christ was tempted to cast Himself off the Temple.
3. MY WILL, I, ego, i.e., self-prominence, self-assertion. Christ was tempted to accept an offer of world empires.

The devastating thing about these devilish tactics is that Satan generally chooses to tempt me in that area of my personality that is not yet under the full control of God's Spirit. He knows full well that I am much more likely to succumb to his inducements where he still can have sway over my person.

And the testing becomes a clear demonstration as to who really holds the upper hand in any given area of my life. Does God or does the devil? Consequently the whole contest for the child of God is one of deciding whether Christ, by His Spirit, controls me, or whether Satan, by means of my old self, manages me.

It is for this reason that Paul wrote so emphatically to the Galatians saying, "Walk in the Spirit, and ye shall not fulfill the lust [passions] of the flesh. For the flesh lusteth against the Spirit, and the Spirit against the flesh; and these are contrary the one to the other, so that ye cannot do the things that ye would" (Gal 5:16–17).

If perchance I find an area of my life in which I repeatedly succumb to temptation, it is because there *self*, my old passions, my old nature, my old desires, hold control rather than God's gracious Spirit.

It is for this reason that any man or woman who really desires to come completely under the control of God's Spirit must turn over all this territory to Him. Unless this is done as a deliberate act of the will, then that ground will be the beachhead from which the enemy will always launch another assault.

And to assert that it is God who allows this temptation to go on is to fail to understand the whole nature of temptation. James, in his usual very practical and pragmatic way, explains temptation this way: "Let no man say when he is tempted, I am tempted of God; for God cannot be tempted with evil, neither tempteth he any man; But every man is tempted, when he is drawn away of his own lust [passions], and enticed. Then when lust hath conceived, it bringeth forth sin; and sin, when it is finished, bringeth forth death" (Ja 1:13–15).

Our Master knew this. Because of the dire consequences attending any defeat in temptation, He urged us to pray that we might not be exposed to it.

I have sometimes wished this petition had a short rider attached to it this way, "And lead us not into temptation, but guide us by Your Spirit."

Of course, our Father does endeavor to do this. The problem is we are not always sensitive or responsive to the overtures of His gracious Spirit. We are not always prepared to give Him control of our conduct. We are not completely sure that He can manage our affairs. We are not always willing to choose His way. So, self reasserts itself, and wherever this happens the terrain is open for Satan to tempt us.

In almost every case where this does occur, it is not our loving Heavenly Father who has led us there. It is our own self-will. It is our own choice. The only exceptions are those instances in which

God allows us to be tested and exposed to hardship in order to enlarge our confidence in Himself. For it is there He demonstrates to us His amazing ability to deliver us triumphant out of the temptation. Our faith in His faithfulness is fortified. And our characters are conformed to His.

Also it is well to remind ourselves, always, that He does not allow us to be tempted above or beyond that which we are able to endure or bear. (1 Co 10:13; Heb 2:18).

There is often confusion and deep disquiet, especially among new Christians who find themselves being tempted. Very often they feel that the inclination to do wrong is in itself evil. This is not so. To be tempted is not to sin. To give ground to the enemy and allow him to control us, contrary to the will and purpose of our Father, is to sin.

There are six steps which follow one upon another that lead to defeat in temptation.

The first step in temptation is often the least obvious. We are given a false impression by Satan that whatever wrong we do really is not serious. Somehow, in very subtle ways, he convinces us that self-will and self-centeredness in counteraction to our Father's will are not crucial matters. "After all," he hints, "is God your Father not loving and forgiving and merciful? What harm is done if you do slip a bit and give ground?"

Second, Satan makes us see (either in fact, or in our minds) something, someone, or some situation which he is sure will appeal to our self life. In other words, he presents a picture to us that arouses some passion or desire in our personality.

Third, this produces, unless we understand his tactics, a powerful response within us. A deep and compelling desire is actively aroused. Often it appears very pleasant or very reasonable or very much to our personal advantage to pursue it.

Fourth, we begin to toy with this idea. We entertain it. We play with it. It appeals increasingly; so we finally reach out to take it. At this point, we have actually fallen for Satan's ruse and given ground. Here we sin against God!

But the action is not over. Temptation, once succumbed to, has dire consequences. We have become a slave to sin and Satan. We are now under his orders in this area.

Fifth, we proceed to act on that which was presented to us in such a subtle, skillfull manner. But the moment we do, we are chagrined and dismayed by our own defeat. We become downcast and discouraged. The devil is delighted!

The sixth and final step is to hide the defeat. We attempt to excuse or conceal the debacle from others and from God. This cuts us off from open communication with our Father. At this point a sense of deep despair and sin and separation overwhelms us.

A careful examination of the sequence of events in Adam and Eve's temptation will show these six steps in action.

1. Satan led them to believe that eating the forbidden fruit would not really have serious consequences (Gen 3:4)
2. Satan presented the picture of them becoming as gods, knowing good and evil, if they ate the forbidden fruit (Gen 3:4–5).
3. This had a tremendous appeal. It aroused the desire to become great and wise. It seemed pleasant and reasonable (Gen 3:6).
4. They actually reached out and took the fruit. They accepted it. They ate it. They took it right in. This was self-will exerted against God's will. This was sin (Gen 3:6).
5. The result was they sensed at once that they had been taken in. They were stripped. They were victimized. They stood naked and ashamed. They were embarrassed and chagrined (Gen 3:7).
6. They attempted to hide from their heavenly Father. They were cut off from open, frank, honest communication with Him (Gen 3:8).

When God came to meet with them, they were in despair, endeavoring to hide from Him. He called out, "Where are you?" Not that He did not know. He did! Here, for the first time, a son of God had succumbed to Satan's tactics. Now he was estranged from his Father. Did Adam know this? "Do you know where you are, Adam?" is really what God was asking.

Do we know where we are when defeated?

Without question, it is because of this sequence in our temptations, leading to estrangement from our Father, that Christ prayed, "Lead us not into temptation." We don't want to be separated from Him who loves us so much. We don't want to walk at a distance. We don't want to be His discouraged, defeated children.

Fortunately we are not left without definite tactics to counter temptation. We are given explicit instructions on how to handle it. And the steps to victory in this field are every bit as clear as those which lead to capitulation and defeat. These will be dealt with in detail in the next chapter.

At this point, one thing should be made very clear. Temptation in itself is not necessarily an evil experience. It is part and parcel of our Father's plan for producing people of strong character and Christlike qualities. When He created us as freewill beings, He knew we would be confronted with never ending choices for good or evil. Our characters as His children are the sum total of the choices we make in a life fraught with temptation. Temptation, from God's standpoint, is our great testing ground. It is the disciplining we undergo as we mature. It can help us grow up into godliness under the guidance of His gracious Spirit.

Dr. J. B. Phillips, in his splendid translation of James 1:2–4, makes this very clear to us.

"When all kinds of trials and temptations crowd into your lives, my brothers, don't resent them as intruders, but welcome them as friends! Realize that they come to test your faith and to produce in you the quality of endurance. But let the process go on until that endurance is fully developed, and you will find you have become men of mature character with the right sort of independence."

Precisely the same sort of view is fully developed in Hebrews 12:1–17.

The picture of temptation presented to us all through Scripture is that it is not an easy ordeal. It is something most of us would prefer to avoid. It is an integral part of the Christian's life. It is something we are to accept as a challenge. We can use it to demonstrate, as did our Lord, that we are determined, with His help, to do God's will. It is an opportunity for us to prove both to ourselves and to a skeptical world, "Greater is he that is in you, than he that is in the world!" (1 Jn 4:4).

It is perfectly proper and legitimate for us to ask our Father in heaven not to lead us into temptation, simply because we know our hearts and their natural propensity to evil. Still, He has made provision for us to be triumphant in temptation. He is able to deliver us from evil. The decision as to whether or not we shall triumph in temptation is pretty much ours.

This is a sobering thought. It shows how much our Father believes in us. He is convinced that if His Son, Christ our Saviour, could overcome, so can we! Bless His name.

# 11
# But Deliver Us
# from Evil

"BUT DELIVER US from evil."

In various translations, this phrase is rendered, "But deliver us from the evil one," or, "Save us from the evil one."

As we saw in the chapter on temptation, the Christian's conflict is essentially a contest with the evil one. It is not just a question of coping with sin or self but rather a matter of being tempted by Satan through our self and its natural inclination to sin.

There is a tendency for us to think of sin, self (or self-will), and Satan as being more or less widely separated from each other. In fact the three are so closely intertwined that they cannot be readily divorced from each other. Or, to put it another way, what it really amounts to is Satan, appealing to self (our self-will), uses it as a means to make us sin. He influences us to exert our wills in contradiction to the expressed will of our heavenly Father. This is to sin.

Because of this, Christ taught us to pray emphatically, "Deliver us from evil [from the evil one]."

It is tremendously encouraging for us to know that this petition can be answered positively. It inspires our spirits to realize that we can be delivered from evil and the evil one. It stimulates our souls and strengthens our resolve to be completely God's children. It is possible to sense the presence and power of Him who can save us from Satan and sin and our own selfish wills. We do not have to be enticed and trapped and tantalized by the enemy of our souls. We can be triumphant in temptation. To know this is to step out of despair into a delightful walk with our Father.

Our Master was not one to indulge in double-talk. He did not say one thing and mean another. He would not teach us to ask our heavenly Father for deliverance from evil if no deliverance was available. He would not instruct us to pray to be delivered from evil situations if our Father was unable to do so. But He *is*. And therein lies a great measure of the glory and joy of really knowing God as our Father.

Let us never, never forget that our Father does not want to see us succumb to temptation. He does not want to see us fall. He does not want to see us down in despair, struggling with self, and stained by sin. He wants us, as His maturing children, to grow up in strength so we can walk serenely with Him in the beauty of a strong, unsullied, intimate companionship.

Sometimes it helps us to understand temptation better if we look at it from our Father's viewpoint rather than ours. Our heavenly Father has precisely the same attitude to us, His children, as a concerned and intelligent human parent has toward his offspring. The concern and the love a good parent holds toward the child is expressed best by a deep desire to have the youngster mature and grow up into a strong, complete person with whom he can have rich rapport.

It is precisely the same with God and His children.

The human parent knows that a child does not grow up in one day. It is common knowledge that before we walk, we crawl. Before we run, we walk. Before we leap or jump, we run. It is a case of learning by degrees. Each stage is a testing, trying, tumbling time. Those of us who have raised children know full well some of the apprehension and dismay and also the joys of watching our young ones grow up.

And so it is with God our Father.

We have seen a wee one struggle to stand up on his own feet. The first few attempts he wobbles and weaves unsurely, inclined to fall to the floor. What does the parent do? He holds the little one's hand, steadies his shaky steps, leads him gently, encourages him to try again and again.

That is just what our Father in heaven does with us.

The little fellow falls flat on his face. He bumps his nose, bruises his head, blackens his eye. Does the parent beat him and berate him for his failure. No! Instead he sweeps him up in his arms, kisses away the tears, hugs him close, and dusts off his clothes.

This is the picture of our heavenly Father.

As the months roll by, and one year follows another, we see the child going on steadily from stage to stage. He walks. He runs. He leaps and jumps. He tackles hard hikes; he climbs high mountains, all with his parent's help, guidance, and encouragement. All the way, he is loved. He is given every assistance to keep on trying, to keep on improving, to keep on until he succeeds. And in every one of his triumphs, the parent shares a keen interest and joyous enthusiasm.

That is how it is in our walk with our heavenly Father.

To see ourselves in this way, endeavoring to mature spiritually, just as a child struggles to mature physically, is to see ourselves in a new light. Every tendency to fall, every temptation to go down, every struggle to stand or walk or leap are not testing situations which we meet alone. Our Father is right there. He is ever responsive, ready, eager, to extend His hand to help us the instant we need it.

Are we surprised then to have our Lord include this petition in His prayer? "Father, deliver us from evil!"

We need to remind ourselves, too, that no matter how often or hard we fall, He is there, waiting to pick us up and restore us. Why? Simply because we are His children, because He loves us, and because He knows that only as we go on do we grow up into His likeness.

Our struggles with sin and self and Satan, seen this way, are not the terrible trials we generally think them to be. Instead they are challenging, testing encounters that can strengthen our determination to go on with God. They inspire within us the resolve to mature into strong men and women with whom our heavenly Father loves to associate.

There are three definite, simple, and positive ways by which our heavenly Father delivers us from the evil one. The first of these has already been alluded to above. It is simply this: He is always there. He is always available. If we are His children, His gracious Spirit resides with us. And when we come into temptation, we need only remind ourselves that He is there and deliberately turn to Him.

It often helps to address Him aloud. Say something like this: "Oh Father, this is a bit beyond me. I can't cope with it. You can! Please extend Your hand, and, by Your Spirit, enable me to stand. Give me such a sense of Your presence by Your Spirit that I shall be empowered to walk through this situation without falling or stumbling."

The response of the Most High God to such a simple, sincere, and humble prayer suddenly provides tremendous strength to the tempted soul. One becomes acutely aware of Christ's presence by His Spirit. At that point the temptation loses its thrust. The impact of evil is dissipated, and an amazing sense of triumph sweeps into the soul. There is sublime power in the presence of God. In this way, God's children are reassured, and evil forces are routed.

The second means by which our heavenly Father delivers us from evil is really a very homespun, happy method. He endows us, by His Spirit, with spiritual common sense which He expects us to use in avoiding temptation. Paul tried to help young Timothy this way by writing to him and saying, "Flee these [evil] things" (1 Ti 6:11).

All of us know full well the areas of our lives where we are most liable to succumb to evil. We know those places and situations where we are most prone to fall for Satan's snares. We know the people that most readily influence us to do, say, or think evil. If we really want to be great, strong people for God it is utter folly and sheer stupidity to go to such places or to associate with such people. We have no right to expose ourselves unnecessarily to evil situations or wrong companions or wicked suggestions.

A child knows full well that he will fall if he plays on the slippery edge of a pond. No doubt, he has fallen there before. He has been warned of the danger by the parent. Still, he sometimes persists in playing there. Suddenly, he slips and falls down. The parent will pick him up again, but there will also be a sharp reprimand as well, with, perhaps, an even sharper smack on the seat. Why? Because the foolish youngster deliberately went into danger. The reprimand and discipline were administered in love and concern for his welfare. So it is with us and our Father. He expects us to use our Godgiven intelligence to keep out of trouble.

If we don't have enough spiritual fortitude to keep away from situations where we know we shall sin, then let us ask God to so invade us by His Spirit that we will. He has promised to give His Spirit to those who ask Him (Lk 11:11–13). The moment we do so in utter sincerity, we will find that He does in fact work in us, both to will and to do of His good pleasure (Phil 2:13). We will find that we do have the grit to get up and get out of evil situations.

At that point we shall find within ourselves both the desire and willingness to go where we should, do what we should, associate with whom we should, think as we should, and avoid what we should.

The Scriptures are replete with stirring accounts of men and women who positively refused to be caught in any compromising situation where they could be enticed by evil. They firmly determined that they would not, if they could help it, be in places or with people where they would be vulnerable to the evil one.

The third method of coping with evil that our heavenly Father has given us is the ability to battle it. There are bound to be times when we suddenly find ourselves struggling with Satan or sin or self, almost without warning. There is no way of anticipating the attack. There is no advance warning so that steps can be taken to avoid it. We find ourselves embroiled with evil, and the fight is fierce. What then?

Sometimes in these situations, we do not sense that quiet, reassuring presence of our Father. It seems as though the very forces of evil surround us so that we are cut off from communication with God. And even when we do call upon Him, there appears to be no response, or, at least, so we imagine. Over and over, people protest that in such a crisis they feel completely overwhelmed and beaten down by the evil one.

Is there any strategy for routing Satan here? Is there anything available to God's child to launch a counterattack and frustrate the foe? Yes, there is.

In James 4:7 we are told very clearly, "Resist the devil, and he will flee from you." There is a sense in which God expects His children to be brave and bold in counterattacking Satan. Far, far too often we give ground to the enemy of our souls without any resistance. We simply slide into sinning without a struggle. This should not be.

The Spirit which God has given to us is not the spirit of fear, but rather, of power and of love and of a disciplined mind (2 Ti 1:7). We should not and need not feel apprehensive about resisting evil and the evil one. When we know full well what is right and proper and in accord with our Father's wishes, we need to be courageous enough to stand for it. And this we can do in the Spirit and by the strength of our Saviour, who Himself demonstrated that evil could be defeated. After all, Christ has vanquished the evil one. We need have no apologies for letting Satan know that we are aware of our powerful position and enormous resources within God's family.

It is worthy of note that whenever Christ was tempted or assailed by Satan, He immediately reacted by addressing Himself directly to His antagonist. With swift, stabbing strokes, using the Spirit's sword, God's Word, He routed the wicked one. It was a demonstration of divine dilligence and spiritual stamina. Generally the encounter was over in a matter of a few brief moments after which Christ emerged triumphant.

If we wish to be armed against the evil one, we must equip ourselves with God's Word. Through reading it daily, thinking about it, and committing it to memory, we become fit to fight, just as our Lord did.

We live in an age when it is commonplace for many Christians to attribute many of their trials and troubles to the evil one. In part, this may be true. But as God's children we should give him less credence than many do. For, though he may be the ruler of this present evil world, though he may be the prince of the power of the air, though he may have cohorts of evil spirits at his command, he has no claim upon God's children, nor does he have the power to tempt or tantalize them, except by express permission from our Father in heaven. "We know [absolutely] that any one born of God does not [deliberately and knowingly] practice committing sin, but the One Who was begotten of God carefully watches over *and* protects him—Christ's divine presence within him preserves him against the evil—and the wicked one does not lay hold (get a grip) on him or touch [him]" (1 John 5:18, Amplified).

It is extremely important for us to understand this. It puts us into an enormously powerful stance. We see ourselves surrounded by the loving, eternal, constant protection of God Himself. We find we are within the great fraternity of God's family, where no assault can touch us, unless it is permitted within the providential purpose of our Father. And then it is allowed only for our own benefit.

The classic example of this truth is the life of Job. It was only by direct permission from God that Satan was allowed to tempt Job as he did. And without that permission he dared not touch either Job's family, his possessions, or his person. And after that dreadful ordeal was over, the end result for Job was enormous benefit and blessing.

Never, never forget that out of what seems to be evil, God our Father can and does bring great good to His children.

When we do encounter evil, we need not feel apprehensive. To the person walking with God his Father, there comes again and again the quiet assurance that all can be well. Our confidence lies, not in ourselves, nor in our ability to counteract evil, but rather in the character and strength of our Father who delivers us. He honors His own commitment to us as His children. He knows exactly why every evil assails us. And, bless His wondrous name, He can free us from it!

"Now unto him that is able to keep you from falling, and to present you faultless before the presence of his glory with exceeding joy, To the only wise God, our Saviour, be glory and majesty, dominion and power, both now and ever. Amen" (Jude 24–25).

# 12
## For Thine Is
## the Kingdom, and the Power,
## and the Glory, for Ever. Amen

"FOR THINE IS the kingdom, and the power, and the glory for ever. Amen."

The benediction appears in only about half of the translations. It is, nevertheless, repeated in the prayer by most people. And because it serves as a beautiful benediction, it is included in this book.

But, over and beyond being a benediction, this part of the prayer is a powerful expression of praise to our Father in heaven. Just as the prayer opened in an attitude of reverence and honor, with the statement, "Hallowed be thy name," so now it closes with the reaffirmation of the greatness of our God. "Thine is the kingdom, and the power, and the glory for ever. Amen."

Do we really believe this?

Are we really sure the kingship of both heaven and earth is vested in our Father? Are we truly confident that He does control the events and destiny of all history? Do we see Him as the One who declares His Son to be King of kings and Lord of lords, before whom, one day, every human heart will bow in utter subjection?

"Wherefore, God also hath highly exalted him, and given him a name which is above every name: That at the name of Jesus every knee should bow, of things in heaven, and things in earth, and things under the earth: And that every tongue should confess that Jesus Christ is Lord, to the glory of God, the Father" (Phil 2:9–11).

Any less view of our Father in heaven is to see Him in a distorted manner. There must sweep over our souls a sense of awe and wonderment and exultation for the God of heaven. It is true, He is our Father; He is the loving One who draws us to Himself by His gracious Spirit with tenderness and compassion. But He is also the supreme Ruler of heaven and earth, before whom we must all one day stand to give account of ourselves. As such, He deserves our utmost respect.

Just as there is vested in Him all authority, so likewise there is vested in Him all power. Everything, and by that simple word *everything* is meant that all creation, be it in heaven or in earth, exists by virtue of His power.

> Now Christ is the visible expression of the invisible God. He existed before creation began, for it was through him that everything was made, whether spiritual or material, seen or unseen. Through him, and for him, also, were created power and dominion, ownership and authority. In fact, every single thing was created through, and for, him. He is both the first principle and the upholding principle of the whole scheme of creation. And now he is the head of the body which is the Church. Life from nothing began through him, and life from the dead began through him, and he is, therefore, justly called the Lord of all (Col 1:15–18, Phillips).

And again the serious, searching question we must ask ourselves is, Do I really believe this? Do I see my heavenly Father as absolute Sovereign of the universe? Do I recognize Him as the ultimate power behind the scenes, who dictates and determines the whole course of history? Do I comprehend, even feebly, that everything that exists does so by virtue of His express permission and ordained will?

If I do, then there is bound to be within my spirit an overwhelming respect for Him. There will steal over my spirit a reverence of profound proportions. And this great regard for my God will color and condition all of my thoughts, actions, attitudes, and motives.

No longer will it be good enough for me to assume rather naively that God my Father is some remote Deity hovering on the periphery of this planet's little stage, a rather benevolent Being somewhere "out there," who can be appealed to in a crisis. Instead, I shall see Him as the central Figure in the whole drama of the universe. I shall see Him as the key Character by whose word the whole world scene can change. I shall see Him as the One who, because of His power, determines the destiny of both men and nations, yes, and much more than this, the Director of the entire universe, both natural and supernatural.

Is it not appropriate then, and very proper, that this prayer, taught us by our Lord, should terminate on a rising theme of exultation and praise? Who else is so truly deserving of our adulation? Who else so merits our most devoted and genuine exaltation?

For most of us, our God is far, far too feeble. Our mental and spiritual pictures of Him, projected before us by our own weak and inadequate concepts of His character, are but caricatures of His true Person. We simply do not see our Father all resplendent in His majesty and power and glory. Few of us have more than a flickering comprehension of His might. At our best we seem to catch only fleeting, passing glimpses of His true greatness.

A few select, and it seems widely separated, human beings have been afforded the great honor to have an intimate view of God. Their reaction has always been the same. They are totally overwhelmed by the utter majesty, the indescribable magnitude, the awesome glory of His Person. Their immediate impulse is to bow low in humble obeisance, to worship, to break out in spontaneous praise and adoration.

It is therefore not the least surprising that Jesus Christ, who, more than any mortal man, knew His Father intimately, would instruct us to ascribe to Him these honors. To do less would be to leave the prayer incomplete.

I say this in great earnestness just here. We are often so preoccupied with our petitions to our Father that we completely forget to praise Him for who He is and what He has done. If we are to have a balanced, wholesome relationship to God, it is imperative that we not only come to Him freely with our petitions but also reverently with our praise and gratitude.

All through the Scriptures, God's people are encouraged to honor, respect, and praise Him. Praise is just as important to God as prayer is to the well-being of humans. I bless God in rendering to Him my reverent praise and genuine gratitude for being who He is. He in turn blesses me by responding to and respecting my prayers and petitions. In essence, such communion between God and man becomes an intimate exchange of enormous benefit to both.

We seldom realize how much we impoverish our own souls and deprive our Father in heaven of deep delight by neglecting to praise Him. Not only does He deserve our praise, He also expects it. Our Lord made this abundantly clear at the time of His triumphal entry into Jerusalem. Some of the Pharisees felt the shouts of praise and cries of approbation given to Christ by the crowds as He rode into the great city were quite out of order. His immediate response was that if the people did not praise Him, then the very stones would shout His praises (Lk 19:28–40).

There is inherent in the very character of God such splendor, glory, greatness, justice, love, generosity, that it demands our deepest adoration and gratitude. It is only when we grasp something of His glorious goodness, greatness, graciousness, generosity in dealing with us as His children, that there begins to spring up from our innermost spirits a clear flowing stream of praise and gratitude to Him. This is the great, great secret to a sublime communion with Him. It is the key to keen, zestful relationship with our heavenly Father.

The interrelationship between me and my heavenly Father finds a parallel in the interaction between a human parent and a child. When a child comes softly and sincerely to a parent, with endearing expressions of gratitude and appreciation for what the parent is or has done, it unlocks that parent's heart in a wondrous way. The parent's spirit is deeply stirred and moved and melted by the child's expression of gratitude, love, and appreciation. The net result is that the parent now, more than ever, is disposed to lavish even more love and care and benefits on the youngster. This is out of gratitude for the praise and appreciation bestowed by the child. So there is set up between child and parent a two-way communication of blessing upon blessing, benefit upon benefit.

This is precisely the relationship which our Father in heaven longs to have with us. After all, the very underlying reason for His making men and women at all was to have sons and daughters with whom He could have intimate communion. It was His longing, in love, for such a relationship that prompted Him to produce a plan of redemption and reconciliation for His wayward children. He desires above all else to have us come into that simple, yet exquisite family relationship with Him, where He can bless us and we can be a blessing to Him. He has endured enormous anguish and suffering to make this possible. But its greatest compensation for Him lies in the praise and love and gratitude of His people. He looks on the travail of His soul and is satisfied because He has brought sons from out the human race to glory. He has found those whom He could transform into His own likeness and character. Therein lies His joy.

Our Lord had all of this clearly in His mind when He concludes on the theme, "For thine is the glory for ever."

As has been pointed out previously in this book, God's great glory is His impeccable character, and His splendid, sublime character is His glory! Nothing we mere mortals know among men can in any way be even remotely compared to the character and person of our Father in heaven. Yet, wonder upon wonders, He deigns to stoop down and impart a portion of that glory to an earnest, searching, seeking soul who longs for His true likeness.

That great poet, David, gives poignant expression to this inner heart yearning, in Psalm 17:15, when he says, "As for me, I will behold thy face in righteousness; I shall be satisfied, when I awake, with thy likeness."

Paul, the grand apostle, put it this way: "But we all, with open face beholding as in a glass the glory of the Lord, are changed into the same image from glory to glory, even as by the Spirit of the Lord" (2 Co 3:18).

There it is. All the glory, all the grandeur, all the greatness of God's character stands vested in our Father forever and forever. Yet through and by the magnanimous generosity of His own self, He gladly, willingly, eagerly imparts it to us by His gracious Spirit. Every good thing we do, every noble impulse we own, every generous thought we think, every praise-worthy attribute we possess, has as its source and fountain the character and Person of our Father in heaven.

Are we surprised, then, that our Lord should end the prayer on this point? He says, "For ever!" It has always been that way. It always will be. God being God, there is neither beginning nor end to the benefits our Father bestows upon His children. They are new every day. They come without interruption or intermission. They come from the inexhaustible supply of His own being. What an assurance, what a consolation, what a strength to those of us, who, in simple, yet sincere and implicit trust, have put our complete confidence in Him.

It is no wonder the psalmist shouts out across the long centuries of time, "This is the day the LORD hath made; we will rejoice and be glad in it" (Ps 118:24).

Today, tomorrow, and every day given to us is a day direct from the hand of our Father. It is a day in which we can fully appreciate all the advantages and benefits He brings to us as His children. It is a day during which we can turn our hearts and minds back toward Him in sincere gratitude and praise. And out of this there flows between us that serene sense of oneness which is so very precious to God's people.

There are some who attempt to live their Christian lives out of a sense of duty to God. It cannot be done. It becomes a dreadful burden and bondage. There are others who endeavor to maintain their relationship to God by ritual and routine. This degenerates to awful boredom. Still others hope to live in spiritual communion with God by indulging in emotional, ecstatic experiences. These are delusive and temporary. A few struggle resolutely to live stoicly with great self-discipline and inner determination of spirit. They grow weary in their well-doing.

But for the soul who understands something of the wondrous goodness of his Father in heaven, who feels his heart warmed with genuine gratitude for the generosity of God, who feels appreciation and love welling up within because of his Father's love, such a soul has found the secret to a serene and enduring relationship with his God. This is forever, unchanging, undiminished!

Such a person discovers that the motivation, the drives, the desires which now determine his relationship to God and others, are not those of his or her own making. They have their origin with God. Their source is the Person of God Himself. In other words, we love because He first loved us.

Our lives, our prayers, our praise, are all bound up in an attitude of gratitude to God our Father. This was the way our Lord lived. In everything, He sensed and knew that His part was to give thanks, even for the cup which spoke of His blood to be shed for us and the bread which spoke of His body to be broken for us. If this then was the attitude of gratitude motivating the very life of our Lord, God's own Son, who taught us this prayer, surely how much more it should be ours!

Only in this way can we live lives that will reflect, even if only feebly, the glory and character of our Father in heaven. These are the lives that will bless Him and benefit others around us. Amen. "So let it be."

"Yes, Father, may all the petitions and all the praise bound up in this brief yet wondrous prayer become a vital part of our very makeup. Grant it, O God, for Your dear name's sake, as well as ours."

"Amen."

# A SHEPHERD
# LOOKS AT
# THE GOOD SHEPHERD
# AND HIS SHEEP

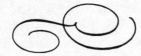

*To*
*Sidney Waterman*
*my friend, brother, and fellow adventurer*
*under God*

# Contents

Preface    269

Acknowledgments    271

Setting the Stage    273

PARABLE I    JOHN 10:1–5    CHRIST IN ME

1    The Sheepfold    280

2    The Shepherd's Entry    288

3    The Shepherd's Voice    296

4    The Shepherd Puts Forth His Sheep    306

5    The Sheep Follow    314

6    A Stranger Will They Not Follow    324

PARABLE II    JOHN 10:7–18    ME IN CHRIST

7    The Doorway for the Sheep    336

8    Entering Into a New Life    346

9    The Abundant Life    354

10    The Hireling    362

11    The Shepherd Knows His
Sheep and They Know Him    372

12    One Flock of One Shepherd    382

13    Christ Lays Down and
Takes Up His Own Life    390

PARABLE III    JOHN 10:25–30    CHRIST IN ME AND ME IN CHRIST

14    To Believe in Christ Is to Belong to Christ    400

15    Eternal Life in the Hand of the Shepherd    408

16    The Good Shepherd Is God!    416

# Preface

IT WAS AT the special request of the publishers that I undertook the writing of this book. It is intended as a companion piece to my previous work, *A Shepherd Looks at Psalm 23*.

That book has been used of God to enrich and inspire thousands of hearts and homes all over the world. It is my deep desire that the same may be true of this volume.

As with *A Shepherd Looks at Psalm 23*, this book also has first been shared in an extended series of lay lectures with my own congregation. In simple yet sincere studies the truths contained in John 10 have been passed on to seeking souls week after week. And out of those sessions our Lord has been pleased to bring enormous benefit to His people.

The fact that the Word of God first "comes alive" in the midst of people in public, reassures the writer that it can likewise "come alive" on the printed page for the reader in private. It was our great Shepherd Himself who stated emphatically, "The words that I speak unto you, they are spirit, and they are life" (John 6:63).

As with the book on Psalm 23, here, too, the Scriptures are explained from the standpoint of one who has been a sheep owner and sheep rancher. But beyond this they are examined by one who has enjoyed the care and companionship of the Good Shepherd, Christ our Lord, for many years.

It is the author's earnest prayer that these pages will open for the reader new vistas and wider horizons of understanding what God our Father, through Christ, by His gracious Spirit intends for His followers—the sheep of His care.

# Acknowledgments

THIS IS TO express my genuine gratitude to my church for recording the messages upon which this work has been based. Those tapes, together with my own detailed study notes, comprise the background material for the book.

A note of appreciation is due also to my courageous wife, Ursula. She has taken great pains to type the manuscript carefully, correcting my wild spelling and making helpful suggestions. She, too, has encouraged me in my writing, when at times the pressure of so many responsibilities seemed almost too great to bear. I am grateful for her good cheer.

Lastly, I must thank Zondervan for their patience in waiting several years for this book to appear. May it be used in the hand of God to enrich and inspire those who read it quietly.

# Setting the Stage

BEFORE WE BEGIN our study of this section of Scripture it is essential to set the stage on which our Lord stated the three parables contained in John 10. Only in this way can we comprehend clearly the truths He was teaching.

His own contemporaries, those to whom He addressed these ideas, were totally baffled by them. In fact, His hearers were so bewildered that some accused Him of being mad, or under the control of an evil spirit. They insisted that such statements as He made deserved death by stoning.

On the other hand there were those who, having just seen Him restore sight to the young man born blind, felt sure that what He said contained truth. It was bound to, since He could perform such miracles.

So it was that a storm of controversy raged around Christ. People were polarized by His parables. Some said He deserved to die. Others hailed Him as a Savior.

Down the long centuries of time since that desperate day in which He declared Himself to be the Good Shepherd, the controversy has continued over what He really meant. Scholars, teachers, theologians, academics, and preachers have all applied themselves to this passage of Scripture. Commentaries and books of various kinds have dealt with these parables. The diversity of views, and explanations given, leave one almost as perplexed as the people of Jesus' own time.

Consequently it is no easy thing to be invited to do a book on John 10. Yet it has been undertaken in humility and with the full knowledge of what others have written previously. It is not intended to discredit what has been drawn from these parables by other teachers. They are fully entitled to their views. But it should be said at the outset that the approach which I have taken is a very distinct, personal one. It is based, not on the concept of the nation Israel, referred to in the Old Testament as God's flock, the people of His fold; nor on the New Testament emphasis of the church being Christ's little flock; but rather on my simply belonging to Him as an individual.

The reasons for this are neither theological nor doctrinal. They are the practical realities of the setting and events in which these statements were made by Christ. And if, with open minds and gently receptive spirits we look at what transpired during the days immediately preceding this passage, it will be seen that the personal approach is valid.

Jesus was nearing the end of His public life. An increasing hostility was building up against Him from the ecclesiastical elite of His time. The religious leaders of His day felt threatened by His enormous popularity and appeal to the common people. The plain people applauded Him openly. His winsome words drew them with magnetic and positive power.

This continuous polarization around Christ created a constant storm center of controversy. The Scribes, Sadducees, and Pharisees tried every tactic to attack Him whenever He appeared in public. The masses on the other hand came to love Him with great affection. His healing, helping, and heartening life had restored and lifted so many of them.

He entered Jerusalem to celebrate the Feast of Tabernacles, or Booths, with His men. It was a festival commemorating Jehovah's care of His people during their long wilderness wanderings after their exodus from Egypt. The Master immediately came under attack. In John 7 we see some claiming Him to be a "good man"; others insisting He was a "deceiver." And they would have lynched Him, if they could, but His hour of arrest had not yet come.

Then, on the last day of the feast He was assailed again. Some asserted He was truly "the Christ." His antagonists on the other hand claimed that Christ could not possibly come from Galilee. Officers were sent to arrest Him but failed to do so, declaring instead, "never man spake like this man!" So once more He was spared from the clutches of His opponents.

On the next day He returned to the city and was confronted by the Scribes and Pharisees with a young woman caught in an illicit sexual relationship. She was to be stoned, but to bait Jesus the frightened girl was brought to Him. Instead of condemning her, He forgave her but instructed her to go and sin no more.

The girl's accusers were furious. They engaged in a dreadful diatribe with Jesus in which He insisted upon His oneness with the Father. For this they again determined to stone Him to death. Yet He eluded them and escaped. All of this is described in John 8.

Later He was met by a man blind from birth. In a remarkable manner He touched the sightless eyes and the blind man saw when he went to bathe them in the pool of Siloam, as instructed. Out of deep gratitude the healed man gave glory and praise to his benefactor. This precipitated another angry controversy with the religious skeptics and leaders.

Because he believed in the Christ the poor fellow was excommunicated from the religious life of his people. Jesus met him again and declared His own identity. The healed man was ecstatic and overwhelmed with adoration.

But to the Pharisees our Lord declared bluntly that they were both blind and steeped in sin and self-righteousness. All their religiosity had done them not one bit of good.

It is on this pathetic theme that John 9 concludes.

In blazing, bold contrast, Christ had personally touched and entered both the lives of the young adulteress and this supposedly sinful, blind man. He had brought them into an intimate, new relationship of abundant living with Himself.

Put into the language of the New Testament, these two individuals had discovered what is meant by "Christ in me," and "I in Christ." They had both entered into that dynamic new dimension of living which Christ Himself later referred to as "[Abiding] in me, and I in you."

To depict and dramatize this remarkable relationship with Himself He then proceeded to tell the three parables of the Shepherd and His sheep in the next chapter.

By contrast, in Psalm 23, David the author writes from the standpoint of a sheep speaking about its owner. In John 10 the approach is the opposite. Our Lord, Jesus the Christ, here speaks as the Good Shepherd. He describes His relationship to His sheep; we, the common people, who have come into His ownership and under His care.

# Parable I
## John 10:1–5
### *Christ in Me*

~

# 1
# The
# Sheepfold

Verily, verily I say unto you, He that entereth not by the door into the sheepfold, but climbeth up some other way, the same is a thief and a robber. (John 10:1)

WHAT IS A sheepfold?

It is an enclosure open to the wind.

It is an enclosure open to the scrutiny of the owner.

It is an enclosure *not* covered in, roofed over, or shielded from the eyes of the shepherd.

It is not a barn, shed, or closed-in structure.

Its walls, open to the sun, the sky, stars, rain, and wind may be made of rough-laid stones, sun-dried bricks, timber, mud and wattle, or even tightly packed thorn brush, called a corral in some places, a kraal in others, and a boma in parts of Africa.

The main purpose of the sheepfold is to provide protection for the sheep—especially at night and in stormy weather. Its high thick walls are a barrier that prevents thieves or, to use a modern parlance, rustlers from invading the flock to plunder the defenseless sheep.

The enclosing walls are also a safeguard for the sheep against all sorts of predators. These vary, depending upon the country in which the sheep are kept. In some areas it is a case of keeping out wolves or jackals. In others, especially parts of Africa, lions, leopards, and even hyenas are guarded against.

Even then, despite the barricade of thorn brush, there are occasions when predators will prowl around a sheepfold stealthily searching for some spot where they can leap over the enclosure to capture and kill their prey. This produces panic among the flock. The carnage is terrifying and the losses among the flock can be enormous. For the sheep owner the raids on his sheep represent serious financial reverses which may take years to recover.

I had a neighbor whose flock was raided one night by a cougar. By daybreak more than thirty of his finest ewes lay dead on the ground. Fences and walls had been cleared by the powerful predator without it ever passing through a gate or open door.

"Sheepfold," besides being the name for an enclosure where sheep are generally kept at night, is also a term for managing sheep. In sheep countries we often speak freely of "folding" sheep. By that we mean the much wider sense in which a flock of sheep are said to be "enfolded" by a certain owner or sheepman. The sheep come under his special management and his direct control continuously. He folds his flock exactly as he sees fit in order that they will flourish and prosper under his care.

Folding sheep is another way of saying a shepherd is managing his flock with maximum skill. It is to say that he handles them with expertise, moving them from field to field, pasture to pasture, range to range in order to benefit them as much as he can, as well as to enhance his own land.

So a sheepfold conveys the idea of the special relationship a sheep has to the ownership and care of a certain shepherd. And when our Lord, who referred to Himself as the Good Shepherd spoke these parables, He saw the overall picture of the unique relationship between Himself and His followers—between Himself and those who had come under His good hand for the management of their lives.

He begins this first parable by asserting that anyone who forces a way into the "sheepfold" other than by the proper doorway or entrance may be a thief or robber. In other words, He is saying that my life is a sheepfold to which He alone, the Good Shepherd, is the rightful owner.

Within the fold of my life there are all kinds of people who come in and out. There are the members of my immediate family circle, my wife, children, grandchildren, cousins, or more distant relatives. Then there are friends, neighbors, business associates, schoolmates or strangers who from time to time pass in and out of the circle of my life.

In reality none of our lives are totally closed in, roofed over, and so completely sealed and safeguarded as to forestall the entry of others. Each of us is a sheepfold in our own private, individual way. We are within a fold, a circle, a life, which really cannot be roofed over.

It is true some of us may have high walls of self-defense erected around us. We may even go so far as to try and enclose ourselves completely to forestall invasion from others, and we may feel we have actually succeeded in this. However, we may fool ourselves into believing that we can withdraw into our own secluded little domain where we are exempt from the entrance and intrusion of others.

Christ's assertion is that in fact this is simply not possible. It is true I am in an enclosure. It is true I live within a limited circle which, however, is shared by others who enter it. But over and beyond this my life is surrounded and enfolded by the encircling care and provision of a providential God. Nor is it closed off from His loving care and concern. It is in fact wide open to the wind— the wind of His gracious Spirit. There is no way He can be kept out, any more than the wind blowing across the countryside can be kept out of an open sheepfold.

The truth that there is no one anywhere who can escape or elude the coming of God's Spirit, is portrayed in exquisite detail in Psalm 139. There is no way known to man in which he can prevent the gracious presence of God's Spirit from making an impact on the fold of his life. We are surrounded by Him; we are found by Him; we are touched by Him. His impact is upon us. We are beneath the influence of His hand . . . His person . . . His presence!

O LORD, thou hast searched me, and known me.
Thou knowest my downsitting and mine uprising,
    thou understandest my thought afar off.
Thou compassest my path and my lying down,
    and art acquainted with all my ways.
For there is not a word in my tongue, but,
    lo, O LORD, thou knowest it altogether.
Thou hast beset me behind and before,
    and laid thine hand upon me.

Such knowledge is too wonderful for me;
  it is high, I cannot attain unto it.
Whither shall I go from thy spirit?
  or whither shall I flee from thy presence?
If I ascend up into heaven, thou art there:
  if I make my bed in hell, behold, thou art there.
If I take the wings of the morning, and dwell
  in the uttermost parts of the sea;
Even there shall thy hand lead me,
  and thy right hand shall hold me.
If I say, Surely the darkness shall cover me;
  even the night shall be light about me.
Yea, the darkness hideth not from thee;
  but the night shineth as the day:
The darkness and the light are both alike to thee.

(Ps. 139:1–12)

In the light of all this we must conclude quietly that though we may be able to exclude others from our lives, to a degree, we cannot do this with Christ. He comes to us again and again seeking entry.

He does not force His way in. He does not gate-crash my life or yours. He chooses to enter by the proper entrance which is really His privilege. Yet He is so gracious in requesting our cooperation in this.

Still, in fear and apprehension we often exclude Him, while at the same time, unknowingly, we are invaded by adversaries.

Many who force their way into my life, who slip in by means that are cunning, who impose themselves by devious and destructive tactics, often are bent on deceiving and destroying me. They are thieves and predators who are determined to plunder and exploit me as a person for their own selfish ends.

We live in a world and society rife with those who hold and propagate false teachings, false philosophies, false ideologies, false concepts, false values, and false standards of behavior. We are approached on every side by those who would penetrate our lives to pillage them if they could. Their aim is to exploit us. They would rob us of the rich benefits which could be ours as the sheep of God's pasture.

Sad to say that in many lives they have actually succeeded. People have been pillaged. Countless lives have been robbed by the enemy posing as proper owners. Yet in those same lives, in those very sheepfolds, the door has never been opened to the Good Shepherd who really does have the right to enter, and who in truth is entitled to their ownership and care.

This is one of the enduring enigmas of human behavior that is so baffling. We human beings will allow all kinds of strange ideologies and philosophies to permeate our thinking. We will allow humanistic standards and materialistic concepts to actually rob us of the finest values that would otherwise enrich us. We permit false aims and ambitions to penetrate our thinking and dominate our desires, scarcely aware that in so doing we are forfeiting the richest values our Good Shepherd intended for us.

On every side we see people robbed, not necessarily of materialistic possessions, but of the much more enduring assets of eternal worth and duration.

The simple solution to this whole dilemma is to discover for ourselves that in truth the only One who really has a right to manage the fold of my life is not myself, but God.

Most of us labor under the delusion that we have every right to our lives; that we have the right to go where we wish, do as we please, live as we choose, and decide our own destiny. We do not. We belong to God. He made us for Himself. He chose us in Christ out of love, from before the foundation of the earth to be His own. He has bought us twice over, both through His generous death and also by His amazing resurrection life.

Every faculty I possess in my body, mind, emotions, will, disposition, and spirit has been entrusted to me as a gift, bestowed by the bounty of a generous, gracious, self-giving, self-sharing God in Christ. There is no such thing as a "self-made" man or woman. To assert this is colossal conceit of the first magnitude. It is an affront to the living Lord who alone has a rightful claim on me.

Even the total earth environment, the biota, of which I am a part, and which sustains me during my brief earth sojourn is God's doing. Only at His pleasure is it maintained in perfect balance and poise. It provides the precise support mechanisms which insure my survival upon this sphere in space.

> Now Christ is the visible expression of the invisible God. He was born before creation began, for it was through him that everything was made, whether heavenly or earthly, seen or unseen. Through him, and for him, also, were created power and dominion, ownership and authority. In fact, all things were created through, and for, him. He is both the first principle and the upholding principle of the whole scheme of creation.
>
> (Col. 1:15–17, Phillips)

In view of the fact that all of life originates with Christ we should be able to see the reasonableness of admitting His ownership of us. We ought to discern the inescapable conclusion that He is entitled to enfold us with His loving care and concern. We should recognize the fact that He is fully and uniquely qualified to manage us with a skill and understanding far surpassing our own.

In spite of all this He does not insist on imposing Himself upon us. He does not override our wills. He refuses to rush into our experience by gate-crashing His way over our decisions. Having made us in His own likeness, free-will agents able to choose as we wish, whether or not we shall be His sheep, enfolded in His care, is ultimately up to us. This is a staggering decision facing each individual.

The amazing generosity of Christ in so approaching us stills our spirits and awes our souls before Him. Yet at the same time He insists anyone else who attempts to invade my life as an imposter, a counterfeit shepherd, is in truth none other than a thief and a robber . . . a plunderer of my life who will impoverish and cripple me.

# 2

# The Shepherd's Entry

But he that entereth in by the door is the shepherd of the sheep. To him
the porter openeth. (John 10:2–3a)

BECAUSE THE SHEEPFOLD belongs to the shepherd who constructed it, he has the right to use and enter it as he wishes. The sheep who occupy it belong to him. The sheepfold is an integral part of his complete sheep operation. The flock moves in and out through the entrance either to find security by night or fresh fields for grazing by day.

Whenever the shepherd comes to the fold it is for the benefit of the sheep. Unlike the rustlers or predators who come to raid or rob the livestock within, he always comes with beneficial intentions. The sheep do not fear him. They do not flee in panic or rush about in bewildered confusion, trampling and maiming each other in blind excitement.

In fact, some of my most winsome recollections of handling livestock during my long life are wrapped around those poignant moments of watching an owner come to his stock. Some come with gentle calls. They alert the sheep that they are approaching. Others whistle gaily as they near the gate so as to set the sheep at ease. Some sheepmen and sheepherders in Africa love to sing soft plaintive tunes as they come to the corral or sheepfold.

All of these approaches are diametrically opposite to the sly, subtle tactics of the predators or prowlers who attempt to pounce on their prey by surprise. They want to catch the sheep off-guard and capture them amid their confusion. It is a crafty, cunning part of their plan of attack.

And when the shepherd reaches the entrance it is customary to tap on the gate, or rattle the latch, or knock on the door loud enough so that all within the enclosure are alerted to the fact that he is outside, ready to enter. More than this, he expects to enter.

When we apply this concept to our own lives we see the striking parallels. So often in our past we have seen our lives exploited by those who had only their own selfish interests at heart. They were not in the least concerned what happened to us as long as their own insidious, greedy ends were gained. They used and abused their prey to promote their own designs, no matter how much destruction they wrought.

By contrast there is none of this in Christ, the great Good Shepherd. Because of His care and concern for us, because of His self-giving love and conduct He comes to us always with peaceable intentions. All through the long and painful history of the human race we see God coming to willful, wayward men in peace.

Always His words of introduction to us are: "Peace be with you"; "Peace be unto you!"; "Be not afraid, it is I"; "Peace, good will toward men!"; "Peace I leave with you . . . not as the world giveth, give I unto you!"

He does not come to men to plunder or prey upon them. God has never exploited any person. Not once has He extracted anything from anyone for His own ends. There is not even a hint of grasping greed regarding the Good Shepherd who approaches us only with our best interests in mind. He does not use people for some selfish pleasure of His own.

And because He comes to us in generous good will He comes gently and graciously. He is Jesus the Christ; "The perfect Gentleman!" He refuses to force His way into our lives. In His magnanimity He created us in His own image with free wills, able to act independently in determining our own decisions.

He stands outside our lives, entreating us gently to grant Him admission. The generosity of such an approach overwhelms us when we pause to reflect that in truth He really has every right to enter.

The enormous pathos of this appeal by Christ to our human hearts is portrayed vividly by the aged and beloved John writing in the third chapter of Revelation. There God's Spirit speaks to us,

See, I am now standing at the door and knocking. If any one listens to
My voice and opens the door, I will come in to him and feast (share life)
with him, and he shall feast with Me. (Rev. 3:20, *Weymouth*)

This One who so entreats us to open our lives to His entrance
is none other than God very God, the Christ, who in the second
parable of John 10 declares emphatically "I am the good shepherd. . . . I am come that they might have life, and that they might
have it more abundantly!"

He comes to us anticipating an entrance. He is entitled to enter
and has that privilege because He is our rightful owner. This will
be explained later in this chapter.

There is a gross misunderstanding among many as to what God's
intentions may be in expecting entry into our lives. They assume
He will make enormous demands upon them which cannot be
fulfilled. They imagine they will be deprived of pleasures or practices which will leave them poorer people. Beleagured by such
misconceptions they are reluctant to grant Him admission.

Yet, the opposite is true of the Good Shepherd. He seeks entry
to enrich us. He desires to put at our disposal all of His wondrous
resources. He wants to inject an exciting new dimension of dynamic living into our days. He intends to share His very life with
us. Out of that life imparted to me as an individual can come all
the noble qualities of a fine and wholesome life which are uniquely
His. These are made real in me, by His presence. They are further
transmitted through me to touch other lives bringing blessing and
benefit to those around me.

Why then are we still so loathe to let Him in?

There are various reasons, of which two far transcend all the
others.

The first of these is fear. Almost all of us have at some time or
other allowed people into our lives who took unfair advantage of
us. They have hurt and wounded us. Sometimes they have abused
us callously and with great cruelty. We started out trusting them
to a degree, and ended up torn and mutilated by the encounter.

The end result is that we begin to build high walls of self-defense
and self-preservation around ourselves. We want to protect ourselves from the onslaught of outsiders. If perchance we have been

injured repeatedly we become even more wary, cautious, and unwilling to open ourselves to anyone whom we regard as an intruder.

We bluntly warn people, "I don't want you in my life!"; "Please stay away, I don't want you interfering in my affairs"; "Just keep out of my business and mind your own"; "Live your life and let me live mine."

And though we may not say so in actual words, we entertain the same attitude toward Christ when He comes to call at the doorway of our hearts (i.e., our wills). We subconsciously attribute to Him the same selfish motives and ulterior designs which characterize selfish human beings.

This is, of course, unfair to God. But it also demonstrates that we really do not know or understand Him, for His thoughts toward us are always good.

For I know the thoughts that I think toward you, saith the LORD, thoughts of peace, and not of evil, to give you an expected end. (Jer. 29:11)

And the ultimate end He has in mind for me is that my will should be aligned with His; my life moving in harmony with His; together sharing in the magnificent plans and purposes He has for His people. To so live is to enter a powerful, positive adventure of selfless giving of ourselves for the good of all. This is the great dynamic of the love of God at work throughout the whole cosmos. It is the divine energy that drives the universe!

Yet most of us will not respond to His overtures. We prefer to draw back, to close ourselves off from Christ, to withdraw within the closely confining circle of our selfish little lives. There we feel more secure and self-assured. It is comfortable and we prefer this confinement—even if we are cramped within the constricting walls of our own making and choice.

The second reason why people will not open up their lives to the Good Shepherd is much more subtle and insidious. It is an integral part of our lifelong conditioning and culture to assume that I, Me, My, are entitled to absolute priority in our thinking, planning, and conduct.

From earliest childhood we insist on having our own way, indulging our own desires, doing our own thing, going our own way with our wishes always paramount. We become veritable little "kings in our own castles," or even worse, "little gods in the temples of our own lives." We resent anyone who dares to enter our domain. We even naively assume at times we can be "the shepherd in our own fold."

There is no doubt in our minds that we are entitled to make all our own decisions, no matter how disastrous the consequences. We are sure we can solve all our dilemmas even though they lead us deeper and deeper into despair. We are determined to run our own lives even if we run them into the ground, ending up in absolute ruin.

In all of this we are positive no one else can manage our affairs nor control our conduct any better than we can. In pride and self-will we view outsiders, God included, as intruders, imposters who dare to try and usurp control. And we adamantly refuse them entrance.

As I sometimes say to people who take up this fortified position, "You have not only erected high walls around your life; you have dug a deep moat outside and drawn up the drawbridge lest anyone ever come in."

In spite of our indifference, our fear, our pride, our determined refusal to let Him in, Christ is very patient and compassionate with us. He keeps coming. He keeps speaking. He keeps standing at the door. He keeps knocking. He keeps rattling the latch.

In the case of a few lives the door is finally opened. Our Lord made the unusual comment that it was really the "porter," the doorkeeper who opens the door. And it may well be asked, "Who is the porter? Who is this One who for the sake and welfare of the sheep opens up the sheepfold to the Good Shepherd?"

He is none other than the gracious Spirit of God Himself. It is He who, unbeknown to us, and long before we are conscious of the presence of Christ, comes to us quietly to begin His gentle work within. It is He who gradually prevails upon our spirits to respond. It is He who, even in our willful waywardness, is at work within us turning us toward the One who stands outside the fold of our lives. It is He who gradually overcomes our fears, our deep subconscious inhibitions toward Christ. He is able in His own wondrous way to pulverize our pride, to lead us gently to see the enormous folly of our self-centeredness. He generates within our wills the active faith needed to comply with and respond to the voice of the Good Shepherd.

It is then and only then that the door is opened to Christ. It is then that the guard, so to speak, is let down. Then the One outside is granted entry. For some this is an act of great apprehension. It involves a definite movement within the will. Yet it is God who works within us to will and to do of His good pleasure. (See Phil. 2:13.)

In his autobiography C. S. Lewis tells how he had long resisted the gentle overtures of Christ to enter his life. One day, while riding atop a double-decker bus to the zoo in London, he sensed he could no longer keep the Lord out of his life. By a definite, deliberate act of his will he literally unfastened the defenses within which he had enclosed himself for so long. Then the presence and the person of Christ moved quietly, but wondrously, into his soul. He was instantly "surprised by joy." And this phrase is the title of his book.

When Christ enters He brings not only joy, peace, and reassurance to the opened heart; He brings also the divine resources of love, life, light, and fullness of character which are uniquely His. These are essential to the new lifestyle He initiates. It is He who assumes control. It is He who begins to manage the sheep. It is He who begins to give direction and purpose to all that happens to them.

Of course it can be asked, "Is He really entitled to do this?" "Is He my rightful owner?" "Does He have the credentials to determine what shall be done with my life?" To each of these the emphatic reply is yes!

First of all, we must be reminded that it is He who made us. The amazing intricacy of our bodies; the incredible potential of our minds and memories; the enormous capacities of our emotions; the unmeasurable impact of our wills; the unplumbed depths of our spirits . . . each and all are glorious gifts bestowed upon us in generosity by God. We did not fashion or form them. They belong rightfully to Him. They are simply entrusted to us for wise use under His direction for the brief duration of our days on earth.

Secondly, though all of us in willful, self-centered waywardness have gone our way to do as we want, we are invited to return to Him and to come under His care. To make this possible, He has brought us back with His own life, given in sacrifice for us. So in reality He has redeemed us, brought us back, made it possible to be accepted again as His own.

Thirdly, He continues ever to intercede on our behalf. He suffers in our stead. He entreats us to become wholly His in glad abandon.

So it is that on this basis it is both reasonable and proper that, as His own people, the sheep of His pasture, we have every obligation to throw open wide the door of our lives, allowing Him to enter gladly as our Lord, our Shepherd.

# 3
# The
# Shepherd's Voice

And the sheep hear his voice: and he calleth his own sheep by name, and leadeth them out. (John 10:3b)

THE RELATIONSHIP WHICH rapidly develops between a shepherd and the sheep under his care is to a definite degree dependent upon the use of the shepherd's voice. Sheep quickly become accustomed to their owner's particular voice. They are acquainted with its unique tone. They know its peculiar sounds and inflections. They can distinguish it from that of any other person.

If a stranger should come among them, they would not recognize nor respond to his voice in the same way they would to that of the shepherd. Even if the visitor should use the same words and phrases as that of their rightful owner they would not react in the same way. It is a case of becoming actually conditioned to the familiar nuances and personal accent of their shepherd's call.

It used to amaze and intrigue visitors to my ranches to discover that my sheep were so indifferent to their voices. Occasionally I would invite them to call my sheep using the same words and phrases which I habitually employed. But it was to no avail. The ewes and lambs, and even the rams, would simply stand and stare at the newcomers in rather blank bewilderment, as if to say, "Who are you?"

This is simply because over a period of time sheep come to associate the sound of the shepherd's voice with special benefits. When the shepherd calls to them it is for a specific purpose that has their own best interests in mind. It is not something he does just to indulge himself or to pass the time away.

His voice is used to announce his presence; he is there. It is to allay their fears and timidity. Or it is to call them to himself so they can be examined and counted carefully. He wants to make sure that they are all well, fit, and flourishing. Sometimes the voice is used to announce that fresh feed is being supplied, or salt, minerals, or water. He might call them up to lead them into fresh pastures or into some shelter from an approaching storm. But always the master's call conveys to the sheep a positive assurance that he cares for them and is acting in their best interests.

When my children were young they saved up their few dollars to purchase their own pet ewes. And it was a delight to watch them go out to the fields and call up their own sheep. Quickly these ewes came to recognize the voice of their owners. When they were called they would come running to be given some special little hand-out of grain or green grass. They would be hugged and cuddled and caressed with childish delight. It was something which both the sheep and the owners enjoyed.

In all of this the key to the contentment of the sheep lies in recognizing the owner's voice. When the sheep hear that voice they know it is their master and respond at once. And the response is much more than one of mere recognition. They actually run toward the shepherd. They come to him for they know he has something good for them.

In examining the Christian life we discover powerful parallels. We find that at some time or other most of us have heard God's voice. We knew the Good Shepherd was calling. As our Lord Himself said so often when He was here among men, "If any man hear my voice," then certain things would happen.

But first the question may well be asked, "How does one hear God's voice?" "Is it possible for Him to communicate with me?" The simple answer is Yes; definitely.

He may speak to me clearly through His Word, whereby He has chosen to articulate Himself. His own gracious Spirit will impress upon my spirit His intentions and purposes for me as a person.

He may do this privately in the quiet seclusion of my own home, in the stillness of my devotions. He may, on the other hand, do it through some message spoken from a church pulpit, through a radio broadcast or a television program.

Christ may come and speak to me through a devout and godly friend, neighbor, or family member. He may call to me clearly through some magazine, periodical, or book I have read. An ever-deepening conviction and awareness that this or that is what I "ought to do," may come to me. This great "I ought to" or "I ought not" is the growing compulsion of His inner voice speaking to me in unmistakable accents by His Spirit.

The Lord has chosen to articulate Himself also through the splendor and beauty of His created universe. The psalmist portrays this for us in exquisite poetry.

> The heavens declare the glory (character) of God; and the firmament sheweth his handiwork. Day unto day uttereth speech, and night unto night sheweth knowledge. There is no speech nor language, where their *voice* is not heard. Their line is gone out through all the earth, and their words to the end of the world. (Ps. 19:1–4)

He also communicates with me clearly through the wondrous character, conduct, and conversation of Christ Himself. He, "the Word," became flesh and dwelled among us. Through His flawless life, His impeccable character, His wondrous words I can hear God's voice. He asserted boldly and without apology, "The words that I speak unto you, they are spirit, and they are life" (John 6:63). On another occasion He insisted, "I am the way, the truth, and the life: no man cometh unto the Father, but by me" (John 14:6).

From the foregoing it is obvious that anyone can hear God's voice; it is possible for us to be reached. But the burning question of communication is, Do we hear? By that I mean much more than merely making contact. This was a perpetual point of pain to our Master when He was among men. Over and over His comment was, "Ears you have, but you hear not!"

Hearing is much more involved, much more complex than it appears on the surface. It embraces more than just being spoken to by God. It involves three very definite aspects of interaction with Him.

If, in actual fact Christ the Good Shepherd has been granted entry into the little fold of my life, then I will have begun to become familiar with His voice. This then implies that I do *recognize* His voice. I learn to distinguish it from the many other voices calling to me amid a confused society and a complex world. I come to that awareness where I am alert and attuned to the special attributes of Christ's call to me personally. I am like young Samuel who, in response to the voice of God, replied, "Speak, Lord, for thy servant heareth."

O great Shepherd, I am listening. I am attentive. I am waiting for Your word to me. I am ready to recognize what You have to say to me.

The second aspect to hearing God's voice is that I *respond* to it. He chooses to communicate with me in order to impress upon me His intentions and desires. He has good intentions toward me. They are in my own best interests and it is incumbent upon me that I recognize this, take them seriously, and respond accordingly.

The instant sheep hear and recognize their shepherd's voice, they lift their heads, turn in the direction from which the sound comes, and cock their ears to catch every syllable. Whether resting, feeding, or fighting, everything else is forgotten for the moment because they have heard their owner's call. It commands their full and undivided attention. Something new and different is about to happen.

The same should be true of us in responding to God's voice. It should command our undivided attention. We should never allow the other interests and demands of our often busy lives to blur the gentle appeals that come to us from Christ. He does not blow mighty bugles to gain our attention. We are not hounds being called to the hunt, but sheep being led in the paths of righteousness. If we are not sensitive to the overtures of His Spirit and quickly responsive to the distinct promptings of His Word, we are not going to go anywhere with Him.

It is often frustrating to a shepherd when he calls his sheep to discover that though they may have recognized his voice and responded to it, they still refuse to move. They simply will not come running when called.

Again and again I have watched a flock of sheep in which there were a few recalcitrant ones. Standing there stupidly and stubbornly they simply shake their heads, waggle their ears, and bleat out a pathetic "blah!" For the shepherd calling them, this is frustrating.

The same thing is too often true among God's people. We recognize His voice, we respond to it to a degree, but we will not move. We will not act. We will not run to Him. We adamantly refuse to comply with His wishes or cooperate with His intentions for us.

Our attitude and actions are as absurd as any "Blah!" bleated by some stupid, stubborn sheep. We stand still, not moving a step toward Him who is so fond of us. We appear to be almost paralyzed . . . impotent to move a step ahead in the will of God.

Now the reader may well ask, "How does a person move toward Christ? How does he, so to speak, 'run to do His will'?" It is obvious that if we are to benefit from hearing His voice we must step out to do what He calls us to do.

This involves much more than merely giving mental assent to what we may have heard. It simply is not enough just to agree with what God's Spirit may have said to us. It goes far beyond even becoming emotionally excited about what we have heard. It is possible for people to weep tears of bitterness or remorse yet never move toward God. It is equally ineffective for individuals to become merely ecstatic about some spiritual issue, for, when the emotion has passed, they are still standing precisely where they were before the call came from Christ.

What then is the step needed to move us? It is an action of our will. It is the deliberate *choice* of our disposition to *do that which we have been called to do.*

We refer to this as the *response of faith in action.* It is the compliance of our will to God's will through straightforward obedience and glad cooperation.

*Truth becomes truth to me, and spiritual life becomes spiritual life to me only when I actually do the thing Christ calls me to do!*

Not until this actually takes place do we move toward the Shepherd or begin to experience the benefits of His care and management. We may know all about Him in a theoretical, doctrinal way. But actually living, walking, and communing with Him in a personal encounter will be something foreign and unknown.

Unfortunately many who call themselves Christians, who consider themselves the followers of Christ, who claim to be the sheep of His flock, are really still strangers to His voice. They have yet to know the precious and special delight of actually *knowing Him.*

Our Lord referred to this in a solemn statement He made in the Sermon on the Mount. It is full of pathos and poignant pain: "Not every one that saith unto me, Lord, Lord, shall enter into the kingdom of heaven; but *he that doeth the will of my Father which is in heaven.* Many will say unto me in that day Lord, Lord. . . . And then will I profess unto them I *never knew you''* (Matt. 7:21–23).

The relationship between the shepherd and his sheep, between Christ and those whom He calls, is one of personal, profound *knowing;* for He knows me intimately, He knows me by name.

Only those who are acquainted with the pastoral life of a sheep owner in the Middle East or Africa are able to grasp how thoroughly these people know their livestock. Their livestock are their very life. Sheep, goats, cattle, camels, and donkeys are both the center and circumference of their entire social scene.

If one goes to visit a village, the order of greeting and salutation is first to ask how the owner himself is faring. Then one inquires after the health of his sheep and cattle. Following that one asks about his children, then lastly his wife or wives. This is not intended as any slur on his family, but it does point up the enormous importance attached to livestock. They are the paramount consideration in the life of the owner.

A second remarkable aspect of the care of animals in these countries is that each one is known by name. These names are not simple common names such as we might choose. Rather, they are complex and unique because they have some bearing upon the history of the individual beast. For example, an ewe might be called: "The one born in the dry river bed," or "The beautiful lamb for which I traded two pots of honey."

During the years when my family and I lived among the Masai people of East Africa I was deeply moved by the intense devotion and affection shown by the owners for their stock. Out in the grazing lands or beside the watering places they would call their pets by name, and it was sheer joy to watch their response as they came to the shepherd's call to be examined, handled, fondled, petted, and adored.

Some of these sheep had literally grown up as members of the family household. From their earliest days they had been cuddled, hugged, fed, and loved like one of the owner's own children. Every minute detail of their lives was well known and fully understood.

A remarkable picture of this is portrayed for us in 2 Samuel 12:3, where the prophet of God rebuked King David for his adultery with Bathsheba, when he likened Uriah to a poor shepherd with only one little lamb.

> But the poor man had nothing, save one little ewe lamb, which he had bought and nourished up: and it grew up together with him, and with his children; it did eat of his own meat, and drank of his own cup, and lay in his bosom, and was unto him as a daughter.

Is it any wonder that such ewes and lambs were called by endearing names? It is little marvel that every detail of their lives, every unusual facet of their character was known intimately.

This is the picture portrayed for us by Christ when He made the terse statement: "He calleth his own sheep by name."

Most of us are totally unaware of just how well God really does know us. We are oblivious to the staggering truth that every aspect of our lives is fully known to Him. If we examine the Word of God on this subject we will discover that even from our conception in our mother's womb all the hereditary factors that combined to make us each the unique individuals that we are have been known to God.

A careful reading of Psalm 139 assures us that we are known far beyond human knowledge, even in the environmental influences that have shaped us, by God who comprehends our complexities. All the multitudinous idiosyncrasies which make each of us distinct individuals are known to our Lord and Master.

The Good Shepherd may well be a stranger to me, but I am no stranger to Him!

When in the process of time an individual opens the sheepfold of his life to Christ, he may feel he is inviting a stranger to enter. Yet the truth is that He who enters is not a stranger at all but the One who has in fact known us from before birth.

This discovery is really double-pronged. It is at the same time both reassuring, yet also alarming. It is wonderful to realize that at last there is someone who does know and understand me. If I have been the type of person who has played games with others and pulled the wool over their eyes, I will find I can't do it with God.

The hypocrisy has to end. I must begin to be open and honest with Him who knows me through and through—who calls me by name.

In calling to his sheep, the shepherd desires to lead them out of the sheepfold. Sheepfolds, especially in the East, are not pretty places. Their names may sound picturesque and romantic, but the enclosure where the sheep spend the night usually is an appalling spot.

Within the enclosing walls of stone, timber, bricks, or brush there is a continual build-up of dirt, debris, and dung. Not a blade of grass survives the eternal tramping of a thousand hooves. And as the seasons come and go the sheepfold lies ever deeper in its accumulated dung. The odors can be atrocious after rain and vile in the heat of the summer sun.

The good shepherd is up early at break of day to fling open the gate and lead his sheep out into fresh pastures and green grasslands. He will not allow his flock to linger within the corral for an hour longer than is necessary. There they can only stand still in the scorching sun or lie down to try and rest in the dirt and dung that clings to their coats and mats in their wool.

Gently the shepherd stands at the gate and calls to his own to come outside. As each animal passes him he calls it by name, examines it with his knowing eye, and, if necessary, searches with knowing hands beneath its coat, to see if all is well. It is a moving interlude at the dawn of each new day: a time of close and intimate contact between the owner and his flock.

The parallel in our own lives is not difficult to discover. It is in the little circle of our own constricted living that most of us feel most secure, most relaxed and perhaps most familiar.

But our great Good Shepherd calls us to come out of the

restricted, petty round of our cramped lives. He wishes to lead us out into fresh new pastures and broad fields, perhaps to new places we have never been before.

The surprising thing is that many of us are not aware of just how drab, soiled, and dusty with accumulated debris our lives really are. We keep milling about in our same little circle. We are totally preoccupied with our self-centered interests. We go around and around, sometimes stirring up quite a dust, but never really accomplishing anything worthwhile. Our lives are cramped, selfish, and plagued with petty pursuits.

The tragedy of all this is that it can apply to every aspect of our lives. It can be true in a physical dimension where we allow ourselves to be cramped within four small walls or within the narrow confines of a city house or apartment. We can be cramped, too, in abused and neglected bodies.

We can likewise find ourselves corralled in a moral and mental dimension. We will not move out into new areas which enlarge the horizons of our minds or new experiences that stir and challenge our souls. We cringe from new vistas and fresh pursuits that will get us off the barren ground of our familiar old style.

Equally so is there a sense in our spiritual lives where God by His gracious Spirit calls us from and leads us out of our cramped experiences. He invites us to move out into the rich, nourishing pastures of His Word. He wants us to roam abroad in the wide ranges of new relationships with others of His flock. He longs to lead us beside still waters; in paths of righteousness; up into the exhilarating high country of the summer ranges where we are in close communion with Him.

The intentions He has for us are all good. His desires and aspirations for us are enormous, full of potential for unimagined benefit to us and others. Because the thoughts He thinks toward us are thoughts of peace and blessing, let us not hold back! It is the truly wise one who will allow himself to be led out into the broad fields of God's gracious blessings and benefits.

# 4
# The
# Shepherd
# Puts Forth His Sheep

And when he putteth forth his own sheep, he goeth before them. (John 10:4a)

As WAS POINTED out in the preceding chapter many sheepfolds are polluted places. Even the environs around the sheepfold often become barren, trampled, and eroded by the passing to and fro of the flock. So if they are to benefit from the outlying fields and meadows they must be put out to pasture.

A good shepherd simply does not permit his stock to linger long on the barren, contaminated ground around the corral. There is nothing of value there for them to feed upon. The corral is essentially a place of protection during darkness.

The diligent owner will be up at dawn to put his flock afield. This is a self-imposed discipline. He must bestir himself before the sun breaks over the eastern skyline, but this he does gladly and willingly for the sake of his sheep.

A reason for this is that because of the aridity of so much sheep country, he simply must get them out on grass early to benefit from the dew that lies on the herbage at dawn. Often this is the only moisture available for the flock. Frequently in these semi-desert countries there are no clear running streams nor placid pools of water where they can be refreshed. The total moisture intake to maintain body metabolism and vigor must come from dew-drenched vegetation.

Another point of interest is that this is the coolest time of the day. The atmosphere is moist and fragrant with the night air that has settled over the land. The heat has mostly dissipated during darkness. Mosquitoes, flies, and other insects are semidormant, less active, allowing the sheep to graze peacefully.

Turning to our lives we find that much the same principles hold true in our quiet times with the Master. It is noteworthy that most of the truly great men and women of God through the centuries are those who have met with Him early in the day. It is significant that so many of His most intimate "saints" have been those who literally allowed themselves to be "put out" into fresh fields of intimate association with Christ at break of day.

It is in these still hours that the quiet dews and refreshing presence of God's gracious Spirit descend upon us. It is then that the frantic world is still. It is then that the clamor and conflicts of our complex lives are quieted. It is then that we sense our own spirits can best be silent, responsive, and sensitive to the stimulus of His own strong Spirit.

Our Shepherd, our Lord, our Master Himself, when He was here among us as a man, delighted in these quiet hours in communion with His Father. The gospel record confirms how often He slipped away to be alone in private prayer and meditation. It was the time of refreshment for His soul; the time of restoration for His body and uplift for His spirit.

It is not always easy to be up and alert at an early hour. It demands a degree of self-discipline which is more than many can meet. But it is the interlude of enormous benefit to those who will allow themselves to be "put out" to this extent. So often, especially when we are weary, the comfort of our warm beds is so appealing. The natural, normal inclination is to simply sleep on.

> Yet a little sleep, a little slumber, a little folding of the hands to sleep: So shall thy poverty come as one that travelleth, and thy want as an armed man. (Prov. 6:10–11; 24:33–34)

The impoverishment which comes to us is often much greater than we are aware of. Not only is it in a spiritual dimension, but it is equally so in mind and body. The reason for saying this is because the early hours are among the best of the day. It is then we are rested. Our minds are alert; our bodies are refreshed; our spirits are still. We are fully prepared for whatever new and fresh experience our Lord may have in mind for us. And if we deprive ourselves of this opportunity for a firsthand encounter with the living God, then our total lives are at a lower level than they could or should be.

It is the alert person who in a positive and distinct way presents himself or herself at dawn to the great Shepherd of the soul, who flourishes under God's care. In a dramatic way the course of the entire day's events are established. A strong, pervading, impelling awareness of God settles over us. We become acutely aware that we are, by a decisive action of our wills, putting ourselves at His disposal, to be put where He wishes during the day. We realize that we are going out into the turmoil of our times; into the chaos of our society; into the broken world of our generation, *not alone but with Him.*

It is because of this knowledge, this awareness, that, as God's people, we can be put out into a troubled generation with strength, serenity, and stability. It is He who puts us into the place of His appointment. It is He who will put us into the green pastures of His choosing. It is He who will make even our most desperate days of benefit to a beleagured world. This He will do even to the refreshing of our own lives.

Why then, it may be asked, are so many of us reluctant to be put out of our little lives? Why are we so loathe to have our life habits disturbed? Why are we so unwilling to be put out either for the benefit of ourselves or the welfare of others—including our Master Himself?

The answer is rather startling, yet simple. It is largely because most of us are stubborn and selfish. We find it much easier and more comfortable to confine ourselves to the familiar little round of our old self-centered lives. We are so enfolded with the comforts and conveniences that have conditioned our existence that we are reluctant to have our constricted circle of living disturbed. Our days may be drab and dry, as barren as any eastern sheepfold with its dust, dung, and debris, but we will not be put out of it.

Some dear souls are fully aware that this is so. In a way they come to almost abhor their own dry existence. But instead of allowing themselves to be put out they turn inward to indulge in endless self-pity and boredom.

Somehow they feel it is no fault of their own that they are caught in a confining little circle of hopelessly selfish living. They are so preoccupied with their own petty interests that the idea of being drawn out to new fields and fresh experiences is both unwelcome and frightening.

They have ears, yet they are deaf to the pleas of perishing people around them. They have eyes, yet they cannot see the broken humanity, homes, and hearts all about them. They have spirits, yet they are shriveled, shrunken, and atrophied with self-interest, unable to sense the needs and heart hunger of a sick society, a world groaning in despair.

To such our Great Shepherd comes, intending to put them out where they can count for something substantial in His economy.

Let us look at this whole concept in a practical and simple way. Let us remind ourselves that because our God has been all over the ground before He knows what He is doing with us. He does not put us out into places or experiences where we are caught in a crisis. There are no crises with Christ. He has all foreknowledge. He is totally familiar with every circumstance that will or can confront us.

It follows then that wherever He chooses to put us it is for Him familiar ground. We are not going out blind. We are setting out under His guidance. Our confidence is in His faithfulness to find the places where not only we, but also He and others will benefit most from our just being there. It is not a case of relying on our wits, intelligence, or insight. Rather, it is a question of unquestioned reliance on His utter reliability to put us into the right place at the right time in the right way. Because He is all-knowing and all-understanding and totally trustworthy we can depend fully on His faithfulness to do that which is best.

Now this applies to every aspect of our lives. In no way is it or can it be confined to just our spiritual experiences. With God, every aspect of life is totally sacred the moment He touches it. There is no distinction in the mind of God, as there is in ours, between secular and sacred when He has a dynamic part in it. He desires that the total round of our little lives be lifted out of the mundane round of impoverished days, to the lofty and broad sweep of living to our fullest capacity under His control. He wants to broaden our horizons.

This is true because He declared unequivocally, "I am come that they might have life, and that they might have it more abundantly" (John 10:10).

What does this involve in basic terms? In Christian thinking there is too often a tendency to deal in abstract values and intangible ideas. Let us get down to basic human behavior. Perhaps we can begin with our bodies, our physical makeup.

If in truth I am God's person; if Christ has in fact entered my life, my body belongs to Him: He resides there. My right to do with it as I choose has been abdicated. It is now the residence of His gracious Spirit who is entitled to be sovereign in its conduct and care. I no longer have any right to misuse or abuse it. It is not to be overworked, overstressed, overfed, overindulged with drink, nor overcharged with sex.

As the sheep of Christ's care this body is to be under His management. It is to be put out of the confining, restricting, damaging environment of just four walls and cramped quarters. It is to be exposed fully and freely to the benefits of fresh air, sunshine, clean water, wholesome food, moderate exercise, and adequate sleep. These are provisions made for it by God. I should be willing to be put out to see they are met. This will benefit not only myself, but also my family, friends, and anyone else who encounters this healthy, wholesome, energetic, vigorous person.

Turning to my soul with its mind, emotions, and will, precisely the same principle applies. This is my person, now indwelt by the living Spirit of the living God. I shall not permit it to be cramped and contaminated by exposing it to such dusty trivia as newspaper propaganda, pornography, cheap debasing literature, hours of low caliber television programs, or rubbish from the mass media.

Instead, God's Spirit will lead me to expose myself to the finest in art, literature, and music. He will put me into situations where my mind can be improved and my soul can be stimulated with that which is beautiful and noble and lofty. I can and will become a person of broad interests, noble aspirations, and enormous enthusiasm because I belong to Him and He wishes to put me out into wide fields of fruitful and useful endeavor to benefit my generation.

The same is true in the realm of my spirit, where I commune with Him. In the deep intuition of my innermost being where I "know him," Christ comes to enlarge my life and the understanding of His will.

He leads me to browse widely and ruminate richly in His Word. He puts me out to touch a hundred or a thousand other lives by His direction. He enriches my fellowship and contact with those outside the little circle of my sheepfold. In short, because He does all this it is possible to make an impact on my generation out of all proportion to my one little life—because He is in it with me.

# 5

# The Sheep Follow

. . . and the sheep follow him: for they know his voice. (John 10:4b)

IN CHAPTER 3 we learned how the sheep come to recognize their shepherd's voice and respond by running when called. Over a prolonged period of time they become acutely aware that it is always in their best interests to do this. They have learned to trust it, to rely on it, but even more significant, to actually enjoy hearing it.

This is simply because the voice and the shepherd are as one. His voice denotes his presence. His voice indicates he is there in person. His voice represents his power, authority, and ability to protect them in danger while also providing for their every need.

In essence the sheep become so acquainted with that voice that they know it intimately. They come to expect it. That voice of that owner speaks peace and plenty to them. To hear and know that voice is to be constantly reassured of the shepherd's care for them. It is evidence of his affection and faithfulness to them.

Precisely the same can apply to the Christian under Christ's control. His voice is not something we shrink from. It does not disturb or dismay us. We do not find it troubles us when He speaks.

We also learn to delight in hearing Him. We look forward to having Him speak to us. We enjoy the increasing awareness of His presence; we relish the individual interest He shows in us; we revel in the close intimacy of communion with Him. We delight in knowing assuredly that He has come to be with us and we can be with Him, ready and eager to follow Him.

Nowhere is there stress or strain in this relationship with the Shepherd of my soul. Its keeping has been deliberately entrusted to Him. A calm, strong, quiet assurance pervades me that in His care all is well. Absent from this commitment of myself to Him is any fear or foreboding. *I know Him. I know His voice. I know all is well.*

And this knowing applies to all of my life. It embraces not only the past and the present but applies equally to the unknown tomorrows. My days need not be charged with anxiety. There is no need to inject unnecessary stress into my sojourn of this day. He is here. His voice speaks strength, serenity, and stability to my soul.

So where He leads me I will follow!

Etched indelibly upon the walls of my memory is one tropical night when all alone, with no one near but God Himself, I went out to walk softly beneath the rustling palms beside the Pacific Ocean. My life, it seemed, had reached an absolute impasse. There seemed no point to pushing on. Everything had ground to a deadly standstill. The future looked forbidding; in fact, it appeared positively hopeless.

From the depth of my being I cried out to Christ. Like a lost sheep bleating in desperation from the thicket in which it was stuck fast, I longed to hear my Shepherd's voice. He did not disappoint me!

He heard. He came. He called. He spoke. And in His voice that night, speaking to me clearly, distinctly through His Word, by His Spirit, my soul was reassured. I could hear Him say, "Entrust the keeping of your soul and life to Me. Let Me lead you gently in the paths of righteousness and peace. My part is to show the way. Your part is to walk in it. All will be well!"

It was so. And it has been to this day.

The question in all of this is, "Do I really *want* to follow Him? Do I really *want* to do His will? Do I *want* to be led?"

Some of us say we do without really meaning it. More than anything else it is like a sentimental wish. It is a half-hearted hope. It is a pleasant idea we indulge in during our better moments. Yet, too often deep down in our wills we still determine to do our own thing and go our own wayward ways.

It is precisely at this point where we come to grief in our walk with God. It is presumption of the worst sort to claim His commitments to us, made so freely and in such generosity, while at the same time refusing to comply with His commands or wishes because of our own inherent selfish desires.

Whatever else happens there remains this one, basic fundamental fact that only the person *who wants to follow* Christ will ever do so. All the rest will become strays.

This word "follow" as used by our Lord implies much more than just the thought of sheep tagging along blindly behind their owner. It has within it the connotation of one who deliberately decides to comply with specific instructions.

For example, if one purchases a complicated clock or other piece of equipment that is to be assembled, along with it will come a sheet of instructions. At the top will be printed in large bold letters, "THESE DIRECTIONS MUST BE FOLLOWED." In other words, there can be no guarantee that it will work unless the directions are complied with and carried out to the minutest detail.

It is the same in carrying out God's commands. His clear instructions for our conduct and character have been laid out for us in His Word and in the life of our Lord, the Word enfleshed. There rests with us then the obligation to comply. As we cooperate and follow through we will find ourselves progressing. New areas of life, exciting experiences of adventure with Him will emerge as we move onto fresh ground. I quote here from *A Shepherd Looks at Psalm 23:* "As mentioned earlier it is no mere whim on God's part to call us sheep. Our behavior patterns and life habits are so much like that of sheep it is well nigh embarrassing."

First of all, Scripture points out the fact that most of us are a haughty and stubborn lot. We prefer to follow our own fancies and turn to our own ways. "All we like sheep have gone astray; we have turned every one to his own way" (Isa. 53:6). And this we do deliberately, repeatedly, even to our own disadvantage. There is something almost terrifying about the destructive self-determination of a human being. It is inexorably interlocked with personal pride and self-assertion. We insist we know what is best for us even though the disastrous results may be self-evident.

Just as sheep will blindly, habitually, stupidly follow one another along the same little trails until they become ruts that erode into gigantic gullies, so we humans cling to the same habits that we have seen ruin other lives.

Turning to "my own way" simply means doing what I want. It implies that I feel free to assert my own wishes and carry out my own ideas. And this I do in spite of every warning.

We read in Proverbs 14:12 and 16:25, "There is a way which seemeth right unto a man, *but* the end thereof are the ways of death."

In contrast to this, Christ the Good Shepherd comes gently and says, "I am the way, the truth, and the life: no man cometh unto the Father, but by me" (John 14:6). "I am come that they might have life, and that they might have it more abundantly" (John 10:10).

The difficult point is that most of us don't want to come. We don't want to follow. We don't want to be led in the paths of righteousness. Somehow it goes against our grain. We actually prefer to turn to our own way even though it may take us into trouble.

The stubborn, proud, self-sufficient sheep that persists in pursuing its old paths and grazing on its old polluted ground will end up a bag of bones on ruined land. The world we live in is full of such people.

Broken homes, broken hearts, derelict lives, and twisted personalities remind us everywhere of men and women who have gone their own way. We have a sick society struggling to survive on beleaguered land. The greed and selfishness of mankind leaves behind a legacy of ruin and remorse.

Amid all this chaos and confusion Christ the Good Shepherd comes and says, "If any man will follow me, let him deny himself, and take up his cross, and follow me" (Matt 16:24). But most of us, even as Christians, simply don't want to do this. We don't want to deny ourselves, give up our right to make our own decisions. We don't want to follow; we don't want to be led.

Of course, most of us, if confronted with this charge, would deny it. We would assert vehemently that we are "led of the Lord." We would insist that we follow wherever He leads. We sing hymns to this effect and give mental assent to the idea. But as far as actually being led in paths of righteousness is concerned, precious few of us follow that path.

Actually this is the pivot point on which a Christian either "goes on" with God or at which point he "goes back" from following on.

There are many willful, wayward, indifferent Christians who cannot really be classified as followers of Christ. There are relatively few diligent disciples who forsake all to follow the Master.

Jesus never made light of the cost involved in following Him. In fact, He made it painfully clear that it was a rugged life of rigid self-denial. It entailed a whole new set of attitudes. It was not the natural, normal way a person would ordinarily live, and this is what made the price so prohibitive to most people.

In brief, seven fresh attitudes have to be acquired. They are the equivalent of progressive forward movements onto new ground with God. If one follows them he will discover fresh pasturage, new, abundant life, and increased health, wholesomeness, and holiness, in his walk with God. Nothing will please Him more, and certainly no other activity on our part can or will result in as great benefit to lives around us.

1) Instead of loving myself most I am willing to love Christ best and others more than myself.

Now love in a scriptural sense is not a soft, sentimental emotion. It is a deliberate act of my will. It means that I am willing to lay down my life, put myself out on behalf of another. This is precisely what God did for us in Christ. "Hereby perceive (understand) we the love of God, because he laid down his life for us" (1 John 3:16).

The moment I deliberately do something definite either for God or others that costs me something, I am expressing love. Love is "selflessness" or "self-sacrifice" in contradistinction to "selfishness." Most of us know little of living like this, or being "led" in this right way. But once a person discovers the delight of doing something for others, he has started through the gate which leads into one of God's green pastures.

2) Instead of being one of the crowd I am willing to be singled out, set apart from the gang.

Most of us, like sheep, are pretty gregarious. We want to belong.

We don't want to be different in a big way, though we may wish to be different in minor details that appeal to our selfish egos.

But Christ pointed out that only a few would find His way acceptable, and to be marked as one of His would mean a certain amount of criticism and sarcasm from a cynical society. Many of us don't want this. Just as He was a man of sorrows and acquainted with grief, so we may be. Instead of adding to the sorrows and sadness of society we may be called on to help bear some of the burdens of others, to enter into the suffering of others. Are we ready to do this?

3) Instead of insisting on my rights I am willing to forego them in favor of others.

Basically this is what the Master meant by denying one's self. It is not easy nor natural to do this. Even in the loving atmosphere of the home, self-assertion is evident and the powerful exercise of individual rights is always apparent.

But the person who is willing to pocket his pride, to take a back seat, to play second fiddle without a feeling of being abused or put upon, has gone a long way onto new ground with God.

There is a tremendous emancipation from "self" in this attitude. One is set free from the shackles of personal pride. It's pretty hard to hurt such a person. He who has no sense of self-importance cannot be offended or deflated. Somehow such people enjoy a wholesome outlook of carefree abandon that makes their Christian lives contagious with contentment and gaiety.

4) Instead of being "boss" I am willing to be at the bottom of the heap. Or to use sheep terminology, instead of being "Top Ram" I'm willing to be a "tailender."

When the desire for self-assertion and self-aggrandizement gives way to the desire for simply pleasing God and others, much of the fret and strain is drained away from daily living.

A hallmark of the serene soul is the absence of "drive," at least drive for self-determination. The person who is prepared to put his personal life and affairs in the Master's hands for His management and direction has found the place of rest in fresh fields each day. These are the ones who find time and energy to please others.

5) Instead of finding fault with life and always asking: Why? I

am willing to accept every circumstance of life in an attitude of gratitude.

Humans, being what they are, somehow feel entitled to question the reasons for everything that happens to them. In many instances life itself becomes a continuous criticism and dissection of one's circumstances and acquaintances. We look for someone or something on which to pin the blame for our misfortunes. We are often quick to forget our blessings, slow to forget our misfortunes.

But if one really believes his affairs are in God's hands, every event, no matter whether joyous or tragic, will be taken as part of God's plan. To know beyond doubt that He does all for our welfare is to be led into a wide area of peace and quietness and strength for every situation.

6) Instead of exercising and asserting my will, I learn to cooperate with His wishes and comply with His will.

It must be noted that all the steps outlined here involve the will. The saints from earliest times have repeatedly pointed out that nine-tenths of being a Christian, of becoming a true follower, a dedicated disciple, lies in the will.

When a man allows his will to be crossed out, canceling the great "I" in his decision, then indeed the Cross has been applied to that life. This is the meaning of taking up one's cross daily—to go to one's death—no longer my will in the matter but His will be done.

7) Instead of choosing my own way I am willing to choose to follow in Christ's way, simply to do what He asks me to do.

This basically is simple, straightforward obedience. It means I do what He asks me to do. I go where He invites me to go. I say what He instructs me to say. I act and react in the manner He maintains is in my best interest as well as for His reputation.

Most of us possess a formidable amount of factual information on what the Master expects of us. Precious few have either the will, intention, or determination to act on it and comply with His instructions. But the person who decides to do what God asks him has moved onto fresh ground which will do both him and others a world of good. Besides, it will please the Good Shepherd.

God wants us all to move on with Him. He wants us to walk

with Him. He wants it not only for our welfare but for the benefit of others as well as His own reputation.

Perhaps there are those who think He expects too much of us. Maybe they feel the demands are too drastic. Some may consider His call impossible to carry out.

It would be if we had to depend on self-determination or self-discipline to succeed. But if we are in earnest about wanting to do His will, and to be led, He *makes this possible* by His own gracious Spirit who is given to those who obey (Acts 5:32). For it is He who works in us "both to will and to do of his good pleasure" (Phil. 2:13).

# 6

# A Stranger
# They Will Not Follow

And a stranger will they not follow, but will flee from him: for they know not the voice of strangers. (John 10:5)

AFTER LONG AND intimate association sheep become beautifully adjusted to their owner. They develop a touching and implicit trust in him and only in him. Wherever he takes them they simply "tag along" without hesitation. In quiet and uncomplaining reliance upon him they accompany him anywhere he goes. In his company they are contented and at rest.

This can be equally true in our Christian experience. Unfortunately for many of us it is not always so. Despite the tendency not to trust ourselves completely to Christ, there are those occasional times when we have. Almost all of us have known what a stimulating delight it has been to respond to the Master's voice, to run to do His will, and thus discover His remarkable provision for us. We call this living or walking by faith.

Because the world is so much with us and we are so much in the world, our responses to Christ are not always as acute as they could be. Because from early childhood we have been conditioned to materialistic or humanistic or scientific concepts, it is not always easy to distinguish God's voice from the many other voices calling to us from the contemporary world. Because we have been taught and trained to be busy, active, energetic individuals, the main thrust of our times is to be people "on the go." This is true even if we really don't have any clear idea where we are going or what our ultimate destination may be.

Modern man is often a frustrated, frantic, fearful person racing madly on his own man-made treadmill.

This is not just true of the twentieth-century western world. It has ever been thus in the history of our race. It matters not whether an individual's life is spent in the feverish, high-pressure atmosphere of a modern executive office in Manhattan or in the feverish, humid, swamplands of the Amazon basin where a primitive hunter struggles to survive. All men know something of the unremitting, unrelenting fever of living.

And to all of us Christ comes with His incredible call, "Come unto me, all ye that labour and are heavy laden, and I will give you rest" (Matt. 11:28).

This invitation is not one to lethargy or indolence. It is not a formula for opting out of life. It is rather the delightful way of walking through the tangled turmoil of our times in quiet company with Christ.

To put this down on paper is fairly simple. To put it into daily practice is much more demanding and difficult. The reason I say this is simply because it is not just Christ who calls us to Himself. It is not just the Good Shepherd who invites us to walk with Him in the paths of right living and right relationships. It is not just the One who loves us deeply and desires our companionship who would have us follow Him.

There are scores of foreign influences appealing to us. On every side there are false pretenders to our ownership. We are sometimes surrounded by counterfeit "shepherds" who would have us believe they have our best interests at heart. When, in reality, they are predators disguised in various cloaks of respectability bent on our destruction. In some cases they are already among us, parading themselves as one of our own, while at the same time plotting our ruin.

In the Scriptures they have been given various names. In the Old Testament they are referred to frequently as "the shepherds which feed themselves and not the flock." Our Lord called them "false prophets" or "wolves in sheep's clothing." Elsewhere they are called "dogs" who devour the sheep.

In some cases these "strangers" have occupied places of prominence in our society. They may be preachers, teachers, writers, lecturers, broadcasters, or people of great influence posing as our protectors. Some may well go beyond even this and parade themselves as "saviours" to their fellowmen. They invite their contemporaries to come along with them and follow in their footsteps.

To a much lesser degree, but just as dangerous, are those common people who in their own quiet, subtle way insinuate themselves into our intimate circle of companions. They may be members of our family, among our friends, in the societies we join, in our business world, amid professional people, or even in the church.

It requires constant alertness on our part not to be victimized by imposters. We simply cannot afford to follow strangers if we are to survive as contented Christians who are attuned only to the call of our Master.

It may seem to the reader that this point is being unduly labored here. But the simple fact is that it is literally impossible to live in serenity of soul if we are torn between trying to follow conflicting calls at the same time. Our Lord was blunt about this. He stated emphatically, "No man can serve two masters: for either he will hate the one, and love the other; or else he will hold to the one, and despise (ignore) the other" (Matt. 6:24).

Too many of us have tried too long to make the best of both worlds. We have tried to live with one foot following Christ and the other following the false ideas and teachings of our times.

And the plain position which the Good Shepherd takes is a simple one: "My sheep—those who *know* Me—simply will not follow strangers." How easy it sounds; how difficult to do!

It is, of course, outside the scope of this book to list or even enumerate the false ideologies, misleading concepts, damaging philosophies, and strange teachings which are so much a part of the contemporary scene. They proliferate on every side. They are spewed out in floods of printed matter, in radio broadcasts and television shows that now engulf the entire planet—to say nothing of the person to person contacts.

But broadly all of these strange and false concepts are based on the following themes.

1) Humanism. Man is master of his own destiny. He is the supreme being in the universe. There is no superior power or intelligence to which he need appeal.

2) Materialism. The chief end of life is the attainment and acquisition of tangible values. The measure of a man's success is not the quality of his character but the quantity of things he has accumulated, or knowledge (human) he has acquired.

3) Scientism. Only that which can be subjected to the scientific method of examination is real. It must be evaluated empirically on the basis of our five fallible finite senses. Any dimension of divinity or deity is ruled out as invalid.

4) Atheism. Insists that there cannot be such a Being as God. All that exists does so by pure chance. Existence which is evolutionary has neither purpose nor meaning nor direction.

5) Religionism. Man's blind, unguided groping after God. The wild guessing at what God may be like. An abortive attempt to interpret the character and conduct of God from the distorted viewpoint of a man still in the darkness of his own sin and despair.

6) Spiritism. All of the occult, including demonism and satanic emulation. This includes all aspects of contact with the realm of evil spirits in opposition to God our Father, God the Son, Jesus Christ, and God the Holy Spirit.

7) Higher Criticism. In Christian circles it denies: the authenticity of God's Word, the deity of Christ, the necessity for the redemption and reconciliation of sinful men to a loving God.

If and when we detect these notes sounding in the voices which call to us as Christians we should be on guard at once. Paul, with his brilliant intellect, broad background of education, and enormous spiritual perception warned the church at Colossae: "Beware lest any man spoil you through philosophy and vain deceit, after the tradition of men, after the rudiments of the world, and *not after Christ*" (Col. 2:8).

Apart from the falsity of strange and unfamiliar teaching there is a second way in which God's people can reassure themselves that these imposters are in fact false shepherds. That is by the actual character and conduct of their lives.

Invariably a man or woman lives what he or she truly believes. Our lifestyle is an unconscious reflection of our inner convictions, and inevitably it will be found that the behavior pattern of the so-called "false shepherds"—"false prophets"—"wolves in sheep's clothing" will be a dead giveaway as to who they really are.

Put in the language of Scripture we say, "By their fruits ye shall know them." No matter how smooth, subtle, or reassuring their words or manner may be, ultimately it is the quality of their lives which will declare their true identity.

As Christians we are wise to not only examine carefully the content of the voice we are called by, but also the character of the one who calls to us. A person's words may drip with honey but be potent poison coming from a corrupt conscience.

It is true we may be likened to sheep because of our mob instincts. But we need not be always ignorant, dumb sheep. If we have heard and known the delight in our Shepherd's voice; if we revel and rejoice in His companionship, we are worse than fools if we do not flee from strangers to Him.

Sheep are among the most timid and helpless of all livestock. Though they will often hammer and batter each other, both rams and ewes, they will run in panic from the least threat of unknown danger. I have seen an entire flock rush away in blind fear simply because one of them was startled by a rabbit bursting out from beneath a bush.

Yet, in a peculiar manner they will sometimes stand still and stare blankly when a powerful predator comes among them. They will huddle up in tight, frightened little knots, watching dumbly while one after another of the flock is torn to pieces by the wolf, bear, leopard, cougar, or dog that may be ravaging them, or similarly they may be stolen by rustlers.

The only sheep that have any chance to escape are those that flee for their lives. They must get out of danger. There is simply no other hope of survival. Somehow they must separate themselves from the attacker who would destroy them.

Our Lord knew all this. He was thoroughly familiar with the hazards of sheep management. No doubt many of the shepherds who had come to His carpenter's shop in Nazareth to have Him build tables and benches for their humble homes had regaled Him with tales about the terrible losses they suffered from predators and rustlers.

This is one of the favorite topics of conversation for sheep men. And always, in the end, they know that the only place of safe protection for the sheep is close to the shepherd himself, within earshot of his voice.

The voice that is such an assurance to them is at the same time a terror to their enemies. That voice, which speaks of safety and well-being in the Master's care, instills fear and respect in the raiders.

To thrive and flourish, the sheep have to be ever under the sound of that familiar, friendly voice. To be lured away or distracted by any other is to face utter destruction or complete loss.

When I was an impressionable young man, one of the jobs given to me was to paint a huge building. At that time, because of a tempestuous boyhood and great adversity in my late teens, I was bitter and hostile toward society. My early life had been a tough struggle to survive amid severe hardships. So my mind was fertile ground for subversive ideas.

Working with me on the big barn, teaching me the tricks and skills of painting, was an old master craftsman. He was a Swede and an excellent painter. But he was also an ardent and avowed revolutionary. Day after day, sitting side by side high on the swing stage, he poured his subversive propaganda into my malleable mind.

It remains a miracle that my entire life was not destroyed by that invidious, crafty campaign. But some twelve thousand miles away, half way around the world, my dear mother, widowed and lonely, poured out her soul in tears that her wayward son would be spared from the snares and attacks of the enemy.

And one day, unable to endure the perverse propaganda poured into my ears by the old painter, I went to my boss and demanded another job where I could work alone. I wanted to be free. I wanted to flee from my foe. Something about that smooth, subtle voice of destruction alerted me to my mortal danger.

I give God thanks that other work was provided for me. It was possible to separate myself from the one who would have ruined me. To flee from a strange voice that brought foreign and damaging ideas was my only salvation.

Later in life, when my own children were teenagers, soon to leave home, I counseled them to do the same. Whenever they found themselves in the company of those who were not God's people, who were endeavoring to destroy them, there was one simple solution: "Just get out of there."

"The sheep will flee from strangers for they do not know their voice."

It is not weakness to do this. It is wisdom. Most of us, sad to say, simply are not skilled enough nor astute enough to match wits with our opponents. We are not sufficiently familiar, nor can we be, to fully understand or master all the devious and destructive devices of false philosophies, cults, religions, and ideologies of our modern world.

But what we can do is to become so grounded in God's Word, so familiar with our Master's voice, so attuned to His will and wishes, so accustomed to His presence, that any other voice alerts us to danger. It is a question of having our souls and spirits in harmony with His. It is a matter of living in close communion with the Shepherd of our lives. Then, and only then, will the threat of strange voices be recognized.

This does not mean that if I live in an environment or culture where one or two false philosophies predominate I am to remain ignorant of them. No, I will learn all about their insidious tactics to take God's people unawares. And in my alertness to their depredations I may well save both myself and others from their ravages.

Engaging the enemy in endless disputes and arguments seldom achieves anything. Paul was aware of this when he wrote to his young protégé, Timothy. Over and over he advised him against becoming embroiled in unprofitable debates with those who posed pointless and false issues.

What Christ asks us to do as His followers is to concentrate on keeping close to Him. Our major distinctive as His disciples should be the unique life we have because of our intimate association with

Him. He resides with us and in us. We likewise live with Him and in Him. Therein lies our strength, our serenity, our stability, and our safety. There is simply no substitute for this wondrous relationship with Him in a warped world.

His audience of that day, except for the young man born blind, and the young adulteress, whose lives He had entered, just could not understand what He said. Nor can most of our contemporaries.

Parable II
John 10:7–18
*Me in Christ*
〜

# 7

# The Doorway
# for the Sheep

Then said Jesus unto them again, Verily, verily, I say unto you, I am the door of the sheep. All that ever came before me are thieves and robbers: but the sheep did not hear them. (John 10:7–8)

IN THE FIRST parable of this discourse, our Lord made clear what He meant when He spoke of entering into the fold of one's life. Now, in the second parable, He proceeds to elaborate in great detail on what it means for a man or woman to enter into His life. By that is implied the way whereby we come into His care, enjoy His management, and revel in the abundance of His life shared with us in gracious generosity.

Again it must be emphasized that His audience did not really understand Him. When He completed His teaching they charged Him with being insane . . . possessed of an evil spirit, and unworthy of a hearing. And since that time millions of others have been bewildered by His teaching.

But the man born blind and the young woman taken in adultery, as well as a few others whose lives He had touched and transformed, understood Him. They knew it was God who had entered their lives. Also they had been introduced into a new life in Christ which was a dimension of living unknown to them before. These few grasped what it was He said.

Perhaps as we proceed to study His statements we, too, can enter into a fuller comprehension of the spiritual truths He shared with His audience. To do so is to have the horizons of our spiritual understanding widened by His words.

"I am the door of the sheep." Put into our modern idiom we would say: "I am the doorway, the entrance, for the sheep." Too often people have the wrong idea that our Lord referred to Himself only as the actual door or gate used to close a passageway into a sheepfold. This is not the picture.

The whole process of sheep management, of folding sheep, is combined with the control of doorways and gateways. It is by means of opening and shutting these passageways that the flock is moved methodically in and out, from place to place. They pass in through it to the protection of the fold within.

A flock has both an interior life within the shelter of the sheepfold and an exterior life outside. It is by means of the doorway, through the opening of the gate, that they enjoy both ingress and egress to a fully rounded and beneficial mode of life.

In the experience of every Christian whose life Christ has entered by His gracious Spirit, there are really two distinct areas of living. There is that inner life which the Quakers sometimes refer to as "the interior life." It is a personal, private, precious communion which a person enjoys within the inner sanctum of his own soul and spirit.

Then there is that outer life in which one is in contact with fellow Christians. It does not just end there, however, for it reaches out to touch all the world around us. This we refer to as our "exterior life," where thousands of contacts are made in a lifetime of interaction with our contemporaries.

The person under Christ's control will sense and know the hand of the Good Shepherd directing him in both areas. He will be acutely aware that it is through Him he passes in and out peacefully wherever He leads us.

Whether it is within the stillness of our own spirits or without in the noisy world around us, He is there. This acute awareness of His presence opening or closing the way before me is a magnificent reassurance to my soul that all is well.

The doorway was of tremendous import in Hebrew tradition and thought; much more so than in our culture. It was against the background of the Hebrew respect for "the door" that Christ made this assertion repeatedly—"I am the door." We do well to examine this briefly in order to fully comprehend what He meant.

Early in her history as a nation, Israel had been enslaved by the Egyptians. For nearly two hundred years her people had been driven by their taskmasters to toil in the dreadful slime pits. There under the broiling sun they made mud bricks with which to build the great, elaborate cities of their enemies.

Though this subservient people lived in their own little peasant hovels by the Nile, they were still prisoners of their Egyptian lords. In desperation they cried out for deliverance. God responded to their cry and sent Moses to wrest them from the land of their bondage.

The final great act of their emancipation had to do with the door of each man's home. A spotless Passover Lamb was to be slaughtered for each household. Its blood was to be liberally sprinkled on the lintel over the door, and on both doorposts. Any person passing through this door to the shelter of the house within was assured of perfect protection and absolute safety from the awesome judgment of the great destroying angel who swept through Egypt in the darkness.

But also by the same door anyone going out entered into the magnificent exodus which was able to deliver the enslaved from their bondage. A person went out through that door to liberty, freedom, and a new dimension of life under God's direction (Exod. 1–15).

It was the blood of the innocent Passover lamb, applied to the owner's doorway, that guaranteed him peace within and protection without. He had come directly under God's care and control within a new life of freedom.

And so it is in the experience of any man or woman who complies with the provisions of Christ. As we come to rely implicitly upon the efficacy of His laid-down life and spilled blood on our behalf, He, God's own Passover Lamb, in very fact becomes the doorway for us. It is through Him that we enjoy a magnificent inner security and through Him that we go out to engage in an adventurous life of new-found freedom under His direction.

Later in the history of the nation Israel, clear and specific instructions were given regarding the doorway to a man's home. The great laws and commandments of God to His people were to be inscribed on long, thin strips of parchment. These were to be carefully wrapped around each of the doorposts through which a person passed in and out of his home. Thus the resident was continually reminded, as were any strangers or visitors who came to call on him, that he and his family lived and moved under the command and control of God. Their going out and their coming in from that time forth were under the guidance of God's Word (Deut. 11:18–21).

Again this was a beautiful concept clearly portraying to God's own people the fact that they were under His care. It was under His hand and under His gracious guidance that in truth they could live securely. As they passed their days going in and out of their humble homes it was to find sweet serenity within and strong safety without. Jehovah God was with them to guide. The Shepherd of their souls was their salvation in every situation.

We see this same remarkable theme and emphasis reiterated throughout the teachings of our Lord. He stated emphatically in His great Sermon on the Mount that the gateway or doorway through which anyone entered into an abundant life of new-found freedom was in truth a restricted one. One could not think that he could pursue any course he chose and still come out right. If he did this he would end up in disaster—a wayward, willful, lost sheep.

No, the way to safety within and security without was only through the gateway of the Good Shepherd's care. Not many would either find or follow that route. Most preferred to go their own proud, perverse path to perdition.

Jesus the Christ was even more specific about this matter when, just before His crucifixion, He stated simply: "I am the way, the truth, and the life: no man cometh unto the Father, but by me" (John 14:6).

Putting this into plain language He is saying: "I am the way in and through which anyone can enter into a splendid new life with God. It is through Me that a man or woman comes to discover truth, reality, purpose, and meaning. It is through Me that one comes into the intimacy of the family of God our Father."

This is the main thrust of the entire New Testament. It is remarkable to see stated over and over the assertion that it is in and through Christ we live.

Through Jesus Christ I have peace with God.

Through Jesus Christ I am justified.

Through Jesus Christ I am forgiven my failures and sins.

Through Jesus Christ I am accepted into God's family.

Through Jesus Christ I am set free from slavery to sin and self.

Through Jesus Christ I am resurrected.

Through Jesus Christ I have immediate access to God in prayer.

And so the list could go on as a paean of praise to Him who has loved us and redeemed us and reconciled us to Himself by His own generous laid-down life.

In a word, it may be said that He, and only He, is the doorway into abundant living.

As in the previous parable, here again the Lord reiterates that anyone who ever preceded Him in our experience was a thief or robber. He was a thief in that if he induced us to do our own thing and go our own way he robbed us of our rightful inheritance.

The reason for this escapes most people. We are conditioned by the culture of our society to believe that we are in the world merely to gratify our own selfish desires and drives. We are taught that to a great degree everything is relative. If my impulse is to push my way to the top of the totem pole, I should do so, even if it means trampling on others along the way. It's just too bad if others are injured. After all, it's a tough world we live in, and life is really a struggle to survive.

So, little by little as time goes on, many of us do not believe that the standards established by God are relative to our age. We discard His directions for living. We ignore His instructions for our conduct. We turn each to his own way only to find that our difficulties deepen. We see ourselves caught up in a worldly way of existence. Life becomes a meaningless mockery. God's absolute values of integrity, loyalty, justice, honor, love, and fine nobility are cast aside. And in their place we find ourselves an impoverished people left only with discouragement and despair. We are robbed blind and left destitute with broken lives, broken hearts, broken minds, broken homes, broken bodies, and a broken society.

Jesus was speaking a truth we should pay attention to when He said that it was possible for us to be pillaged and plundered by the false philosophies and crass materialism of our times. Unhappily most people simply won't believe Him. They know better, or so they think. But they end up broken and beaten.

There is a second, and even more subtle way in which we ignore Him as the "way" and put others "before Him." It has to do with our basic priorities in life.

Again it is helpful to go back into the early Hebrew teachings and traditions. The first of the Ten Commandments given by God to Moses in Exodus 20 states explicitly, "Thou shalt have no other gods before me!" God knew that to do so would spell certain disaster. No one, no thing, no human ideology could begin to compare with God Himself in wisdom, might, love, or integrity. In Him resided all that was selfless, noble, and glorious.

For us to give ourselves or our allegiance to any other is to impoverish and demean ourselves: it is never to know *the best*.

Yet, in our blindness, ignorance, and folly all through the long and tragic tale of human history, men have sold themselves short to all sorts of strange and stupid gods. We have bartered away our birthright for a meager mess of unsatisfying substitutes.

God made us for Himself. In love and concern He intended us to be the children of His family, the sheep of His flock, the bride for His bridegroom.

Instead of seeing, longing, and devoting ourselves to Him, we have turned away and have put all sorts of other gods before Him. Other interests, ideas, people, and pursuits have been given prior place in our lives and affections. They have all "come before" Him.

Whatever it is to which I give most of my attention, time, thought, strength, and interest, becomes my God. It may be my home, my health, my family, career, hobby, entertainment, money, or person.

But our Lord says that if they come before Him, we are robbed. We have been stolen blind. We are poorer than we think. Our plight is pathetic, and we have settled for second best.

Our Lord points out in our text that those who are truly His people, the sheep of His pasture, will not allow themselves to be subverted by false gods. In the history of the people of Israel this had always been one of their greatest difficulties. Often they had been warned not to follow after the pagan gods of the races around them. Whenever they gave an ear to their subtle attractions they were drawn into dreadful practices that led them to utter ruin.

It did not matter whether they did this collectively as a nation or privately as individual citizens. The end result always was retrogression and remorse. But in spite of the repeated warnings there always seemed to be those who were oblivious to the dangers of thieves and robbers. In stubborn, sometimes blind folly they would fall prey to the predators among them or around them. And the same is still true today.

It reminds me of the behavior of a band of sheep under attack from dogs, cougars, bears, or even wolves. Often in blind fear or stupid unawareness they will stand rooted to the spot watching their companions being cut to shreds. The predator will pounce upon one then another of the flock raking and tearing them with tooth and claw. Meanwhile, the other sheep may act as if they did not even hear or recognize the carnage going on around them. It is as though they were totally oblivious to the obvious peril of their own precarious position.

We see this principle at work even among Christians. We as God's people are continually coming under attack, either from without or within. Yet many are unable to detect danger among our number. It is as though we cannot hear or see or sense our peril. Often the predation is so crafty and cunning that fellow Christians are cut down before our eyes by the enemy of our souls.

Sometimes those who do the most damage are already among us. They insinuate themselves into our little folds. They may be in our family, among our friends, in our neighborhood, in some small Bible class, in the community, or even in the church itself. They come bringing discord, divisions, and dissension. They rob us of the enrichment we might have from our Master by redirecting our attention to lesser issues. We get caught up in conflict and confusion that can lead to chaos. Instead of our focus being centered in Christ they get us embroiled with false and destructive ideas that may eventually lead to our downfall.

Almost invariably those who come as thieves and robbers divert our attention from the loveliness and grandeur of our Good Shepherd. They manage to redirect our interests to peripheral issues of minor importance. They will get us to expend our time and energy and thought on trivia. And while we are so preoccupied with following their "will-o'-the-wisp" suggestions we fall prey to their deceptive and destructive tactics. We see this in such things as over-emphasis of questionable doctrines, humanistic philosophies, undue desire for feelings rather than faith in the Christian experience, disputes over biblical interpretations, excesses in legalism, worldly ways of living or doing God's work, pandering to certain popular personalities or programs.

Throughout the teachings of our Lord, and later in the writings of the New Testament apostles (see 2 Tim.), we are warned "not to hear" such false teachers. We are urged to turn a deaf ear to them. We are told to flee from them. If we are to survive we must disassociate ourselves from them. We do not respond to those who treacherously try to tickle our ears while cutting our throats.

This is not always easy to do, but if we are following Christ in an intimate communion, we will be aware of our danger. We will turn from those who would maim and mutilate us. We will be acutely sensitive only to the gentle voice of the Good Shepherd.

# 8

# Entering Into
# a New Life

I am the door: by me if any man enter in, he shall be saved, and shall go in and out, and find pasture. The thief cometh not, but for to steal, and to kill, and to destroy. (John 10:9–10a)

OUR LORD MAKES it clear that He is the door, the way, the entrance into a new life. This life in which He controls both my interior and exterior life is totally different from any lifestyle I may have known before.

It implies a new two-way interpersonal relationship. He has come into the little fold of my life there to exercise His management of my affairs. He leads me out in due course to wider fields of contact and adventure with others in new dimensions of spiritual growth.

Yet, at the same time I find myself entering into an exciting and stimulating lifestyle within the *enfolding control* of His presence. He has become the paramount and preeminent person in my daily experience. He occupies a place of greater priority in my thoughts, emotions, and decisions than any earthly companion. This applies to my family, friends, or other intimate associates.

This process of gradually allowing God to govern my life, permitting Christ to control my conduct, coming gently under the absolute sovereignty of His gracious Spirit is to enter into the remarkable and restful salvation He provides for His people.

It is a case where I am no longer enslaved to my own small, self-centered wishes. I am set free from the tyranny of my own destructive emotions. I am liberated from the bondage of my own bungling decisions. It is a case of being set free from the terrible tyranny of my own selfish self-centeredness. He, the Good Shepherd of my soul, takes over the welfare of my affairs. He delivers me from the dilemma of my own self-destructive drives. I am free at last to enter into the joyous delight of just doing His will.

Sad as it may seem, many Christians do not enter into the rest and repose of this life in Christ. They may have heard about it. They may have read about it. They may even have seen it in the experience of one or two of their contemporaries, but for themselves it is as elusive as a passing daydream.

Perhaps if a parallel is drawn from the relationships between a shepherd and his sheep we can understand how one enters into this wondrous life.

Any sheep, if treated with kindness and affection, soon attaches itself to its new owner. Sheep are remarkably responsive, for the most part, to the attention and care given to them by a good shepherd. This is especially true in small flocks where the owner has opportunity to bestow his personal affection on individual animals. They quickly become his friends. A select few are actually pets. They follow him as faithfully as his own shadow. Wherever he goes they are there. It is in his company, and because of his presence, that they are ever secure and at rest.

The same truth applies in our relationship to Christ. We can in truth enter into a new life with Him whereby we enjoy the safety, surety, and security of His presence. This is not some superspiritual, once-for-all, ecstatic experience. Rather it is the quiet, gentle hour-to-hour awareness of "O Lord, You are here!" It is the keen knowledge, "O God, You are guiding me!" It is the calm, serene assurance, "O gracious Spirit, in Your presence there is peace!"

There is nothing mystical or magical about this. It is the winsome, wondrous knowledge of realizing the person, presence, and power of Christ in every detail of my day. This is the meaning of salvation in its full-orbed splendor.

The entering into this life in Christ lifts me above the low level of trying to struggle with the down-drag of sin that leads so many into the deep ditch of despair. It frees me from the fret of fighting with the old selfish impulses that generally govern my life. It delivers me from the dominion of the enemy of my soul who wishes to ensnare me.

The focus of my attention has been shifted away from myself to my Shepherd. The movement of my soul has been brought to Him for direction rather than left in the dilemma of my own decision making. The responsibility for my activities has been placed squarely in His care and taken out of my hands. This means subjecting my will to His wishes, but therein lies my rest and relief from my own stressful way of life.

Such people, our Lord said, would go in and out freely and find pasture.

Many people assume that to become a Christian and follow Christ calls only for self-denial, privation, poverty, and hardships. It is a distorted picture, for in fact, though we may relinquish our old selfish lifestyle, we discover to our delight an entrance into a much greater and broader dimension of living.

Who is the person rich in friends, loved ones, and affection? The one willing to give himself away to others. Who is the individual who finds life full, rewarding, and deeply satisfying? The person who loses himself in a cause much greater than himself, who gives himself away for the greater good of all.

And it is to this caliber of life that Christ invites us. He calls us to enter into great commitments and noble causes. He leads us into a broken world there to expend ourselves on behalf of suffering, struggling, lost humanity.

Life is too magnificent, our capacities too noble, our days too few and precious to be squandered on just our own selfish little selves. God has made us in His own great image for great purposes. Only in coming into harmony with His will and wishes can we ever begin to realize or attain the tremendous aspirations He has for us. It is in complete and implicit cooperation with His ongoing purposes for the planet that any of us ever attain even a fraction of our potential for eternal service and salvation.

Too many of us are too provincial, too petty in our outlook. We see only our own little problems. We are obsessed with only our own little objectives. We go through life cramped and constricted by our own small circle of contacts.

Christ the Good Shepherd calls us to go in and out and find wide, broad pastures of practical and abundant service; not only for our own sakes but also for the sake of others who are as lost as we once were.

He gave us this broad view in graphic terms Himself when He

sent out His twelve disciples as missionaries to the lost sheep of Israel.

A careful and intelligent reading of Matthew 9:35–10:16 discloses a delightful scene of an eastern shepherd gathering up stray sheep. Jesus had been moving from village to village, town to town, teaching, preaching, healing, and ministering to men's needs in every area of life. Seeing the innumerable multitudes of struggling souls He was moved with enormous concern and compassion for them. They were as sheep without a shepherd. They were weary, apprehensive, distraught, and scattered afield in every direction.

Turning to His twelve companions He made the comment, so often misunderstood and misinterpreted by missionaries. "The harvest truly is plenteous, but the labourers are few." He was not speaking of a harvest of wheat or corn or other grain, but rather a crop of lambs, a crop of lost sheep scattered by the millions, milling aimlessly across the surface of the earth.

Who and where were the workers, the laborers who could gather in the lost? There were so few able to do this difficult and delicate task.

How does an eastern sheepman gather up his stray sheep? How does He bring home the wanderers and stragglers?

He does not use dogs the way western sheepmen do. He does not resort to horses or donkeys to herd them home or round them up. Nor does he employ helicopters or Hondas as some western ranchers do.

No, the eastern shepherd uses his own pet lambs and bellwethers to gather in lost sheep. Because these pets are so fond of being near him and with him, he has to literally go out into the hills and rough country himself taking them along, scattering them abroad. There they graze and feed alongside the wild and wayward sheep.

As evening approaches the shepherd gently winds his way home. His favorite pet lambs and bellwethers quietly follow him. As they move along in his footsteps, they bring with them the lost and scattered sheep. It is a winsome picture full of pathos.

In Matthew 10 Christ actually took His twelve men and scattered them out among the lost sheep of Israel (v. 6). He warned them that He was sending them out as sheep in the midst of predators who might try to prevent them from bringing home the lost (v. 16). But they were to go anyway, because the presence of His Spirit would be with them to preserve them in every danger.

This is a precise picture drawn for us in bold colors of what our Good Shepherd requires of us. He does not demand that we embark on some grandiose schemes of our own design to do His work in the world. He does not suggest that we become embroiled in some complex organization of human ingenuity to achieve His goal of gathering in lost souls.

He simply asks me to be one who will be so attached to Him, so fond of Him, so true to Him, that in truth I shall be like His pet lamb or bellwether. No matter where He takes me; no matter where He places me; no matter whom I am alongside of in my daily living, that person will be induced to eventually follow the Shepherd because I follow Him.

Put in another way it may be said that any Christian's effectiveness in winning others is directly proportional to his own devotion to the Master. Show me a person to whom Christ is absolutely paramount and I will show you one who gently but surely is gathering in others from the pastures of the world.

This is the individual who has entered into an exciting, adventuresome, fresh mode of life in God. Day after day, under the guidance of the Good Shepherd, he goes in and out to find fresh pastures of new experience. His life touches other lives, and all the time here and there he sees others gently gathered in, because he was willing to be sent forth wherever the Shepherd best saw fit to place him.

It all sounds fairly simple. It is, if we faithfully follow Christ. It is He who assures us of effective success in helping to save the lost and scattered sheep in a shattered world. We are His co-workers, colaborers in His great ongoing plans for rescuing the lost.

Nor is such labor without its rewards. Our God is the God of all consolation and compensation. He is no man's debtor. Those who honor Him, He will honor. If we put Him and His interests first, there will ever be ample provision for all of our needs. This is not theory. This is the truth testified to by uncounted millions of men and women who, having entered into this new life with God, have found Him to be ever faithful to them.

Any life He enters is always enriched, never impoverished. Any of our days He touches are transformed with the light and joy of His presence. To sense and know Him is to have tasted life at its sublime best.

Yet amid such living our Lord warns us that there can still be thieves and robbers present. There are always predators prowling around the periphery of our lives, waiting and watching for opportunity to plunder and impoverish us.

In previous chapters these have been dealt with in some detail. Emphasis has been placed especially upon those aspects of our Christian lives where we can be seriously endangered by false teaching, philosophies, or ideologies.

Here, very briefly, I would like to mention just two of the more practical aspects of our times which literally come into our lives and impoverish us. Not only are we poorer because of them, but God's work is hindered from being carried out as well as it might be.

The first is idleness. We live in a culture given to greater leisure. The shorter work week means more leisure time. Indolence is an outgrowth of this. The discipline of diligent duty is disappearing. Consequently the character of our people becomes increasingly casual, careless, and irresponsible.

For young people especially, excess ease is debilitating. The sense of challenge and achievement is lacking. They are impoverished because there is so little attained to satisfy them with a sense of worthwhile accomplishment. Too often the young toss away their days while the older loaf away their lives.

As God's people we should give ourselves completely, gladly, and wholeheartedly to His enterprises upon the earth. There is much to achieve!

Then there is affluence and luxury. The world is so much with us. We have been conditioned by our culture to believe that an individual's worth is measured by his material assets. Yet Christ declared, "A man's life does not consist of the abundance of things he owns" (Luke 12:15).

Still, there is a tendency for us to allow our attention to be centered on the acquisition of material wealth, or even academic attainments, or personal power and prestige in one form or another.

This is not to say that as Christians we are not entitled to pursue excellence in any of the fields into which God may guide us. We should strive to excel for His sake, not our personal pride. But at no time should these become a prior claim upon our thought or time or strength. If we allow this to happen we will soon discover that in truth we are being robbed of the best. We are being deprived of His presence, power, and peace in our lives. We will have settled for second best. We will be poorer than we know. This will constrict our effectiveness for Christ and will cramp our personal relationship to Him.

The Spirit of God speaking to the church of Laodicea in Revelation 3:16–20 put it this way:

> So then because thou art lukewarm, and neither cold nor hot, I will spue thee out of my mouth. Because thou sayest, I am rich, and increased with goods, and have need of nothing; and knowest not that thou art wretched, and miserable, and poor, and blind, and naked: I counsel thee to buy of me gold tried in the fire, that thou mayest be rich, and white raiment, that thou mayest be clothed, and that the shame of thy nakedness do not appear; and anoint thine eyes with eye-salve, that thou mayest see. As many as I love, I rebuke and chasten: be zealous therefore, and repent. Behold, I stand at the door, and knock: if any man hear my voice, and open the door, I will come in to him, and will sup with him, and he with me.

What the Good Shepherd desires above all else is that He might have the wondrous delight of entering *fully* into my life, there to share it with me. And I in turn can enter wholeheartedly into His great life, there to experience the remarkable fulfillment which He intended for me as His person. All of this is the purpose of His love for me.

# 9

# The

# Abundant Life

I am come that they might have life, and that they might have it more abundantly. I am the good shepherd: the good shepherd giveth his life for the sheep. (John 10:10b–11)

ANY SHEPHERD WHO is a good manager always bears in mind one great objective. It is that his flock may flourish. The continuous well-being of his sheep is his constant preoccupation. All of his time, thought, skill, strength, and resources are directed to this end.

Nothing delights the good shepherd more than to know his livestock are in excellent condition. He will stand in his pastures amongst his sheep casting a knowing eye over them, rejoicing in their contentment and fitness. A good stock man actually revels in the joy of seeing his animals flourishing.

There are several reasons for this. First, and perhaps foremost, is the simple fact that sheep that are in good health are free from all the trying and annoying ailments of parasitism and disease that so frequently decimate sheep. He does not have to worry about sick or crippled animals. They are thriving under his care.

Second, it means that most of his time and attention can be devoted to the development and care of the entire ranch. This will assure his stock of an ideal environment in which they can prosper. He can supply abundant pasturage, clean water supplies, proper shelter, protection from predators, ample range, and ideal management in every area of the ranch operation.

This is the best guarantee that the flock in his ownership will derive maximum benefit from his expertise.

Third, his own reputation and name as an esteemed sheepman is reflected in the performance of his flock. All of his expertise and affection for the sheep is shown by how they prosper under his watchful eye. When they are thriving he also benefits. Not only does he prosper but he feels richly rewarded in soul for all his strength and life actually poured into them.

Put another way it may be said that the outpouring of his own being is to be seen in the excellence of his stock. It is very much a demonstration of the eternal principle that what a man gets out of life is what he puts into it.

Reflecting back over my own years as a sheepman I recall clearly those happy, contented times when I literally revelled in the well-being of my sheep. Visitors would often remark how contented and flourishing my flock appeared. But only I knew how much work, effort, tireless attention, and never-ending diligence had been expended on my part for this to be possible.

My sheep had literally been the recipients of my life. It had been shared with them abundantly and unstintingly. Nothing was ever held back. All that I possessed was in truth poured out unremittingly in order that together we should prosper. The strength of my young body, the keen enthusiasm of my spirit, the energy of my mind, the alertness of my emotions, the thrust and drive of my disposition were all directed to the well-being of my flock. And it showed in abundant measure.

This is the graphic picture our Lord had in His mind when He stated simply, "I am come that they might have life, and that they might have it more abundantly. I am the good shepherd: the good shepherd giveth his life for the sheep."

If we pause to reflect here a moment we must see that any person is "good" in whatever he undertakes to the degree in which he devotes and dedicates himself to it. A "good violinist" becomes a good violinist only by putting his time, talents, and attention into his art and instrument. Likewise a "good runner" becomes a top athlete only to the extent that he will invest his strength and energy and interest in his sport. And the degree to which anyone becomes "good" is the length to which he will go in giving himself unhesitatingly to his chosen vocation.

Thus, in speaking of our Good Shepherd we are compelled to consider the enormous generosity with which He gives Himself to us without stint. The very nature and character of God, exemplified in Christ, convinces us beyond any doubt that He literally pours Himself out on our behalf. All of the eternal, ongoing activities and energetic enterprises of God have been designed that we might share His abundant life.

We are not, as the people of His pasture, merely the recipients of good gifts which He dispenses to us in random fashion from afar. To think this way is to be terribly impoverished in our lives.

For much of my early Christian life I labored under this delusion. To me God was a distant deity. If perchance I needed extra strength or wisdom or patience to face some perplexing problem He who resided off in the immensity of space somewhere could be appealed to for help and support in my dilemma. If my conduct was commendable He would probably, hopefully, cooperate. He would condescend to comply with my requests. If all went well He might just drop down a bit of wisdom or strength or patience to meet my need for the moment.

To imagine or assume that this is abundant life, or abundant living, is a caricature of the true Christian life. Yet multitudes of God's people struggle along this way. Their lives are impotent and impoverished because of it.

The simple truth is that the abundant, dynamic life of God can be ours continuously. It is not something handed out in neat little packages as we pray for it sporadically.

*A man or woman has the life of God to the extent that he or she has God.* We have the peace of God to the extent that we experience the presence of Christ. We enjoy the joy of the Lord to the degree we are indwelt by the very Spirit of God. We express the love of God to the measure we allow ourselves to be indwelt by God Himself.

God is not "way out there somewhere." He is here! He not only resides within anyone who will receive Him, but equally important is the fact that He completely enfolds and surrounds us with His presence. He is the essence of both our inner life and outer life. "O God, You are here! O Christ, You have come that I might have abundant life. O gracious Spirit, You are as invisible as the wind yet as real as the air that surrounds me, which I inhale to energize my body! You are within and without.

"It is in You, O my God, that I live and move and have my being.

You are the environment from which my total life is derived. You are the energy and dynamic of my whole being. Every good and every perfect bestowal is derived from You. The vitality of my spirit, the energy of my emotions, the drive of my disposition, the powerful potential of my mind, the vigor of my body; in fact, every facet of my total, abundant life is a reflection of Your life, O Lord, being lived out in me and through me."

To become aware of this is to become charged mightily with the abundant life of God, in Christ, by His Spirit. This is to experience being "in Christ," and "Christ in me." This is to *know* God. This is to enjoy eternal life, the life of the eternal One being expressed through my person. This is, as Paul put it, "knowing Christ and the power of his resurrection."

This life of God, given so freely to us in an undiminished supply from an inexhaustible source, is not intended to end in us. We are not an end in ourselves. The abundant outpouring of God's life to His people is intended to be an overflowing, out-giving, ongoing disposal of His benefits to others around us. More than this, it is designed to bring pleasure, delight, and blessing back to our Lord Himself. It is not just a case of His blessings being bestowed on us, but also our abundant lives in return being a blessing to Him.

> Bless the Lord, O my soul: and all that is within me, bless his holy name.
> Bless the Lord, O my soul, and forget not all his benefits (Ps. 103:1–2).

The full and complete awareness of this concept of abundant Christian living can come to us only as we grasp the nature and character of God, our Father. The Scriptures reveal Him to be love. By that is meant not a selfish, self-indulgent, sentimental love, but its opposite.

The love of God spoken of so extensively is total selflessness. It is God, in Christ, sharing Himself with us unhesitatingly. It is He giving Himself in glad, wholehearted abandonment to us. It is God pouring Himself out for His people. It is God losing Himself in our little lives that we might know the abundance of His life. It is God giving Himself to us without measure in overflowing abundance so that in turn His life spills out from ours to go running over our weary old world in streams of refreshing.

The life of God comes to us in many ways. So majestic and marvelous are they that this little book cannot begin to list or catalog them all. The life of God given to men is the same life that energizes the entire cosmos. It sustains the universe. It is the essence of being.

The best a mere mortal can do is to go quietly to some place, still, alone, there to meditate before the splendor of our God.

I sense something of His glory in the wonders of the world He made: the flaming sunrises and sunsets that still the soul; the awesome grandeur of mighty mountain ranges and sweeping plains; the restless roar of ocean waves and winds and tides; the fragrance of forests or the green glory of rich grasslands; the austere stillness and rugged solitude of gaunt deserts; the delicate beauty of flowers, trees, and shrubs; the incredible diversity of insects, birds, and mammals; the beauty of sun and cloud, snow and rain.

All of these contribute something to the total environment which supports and sustains me. Each in its own way contributes to the well-being of my person. They energize and feed my body. They stimulate and quicken my soul. They enrich my spirit. They make me what I am . . . a man sensitive, receptive, and alive to the world around me—my Father's world—His provision for my well-being, joy, and abundant life. He has come. He has made it all possible. He has put it at my disposal for full and enriched living.

All that is sublime, beautiful, dignified, noble, and grand has this as its source. The finest in our literature, music, arts, science, and social intercourse has its base in the generous giving of our Lord. All that contributes to our physical health, energy, and acumen as individuals is grounded in the good gifts and undiminished life of God poured out to us upon the planet.

And yet in His magnanimous and magnificent generosity He does not just leave it at that. God has deliberately chosen to articulate Himself in terms I can comprehend. He has spoken. His Word has been received, recorded, and reproduced in human writing. He has not withheld His will or wishes from us earthlings in mystical obscurity. It is possible to know precisely what He is like. He has articulated Himself in meticulous terms understandable to man. He has given us clear and concise self-revelations as to His gracious character, impeccable conduct, and friendly conversation. We know who it is with whom we have to do. He does not deal with us according to our foibles and failings, but in amazing mercy and gracious kindness, as our Father.

As though all of this is not enough, He has gone even further in coming to us as God in man. He, the living God in Christ, has come among us, wholly identified with us in our human condition and human dilemma. He has not spared Himself. He was born among us, lived among us, worked among us, served among us, taught among us, died among us, rose among us, and ascended among us to reclaim and repossess His place of prominence.

All of this He did willingly and gladly to deliver us from the plight of our own peril upon the planet. He came to set us free from the folly and foibles of our own perverseness and pride. He gave His life to redeem us from our slavery to sin and selfish self-interests and Satan. He gave Himself to seek and to save us who were lost. He came to call us to Himself. He came to gather us into His family to enfold us in His flock. He gave Himself to make us His own, the recipients of His own abundant, abounding life.

To those few, and they are relatively few, who have responded to His overtures, He still comes, even today, and gives Himself to us by His gracious Spirit. He is with us. He is our counselor. He is our companion. He is our "alongside one." He is our comforter. He is our closest friend. He is here in rich and wondrous intimacy.

"I am come that you might have life, My life, and that you might have it in overflowing abundance." These are still His words to us today.

# 10

# The Hireling

But he that is an hireling, and not the shepherd, whose own the sheep
are not, seeth the wolf coming, and leaveth the sheep, and fleeth: and the
wolf catcheth them, and scattereth the sheep.
The hireling fleeth, because he is an hireling, and careth not for the sheep.
(John 10:12–13)

OUR LORD USED contrast for dynamic effect. It was one of the secrets of His remarkable, arresting teaching. He used contrast to display in bold, bright strokes the great truths we human beings have such difficulty in comprehending.

He told about the rich man and the poor beggar Lazarus who lay at his doorstep. He recounted the incident of the haughty, proud Pharisee praying while the contrite publican struck his breast begging for mercy. He contrasted the prodigal with his very "proper" elder brother. And now, in this parable, Christ brings before us the behavior of a hireling as it is contrasted with the Good Shepherd in caring for sheep.

Our Lord previously pointed out how the people of God's pasture could, under His control, enjoy an abundant, rich life with Him.

He made clear how God's life, poured out in rich measure on my behalf, enables me to enjoy abundant living in every area: physical, mental, moral, emotional, and spiritual. He told how life in Him contributes to a wholesomeness and holiness of unique quality; that it is entirely possible for a man or woman to be so intimately associated with God as to reflect His character to a skeptical society.

Yet, in bold contrast to all of the foregoing, Jesus made it clear that not all sheep were under a good shepherd. Some suffered because of the bad behavior of hireling shepherds.

During the time of our Lord's sojourn in Palestine, servants were of two sorts. They were either bond or free. They were either slaves owned outright by their masters or free people who worked temporarily for meager wages. In fact, because of slavery, the worth and dignity of a human being was much less esteemed than it was in a free society. After all, if people could be bought and sold at random in a slave market they were really not of much more value than cattle or furniture.

It will be recalled that when Judas bartered with the high priests for the betrayal of his Master, the price of thirty pieces of silver was agreed upon. This was the going price, then, of a slave in the slave market.

If a slave served his owner well and the two became attached to each other, the master often offered to set him free. The slave could then choose either to go free or become a bond slave or bond servant. Of his own free will he could choose to remain, for the rest of his life, as a servant who, because of his love for the master, chose to remain in his family.

To confirm this the owner would take his slave to the doorpost of his home. Placing the slave's ear against it, he would pierce the lobe with an awl, pinning it momentarily to the post. This drew blood. This indicated that a bond was sealed for life, and that this slave had in fact become a love servant for the remainder of his days. He would never leave that family. He would be ever faithful to his owner. He was a part of that household. Their life was his. His life was theirs.

There was none of this devotion about a hireling. A hireling had no permanence. He was a casual laborer who came and went at will in a rather haphazard way. He would be here today and gone tomorrow. He was essentially a transient worker. He took no special interest in his job. As soon as a few shekels jingled in the deep folds of his loin cloth he was gone. He would seldom settle down or take any responsibility seriously. His average wage in Jesus' day was a penny a day. The less work he could do to earn this the better it suited him. Like a dandelion seed drifting on the wind he floated about the country looking for the softest spot to land. And if the place did not please him he would soon take off for another.

Sometimes, but not often, one of these drifters would be employed to tend sheep in the owner's absence. It was seldom a satisfactory arrangement. For that reason our Lord used the hireling to represent those who were entrusted with the sheep, but had no real love or concern for them. The secret to successful livestock husbandry is an essential love for the animals under one's care. And this the hireling lacked. He had no stake in the flock. They were not his. He could care less what became of them. They were but the means whereby he could make his "fast buck," and then get out.

As a young man of twenty-five I was entrusted with the management and development of a large livestock ranching operation in central British Columbia. There were thirty-six men on the various crews hired to run the ranch. We were in a rather remote, though choice, area, where the glamor and glitter of cities seemed far away.

Among us there was a common joke that we really had three crews: one was coming; the second was working temporarily; and the third was leaving. These were all hired men, passing through, who stayed in this remote and lonely location only until they had gathered up enough to move on to a more desirable job.

In bold contrast I recall vividly the love, loyalty, and undivided devotion of the Masai in East Africa to their animals. For the years we lived among them I never ceased to marvel at the incredible fortitude of these people in providing the best care they could for their livestock. No price was too high to pay to protect their stock from predators. Why? Because they owned them. They had a stake in them. They loved them. They were not hirelings.

Just a few days after we moved into the Masai country, a small, slim boy about ten years old was carried up to our house. He had, single-handed, tackled a young lioness that tried to kill one of his flock. In total self-abandonment and utter bravery he had managed to spear the lion. The mauling he took almost cost him his life. We rushed him to the nearest hospital twenty-seven miles away where his young life was spared, as by a thread. But why did he do this? Because the sheep were his. His love and honor and loyalty were at stake. He would not spare himself. He was not a hireling.

God has, all through history, entrusted the care of His sheep to so-called undershepherds. And not all of them have proven to be as loyal as the Masai lad, nor as brave as young David, later Israel's great king, who slew the lion and the bear that came to raid his father's flock.

Inevitably in the nature of human affairs there appear those who pretend to be genuine but are not. The ancient prophets of Israel cried out again and again against those who posed as shepherds to God's people, but who instead only plundered them for their own selfish ends.

> And the word of the LORD came unto me, saying, Son of man, prophesy against the shepherds of Israel, prophesy, and say unto them, Thus saith the Lord GOD unto the shepherds; Woe be to the shepherds of Israel that do feed themselves! Should not the Shepherds feed the flocks?
> Ye eat the fat, and ye clothe you with the wool, ye kill them that are fed: but ye feed not the flock. The diseased have ye not strengthened, neither have ye healed that which was sick, neither have ye bound up that which was broken, neither have ye brought again that which was driven away, neither have ye sought that which was lost;
> But with force and with cruelty have ye ruled them.
> And they were scattered, because there is no shepherd: and they became meat to all the beasts of the field, when they were scattered.
> My sheep wandered through all the mountains, and upon every high hill: Yea, my flock was scattered upon all the face of the earth, and none did search or seek after them. (Ezek. 34:1–6)

The same situation prevailed in Jesus' time. Those who posed as the protectors and leaders of the people, the priests, Pharisees, scribes and Sadducees, were but rank opportunists who plundered and abused the people. The rake-off in the temple trade alone in Jerusalem exceeded $35,000,000 a year. Most of it went to line the pockets and oil the palms of the oppressors. Little wonder Christ went storming through the temple to clear it of its counterfeit activities shouting, "You will not make my Father's house, a place of plunder . . . a den of thieves!"

His confrontation was always with the ecclesiastical hierarchy of His times. They were not true shepherds. They did not love their charges. They did not care deeply for those in their care. They never wept over the plight of their people who were sheep gone astray. They were hirelings. They were there to grab what they could get for themselves.

Is it any wonder our Lord thundered out His great imprecations against them? Here, He the great Good Shepherd, saw His people abused and betrayed by those who had no interest in them whatever.

And the same applies to all church history since His day. God's people have always been parasitized by imposters. Men have worked with the flock only for what they could get out of it, not for what they could contribute to the well-being of their people.

It was this sort of thing that nearly ruined me as a young man. There was within my spirit a strange, powerful, deep desire to *know* God. I literally thirsted and hungered for spiritual sustenance. I longed to be fed truth that would satisfy my innermost craving.

Sunday after Sunday my wife and I would attend whatever churches we could. Some of them were small and struggling. Others were large and pretentious. Some of the preachers were proper and orthodox but seldom shepherds. Again and again I came hoping to be fed, but there was nothing.

Frustrated and angry I would storm home, and vow never to enter a church again. "I'm like a sheep going to the feed trough hoping to find hay or grain, and there is only dust and chaff!" I would storm to my gentle wife. In her wisdom, kindness, and patience she would prevail on me to keep going, for sooner or later she was sure a few straws would be found here and there.

Why was this? Because many of the men who were supposed to be shepherding God's people were only hirelings. They were in the job for what they could get out of it. It was obvious they spent no time communing with Christ. It was clear the Scriptures were not a *living* Word to them. They had no great love either for God or for His people. What happened to their charges really did not seem to matter.

Eventually some of these men came to know me personally, but even after they had entered into our lives, their casual indifference and lack of genuine concern astonished me.

In one community I attended services diligently for nearly four years. At the end of that time I had been taught virtually nothing. I was a stranger in a far country, away from my home land, but no shepherd seemed to care for my soul.

At that period in my life I was under tremendous attack from the enemy of my soul. Almost daily I was exposed to onslaughts against the great truths of God's revelation in His Word. Subtle suggestions and crafty cynicism were working havoc in my convictions. The wolves were at work on me but there was no shepherd around who really seemed to be concerned about this wandering sheep.

Alone and unattended I fled for safety. I knew not really where to run. Like a sheep blinded with fear and seized with panic I simply turned to run in my own stupid way. And the result was that I went far astray. I ended up far from my Good Shepherd. The hirelings had literally let me fend for myself.

The net result can be expressed in the words of the grand old prophet Ezekiel:

> For thus saith the Lord God, Behold, I, even I, will both search my sheep, and seek them out. As a shepherd seeketh out his flock in the day that he is among his sheep that are scattered; so will I seek out my sheep, and will deliver them out of all places where they have been scattered in the cloudy and dark day. (Ezek. 34:11–12)

Only the tender compassion of Christ, only the understanding of the true Shepherd of my soul, only the gentle overtures of the gracious Spirit of God could ever retrieve this wild and wayward one from the cloudy and dark days of his despair. Because in His patience and perseverance He pursued me along my wayward path, because He gathered me up again and drew me back once more in selfless love, was I saved. And for this I shall be eternally grateful to my God.

But what desperate despair I could have been spared if only someone had cared for my soul at that stage of my life. Those to whom I looked for help were only hirelings. They would not stand up to the enemy. They would not engage the wolves that were raiding my life and the lives of others. They would not risk a confrontation. They simply turned tail and left us to be torn and scattered.

The same is still true. There are ministers, teachers, scholars, writers, and leaders who pose as champions of Christianity. But when the enemy comes in they are shown in their true colors. They back away rather than risk a confrontation. They settle for withdrawal rather than beard the lion or bear, or assail the wolf.

They turn and flee in the face of violent attack. Others remain silent while their people are deceived, harried, and driven to despair. Only the Good Shepherd cares enough for His own to lay down His life for them.

It must be He who, living His life through and in His true undershepherds, enables them also to lay down their lives for the sheep. They must be prepared and willing to be expendable for the sake of others. They are not hirelings, they are His slaves of love. Paul calls himself "a bondservant of Jesus Christ."

Men or women who enter God's service should regard this as an enormous responsibility not only before God but also to those whom they serve. It is something which is not undertaken lightly or casually for personal gain, but with an eye to eternal consequences.

In any enterprise where we are coworkers with Christ there is incumbent upon us the obligation to realize that this is not a hit-or-miss affair. His view of His work in the world is a sincere and serious one. And He expects that those who enter His enterprises will take a similar attitude.

When we give ourselves to serve the Lord, the primary motivation should not be one of personal gain or advantage. Rather, the predominant desire ought to be one of serving the Master out of love and gratitude for His goodness to us. We are freely, willingly choosing to be a benefit to others, not just for their sakes or our own self-gratification, but for His sake.

It is only the undershepherd, whose first and foremost devotion and consecration is to Christ, who can stand up to the strains and stresses of shepherding. If one's devotion is only to people, deep, disappointing disillusionments are bound to come. But for the one whose service is centered in Christ there comes the strength and serenity to meet all the storms.

We love Him because He first loved us.

We love others because He first loved us.

We love at all because He first loved us.

This is what it means to be a love slave and not a hireling.

# 11
# The Shepherd
# Knows His Sheep
# and They Know Him

I am the good shepherd, and know my sheep, and am known of mine.
(John 10:14)

IN ALL OF Scripture this must surely be one of the most reassuring statements made by our Lord to His people. Oh, the wonder and joy of being known by God! The strength and consolation of being in the care of Christ who fully and completely understands us!

Such awareness and such knowing stills our spirits, soothes our souls, and fills us with quiet awe. "O God, You do know me through and through."

The ultimate measure of a good shepherd is how well he knows his sheep. Just as we might say that the measure of a good artist or a good gardener or a good mechanic is the extent to which he "knows" the materials with which he works.

This "knowing" implies much more than just mere acquaintance or contact with sheep. It means the shepherd is so familiar with his sheep, has handled them so much, that he knows their every trait, habit, and characteristic. He can predict their behavior under any given set of circumstances. He understands all their peculiarities. He is never surprised or taken aback by their unusual idiosyncrasies. He is at ease with them, comfortable in their company, delighting in their management.

The full impact of this unique relationship between livestock and their owners came home to me with enormous impact during the years my family and I lived among the Masai people of East Africa. These nomadic livestock owners believed implicitly that to them, and only them, had God given the original responsibility for husbanding livestock.

The Masai were tremendously proud of their supposed management skills with sheep and cattle. They entertained a haughty superiority toward anyone else who tended stock. And much of their claim to fame in this field was based on their knowing individual animals intimately.

In part their pride was justified. The animals under their care were their very life. They gave themselves to them with unstinted devotion. No demand was too tough nor any risk too hazardous to insure their well-being. They would go to any lengths, day or night, to protect them and care for them.

But over and beyond all this lay the incredible intimacy and personal awareness each owner had for his own charges. Many of the lambs, kids, and calves had been hand-reared within the affection of the family circle. They were fondled, hugged, caressed, and called by cute pet names. Bonds of enduring affection were forged from birth that the ensuing years could never break.

Again and again I would watch, awe-struck, as one of the Masai would go up to one of his favorite beasts in the field and spend time caressing it. He would speak to it in endearing terms. He would examine and scrutinize it carefully, checking to see that all was well. This was not something done only on rare occasions. It was a normal part of the appealing relationship between shepherd and sheep.

Some of the fondest memories that came back to me from those years on Africa's sun-drenched plains are wrapped up in small boys shepherding sheep. I can still see them holding lambs gently in their arms. I can see them calling to their pets who came running at the sound of their voices. I can see the obvious pleasure and delight with which the sheep reveled in this attention. They sensed and knew all was well when they were in their owner's embrace. Here was safety and assurance. They were known.

When we turn our attention to our own lives in the care of the Good Shepherd we discover some powerful parallels. If we can grasp them they may well revolutionize our whole relationship to God.

It is essential for us to face the fact that God has known us from our earliest beginnings. By that I do not mean just collectively as a race of people upon the planet, but in a much more private and personal way as an individual human being from the hour of my conception in my mother's womb.

Such knowledge alone startles some of us.

In fact some find it alarming.

Amid a society where, especially in large urban centers, it is possible to live almost anonymously, this is shattering.

We in the western world have become extremely skilled at living behind a false facade. We wear masks. Seldom do we disclose our true identity. We try to present a brave front to the world, even though within we may be shattered, broken people. We proceed on the assumption that most people really don't know us and don't care. We often run a bluff on others, based on the premise that they will not or cannot be bothered to really find us out.

The net result is that for many, life becomes a sham. It is almost playacting. It is played by people playing little games with each other. Much of it is really make-believe. It lacks depth, honesty, or sincerity. People become phonies, they are riddled with skepticism and cynicism. They really don't know where they are at.

Against this background of confused and bewildered life God steps onto the stage and states dramatically, surely, and without apology, "I know you! I understand you! I have known all about you all the time!"

Just the thought of such "knowing," of such insights terrifies most people. In their phony pretense they want to run, to flee, to escape, to hide behind their masks.

But for others of us, this knowing comes at long last as a great relief, a great release from our restless roaming. "O Lord," our spirit cries out, "at last I have been found. Now I am found out. I am known! I can step out of the shadows of my own stumbling steps into the full splendor of Your knowledge. Take me. Search me. Examine me carefully. Put me right. Let me be Yours. And please, You be mine!"

It is only when a person sees himself as known before God that he will get serious with Him. Until this happens we go on playing our pathetic little games with Him. We behave as though we were indeed doing Him a great favor to allow Him to draw near. What colossal conceit! What incredible stupidity. How long will we delude ourselves?

In contrast David, himself a shepherd, cried out exultingly in Psalm 139

> O LORD, thou hast searched me and known me. Thou knowest my downsitting and mine uprising, thou understandest my thought afar off. Thou compassest my path and my lying down, and art acquainted with all my ways. For there is not a word in my tongue, but, Lo, O LORD, thou knowest it altogether. Thou hast beset me behind and before, and laid thine hand upon me. Such knowledge is too wonderful for me; it is high, I cannot attain unto it. Whither shall I go from thy spirit? Or whither shall I flee from thy presence? If I ascend up into heaven, thou art there: If I make my bed in hell, behold, thou art there. If I take the wings of the morning, and dwell in the uttermost parts of the sea; Even there shall thy hand lead me, and thy right hand shall hold me. If I say, Surely the darkness shall cover me; even the night shall be light about me. Yea, the darkness hideth not from thee; but the night shineth as the day: The darkness and the light are both alike to thee. For thou hast possessed my reins: Thou hast covered me in my mother's womb. I will praise thee; for I am fearfully and wonderfully made: marvellous are thy works; and that my soul knoweth right well. (vv. 1–14)

Before such affirmations we are stilled. In wonder and joy we are awed. "O Great, Good Shepherd of my soul, how wondrous to know that You know me!"

For the Christian this awareness can become a potent power in his walk with God. An enormous desire to be open and honest with his Master will descend upon him. The mask will be removed from him by the Spirit of God as He works in his life. A sense of earnestness and simple sincerity will replace the superficiality of his former lifestyle.

He will take God seriously. He will begin to obey His Word. He will be sensitive to the voice of His gracious Spirit. He will allow no petty pride or other obstacle of self-will to obstruct the movement of God's Spirit in his life. He will allow himself to come under Christ's control.

In contrast to the world's way of working, God, by His Spirit, begins to do His work at the center of our beings. The world's view is that if an ideal environment of better housing, hygiene, health, and nutrition is supplied, along with improved education, man will become better and better. History has repeatedly demonstrated the fallacy of this idea.

God's approach is the opposite. His gracious Spirit touches and enlivens man's spirit. If allowed to, He will illuminate the whole inner life. He will permeate the total personality transforming the disposition, emotions, and mind. The net result will be that the remade man will alter his whole environment.

A good environment does not guarantee good men.

But noble men do generate an improved environment.

So God's Spirit begins His re-creative work within us by touching our spirits. He makes us alive to what is right and what is wrong. He impresses upon us what we "ought to do" and what we "ought not do." We become acutely God-conscious. We are aware of what He wants. We know His wishes. We are alerted to His aims and ambitions for us.

This is what it means to have a Christian conscience. We wish to cooperate with Christ. He knows us. We know Him. We have common interests.

Likewise in the area of our communion with Him, we begin to discover that there can be an ongoing discourse between us. He speaks to me. I speak to Him. This intercourse finds full expression in prayer, praise, petitions, and personal awareness that He is ever present.

It takes time to do this. It is profound. It cannot be hurried or rushed. The man who would know God must be prepared to give time to Him.

It is tremendously helpful to speak privately but audibly to the Lord. Let Him know you love Him, that you are fond of Him, that you are deeply grateful for all His kindness.

Not long ago I visited an elderly lady who claimed she had known Christ for more than thirty years. I asked her if she enjoyed conversing with Him quietly in the privacy of her own elegant home. I inquired if she ever told Him how much she loved Him.

Her response was an outburst of embarrassed laughter. "Oh," she blurted out blushingly, "only you would ever suggest such a thing,

Phillip." But I left her home wondering just how well she really knew the Good Shepherd.

In his first epistle the apostle Peter put it this way: "Unto you therefore which believe he is precious" (1 Peter 2:7).

Why? Because I am His and He knows me through and through. And even though He knows the worst, He still loves me with an everlasting love.

This knowing is the great central theme that runs like a chord of gold all through John's first epistle. To know the love of God. To know that we have His life. To know that He hears us. To know that we belong to Him, etc.

Such knowledge is strength. It is stability. It is serenity. It is the solid assurance upon which my relationship to the Good Shepherd stands secure.

There is nothing ambiguous or vague about it. There are no ifs, maybes, perhaps, supposes, or assuming it may be so. I know!

As the Spirit of Christ expands His influence within my life He will begin to penetrate my personality. If allowed to do so He can pervade my mind, emotions, and disposition.

No doubt the ultimate, acid test of Christianity is the dramatic and beneficial changes wrought in the personality and character of people. Weak become strong. Deceivers become honest. Vile become noble. Vicious become gentle. Selfish become selfless.

Perhaps the area in which there is the most coverup is that of our minds. Most people live very private thought lives. Even within the intimate family circle it is possible to retire and withdraw into the inner sanctum of our minds and imaginations.

Were some of the scenes there enacted, to be exposed, it would shock and startle our family and friends to find what sort of world we moved in mentally.

It is sobering to realize, "O God, you know all my thoughts." It is equally solemnizing to remind ourselves always, "And, O God, I know You know!"

This is a purifying discipline. In the presence of His impeccable person it humbles, cleanses, and converts me, turning me from the wickedness of my ways to walk softly in His sight.

As He is allowed to move into my emotions the same process is at work. The same eternal promise holds true. There can be no pretext, no pretense, no playing around, pretending to be so pleasant or pious while within we seethe and boil with pent-up perverseness. "O Lord, You know me!"

With other human beings ill will, hatred, bitterness, envy, old grudges, jealousy, and numerous other heinous attitudes may be masked with a casual shrug of the shoulder or forced half smile. But we simply cannot pull the wool over God's all-seeing eyes. We may kid ourselves that we are getting away with the cover-up, but we don't kid God.

Over and over, when our Lord moved among us as a man, He emphasized the importance in His estimation of our inner attitudes. They were the ultimate criteria to a man's character. He simply could not tolerate false pretenders, who, though appearing to shine like mausoleums in the sun, were filled with dead men's bones.

"O God, You know my anger, resentment, impatience, hostility, and many other evil emotions; I know You know."

What is the solution? Somehow my soul must be cleansed. The debris and dung of a thousand terrible thoughts and imaginations must be swept from my life. It is my sins and iniquities which have come between me and my God. Where is the solution?

I am ever reminded of Hercules who was given the impossible assignment of cleansing the gigantic Aegaen stables. Thousands of horses had deposited their dung within its walls until a literal mountain of manure engulfed the place.

Hercules knew full well, even in his own great strength, that he could never remove the accumulated filth. Instead, he went high into the hills and there found a rushing mountain stream. He diverted it from its course and directed its clear flowing waters through the huge stables. In a short time the surging stream had flushed away all the dung. The stables stood clean because of the sparkling water from the high country.

It is a sublime picture of the wondrous work God's gracious Spirit can effect in a Christian's life. Only as He is allowed to surge freely through the rooms and galleries of my inner life can they ever be cleansed from the dark thoughts, the evil imaginations, the angry emotions, and evil decisions of my disposition.

If in open honesty and genuine earnestness I come to Christ and open my person to Him, He will come in. He will penetrate every part of me. He will purify. He will fill with His presence. His peace will permeate me. His power will be mine in inner strength.

This power will enable me to make proper decisions. His presence at work within me will empower me to both will and do His good pleasure. I shall find harmony and unity between Him and myself. There will be common purposes, common aims, common joys we share. Why? Because He knows me and I know Him.

These titanic changes which can be effected within my spirit and soul by God, can likewise be accomplished in my body. It is He who designed and fashioned men and women in all of their complexities. He knows and fully understands all the instincts, desires, and appetites of our physical makeup.

As we allow ourselves to come gently and increasingly under His control, we will find it affects how we handle our bodies. They will be nurtured and treated with respect. They will not be abused or misused. We will find it possible to so discipline ourselves and direct our activities that even in our bodies there will be a blessing, and that not only a benefit to us but also a benediction to others.

It is possible for God's people to live in moderation, wisdom, and exuberant joy. We can so conduct ourselves amid a corrupt society and sick culture that we are a credit to our Master.

We can practice moderation in our daily habits. It is as much God's good will for me to eat wholesome food, drink pure drinks, enjoy regular rest, revel in regular exercise, and relish the beauty of His creation as it is to go to church. All is sacred and sublime when touched by the delight of His presence with me.

I do not know Him only within the confines of a cathedral. I do not meet Him only within the pages of a Bible or in the still moments of meditation. I can encounter and commune with Christ my Shepherd anywhere along the long winding trails of life that we walk together.

My walk with God need not in any sense be a spectacular display of special dedication. It need not have any carnival atmosphere about it to be convincing. I don't have to indulge in theatrics to impress either Him or other human beings.

What He desires most is that I walk with Him humbly, quietly, and obediently. The communion between shepherd and sheep is sweet and secure because *He knows me* and *I know Him!*

# 12
# One Flock
# of One Shepherd

As the Father knoweth me, even so know I the Father: and I lay down
my life for the sheep. And other sheep I have, which are not of this fold:
them also I must bring, and they shall hear my voice; and there shall be
one fold (flock), and one shepherd. (John 10:15–16)

THIS IS AN appropriate point at which to pause for a moment in studying this parable. Always it is important to keep in mind a clear picture of the setting in which our Lord made His statements.

A young man was born blind. His eyesight was restored by Christ and then he discovered who his benefactor was. In his incredible gratitude the healed man rejoiced not only in new-found physical sight, but also in new-found spiritual sight. He actually *saw* Jesus as his great deliverer, his Savior, his Redeemer.

Though he had been excommunicated and cut off from any further association with the religious leaders, this was only a small loss—for he had found the Christ. He had come to know Him who could give great meaning and direction to his previously derelict life. In humble awe he believed. And with touching appreciation he worshiped Jesus, bowing down before Him in glad submission.

This act of obeisance scandalized and horrified the Jews. They were infuriated even further when the Master made it clear that it was in fact they, who thought they saw and knew and understood spiritual realities, who were blind. The accusation enraged them. Like a pack of bloodhounds closing in on their prey, they encircled Him, bent on His destruction. Their blood boiled. Their eyes blazed with hate.

This next statement Jesus makes—"As the Father knoweth me, even so know I the Father"—was outrageous enough that they charged Him with being utterly insane, if not possessed of a demon.

Of course, it was proof positive of their own self-delusion. They stood confronted by the One who was the light of the world but whose presence only accentuated their own dreadful darkness.

They were encountering heaven's royalty in disguise. Yet they rejected God's anointed Prince of Peace with impassioned pride. He who stood encircled by them came from God, knew God, was very God, but they were totally blind to His being.

In just a few more moments they would pick up rocks from the ground ready to break His bones and dash out His brains. If they could not still Him with spiritual arguments, they could slay Him with stones. Men forever try to silence God, but He does not go away that easily. He always has the last word.

It was not within man's power, nor will it ever be, to do away with God. If His life was to be put on the line, it would be at the time of His own choosing and in the manner of His own choice. No man would deprive Him of this honor or privilege. Jesus later made this clear to His would-be assassins.

What so enraged them was His claim to divinity. "I know the Father. The Father knows me." There was nothing vague or tenuous about this intimate relationship. It was not a knowing of hearsay or second-hand acquaintance. It was in truth a knowing of the most profound, personal sort. It implied the interaction of coequals, the unequivocal unity of total oneness. Jesus, in His final statement to His foes on this important occasion, said, "I and my Father are one!"

This straightforward claim to deity completely undid His audience. And it has been the stone over which uncounted millions have stumbled since.

Unless we grasp the profound and enormous implications of this claim of Christ to being known and knowing God, all the other remarks made later will have no relevance. I say this in sincerity to remind the reader that our Lord was not just a good man; He was also the great God in human guise. His claims to a special knowledge and relationship with His Father were recognized by the Jews as outright insistence on His personal deity.

Not only were they unwilling to accept Him as such, but the same has been true for most men during the past twenty centuries.

If we are to "see," if we are to "understand," we must face the formidable fact that this One was none other than God. He was the God of the Godhead who knew from before the creation of planet earth what plans were made to preserve and restore human beings to a proper relationship with Himself.

He was the God who would have to identify Himself with men in their darkness and dilemma of despair and deception. He would have to interpose His own pure and impeccable life on their behalf, as a substitute for their grievous sins that incurred the judgment of a righteous God. He who knew no sin, of necessity had to be made sin with our wrongdoings, in order that we might be made right with His amazing righteousness.

Only as He Himself, in His own person, exhausted and absorbed the penalty for our wrongs in His death, could we be acquitted and set free. This freedom to be His, to follow Him, to become the people He intended, must of necessity be bought for us at an appalling price.

The price paid was His own life. It was His righteous, sublime life poured out as a supreme propitiation for our pride, perverseness, and pollution. This satisfied the awful abhorrence of a selfless God for our selfish sins, but also delivered us from death, alienation, and the despair of our dreadful dilemma.

Like the young man born blind, only a tiny handful of human beings have ever seen or grasped this truth.

In his simplicity and sincerity he had allowed the great Shepherd of his soul to enter the fold of his young life. He had allowed Him to take control. He had allowed the Good Shepherd to claim him as His own.

The cost to him, too, had been great to come into the care of Christ. His contemporaries had cut him off from the synagogue. They had ostracized him from their company. They had heaped scorn and abuse upon him. He had done no wrong. His only misconduct was to come into Christ's care, to become one of His flock.

The flock of God has never been very large.

Our Lord made it clear few would come into His care.

Most of us are sheep who turn to our own way and go astray.

Yet scattered across the world are those who are His.

Down the long avenues of human history the Good Shepherd has been out among us, gathering up those who would come.

With enormous compassion and great tenderness He looked at the young man whose sight had just been restored. "Other sheep I have, which are not of this fold." All over the earth there are other lives, individual sheepfolds, scattered like so many sheep astray, whose intimate folds He is eager to enter. This young man's life was but one tiny fold out of uncounted thousands which in their sum total would make up His final flock.

It is important to recognize the difference between a flock and a fold. The shepherd is said to have only one flock. This flock is the sum total of all the sheep which belong to him. But almost always his flock is distributed widely, especially if he is a wealthy owner, among many folds across the country. Put another way, we can say that one sheepman's flock is made up of many different folds. The modern rendering of John 10:16 is much more accurate than the King James version which confuses the reader by stating "There shall be one *fold*," rather than, "There shall be one *flock*," which is correct and clear.

When we lived among the Masai people of East Africa it impressed me how one livestock owner would have his animals scattered in small groups all across the countryside. One very wealthy man whom I came to know quite well actually owned more than 10,000 head of stock. But these were not all cared for in one place. They were distributed in little clusters here and there, scattered widely among many kraals.

Yet, the sum total of them all comprised his one unit, one herd, one flock under one owner.

It will help the reader to understand this concept if we look at modern farming practices on the prairies. During pioneer days it was common for each individual family to own and operate its own homestead. These small holdings of land comprised either a quarter (160 acres) or half (320 acres) section of land, a full section being one square mile or 640 acres.

With the advent of power equipment and expensive machinery most farmers found they needed more land to justify the investment made in expensive tractors, plows, drills, and combines. The upshot was that the more prosperous and efficient farmers began to buy up random quarter or half sections their neighbors might sell them.

The final result has been that today one man's farm may well include numerous pieces of land scattered all across the country at random. Yet he refers to them in total as "my farm."

I knew of one wealthy grain grower who owned seventeen different quarter sections. Separately, each was a unit of its own. Collectively they comprised his one farm. The same is true with sheepmen. All their folds together become their one flock under one owner.

Looking now at Christ's flock, we see clearly that it is composed of many different lives (little folds) scattered at random all across the earth. He is ever active and at work bringing men and women into His care and under His control. He gathers them up from the far-flung corners of the world. He has been energetically engaged in this enterprise since the beginning of human history.

A magnificent and splendid overview of Christ's achievements through the centuries is painted for us by John in the Book of Revelation. Under the unction and inspiration of God's own gracious Spirit he writes glowingly this great song.

> You are worthy to take the scroll and to open its seals, because you were slain, and with your blood you purchased men for God from every tribe and language and people and nation.
> You have made them to be a kingdom and priests to serve our God, and they will reign on the earth. (5:9–10, NIV)

And so the eyes of our spiritual understanding are opened to see our Good Shepherd, relentlessly, tirelessly, eagerly calling to Himself those chosen ones who will respond to His voice and come to His call. He brings them in from every tribe, every language, every race, every nation.

His majestic voice has rung out over all the earth. In unmistakable sounds He calls out to any who will come. With enormous compassion He cries out to men "Come unto me, all ye that labour and are heavy laden, and I will give you rest."

None other has ever extended to wayward wanderers such a winsome, warm invitation. But most men spurn it. They turn instead each to their own perverse path that leads into peril and ultimately to perdition.

Yet from out of earth's milling masses a small flock is being faithfully formed. We find members of that flock scattered here and there. By no means are they confined to any one church, denomination, or sect. Rather, they are distributed widely, and spread rather thinly through a multitude of groups and gatherings of diverse doctrines.

It has been my great privilege through the years of my long life to have rich fellowship with other Christians all over the world. My travels have taken me to some forty different countries. The places where I met other people who knew Christ as their Good Shepherd would take a whole book to describe fully. I have stood solemnized in some of the most impressive cathedrals ever erected by man and there sensed and known that others of His flock were with me in the care of Christ. By the same measure I have sat in tiny mud huts in Africa and grass thatch houses in southeast Asia where the Good Shepherd had also gathered up some of His sheep.

You see, the ultimate criteria is not the church, the creed, the form of communion, or even the cherished and contested claims to special spiritual insight which determine a person's position. It is simply this: "Do they or do they not hear Christ's voice?"

He Himself said emphatically, "Other sheep I have. Them also I must bring. They shall hear My voice."

To hear Christ's voice, as was pointed out in a previous chapter, means three essential things.

1) I recognize it is God who calls me to Himself. He graciously invites me to come under His care, to benefit from His management of my life, to accept His provision for me.

2) I respond to His overtures by taking Him seriously. I alert myself to act. I open my life to Him so He may in truth and reality enter to share it with me.

3) I then run to do whatever He wishes. I cooperate with His desires. I regularly do His will. Thus I enter fully into the greatness of His life, grateful for His care.

This is to "hear" Christ's call and to respond.

Any man or woman who does this belongs to Him, is a member of His flock, a sheep of His pasture. Our Lord has them here and there in ten thousand times ten thousand tiny folds, each flourishing under His infinite love.

# 13

# Christ Lays Down
# and Takes Up
# His Own Life

Therefore doth my father love me, because I lay down my life, that I might take it again. No man taketh it from me, but I lay it down of myself. I have power to lay it down, and I have power to take it again. This commandment have I received of my Father. (John 10:17–18)

OVER AND OVER in this book the point has been made that the hallmark of the Good Shepherd is His willingness to lay down His life for His sheep. It cannot be otherwise. The essential nature of Christ demands it. Because He is love, selfless love, this must be so.

This love of God is the most potent force extant in the universe. It is the primal energy that powers the entire cosmos. It is the basic driving initiative that lies behind every good and noble action. Without it all men of all time would languish in despair. They would grope in darkness. Ultimately they would know only separation from the goodness of God which is death.

But—and it is a remarkable "but"—Christ was willing to leave His glory; to come among us expressing that love, giving tangible form to it in a sacrificial life. I have written of this love at great length in *Rabboni*. Here I quote from its pages without apology: "With our finite minds we cannot probe but a short distance into the vastness of Christ's pre-earth existence. But with the enlightenment that comes to our spirits by His Spirit we sense and feel the magnitude of His enterprises in arranging and governing the universe.

"Such enlightenment comes from His Spirit. He the Eternal Spirit of the Infinite God; the same Spirit of the Eternal Christ; was simultaneously in everlasting existence with both the Father and The Son, Our Christ. He like them was engaged in the enormous activities that long preceded even the appearance of the planet earth.

"In all the enterprises which engaged this tremendous triumvirate, there was perfect coordination of concept and ultimate unity of purpose in their planning. Unlike human endeavours there was never any discord. Friction was unknown simply because there was no selfish self-interest present. Between God The Father, God The Son (Jesus Christ) and God The Spirit, there flowed love in its most sublime form. In fact this love was of such purity that it constituted the very basis of their beings.

"We earth men can barely conceive of a relationship so sublime that it contains no trace of self-assertion, no ulterior motives for self-gratification. But that is the secret to the strength of God. Here was demonstrated the irresistible force of utter self-lessness. In the total giving of each to the other in profound 'caring' for each other lay the love of all eternity. This was love at its loftiest level. This was love at its highest source. This was love, the primal source of all energy.

"Just as there is stored within an atom enormous power because of the inter-action between neutrons, protons and electrons, likewise there was inherent unlimited energy in the Godhead because of the inter-relationship between Father, Son and Spirit. And the essence of this energy was love.

"In that outer world love was the moving force behind every action. Love was the energizing influence at work in every enterprise. It was the very fabric woven into every aspect of Christ's life. It was in fact the basic raw material used ultimately to fashion and form all subsequent matter.

"To the reader this may seem a bit obscure, a bit beyond belief. But if we pause to find parallels upon our planet, earth, we may soon see the picture in practical terms. What is the most irresistible force upon the earth? Love? What pulverizes strong prejudice and builds enduring allegiance? Love? What binds men together in indestructible devotion? Love? What underlies all generous and magnanimous actions? Love? What is the source of strength for men and women who gladly serve and die for one another? Love? What energizes the loftiest and most noble enterprise of human hearts and minds? Love? If this be true of selfish mortal men, then how much more is it the very life of God—And this is the life of Christ.

"It was in the setting of a realm permeated by love that the generous thought of sharing it with others came into being. Of course it could scarcely be otherwise. For if heaven was such a happy home it would scarcely have been consistent for God to want to keep it to Himself. Love insists on sharing.

"So the concept was born of love that other sons and daughters should be brought into being who could participate in the delights of paradise. That such a remarkably generous endeavour was even considered is in keeping with the character of God. He chose to do this in love and out of love simply because of who He is.

> Praise be to God and Father of our Lord Jesus Christ for giving us through Christ every possible spiritual benefit as citizens of Heaven! For consider what he has done—before the foundation of the world he chose us to become, in Christ, his holy and blameless children living within His constant care. He planned, in his purpose of love, that we should be adopted as his own children through Jesus Christ—that we might learn to praise that glorious generosity of his which has made us welcome in the everlasting love he bears toward his Beloved. (Eph. 1:3–6, *Phillips*)

"Like all other divine enterprises it undoubtably first found expression in the mind of God The Father. Yet it was agreed to completely by God The Son and fully endorsed by God The Holy Spirit."

All of this Christ did deliberately, freely, gladly out of His own generous good will toward us. It was not that we deserved or merited such magnificent mercy, but it was because of His own inherent character. He really could not do otherwise. There was nothing in us to earn His gracious attention. *The only compulsion upon Him was the compulsion of His own wondrous love.*

Are we surprised then that it is for this reason He stated He was loved so dearly by God the Father. This love was not and never can be anything soft or sentimental or insipid. Rather, it is strong as steel, tough as tungsten, yet glittering with the incandescent brilliance of a diamond.

It had to be for Him to endure the abuse and calumny of His earth days at the hands of wicked, selfish men. His entire interlude upon the planet represented the utmost in ignominy. Born into a peasant home, surrounded by the appalling filth of an eastern sheepfold, His birth could not have been more debasing. The long years of His youth and early manhood were spent in the most wicked town in Palestine. Nazareth was notorious for its wicked ways. Yet there He toiled, sweated, and hewed out a meager living working in wood to support his widowed mother and siblings.

He lived in abject poverty without a home to call His own. He literally laid Himself out for others. His strength and stamina flowed out to those who followed Him. His great vitality restored the sick, raised the dead, fed the masses, ministered to those in sorrow, and propelled Him from one end of the country to the other with incredible energy. Everywhere He went, men and women sensed the touch of His strength, the impact of God's love upon them.

Inherent in Christ in perfect poise were the divine life of undiminished deity and the delightful life of untarnished humanity. Though He was the suffering servant, He was also the magnificent Lord of glory—God, very God.

At His death this became supremely evident. In that terrible agony of the garden, in the ignoble lynching by the mob under cover of darkness, in the atrocious trials and beastly behavior of men determined to destroy Him, in the crucible of His cruel crucifixion, He emerges ever as the One in control. He chose to die this way. He chose deliberately to lay down His life in this manner. It was all His doing and His dying for dreadful men.

No matter what the scoffers and skeptics may say, He stands at the central crossroads of human history as its supreme character. No other individual, with so little ostentation, so shaped the eternal destiny of men.

But His death was not His end. It was but the conclusion of a magnificent chapter in the story of God's plan for man.

Death could not hold Him. Decay and decomposition could not deteriorate Him. The spices and wrappings and grave clothes that enfolded Him were for naught. They were powerless to prevent His resurrection. With majesty and growing grandeur He took His place of power. His position of omnipotence was reinstated. His coronation as King of Kings and Lord of Lords was celebrated in the throne room of eternity.

All of this Jesus foreknew and declared fearlessly to the young man born blind. He stated these facts with calm assurance to any who would listen—the Pharisees, Scribes, and others who now encircled Him.

They knew full well what it was that He implied. He was in truth telling them that He was none other than God. He was declaring unashamedly that He, their Messiah, the anointed One of God, their Promised One, was now among them. He had chosen to come to His people. It would be but a brief sojourn, and then He would return to the splendors from whence He came.

But why had He come? Why suffer? Why lay down His life? Why endure such agony for sinners?

Because men were lost. And His commission from His Father was that He should come to seek and to save those who were lost. He knew this to be His unique responsibility in the redemptive enterprises of God. He recognized it was His responsibility to carry out and execute in precise detail this executive order of the Godhead.

His audience then, and most men ever since, refused to believe they were lost. In truth it is exceedingly difficult to convince human beings that they are in peril. Like the Scribes and Pharisees of Jesus' day, we are prone to pride ourselves upon our religiosity, our cultural achievements, our educational attainments, our material possessions, or any other attributes which we naively suppose are indicators of our success in living.

We who are in the family of God, who have been found by the Good Shepherd, often seem to forget just how "lost" we really were. As we look out upon a confused society and bewildered world we allow its trappings and trumpetings to blind us to the lostness of our families, friends, or acquaintances. We are dazzled by the glittering exteriors and flashing facades put on by people in desperate peril away from God. Fine language, impressive homes, beautiful cars, elaborate furnishings, glamorous holidays, affluent incomes, sharp clothes, and clever minds are no criteria for having either succeeded or found the reason for our being. We can have all these and still be far from God.

This explains why God, in Christ, by His Spirit, continues to pursue men. His approach to them polarizes people. He is willing to lay down His life for them in order that He might also take it up again in them. Some are delighted to discover He has drawn near, ready to pick them up in His own strong arms. Others turn away, go their own way, and refuse adamantly to have anything to do with Him. To those who respond He gives Himself in wondrous ways.

> Behold, the Lord GOD will come with strong hand, and his arm shall rule for him: Behold, his reward is with him, and his work before him.
> He shall feed his flock like a shepherd: he shall gather the lambs with his arm, and carry them in his bosom, and shall gently lead those that are with young. (Isa. 40:10–11)

What a remarkable portrait this is of our Lord, laying down His life for His sheep. He feeds them; He leads them gently; He gathers them up in His strong arms; He carries them close to His heart.

It is in this way that He also takes up His life again in us. Caught up into His care, encircled by His strong arms, enfolded within His love, we find ourselves *in Him*. This is part of the great secret to sharing in His life.

Much more than this, however, is the fact that it is to Him an endless source of satisfaction. He looks upon the outpouring of His life, the travail of His soul, the generous giving of Himself repaid and returned in sons and daughters brought to glory. Men and women, retrieved from their utter lostness and dereliction, are restored to the grandeur of wholesome godliness and new life in Him.

Often as I let my mind wander back to the great storms and blizzards that we went through on my ranches I recall scenes full of pathos and power. Again and again I would come home to our humble cottage with two or three tiny forlorn, cold lambs bundled up against my chest. They would be wrapped up within the generous folds of my big, rough wool jacket. Outside hail, sleet, snow, and chilling rain would be lashing my face and body. But within my arms the lambs were safe and sure of survival.

Part of the great compensation for enduring the blizzards, fighting the elements, and braving the storms was to pick up lost lambs.

And as I picked them up I realized in truth I was taking up my own life again in them; my life that had been expended freely, gladly on their behalf.

It is as I am found in Him that He, too, revels and rejoices in my being found. No wonder there is such rejoicing in heaven over one lost soul who is brought home.

Sad to say, many of Jesus' hearers did not and could not understand. In fact, they went so far as to say He was insane.

Parable III
John 10:25–30
*Christ in Me and Me in Christ*

# 14

# To Believe
# in Christ Is to
# Belong to Christ

Jesus answered them, I told you, and ye believed not: the works that I do in my Father's name, they bear witness of me.
But ye believe not, because ye are not of my sheep, as I said unto you. My sheep hear my voice, and I know them, and they follow me. (John 10:25–27)

THIS IS AN appropriate point at which to reflect on the polarization produced by Christ. This aspect of His life has ever proven to be an enigma to human beings. The unchangeable, irrefutable truth manifest in this One inevitably polarizes people. There is no middle ground. There can be no straddling the fence of neutrality. Either we believe in Him or we don't.

Perhaps polarization should be explained briefly. Whenever truth, that is to say absolutes, or eternal verities are presented to a person they produce one of two reactions. The first reaction is that the soul and spirit in search of God responds positively and promptly. There is an immediate move toward the truth. The spirit lays hold of, and takes to itself, the verities presented. They become a veritable part of one's life. They are the vitalizing, energizing, invigorating life of God moving into human character, human conduct, human conversation. They change, color, and condition a person until he is conformed to Christ.

The alternative is the opposite; it is a negative reaction. The end result is a rejection of truth, which of course implies ultimately the rejection of Christ.

This was eminently true in His days upon earth, and it is the same today. And on this occasion his attackers went so far as to declare Him either a raving maniac or one possessed of a devil. Eventually their animosity and reaction to Him became so violent they schemed to destroy Him. Several times He slipped through their clutching fingers, but eventually, like bloodhounds, they brought Him to bay. Nor were they satisfied that He was stilled until they saw Him suspended on a cruel Roman gibbet. There, hanging midway between earth and sky, writhing in agony, they were sure His disquieting and disturbing declarations would terminate in His death.

But truth simply does not die that way.

Truth does not disappear in the face of evil.

Truth is indestructible just as God is indestructible.

Truth endures forever.

Truth remains eternal.

So down the long avenues of time men have turned angrily amid the darkness and despair of their dreadful deeds to attack truth. They have derided it, despised it, and tried to demolish it. Or better, we should say that in their blindness and ignorance they have so desired. Why?

The clearest and most concise answer to that enormous, unending question is given by Christ Himself:

> For God so loved the world, that he gave his only begotten Son, that whosoever believeth in him should not perish, but have everlasting life. For God sent not his Son into the world to condemn the world; but that the world through him might be saved. He that believeth on him is not condemned: but he that believeth not is condemned already, because he hath not believed in the name of the only begotten Son of God. And this is the condemnation, that light is come into the world, and men loved darkness rather than light, because their deeds were evil. For every one that doeth evil hateth the light, neither cometh to the light, lest his deeds should be reproved. But he that doeth truth cometh to the light, that his deeds may be made manifest, that they are wrought in God. (John 3: 16–21)

On this particular occasion our Lord's adversaries ranted and raged at Him. "How long are You going to keep us in doubt?" "If you really are the Christ tell us plainly!"

The pathetic aspect of the whole scene really was their own positive refusal to accept what He had said as truth.

Repeatedly He had declared His identity. They knew from their familiarity with the Old Testament Scriptures that this One who now stood before them was none other than the promised Messiah. He was God's Anointed. He was the Great, Good Shepherd foretold by the prophets and seers of their people. David, Isaiah, Ezekiel and others had predicted that the true Shepherd would come to gather up and restore the lost sheep of Israel.

Over and over Christ had asserted that He was in fact that One. He was here. The Good Shepherd was among them. He was calling to His own. He was gathering them up . . . those who would come.

But they adamantly refused to believe Him.

They simply would not accept Him.

They rejected and repudiated all He said.

Yet, over and beyond all of this He endeavored to convince them of His credentials by repeated demonstrations of His deity.

He performed all sorts of remarkable miracles that were positive proof and incontestable confirmation of His divinity. They had heard Him preach good tidings to the meek and poor. They had watched Him bind up the broken-hearted. They had seen Him liberate those who were captive to evil spirits, disease, or their own deranged minds and emotions. They had been there when He spoke comfort to those who mourned. They had seen sorrow turned to gladness.

They had been witnesses to the full and total fulfillment of all that Isaiah predicted in 61:1–3

> The spirit of the Lord God is upon me; because the Lord hath anointed me to preach good tidings unto the meek; he hath sent me to bind up the broken-hearted, to proclaim liberty to the captives, and the opening of the prison to them that are bound; To proclaim the acceptable year of the Lord, and the day of vengeance of our God; to comfort all that mourn; To appoint unto them that mourn in Zion, to give unto them beauty for ashes, the oil of joy for mourning, the garment of praise for the spirit of heaviness; that they might be called trees of righteousness, the planting of the Lord, that he might be glorified.

And still they would not believe. Still they would not receive Him.

Accordingly it is absolutely essential for us, as it was for them, to grasp fully what it really means "to believe," "to receive," for by Christ's own simple statement He insisted that only those who do believe belong to Him.

"To believe" implies much more than merely giving my mental assent to truth. It is much more than merely agreeing to what God has to say.

There are literally hundreds of thousands of people who profess to be believers who do this much. They agree in a formal manner to the truth as it is revealed in the Scriptures. They subscribe in a rather ambiguous way to the teachings of Christ. They believe that in some rather obscure way He was a historical character who came to earth to reveal truth to us. He was really no more than another of the great prophets or teachers who claimed divine attributes and abilities.

But this simply is not enough!

Even the evil spirits believe this much and tremble.

Without a doubt the greatest single weakness in Christendom the world around is so called "believism." It is an anachronism that millions who claim to believe are in reality a repudiation of the living Christ. Their characters, conduct, and conversation are a living travesty of the truth they claim to exemplify.

This is why Christianity and the church is eternally being charged with hypocrisy. It is why so many who are outside claim that those inside the church are charlatans. It is why to be a true believer is difficult, simply because so often the behavior of our so-called brethren betrays them and us. We are all lumped together and labeled as imposters. And our dilemma only deepens when all around us, amid the confusion and criticism, men and women insist they are all believers, when in truth their behavior may well be a reproach to Christ.

In our Lord's discourses He equated believing with drinking. To believe truth, to believe Him, was in fact to imbibe truth, to imbibe Him.

> . . . He that believeth on me shall never thirst. (John 6:35)
> If any man thirst, let him come unto me, and drink. He that believeth on me, as the scripture hath said, out of his belly (innermost being) shall flow rivers of living water. (John 7:37–38)

To believe in Christ is not just to give endorsement in an objective manner to what He has done and said on my behalf.

To believe in Christ is to fully accept both Him and His truth so that I actually take Him into my life in deliberate, volitional action, that goes on continuously.

Put another way it means this: He, the living Christ, is actually allowed to so enter the whole of my life that He shares it with me, lives it with me, becomes an integral, vitalizing part of it. In other words, He is in me and I am in Him.

The closest parallel to this is marriage.

It is possible to read about marriage, talk about it, discuss it, and debate it. But until you find another whom you implicitly trust and love enough to invite into your life to share it with you, you know virtually nothing about the truth of all that marriage implies. It must be experienced to be known. It must be tried to be understood. It must be undertaken to be enjoyed. It must be engaged in to be believed.

It is the same with Christ. He is referred to in Scripture as the Bridegroom and we His bride.

The second closest parallel to this is the intimate interrelationship between a shepherd and his sheep.

We can discuss shepherding, read about it, study it, observe it, and even enjoy watching it. Yet until we actually participate, we really know nothing about it except in a very remote, detached, and impersonal way.

And this is precisely the point Jesus made when He said: "You don't believe, simply because you don't actually belong to Me. You aren't My sheep."

All through this book and also in A *Shepherd Looks at Psalm* 23, I have endeavored to point out in unmistakable language what it really means to "belong" to Christ. I have tried to show what is involved in "coming under Christ's control." I have indicated the great joys and benefits and advantages of allowing our lives to actually be managed by Him who made us, who bought us, and who is legitimately entitled to own us.

Yet, the point must be made again here that the decision as to whether or not this will happen rests with us. Christ comes to us. He calls to us. He invites us to turn to Him. He offers to take us under His care. He longs to lead us in His ways. He desires to share life with us. He wants us to enter fully into the joys of His owner-ship. He delights to give us all the advantages and benefits of His life.

In short, He wants to be in our lives and for us to be in His.

Are we or are we not prepared to have this happen?

It is an intimate association from which most of us shy away. We really are afraid of this involvement. To speak of "believing" in this way makes most of us uneasy. We are not at all sure we wish to be so completely committed. There is so much at stake! Yes! all of this life; all of eternity; all of myself is at stake.

It is only the person prepared to become open and available to God, who positively responds to truth as it is revealed in Christ, the Great, Good Shepherd, who will "hear" His voice.

To hear Him is to "recognize" that this One is in truth none other than God, very God.

This being so, what He says and what He does will be taken seriously. We will respond to Him in powerful ways of acceptance and total personal commitment.

Evidence of this will be apparent in a deliberate and eager will-ingness to do whatever He requires. This "running" to do His bid-ding demonstrates faith and confidence in Christ of a potent sort. This is to believe in Christ—to know God!

It is this intimate interchange and private interrelationship be-tween Christ and me that becomes such a unique relationship. It is in truth the "knowing," of which Christ as the Good Shepherd speaks with such affection. He is in my life; I am in His. He knows me; I know Him. He is mine; I am His.

This is a precious relationship. The acute awareness that He knows me and I know God in Christ is the most profound and potent influence I am privileged to know as a man. In its aware-ness lies great rest.

There is about this knowing an element of elevation that induces me to attain lofty living and noble conduct far beyond anything I might otherwise have thought possible. This knowing is the pow-erful, potent presence of the very person of Christ made real in my everyday experience by His gracious Spirit.

Finally, there is the inescapable reality that this knowing has a profound purifying effect upon my life in all its activities. I live and move and have my being in company with Him who is altogether noble. He is royalty. He is my Lord, my Owner, my Master, and in His close company I scorn that which is corrupt.

Only those who know Him in this manner, who believe on Him to this extent, who receive Him without reservation in this way find it appropriate to follow Him.

I have used the word appropriate deliberately here. It implies that to follow Christ, as following Him has been explained previously in this book, is not something absurd or unrealistic or unreasonable. Rather, to follow Him becomes the proper, reasonable, and appropriate thing to do.

To follow Christ means I become intimately identified with His plans and purposes for the planet and for me as a person. His wishes become my wishes. His work becomes my work. His words become my words. His standards, values, and priorities become mine. His interests become my interests. His life becomes my life.

In a word: He is in me; I am in Him. There is the place of peace. Here lies serenity, strength, and stability amid earth's troublous times.

# 15
# Eternal Life
# in the Hand
# of the Shepherd

My sheep hear my voice, and I know them, and they follow me:
And I give unto them eternal life; and they shall never perish, neither
shall any man pluck them out of my hand. (John 10:27–28)

AT THE HEAD of this chapter, John 10:27, 28 have been deliberately set down together. They cannot be separated. These verses constitute one continuous concept.

The incredibly beautiful relationship between the Shepherd and His sheep can be and only is possible provided the sheep hear His voice, are known of Him in intimate oneness, and so follow Him in quiet, implicit confidence.

The eternal life inherent in Him, whereby they shall never perish, within which they can enjoy endless security under His hand, are benefits made possible only in constant communion with Him.

If for a moment we turn our attention to a human shepherd and his sheep we will see this to be self-evident.

Those sheep which remain in the shepherd's personal care are the ones which derive and draw their very life from his provision and possession of them. They have at their disposal all the resources of his ranch. They thrive under the expertise of his skilled management. They enjoy the eternal vigilance and loving protection of his care. Under his hand they flourish because they are "handled" with affection by one who is tremendously fond of them. In fact, they are his very life. In turn he becomes to them their very life.

Looking back in gentle reminiscence across the distant years of my own life as a sheepman this remains its most memorable aspect. There was a profound and deeply moving sense in which all my life, all my strength, all my energy, all my vitality was poured into my flock. It simply had to be so if they were to enjoy an optimum life under my management.

The "life" which they had in such rich measure and overflowing abundance was but an expression of my own life continuously given to them day after day. The lush green pastures, the lovely wooded parkland where they could shelter from summer sun and winter winds, the clear cool water to slake their thirst, the freedom from predators or rustlers, the protection against disease and parasites of all sorts, the loving attention and intimate care of one who delighted in their on-going well-being all reflected my own life lived out through them.

They came to be known and recognized uniquely as being "Keller's sheep." They had upon them the indelible, unmistakable mark of belonging to me. Their health, quality, and excellence were a declaration of whose they were.

Yet, it must be emphasized that this life, this special care, this exquisite sense of security and well-being was theirs only as long as they remained on my ranch and under my hand.

In my book on Psalm 23 I told in detail of certain sheep which were never really satisfied to stay in my care. They were always looking for a chance to slip out through a hole in the fence. Or they would creep around the end of the enclosure that ran down to the seashore at extreme low tide. Once they had gotten out, they were exposed to enormous perils. Some wandered far off to become lost up the road or into the woods. And there they fell prey to all sorts of disasters.

With all of this in mind our Lord made it clear that our own relationship to Him is the same. The remarkable eternal life which He gives to us is His own life transmitted to us continuously as we remain in close contact with Him. His vitality, His vigor, His view of things are mine as long as the communion between us is constant.

It is a mistake to imagine that eternal life, the very life of the risen Christ, is some gift package dropped into the pocket of my life at some specific point in time; that once it has been bestowed I automatically have it forever.

Life, any kind of life, physical, moral, or spiritual, simply is not of that sort.

Life is correspondence between an organism and its environment. Life goes on only so long as the organism is deriving its sustenance from its surroundings. The instant it no longer draws its support from its environment, life ceases. At that point the organism is declared to be dead.

This principle applies in the realm of my body—physical. It holds true in the region of my soul—moral. It is so in my spirit—spiritual.

All of life originates with God irrespective of whether it be physical, moral, or spiritual. To assume that He bestows only spiritual life to human beings is a distortion of truth.

The whole of the biota, the total physical, chemical, and biological environment which supports my physical body comes from Him. He designed it. He programmed it. He set it in motion. He sustains it. He maintains its meticulous functions. He enables me thus to derive my physical life and well-being from His wondrous world around me. The moment I can no longer do this I am said to be physically dead.

Precisely the same principle operates in my soul. My mind, emotions, and will are stimulated and sustained by correspondence with the moral environment that surrounds me. This is the realm of human relationships and ideologies. It is the world of ideas, concepts, and culture expressed in literature, science, the arts, music, and accumulated experience of the human race.

A person can be acutely, vividly alive to all of this. Or he can be likewise virtually dead to it. For some it is well nigh life itself. Yet even here every capacity anyone has to correspond or communicate with this total soulish environment comes from God. It is He who has arranged, ordered, and programmed all that is excellent, beautiful, and noble in the arts, sciences, and humanities. Man has only just gradually uncovered all that formerly lay hidden from his restricted vision.

So in truth, all moral, all soul life is derived from our Lord, for without the capacities of mind, emotion, and will bestowed upon us by Him, we would have no way of enjoying even this life.

Again, it may be legitimately stated that the moment I can no longer derive moral stimulation and uplift from this realm I am said to be dead to it. What is more, it is perfectly possible to be physically alive yet morally dead to one or more or all of God's life in this region.

I am said to be morally alive only so long as I draw life from those generous and godly gifts bestowed upon me by a benevolent and loving Master. He so designed me as to live on this noble lofty plane as His person.

What has been said of physical and moral life also applies in the region of my spirit. There, deep within my inner life, lies my conscience, my intuition, and my capacity to commune with God by His Spirit.

I am said to have spiritual life only so long as there is being derived directly from God a measure of His life. It is He who in the realm of my conscience alerts me to absolute verities, ultimate truth. It is in this way I know what I ought to do, what I ought not to do. I am alive to what is appropriate and proper behavior before Him and what is not.

It is in the realm of my intuition that I enjoy that ultimate dimension of living, in knowing God. It is in the unique awareness of being alive to Him that I enjoy life at its loftiest level. There steals over my stilled spirit the sure knowledge that it is in Christ I live and move and have my being. This is to know also that I am known of Him, intimately, personally, and with profound affection.

So there flows between His gracious Spirit and my spirit an interchange of life—His life. I am in Him; He is in me. There is an ongoing, continuing interrelationship whereby He imparts His life to me and takes up my little life into His.

To know, experience, and enjoy this communion with Christ is to have eternal life. This is what Christ meant when He said unashamedly, "I give unto them eternal life."

He went on to add emphatically, "They shall never perish."

As long as my communion with Him continues, His life is imparted as a clear flowing stream from the fountain source of His own magnificent, inexhaustible self. He comes to me continuously in neverending life to energize and invigorate me. I am His, to be the recipient of an ever-renewed life. He is mine to be the bestower of every good and perfect gift needed to sustain me through all eternity.

He has no other intention than that this relationship should be one of eternal endurance.

My part is to remain ever open, responsive, and receptive to the inflow of His life to mine. It is His life that surrounds and enfolds me on every side. In any situation, at any time, in any place I can breathe quietly, "O Christ, You are here. You are the ever-present one—the great 'I Am.' Live Your life in me, through me, in this moment, for I, too, am in Your presence ready to receive You in all Your splendor."

The person who so lives in Christ's presence shall never perish. He it is out of whose innermost being cascades clear streams of life-giving refreshment to those around him. This is the individual who is an inspiration and blessing to his generation, and to his God.

Those who live this joyous and serene communion with Christ are the men and women who know they are in God's hand. Nor will they ever make a move or entertain a thought that would take them out of His hand.

To know that God's hand is upon me for good is perhaps the most precious awareness a human being can savor in his earthly sojourn. To be acutely aware—"O my Shepherd, You are enfolding me in Your great strong hand!"—is to sense a sweet serenity that nothing can disturb. To realize the intimacy of the Master's touch upon every minutiae of my affairs, to experience His hand guiding, leading, directing in every detail of each day, is to enter a delight words cannot describe.

My part is to be sensitive to His gentle Spirit. My part is to obey instantly His smallest wish. My part is to wait quietly for the unfolding of His best purposes and plans. In harmony, unity, and mutual pleasure we commune together along the trails of life. He becomes my fondest friend and most intimate companion. More than that, He becomes my life.

This is the life of serene security. This is the relationship of quiet relaxation. This is the life of rest and repose; for the person willing to be led of the Lord there is endless enjoyment in His company.

The ancient prophet Isaiah portrays this for us in an exquisite word picture of the Great Shepherd of our souls.

> O Zion, that bringest good tidings, get thee up into the high mountain; O Jerusalem, that bringest good tidings, lift up thy voice with strength; Lift it up, be not afraid; Say unto the cities of Judah, Behold your God! Behold, the Lord GOD will come with strong hand, and his arm shall rule for him: behold, his reward is with him, and his work before him.
> He shall feed his flock like a shepherd: he shall gather the lambs with his arm, and carry them in his bosom, and shall gently lead those that are with young. (Isa. 40:9–11)

It has always been our Lord's intention to hold His people in His own strong hand. It is the most profound longing of His Spirit to lead us gently in the paths of right living. He is eager and happy to gather us up into His powerful arms where no harm can molest us.

The intentions of God toward His own are always good. He ever has their own best interests at heart. His desires are only for their well-being. He is a Shepherd of enormous good will and deep compassion for the people of His pasture.

It is ever He who holds us in His hand, if we will allow ourselves to be so owned and loved. We do not have to "hold on to Him" as so many wrongly imagine. How much better to rest in the quiet assurance of knowing His hand is upon me rather than doubting my feeble efforts to hold onto Him.

This is one of the great secrets to a serene life in Christ. It does not come instantly, overnight so to speak. It is the gradual outgrowth of a life lived quietly in gentle communion with Him.

Imperceptibly there steals over my spirit the assurance that with Him, all is well. He makes no mistakes. He is ever here. And so long as I remain acutely aware of His presence, nothing can separate me from His love and care.

> Who shall separate us from the love of Christ? shall tribulation, or distress, or persecution, or famine, or nakedness, or peril, or sword? As it is

written, For thy sake we are killed all the day long; we are accounted as sheep for the slaughter. Nay, in all these things we are more than conquerors through him that loved us. For I am persuaded, that neither death, nor life, nor angels, nor principalities, nor powers, nor things present, nor things to come, Nor height, nor depth, nor any other creature, shall be able to separate us from the love of God, which is in Christ Jesus our Lord. (Rom. 8:35–39)

# 16
# The
# Good Shepherd
# Is God!

My Father, which gave them me, is greater than all; and no man is able
to pluck them out of my Father's hand. I and my Father are one. (John
10:29–30)

THERE ARE OCCASIONS on which it is imperative that an author share his own inner struggle in search of spiritual truth. For all of us there are sections of the Scriptures where we have found difficulty in arriving at veracity. All of us are pilgrims on the path, and no matter how sincerely we endeavor to follow our Good Shepherd, there are times when we stumble.

For me the two verses above, taken together, "seemed" to pose an insurmountable problem. In verse 29 our Lord states that His Father "is greater than all." In almost the next breath He asserts He and His Father are one.

The false cults who eternally deny the deity of Christ have capitalized on this "apparent" contradiction. In fact, it is a passage they exploit to the maximum in order to undermine the faith of those who have placed their simple confidence in Christ as God, very God.

It was not until I undertook a deep study on this section that at last the clear light of its meaning began to break through. What previously was puzzling has now become exceedingly precious. And it is with distinct joy and a sense of triumph that the closing chapter of this book can be written.

Once more light has replaced darkness, love has taken the place of despair. The result is that I am much richer for it, and I trust you the reader will be as well.

In Dr. Weymouth's remarkable translation this reads, "What my Father has given me is greater than all, and no one is able to wrest anything from my Father's hand. I and the Father are one."

In the translation by Knox the meaning is made even more clear.

"This trust which my Father has committed to me is more precious than all else; no one can tear them away from the hand of my Father. My father and I are one."

What is this trust of such supreme importance?

What is this enormous responsibility?

What is greater than all else in God's estimation?

Wonder of wonders, and marvel of marvels, it is His own keeping of His own sheep!

This disclosure humbles my spirit and draws me to Him with bonds of love stronger than steel, tougher than tungsten.

To realize that from God's standpoint the most precious thing is the preservation of His people, those who have come to put their confidence in Him, who have come under His control, overwhelms our hearts. In response to such compassion and caring for me there springs up within my soul an overflowing stream of gratitude. "O my God, how great You are! O my Shepherd, how wondrous are Your ways!"

I really know of no other declaration by our Lord that so stills my spirit in quiet adoration and gentle awe. To know that though I am weak and wayward and often downright difficult to handle, to Him who loves me I am very precious. This pulverizes my pride and draws me to Him.

There is something tremendously touching in this truth. It strips away all the misgivings I may have about belonging to the Shepherd of my soul. It overwhelms me with confidence and joyous assurance. "O Christ, to You I am precious!" "O great Shepherd, to You I am special! O Father, to You I am the supreme object of Your care and affection! I have been accepted, beloved, and wanted above all else."

Is it any wonder that He will do everything possible within His power to preserve and keep me in His hand? Am I surprised to see that the supreme price paid for my reconciliation to Him, was paid gladly and freely with His own life? It was His precious blood shed so willingly for us that now makes us so valuable. It is His touch upon my life and its transforming power to take a sinner and change him into a joyous son that makes me so precious to Him.

It is not who I am that makes me special to God.

Rather, now, it is *whose* I am that makes me precious.

There is no intrinsic merit in my makeup that He should esteem me as someone significant. In fact, the opposite is the case, for by His revelation He declares me to be undone before Him.

But bless His dear name, it is the impact of His life upon mine that makes all the difference. It is the immense emancipation of His salvation that sets me free to follow Him. It is the joyous sharing of Himself with me by His Spirit that empowers me to do His will. It is the strong touch of His mighty hand upon my life that changes my character, alters my conduct, and conforms my lifestyle to His.

This is to become His person. This is to become the sheep of His pasture. This is to become a member of His family. This is to enjoy an exquisite, intimate relationship in which I am His and He is mine. No wonder then that to Him I am exceedingly precious.

Of course, to our contemporaries we may not seem to be very special. In fact, some may even look upon us with a jaundiced eye, calling us "odd," "religious fanatics," or even "square." But let us never forget that they do not see us as God does. They can, at best, observe only our outward appearance and behavior, whereas our Shepherd knows us through and through. And though knowing even the worst about us still loves us with an enduring love— because we are His.

This truth came home to me with tremendous impact as a young man when I started to build up my first sheep ranch.

Because all my life previously I had worked with cattle, sheep seemed strange and unfamiliar. So I sought expert advice and help from anyone who would give it to me. I was determined that I would keep only the finest stock and breed the best animals it was possible to produce. There would be no half-way measures. My sheep were special and would become increasingly precious.

I went to see an elderly, white-haired, highly esteemed sheep breeder who lived about thirty miles away. He was a Scot, who, like so many livestock men from Scotland, stand tall among the world's finest breeders of quality animals. Gently and graciously he led me out to his fields where his flock was grazing. In a small pasture about a dozen superb, big, strong rams were resting in the shade.

An endearing look of comingled love, affection, pride, and delight filled his soft brown eyes as he leaned on the fence rail letting his gaze run over his rams.

"Well," he said softly, "pick out whichever ram you wish, son." He smiled at me warmly, "You are just a young man starting out with sheep. I want you to have the best!"

I replied that only he knew which was the finest ram. It was he who had poured the long years of his life and skill and expertise into these sheep. It was he, who, with infinite care, patience, and perseverance had selected those which ultimately would become the finest stock on the whole continent. Only he knew which was the most valuable ram in his possession. Only he knew how great and precious it was to him.

Not hesitating a moment he swung open the gate with his big gnarled hands and strode in among the rams. Quickly he caught hold of a fine, handsome ram with a bold, magnificent head and strong conformation.

"This is Arrowsmith II," he said, running his hands gently over the ram. "He is the supreme Grand Champion Suffolk Ram and has won all the top awards across the country!" He rubbed the ram's ears softly in an affectionate caress. "No one else has ever handled him but me. He's my top prize ram . . . tremendously valuable . . . more than that . . . . very precious to me in a very personal way!"

I could understand exactly what he meant. I was not surprised to see a misty look steal across his eyes. And I considered it one of the greatest honors of my life that he would permit me to take the ram home to become the top sire for my flock.

That day it came home to me with great clarity that what made the difference between one sheep and another was the owner. In whose hand had they been? Who was responsible for breeding, raising, and shepherding them? Was it a grand flockmaster? Was it a superb sheepman?

And so it is with us. Are we in God's hands? Who is handling us, shaping us? Whose are we? Whose life is molding mine?

Jesus said, "I and the Father are One!" It matters not whether we speak of being in the hands of God our Father, or under the control of Christ our Good Shepherd, or guided gently by the gracious Holy Spirit; we are inevitably in the hands of God.

To us today this is fairly understandable. We accept this concept without question. To us who believe He is precious (1 Peter 2:7).

But in speaking to the Pharisees, His straightforward declaration that He was one with His Father immediately alienated His audience. His simple, honest, legitimate claim to deity antagonized His hearers. He was declaring Himself to be God, very God, and they determined to destroy Him for it.

On that dark day when the mob grabbed up rocks from the ground to stone Him, they recognized that He had answered their query: "If Thou be Christ—tell us plainly!"

He had, and they rejected His claim.

He said He was One with God the Father, and they were furious.

He had come to them as the Good Shepherd, prepared to lay down His life for His sheep, but they would not have Him.

Only two young people from among this angry, hostile crowd had responded to His invitation: the young woman taken in adultery and the young man born blind. Both had felt the touch of His hand on their lives. Both had turned to Him for restoration. Both went on from there exulting in a new dimension of life. They were remade in the Shepherd's care.

The same choice still confronts mankind.

The majority still spurn the Good Shepherd.

Yet to those who hear His voice, respond to His call, come under His care, follow Him, His commitments come true. They find life, overflowing life, fulfilling life, and they find it in rich measure. It is *life in Christ and Christ in them.*

# A GARDENER
# LOOKS AT
# THE FRUITS
# OF THE SPIRIT

*To*
*Ursula*
*My Courageous Companion*
*Along Life's Tough Trails*

# Contents

Introduction     427

*PART I: FOUR TYPES OF SOIL*

1   Pathway People—for the Birds     432
2   Rocky People without Deep Roots     442
3   Thorny People, Lost in the Weeds     456
4   Productive People, Good Ground     468

*PART II: THE NINE FACETS OF GOD'S LOVE*

5   Love—the Life of God     482
6   Joy in the Christian's Life     492
7   Peace and "Peacemakers"     502
8   Patience     512
9   Kindness—Love Showing Mercy     520
10  Goodness—Grace and Generosity     530
11  Faith and Faithfulness in Christians     540
12  Humility—Meekness and Gentleness     550
13  Self-Control (Control of Self)—
    Temperance—Moderation     560

# Introduction

IT WAS AT the special invitation of Mr. Al Bryant, senior editor of Word Books, that this book was written. He has waited patiently during its preparation. I am grateful to God that the material shared in the pages that follow, when first shared with my congregation, was used by God's Gracious Spirit to lead some into a more intimate life with Christ. May the same be true for you the reader.

Various books, pamphlets, and articles have been published dealing with the fruits of God's Spirit. These have been very beneficial to Christians and have contributed richly to the lives of those who earnestly longed to be conformed to the character of Christ. It is my genuine hope and prayer that this will be true of this book.

The approach taken in this work, rather than being predominantly doctrinal, is very practical and deals more directly with the *how* and *why* of fruit production in our lives. As with some of my other books such as *A Shepherd Looks at Psalm 23*, *A Layman Looks at the Lord's Prayer*, *Rabboni*, *A Shepherd Looks at the Good Shepherd and His Sheep*, *As a Tree Grows*, and so on, it is written in plain layman's language.

The approach taken here is based upon the overall teaching of both the Old and New Testaments. There God's people are likened to a carefully cultivated garden. This piece of ground is tended and tilled with tender, loving care. It is watered, hedged, and husbanded with undivided devotion. God Himself in Christ by His Spirit is the Gardener. He comes looking for fruit.

Sometimes He gathers a bountiful harvest.

Sometimes the returns and response to all His efforts are minimal.

The reasons for this are dealt with in great detail in the first four chapters included under *Part I: Four Types of Soil*. This section is based on our Lord's own teaching in the parable of the sower found in the Gospels.

The individual fruits of the Spirit, and how they are produced, are then treated in *Part II: The Nine Facets of God's Love*. This section is drawn from the writings of Paul based particularly on the well-known passages in 1 Corinthians 13 and Galatians 5, where the fruits are listed.

In each case the individual attribute of God's own love, of His very life, is examined from three aspects:

1) Its function in God's own character, and how this determines His attitudes and actions toward us.

2) The growth of this fruit in our own lives and its effect upon both God Himself and others around us.

3) How it can be encouraged and cultivated in abundant measure.

From the foregoing it will be seen that a study is made of both the quantity and quality of fruit production in a Christian's life. An earnest endeavor is here made to instruct the reader in the great basic principles of fruit production.

As Henry Drummond stated clearly so long ago, fruits and flowers do not just grow by caprice in the natural realm, nor do the fruits of God's Spirit flourish in our own lives by mere whimsy or accident. Certain causes produce certain effects both in the natural and spiritual realms. It is as we begin to see that concept in Christian living that a whole new exciting life like Christ's can open up to us.

Because unnumbered millions of men and women (whether in the country or in the city) are gardeners, they will readily identify with the ideas presented here. Anyone who, like myself, loves the soil, enjoys gardening, revels in plants and shrubs, crops and trees will follow these pages with ease—and I trust pleasure.

Most of all may this book enrich your life in God beyond measure!

# Part One
*Four Types of Soil*

# 1
# Pathway People—
# For the Birds

IN THAT DELIGHTFUL romance, "The Song of Solomon" in the Old Testament, we are given a glimpse of God's view of His garden. He calls His chosen people, His bride, the Church, you and I, His garden.

There in pure, powerful, poetic language He draws for us a word picture of the enormous pleasure and delight He derives from His garden of herbs and spices, fruits and flowers. He longs for it to be a rich source of satisfaction to Him who loves and tends us with His everlasting diligence and care:

A garden inclosed is my sister,
my spouse; a spring shut up,
a fountain sealed.

Thy plants are an orchard of
pomegranates, with pleasant fruits;
camphire, with spikenard,
Spikenard and saffron; calamus
and cinnamon, with all trees
of frankincense; myrrh and aloes,
with all the chief spices:

A fountain of gardens, a well of
living waters, and streams from Lebanon.

Awake, O north wind; and come,
thou south; blow upon my garden,
that the spices thereof may flow out.
Let my beloved come into his garden,
and eat his pleasant fruits.
Song of Solomon 4:12–16

Like so many things in life, this is the ideal, the ultimate which God has in His heart for us. It is the deepest desire of His Spirit for us—that toward which so much of the energy and activity of His life is directed. He comes to us seeking for the fruits, the fragrant attributes of His own careful cultivation in our characters.

Sometimes He is distinctly disappointed.

There is no fruitage.

Or if there is, it is sparse and sickly.

Despite His most diligent endeavors there is a dearth of production.

In fact, again and again He bemoans the feeble growth and the fickle flowering which results in only meager, shrunken, shriveled fruit.

At times there spring up wild varieties in the garden of our lives: wild vines and untamed weeds.

On other occasions there is simply no crop at all. Why? Because basically there are such things as nonproductive soils and marginal land.

Of these, the first which our Lord described were the wayside soils: the land along the paths that had been beaten hard by the passing feet of those who crisscrossed it in their travels.

Anyone familiar with Africa, the Middle East, or the Orient, will quickly grasp the picture. Here multitudes of poor people struggle to wrest a meager living from tiny plots of land. Scattered across the countryside in an irregular patchwork the little gardens are transected and crisscrossed with a weblike network of tiny footpaths.

It is along these thin trails that men and women bear their burdens traveling to and fro across the countryside. Along these primitive paths, beaten hard as pavement by uncounted passing feet, children race and run and play their games. Along these paths, back and forth, move the donkeys, mules, camels, and caravans of commerce.

It was along these pathways as a boy that I ran barefooted and carefree, like the wind, growing up in Africa's sunshine.

It was along these trails that I later strode, traversing the country in search of game to feed my family. These paths were the trails leading into new terrain and high adventure over beckoning hills on the horizon.

But the soil trodden by my feet and those of ten thousand other passers-by, had become hard as brick, solid as cement, and impervious to the thrusting young roots of any seed sown upon it.

Jesus Himself had tramped hundreds of miles under the heat of the summer sun along such paths.

His feet had become dusty with the soil scuffed up under His sandals. Often He had seen the stray seed lying loose along the path. There it remained ungerminated, unmoving, unproductive.

It was a waste of seed, a waste of the gardener's energy to scatter it on such soil. It was a waste of hope to think there would ever be any crop. Such ground was good only for the birds. There they quickly spotted the seed lying bare and exposed. It was easy to fly down and snatch it away. The end result was bareness.

Jesus said some of our lives were like that soil.

He called us "Pathway People." The garden of our lives had, in places, been beaten hard as rock by the passing to and fro of other people and influences in our experience.

He did not elaborate upon who those strangers and visitors may have been. Obviously He could not begin to enumerate or catalogue them all. For with each garden plot they would differ. But for all of us there are certain people and influences that beat a path through our lives. Here are some of them. All can harden our hearts in such a way that there is little or no response to the Word of God which may have been planted there. The first includes:

*1) Our friends and associates.*

It may well be asked, "Who are the people who most frequently pound a path through my life?"

"What sort of impact do they make upon my mind?"

"Are they hardening me against God?"

"Do they compact and compress my convictions against Christ?"

"Are they slowly solidifying my sentiments against the Gracious Spirit of God?"

These are perfectly proper and appropriate questions which we need to face. Often, quite unknown to ourselves, our souls are being set against the very One who tends us with such loving attention.

Christ comes to us in compassion to implant the seed of His own special Word. He endeavors to cultivate the soil of our lives by the inner working of His own gentle Spirit. But He runs into resistance. The soil has been hardened by the impaction of a thousand other passers-by.

The trail that has been trodden across my spirit and soul is solidified by the world's ideologies and thoughts. I become conditioned by the culture of my society.

When God's view of things is laid upon my heart, when His claims are brought to bear upon me, my initial response often is, "Forget it—that's strictly for the birds."

This is why, whenever it is my joy to lead someone to Christ, one of my greatest concerns is that they should quickly establish a new circle of Christian friends and associates. They can no longer afford to allow just any strangers or alien associates to beat a path through their lives.

If they do, the results can be disastrous both for them and for God. Those who do not know Christ can so condition their outlook and set their minds against the Savior that there is stern resistance to God's Word when presented to them. There is no warm response of obedience to the overtures of the Gracious Spirit. So the ground of their lives lies bare and unproductive. The good seed of God's Word cannot germinate in such a situation. Whatever is said is snatched away by the enemy of men's souls. There is no fruit.

The attitude is one of total indifference. "That's just a bunch of nonsense—forget it—it's for the birds."

*2) The literature that we read and the T.V. programs we watch.*

The second strong influence which beats a path through our lives is the reading or viewing material to which we allow our minds and emotions to be exposed. What sort of books do I read? What kind of magazines, journals, and newspapers do I digest? What type of television or radio programs do I follow?

In this whole area we are more often than not creatures of habit. We acquire certain insatiable appetites and preferences for special periodicals, programs or professional performers. In fact, they become almost a mania. We allow ourselves to be manipulated by the mass media, becoming like clay in the hands of the author, writer or producer. We are pounded and compacted by the relentless pressures that play upon us until our convictions set like cement.

Many of the men and women who dominate the media either in publishing or programing are non-Christians. Some are violently anti-God. Such set out in subtle but severe ways to undermine and destroy the quiet faith of God's people. Through means of insidious suggestions, doubt, disparagement, and despair they endeavor to undermine our confidence in Christ.

The total tragedy of all this is that steadily and surely certain patterns of worldly thought and philosophy beat their way through our lives. As Solomon, the great Sage, wrote long centuries ago: "There is a way which seemeth right unto a man, but the end thereof are the ways of death!" (Prov. 14:12).

In the garden of our inner lives that death is utter fruitlessness. God's ideas, God's economy, God's view of life, God's standards of behavior, God's priorities simply cannot penetrate our hard hearts. There is no way the good seed of His Word can ever germinate or take root in such stubborn soil set against Him.

In the end, we are the sum total of all our own choices. The decisions as to what I shall allow my mind, emotions, will, and spirit to be exposed to rests with me. Whether or not my life shall be intractable or mellow under God's good hand in large part depends upon who I permit to beat a path through it.

*3) The music we listen to constantly.*

This constitutes a third problem area. It may come as somewhat of a shock to some readers to discover that the wrong sort of music can harden us against God.

Many kinds of music are highly commendable. Some of the very first music played out upon the planet was composed under the exquisite inspiration of God's own Spirit.

The majestic sounds of surf on sand or thundering waterfalls and tumbling streams. The mellow melodies of wind in the trees or breezes blowing across the grasslands. The gentle notes of bird song, insects in the meadow, a child's laughter or an old man's plaintive whistle all can lift our spirits.

Yet at the same time there is hard, harsh music. Coming out of the contorted culture of men apart from God, it depicts and reflects the fierce emotions and passionate despair of men in darkness. It creates enormous stress and impassioned emotions with its relentless beat.

If allowed to do so, it also can beat its way into the very personality of people. In the hands of evil men it is capable of enormous damage to the minds and emotions of the young. Noble convictions and lofty restraints can be broken down through the implacable pounding of "mad" music.

One of its most insidious dangers is that it distracts men and women from the things of God's Spirit. Instead they become fascinated with the old natural life. Their emotions are aroused and their passions inflamed. The whole personality may be set upon a perverse way of conduct contrary to God's best intentions for His children.

Unfortunately some of this music now passes amongst God's people as acceptable. Little do some realize how seriously they have been deluded. Their affections have been taken captive and their wills have been set hard against God.

*4) The pursuit of pleasure.*

It is true to say that in large measure we of the west are a hedonistic society . . . a people totally given over to the pursuit of pleasure, ease, and luxury. For many, pleasure itself has become the main preoccupation in life. To indulge one's self in some sort of sensual experience has become a mania.

As with music, so with pleasure, some pursuits are noble, commendable, and inspiring. Others can be decidedly debasing and destructive. The parent fondling and loving a child experiences pleasure and benefits both himself (herself) and the family. But the parent who gambles away his (her) earnings does a serious disservice to the whole home.

Pleasures of so many sorts can become an obsession. They tyrannize our time and dominate our days. Their constant demands upon us begin to beat a path through the brief span of our little lives. Such pleasures command so much of our thought, energy, and means that those areas they control are land in our lives lost to God.

If the resources devoted to pleasure were given over instead to Christ's interests in the world, we would indeed be amazed. Congregations would flourish. Churches would be crowded. Missionaries would multiply. The poor would be helped. The downtrodden would be lifted up. The suffering of earth's men and women would be alleviated. And like our Master Himself, many would go about doing this weary old world a great deal of good.

Our Father, the Gardener of our lives, looks for friable soil in which to produce such graces. But sad to say, sometimes our days are so packed with pleasure they pass without producing a single fruit of benevolence that will endure throughout eternity. We are too preoccupied.

5) *Our personal ambitions.*

The whole subject of personal, private ambitions poses an enormous problem for many Christians. They struggle relentlessly to accommodate their own desires to the great will of God. There is within them a tension between attaining their own ends and serving Christ.

Ambition of the right sort—putting God first in all of our affairs—seeking above all else to please Him while serving others—is a powerful implement in the hand of God for producing rich fruit in our lives and the lives of others. It breaks up the hardness of a heart set on only selfish ends. It redirects the enthusiasm and energy of the whole person into fields of usefulness.

But by the same measure the individual with strong personal ambitions of self-centeredness is soon set against God. It is an inexorable principle that any ambition established deep within our wills becomes the polestar of our daily decisions. All our choices, whether conscious or unconscious, are trimmed toward that one end. It becomes the overriding consideration that pounds out a predominant path through all our activities.

All else becomes secondary, even Christ's claims upon us.

It is for this reason that the word of the Lord through Jeremiah was: "Seekest thou great things for thyself? Seek them not" (Jer. 45:5).

In bold contrast our Lord's admonition was: "Seek ye first the kingdom of God, and his righteousness; and all these things shall be added unto you" (Matt. 6:33).

*6) Our private thought life.*

It has been well said that "I am what I think about when alone—not what I pretend to be in public." That is a most sobering and searching statement. It strips away the facade and false front.

This is the way God, our Father, knows and sees us.

He alone has carefully examined, explored, and investigated every square foot of the little garden of our lives. Having gone over all the ground with great care, He alone knows that there are some areas, some beaten pathways where He simply cannot get a single seed of His own gracious life to grow.

Perhaps more often than anything else, the ground of our persistent old thought patterns is the toughest soil He has ever had to tackle. Some of us harbor places where unforgiven grudges and grievances have hardened against others across the years. Even the dynamite of His Holy Spirit can scarcely break up the compacted clods of scorn, censure, and cruel hostility that harden us.

In some lives belligerence, animosity, and illwill have beaten a trail through our thinking for so long that not a single good seed dropped there by the Gracious Spirit of God can ever grow. The same wretched old thoughts have set our souls brick hard.

If anyone suggests to us that we should change our inner attitudes or animosity we grunt in disgust and shrug off the idea with the crass comment, "That's strictly for the birds."

God's Word states pragmatically: "As he thinketh in his heart, so is he!" (Prov. 23:7). For those who think hard thoughts, there lies hard soil that will not yield to God's good care.

Only the deepest convicting work of God's Gracious Spirit in the soul can begin to alter such tough soil. And until that happens no fruit of godliness can come from that ground.

7) *The Master's footprints.*

There is a very ancient saying in agriculture that "The finest fertilizer on a gardener's ground are his own footprints."

The attentive, enthusiastic gardener does not, like strangers and outsiders, limit himself just to the pathways. His feet do not pound and abuse the same places with their persistent passing. Rather he moves gently, tenderly, and carefully over every square foot of ground. He knows each tree, plant, shrub, and flower that flourishes on his land. He literally loves them into abundant profusion and rich production.

If anyone is to walk through my life, it should be He who tends me, cares for me, knows all about me, and longs to improve the garden of my life. This is none other than God Himself. He is the great and good gardener, the Husbandman who loves me.

This is a picture of Jesus Christ. By His gracious, kindly Spirit, He moves in our lives sharing His very own life with us. Pouring out His benefits and blessings upon us, He works deep within our spirits to mellow us and make us receptive to His own good seed. He enables us to respond to the implanting of His own new life from above. As He introduces the exotic fruits of His own person into the prepared soil of our hearts, there they take root and flourish.

The final choice as to who or what shall dominate the garden of my life pretty much depends on me. God does not choose my friends, my reading material, my music, my pleasures, my ambitions or my thoughts for me. I do this.

The ultimate question simply is: "Do I or don't I want to be a 'pathway person'? Will I allow the Master's footprints to enrich the soil of my soul? Or do I prefer to let worldly ways harden my soul against His good plan for my life?"

# 2
# Rocky People
# Without Deep Roots

THE SECOND TYPE of soil which our Lord discussed was rocky or stony ground. In modern terminology we would refer to this as marginal soil. This is soil which, even though cleared and cultivated at enormous cost and with infinite care, often produces only pathetic results. This is true because it is so stony.

One can find fields of this sort all over the earth. In my travels to some forty countries around the world I have always been deeply moved by the enormous labors of peasant people to clear rocky land for crops. I have seen this throughout the Middle East, in parts of Africa, along the Mediterranean littoral, in the British Isles, in the Eastern Provinces of Canada, in Mexico and even the Hawaiian Islands, to name a few. Small parcels of stony soil are surrounded with sturdy walls of rock lifted and cleared from the difficult ground with enormous toil, sweat, and diligence by the loving owners.

Christ was familiar with scenes such as these. Often in His travels across the Palestinian countryside He had tramped the dusty tracks that traversed the rocky hillsides where farmers fought to wrest a few meager handfuls of grain from the stony ground. He had sometimes seen a small patch of rock-riddled land glow green with the empty promise of a flourishing crop. Yet a few days or weeks later under the blazing summer sun the crop had shriveled, scorched and seared. Without deep roots the planting perished, leaving the work-worn owner with nothing but broken hopes and a mere remnant of shrunken produce.

No doubt, too, while working in His dusty little carpenter shop in Nazareth, He, the Master Craftsman, had been asked to repair and rebuild many a plow broken and battered on the boulders of some tough hillside land.

Surrounded by such reminders of rocky ground He had often reflected on the winsome Old Testament passages where, through the prophets, God had likened His people to stony ground.

A new heart also will I give you, and a new spirit will I put within you: and I will take away the stony heart out of your flesh, and I will give you an heart of flesh. And I will put my spirit within you, and cause you to walk in my statutes, and ye shall keep my judgments, and do them. And ye shall dwell in the land that I gave to your fathers; and ye shall be my people, and I will be your God. I will also save you from all your uncleannesses: and I will call for the corn, and will increase it, and lay no famine upon you. And I will multiply the fruit of the tree, and the increase of the field, that ye shall receive no more reproach of famine among the heathen. Then shall ye remember your own evil ways, and your doings that were not good, and shall loathe yourselves in your own sight for your iniquities and for your abominations. Not for your sakes do I this, saith the Lord God, be it known unto you: be ashamed and confounded for your own ways, O house of Israel.

Thus saith the Lord God; In the day that I shall have cleansed you from all your iniquities I will also cause you to dwell in the cities, and the wastes shall be builded. And the desolate land shall be tilled, whereas it lay desolate in the sight of all that passed by. And they shall say, This land that was desolate is become like the garden of Eden; and the waste and desolate and ruined cities are become fenced, and are inhabited. Then the heathen that are left round about you shall know that I the Lord build the ruined places, and plant that that was desolate: I the Lord have spoken it, and I will do it. (Ezek. 36:26–36)

There in majestic language and heart-stirring strains the great prophet of His people had predicted what He Himself would accomplish for those whom He referred to as His garden. The land which lay desolate would be redeemed, restored, brought back into productivity. The stony soil of their souls would be salvaged and made soft and friable. An incredible transformation would take place in the tough terrain of their hard hearts. And this bit of barren ground would eventually flourish like a glorious garden of Eden.

As our Lord pondered these great prophecies He knew they would come true. It could not be otherwise under the deep and diligent care of the divine gardener. It was He who saw the potential productivity lying dormant in desolate human hearts. Only He could transform the toughest soul into a gorgeous garden. As the Great Gardener He was prepared to tackle this task for His own name's sake. His reputation was at stake in the project.

These were the thoughts uppermost in our Lord's mind when He declared flatly that some of us were hard, rocky people. The reason virtually no fruit was produced in our experience was simply that we are such stony souls.

Now you may very well ask in sincerity, "What constitutes a 'stony soul'? What are the characteristics of a rocky character? What sort of conduct or behavior belies the boulders buried beneath the surface of an unproductive life? What are the earmarks of 'marginal land' that spell out crop failures?"

Before dealing with these difficulties in our lives we must pause briefly and reflect on God's view of the absolute necessity for fruit production in the lives of His people. On a number of occasions our Lord made it abundantly clear to His hearers that the final criteria by which His own were known was fruitfulness. "You shall know them by their fruit."

He told various parables portraying the care, love, and expertise applied by the Divine Gardener to His orchards, vineyards, fields, and crops. He emphasized dramatically that the husbandman, the cultivator, came looking for a crop. And unless there was fruitage the whole enterprise was a total disaster. Crop failures simply could not be tolerated.

In the Christian experience, and in the church as a whole, this fact has often been forgotten. There is a distinct tendency to sidestep this whole issue by involving ourselves in other activities which we seem to believe will cover up our barrenness.

We are not known, either to God or to a skeptical society around us, as Christians based on what we claim to believe. Nor are we identified with Christ just by the creed to which we may subscribe. We are not recognized as God's garden by some special ecstatic or supernatural experience we may have enjoyed. Our profound biblical insight or great grasp of Scripture does not make us of consequence in His economy.

We are identified and known by the sort of fruit, the quantity of fruit, and the quality of fruit borne out in our daily conversation, conduct, and character. There is no greater criterion for Christians. It is the paramount gauge of God's people.

This being the case, what then constitutes rocky ground—unproductive soil? As in nature, so in our lives, there are three major types of marginal land.

The first of these includes those deceptive areas where only a thin layer of soil lies over a vast expanse of basement rock (so-called bedrock). Millennia of weathering of the original substrata of stone has served to sheath the basement formations of rock with a shallow skin of sickly soil.

Seed dropped into such shallow soil will spring up quickly. Rocks retain both heat and moisture. So in this apparently favorable ground the seedlings appear to get off to a quick start.

Sad to say, the sudden burst of green growth is short lived. The fragile roots of the young plants run into rocky resistance. They cannot grow. There is no place to go—no depth of nourishing soil from which they can derive nourishment. There is no space in which to spread and expand their root system.

Under the heat of spring sunshine and the searing rays of intense sunlight the tender plants soon succumb. They wilt, begin to turn gray, then yellow, then brown until finally bleached and beaten by the heat, they collapse—a crop failure.

Jesus said some of us are like that.

The good seed of His Word is dropped into the shallow soil of our superficial souls. It seems to be an attractive area. At first there is a positive response. We seem to flourish. Our new Christian friends; our warm loving fellowship; our somewhat ecstatic experiences; our fresh encounters produce a sudden flush of new growth that just as quickly starts to shrivel up and wither away.

Suddenly we realize that it has been a superficial show, a "surface experience." The whole process has been painfully pathetic. The person who started off with such promise has petered out. The one who appeared to have such enormous potential for fruit production has fallen by the way. We are dismayed, and God, the Good Gardener, is disappointed.

What is the profound problem here?

What is the difficulty lying below the surface of our apparently spiritual lives?

It can be stated in a single word—*Unbelief:*

Unbelief is one of the most difficult subjects to deal with in a book of this kind. Like the massive formations of bedrock that underlie some marginal land, because it is out of sight, hidden from view, it almost defies exposure. Yet it underlies so many of our lives.

An honest attempt will be made here to deal with what unbelief is and how it stunts and shrivels us.

There are three formidable dimensions to unbelief which, if we can grasp them, will enable us to see what our spiritual soil is really like.

The first of these is this: when we come into contact with Christianity initially our belief is not really in Christ, but rather in the church. By the church I mean the pastor, the preacher, the evangelist, the counselor, the congregation, the liturgy, the fellowship, the friendship, the experiences, the sharing, the love of other so-called Christians, the acceptance and concern of God's family.

All of these are to be commended. Each plays its part in leading us to Christ. All nurture us as newborn people. But these factors are not and can never be used as a substitute for God Himself. Our faith, our belief, our trust, if invested only in the church, its people and its programs will lead to disillusionment, discouragement, and despair.

Our belief, our trust, our confidence, our faith must find its foundation in God. He is the only ground of our salvation, of our deliverance, of our hope, of our peace, of our very life.

So many of us have the roots of our faith in the shallow soil of the social life of the Christian community of which we are part. Because of this we are sure to be shaken. Preachers and teachers may prove to be less than perfect. The support and friendship of other Christians may play us false. The liturgy or social functions of the church may go flat. And since we ourselves are a part of all this the spiritual soil of our lives is soon seen to be shallow.

When things go wrong we grow hard and cynical. We find ourselves being set like stone against that which is godly. Basically all of this happens because our hope, our trust, our confidence was not in Christ, but in the church. And often when the heat is on, the church simply does not sustain us in the stress of our society and times.

On the other hand, Christ has never betrayed any confidence placed in Him. He always validates any faith or trust vested in Him. Yet most of us simply do not believe this or Him. This is what makes it so difficult for Him to produce His fruit in our lives.

Christ comes to us continually by His Gracious Spirit, inviting us quietly to put our implicit and undivided confidence in Himself. But this we decline to do. We are reluctant to trust Him— even with the most common details of our lives. We will trust and we will try almost anything or anyone else . . . but not Him.

This bedrock of unbelief in the living person of the living God is what makes it virtually impossible for Him to produce any sort of eternal, enduring results (fruit) in our lives.

The second dimension of unbelief is our refusal to actually believe God's Word. Because we do not really consider the Bible to be a valid, documentary declaration of divine truth, we question the credibility of the Scriptures. We refuse to recognize them as a supernatural revelation of spiritual integrity.

Too many of us equate the Scriptures with other writings of human origin. Naively we assume that it is our personal prerogative to accept or reject them. We consider it really not mandatory that we respond to their declarations by prompt and positive action.

The net result is that at every point where they have spoken to us and we have neglected to react as we should, the unbelief of our hearts (our wills) hardens us. It is no small wonder that Scripture repeatedly speaks of the hardness of men's hearts . . . the unwillingness of their wills to cooperate and comply with the will and wishes of God.

The enormous subsurface resistance of our subconscious minds and wills to the best intentions of God is terrifying. It is little wonder that in some lives, despite His most tender care and concern, there is nothing but a crop failure.

Let me illustrate. The Word of God instructs us emphatically to live at peace with others, in so far as it is possible. This admonition is repeated over and over. If in defiance of such directives we deliberately determine to have an ongoing vendetta with someone else, there will be *no peace.*

This fruit of God's Gracious Spirit will not be present. It will be a total failure. Not because God is an incompetent gardener, but because of the rocky resistance of my own hard will.

The third dimension to *unbelief* is our formidable preoccupation with *self.* From earliest childhood we are taught and trained to be self-reliant, self-confident, self-promoting people. *I* and *me* and *my* are the triune epicenter around which our little lives revolve. We build our entire earthly sojourn upon the premise that *myself* is the most important person upon the planet. The net result is *self-centeredness* of appalling proportions.

Moving in a diametrically opposite direction comes the call of Christ to us to forget ourselves (lose our lives); to follow Him (that is, put Him at the heart and center of our affairs); and give ourselves in glad service to others.

It all goes very much against our grain. We may not say so publicly, but privately we are convinced this is the sure path to oblivion and nothingness. *We really do not believe that God in Christ has the only formula for a fulfilling and abundant life.*

The simple consequence is that though mentally and perhaps even emotionally we may claim to believe Christ, deep down in our wills, dispositions, and spirits we do not. We regard Him as an idealist not truly worthy of our undivided allegiance, loyalty, and confidence. In such stony souls underlain by incredible unbelief the Spirit of God strives in vain to produce the fruits of His own winsome character.

There are three simple steps that can be taken to break up our unbelief under the dynamic impulse of God's Spirit.

*1) Ask God in sincerity to show you Himself.* Ask Him to let you see what He is really like. When you discover that He is the Good Gardener who loves you immensely and longs to make your life productive it will pulverize your proud stony heart.

*2) Ask Christ by His Spirit to show you yourself and the hard condi-*

*tion of your own inner will.* When it dawns upon your dull soul how defiant and difficult you can be, it will break your heart and prepare it for His deep work.

*3) Ask God by His Spirit to impart to you great faith*—the faith to trust Him implicitly; the faith to have complete confidence in Christ and in His commitments to us; the faith of obedience to simply step out and do whatever He asks by His Spirit through His Word.

The second type of rocky ground is what we generally call stony soil. This is land littered with loose stones and boulders varying in size from that of large eggs to random rocks weighing hundreds of pounds. Frequently this is very fertile soil which requires enormous labor and expense to clear for proper cultivation.

My boyhood home in the heart of Africa was located on such land. My father had acquired 110 acres of desolate land on a high ridge. With tremendous toil, using teams of oxen, he literally tore thousands of stones from the ground. In fact they were numerous enough to build all the walls of all the buildings he erected on the property. And where the stones had lain there were planted thousands of trees of all sorts—fruit trees, coffee trees, ornamental trees, and firewood trees. Gorgeous gardens, too, and luxuriant pastures for cattle, replaced what previously had been desolate and derelict land. It was in fact a down-to-earth demonstration of the prophecy foretold by Ezekiel. It was a garden of Eden flourishing where before there had been nothing but stones, scrub thorn, and the cry of the jackals in the wilderness.

In the Christian experience there are likewise wilderness areas. There are areas of stony soil, ground in which the good seed of God's Word has been dropped. It germinates, flourishes briefly, comes up against rocks of resistance, then withers away to nothing.

Any point or any place in life where a person prefers to disobey God, to go his own way and do his own thing is stony soil. This is what it means to have a hard heart. It is the kind of ground where the good gardener encounters enormous grief and labor to get anything to grow.

Those areas in which we stubbornly refuse to comply with

Christ's commands are barren, boulder-strewn soil. We block the movement of His Spirit in our affairs, hindering the action of His Word. There is no growth. Nothing happens. Our souls are impoverished and our lives languish. And there is no ongoing growth that will produce fruit.

By His Gracious Spirit, God wants to clear the stony, stubborn soil of our souls. He wants to plant the trees of His own righteousness in every spot from which a stone of disobedience has been dug. Our Divine Gardener wants to cultivate a gorgeous garden where before there were only barren boulders of bald resistance to His Word.

If this is to happen we must want it to take place. By faith in Christ we must believe that He actually can take the waste land of our lives and transform it into a garden of God. We must ask Him to give us a vision, a preview, a glimpse of what He can do with a hard heart, a stony will, a stubborn and wayward disposition. Perhaps He will show us the miracle of transformation He has performed in another person's character.

This is basically what happened to me as a teenager. My earliest childhood impressions of my Dad were of a tough, demanding man. He was hard with himself, hard on others, and difficult for God to handle. But as the years rolled by, the Lord in His own persistent, powerful way was clearing the stony ground in my father's life, just as he himself was removing the boulders from his own hillside acres.

The result was that throughout my teens I watched, awestruck, the transformation that took place in Dad's character. Gradually, surely and steadily he mellowed into one of the most lovable men I ever met. He became gracious, gentle, forbearing and thoughtful. His entire life was fragrant with the fully ripened fruitage of God's Spirit.

If in truth we want such a change of character it can take place. We will earnestly and honestly determine to do God's will, setting ourselves to comply with Christ's commands. Attuning ourselves to be sensitive to His Spirit as He speaks to us through His Word, we will take time to meditate over the Scriptures. We will take them seriously and will respond to the call of Christ. We will allow ourselves to be open and available to the inner working of God Himself. And we will be amazed at our growth in godliness.

*"For it is God who worketh in you both to will and to do of his good pleasure" (Phil. 2:13).*

The third type of rocky soil is what is known as gravelly ground. It is land interlaced with layers of gravel or streaks of sand. Frequently a thin cover of top soil conceals the true condition of the ground beneath the surface.

Seeds or plants that take root here will generally spring up swiftly. They show rather sudden, spectacular growth, but a few days of hot sun and wind soon wipe them out as they wither away. The substrata of sand and gravel is like a sieve through which all the moisture and nutrients drain away. Roots shrivel and die. And only desolation remains.

Our Lord had often seen fields of this sort. They were common on the ridges and slopes of marginal land that often left their owners impoverished. He said some of us were like that gravelly ground. Little or nothing would grow there successfully.

What is the parallel in our personal lives?

There are two.

The gravel layer that lies below the surface with so many of us is the ground of our *ingratitude*. It is the deeply ingrained grumbling in which so many of us indulge. We complain against God for the way in which He handles our lives and arranges our circumstances. Peevishly we protest our lot in life, finding fault with the way He leads us and the places He puts us.

Of course most people do not proclaim their petty grievances in public hearing. Quite the opposite. Most prefer to put on a fine front. They pretend that all is well behind their false façade. But deep beneath the surface of their superficial smiles lie hard, resistant, sometimes defiant attitudes of resentment toward God's arrangement of their affairs.

This is absolutely fatal to any sort of Christian growth. It grieves God's Gracious Spirit. In fact, He simply cannot produce His fruit in such grumbling, gravelly ground. In Hebrews 3:12–19 we are warned solemnly not to harden ourselves against God by complaining. This is what the nation of Israel did when delivered from Egypt. It provoked God to great anger.

The streak of sand in our experience is the habit of fault-finding, criticism, and censure of others. Unless we are alerted to this, it can easily become a chronic condition. We can develop a *mindset* that habitually sees only the dark, difficult side of life. Conditioned and accustomed to hard attitudes of condemnation that invariably put other people in a bad light, we become tough, demanding, and abrasive. This is not good ground in which the Divine Gardener can grow His sunny fruits.

He comes to us and urges upon us several steps for dealing with our grumbling against God and our fault-finding with others.

Instead of raging against the Lord for the way He manages our lives, let us carefully consider all the benefits He bestows. Take a piece of paper; sit down alone in a quiet spot; write down one by one all the good things—the delights and pleasures He has made possible for you. List everything—the sound of music; the laughter of children; the sunrise; the scent of a rose; the clasp of a friend's hand; the loyalty of a dog. If one is honest, there is no end to the list. It is an exercise that will break our grumbling, pulverize our pride and humble our hard hearts before a gracious God.

Look for and deliberately seek out the lovely, beautiful, noble, honest, and gracious aspects of life. Search for the best in others. We are told pointedly to do this in Philippians 4.

Lastly use the three great words that spell out growth in godliness.

*1. Acknowledge*—"O God, You are very God. You know exactly what You are doing with me. It is for my best. All is well."

*2. Accept His Management.* Herein lies peace and rest. No longer will I resist or resent Your work in my life. You are the Good Gardener.

*3. Approve of Christ's Arrangement of Your Affairs.* It is Your intention I should become fruitful. Under Your good hand this will happen. Thanks for everything.

This will turn pouting into praise—grumbling into gratitude. It is the key to releasing all the energies of God the Holy Spirit to move fully and freely through my daily life. He will do exceedingly more than I can ever ask or think (Eph. 3:19–21).

# 3
# Thorny People,
# Lost in the Weeds

THE THIRD TYPE of soil which Our Lord referred to as being *non-productive* was thorny ground. Such ground was infested with weeds and thistles. Any garden riddled and choked with noxious plants simply was incapable of fruit production.

Because of its diverse topography and terrain, some of it semi-desert, Palestine was notorious for its wide variety of thorns, thistles and briers. Over 200 species of undesirable weeds invaded cultivated land to compete with the crops planted with such painstaking care. It was a never-ending struggle to grow good gardens and keep fields free of foreign plants.

Both in the Old Testament Hebrew text and the New Testament Greek some seventeen different words are used to describe this undesirable, thorny sort of growth. In the English language a variety of words are likewise used to translate the meaning. We find such nouns as *thorns, thistles, briers, brambles,* and so on appearing in the scriptural account.

Always, the picture portrayed in connection with gardening or farming is that of the enormous problems posed by the growth of these undesirable plants. Jesus was very familiar with the people's struggle to produce a harvest of fruit or grain in the face of competition from thistles and thorns in their crops.

He used pointed parables to illustrate this fact. In His mighty Sermon on the Mount, He asked the point-blank question, "Do men gather grapes of thorns, or figs of thistles?" (Matt. 7:16). If one's vineyard was choked with brambles, he did not look for a bumper crop of grapes. It was a straightforward case of one or the other.

Brambles and briers, thorns and thistles had the nasty capacity to so crowd and choke the grower's planting that the crop was utterly smothered and stifled. There was virtually *no production— no fruitage.*

Our Lord made the point that some of our lives were just like that. They were so infested with noxious weeds that there could be no harvest.

Unlike our modern agricultural techniques where all sorts of selective herbicides are used to control weeds in crops, primitive people had only one remedy—clean cultivation of the ground. And this was a well-nigh impossible task. Thistle seeds could be blown in on the wind from miles away. Wild birds that had fed on berries and brambles could drop their dung on any garden depositing foreign seeds in their droppings. Wild animals and domestic beasts could carry all sorts of burrs and weed seeds in their coats across the countryside.

So there was no such thing as an eternally clean garden. It was only the owner's constant diligence and care that could guarantee a beautiful and productive piece of ground. And often even then, in spite of his most persistent efforts, the invaders would be present to prevent full fruitage.

Jesus likened some of us to this sort of weed-infested soil. He declared very forthrightly that such a garden was simply *unfruitful.*

The question which we must therefore ask ourselves is solemn and searching. *"What is growing in the Ground of my life?"*

Putting it another way we might ask, "What takes up the most space in my life? What occupies most of my time and attention? What has gained prime place in my priorities? What has become the chief outgrowth and production in the overall performance of my life? What is the net result of my living—worthless weeds or fine fruit of eternal value?"

Christ made it clear that there were three types of weeds:

1) The cares, anxieties, worries or interests of this world.
2) The deceitfulness of wealth; the attraction of affluence.
3) The covetousness for things; the magnetism of materialism.

Because of the intense competition from some of these influences, our lives are total crop failures. The good seed of God's Word implanted in us by His Gracious Spirit simply comes to nothing. It is simply smothered by fierce and formidable competition from foreign ideals. Of these the first Jesus named would appear to be the least dangerous.

## 1. Worldly Cares

Like death and taxes, the cares of living are just an integral part of the very warp and woof of life. We delude ourselves if we believe that somehow the children of God are exempt from the stresses and strains of the human family.

Those preachers and teachers who would lead us to think that a Christian's life can be a trouble-free trip do us all a great disservice. It simply is not so. The Word of God makes it abundantly apparent that "many are the afflictions of the righteous" (Ps. 34: 19). Our Lord declared flatly, "In this world ye shall have tribulation—but be of good cheer, I have overcome the world" (John 16:33).

All of us, without exception, have laid upon us the responsibility to earn a proper and appropriate living. Whatever our lot in life may be, we are instructed to work diligently and heartily. We are taught to provide adequately for our families, and we are told to pay our taxes, to meet our moral obligations as law-abiding people. We have clearly defined guidelines laid down in God's Word as to what our behavior should be in the human community of which we are an integral part.

It follows, therefore, that life does make definite demands upon us. If we are to live well-rounded, balanced, fruitful lives we must meet the responsibilities placed upon us by both God and man. How do we do this? How do we avoid becoming eccentric ascetics who desire to withdraw entirely from the challenge of society? How do we keep from engrossing ourselves in the world so that we become engulfed and smothered by its deceptive and destructive philosophies or ideologies?

Our Lord dealt with this dilemma in great detail in His majestic Sermon on the Mount in Matthew 6. There He reassures our questing hearts that our Heavenly Father does know the needs and demands laid upon us by life. He knows we require food, shelter, drink, and clothing. Since He provides adequately for birds and lilies, He likewise provides for His people upon the planet.

The crux of the issue is my preoccupation with those cares which press in upon me. Do I really believe that my Heavenly Father, if I trust Him fully, will care for me? Where are my priorities in the picture? Is the focus of my attention upon earning my living by the sweat of my own endeavors—or is it upon the trustworthiness of God?

As a word of personal witness to the reliability of the Lord I would like to share my own experience here. Up until I was nearly forty I worried incessantly about making a living, providing for my family, success in my endeavors, security for the future. And even when all of these were taken care of my dear wife would say, "Phillip, even if you haven't anything to worry about you will soon invent something to fret over."

It was at that advanced age in life, through a most traumatic experience, which I shall not describe here, I was virtually stripped of all I had struggled to secure. In total abandon and trembling, childlike faith I flung myself upon the care and commitments of my Heavenly Father. The past twenty years have been a most powerful demonstration of His willingness to provide in a remarkable manner for my every need in all areas of my life. This is not to boast but to give hearty thanks for His total trustworthiness.

It is a straightforward question of priorities. The instant an individual determines to put Christ at the center of his life, to give Him the place of priority and consideration, he is out of the woods. He is no longer lost among the weeds of worry and concern. The ground of his being is cleared of the confusing entanglements of his contemporaries. There is now time and space to produce fruit for God of eternal consequence.

A second aspect which we need to discover in this dilemma of worldly cares is the time factor. Christ emphasized strongly that each day did have its difficulties. "Sufficient unto the day is the evil thereof" (Matt. 6:34).

We cannot afford to drag the distress of either yesterday or tomorrow into today. I cannot allow myself to "borrow sorrow from tomorrow." I must not permit the sure joy of this day to be jeopardized by the uncertainties of the future or the empty regrets of the past.

In very truth I have only today. Yesterday is gone forever. There is no guarantee I shall be here tomorrow. So in reality I am locked into a single *day-tight* time and space concept. I have the choice—either I can worry my way through it or I can revel and rejoice in this interval of time provided by my Father.

One of my favorite phrases is, "Relish the moment." This is the day the Lord has arranged for me so I will rejoice and delight in it (See Ps. 118:24).

Living in this attitude of carefree goodwill frees our spirits from the stress and tension of worldly cares. Like the continual cultivation of a garden to keep it clear of weed growth, so this daily discipline of delighting in God's faithful provision for us is a soul-liberating process.

As I live this way the ever present would-be weeds of worry, anxiety, and preoccupation with petty concerns wither away. They cease to dominate my days. Instead, I become engrossed with the great and joyous purposes of God for both the planet and His people. My focus is transferred from my needs to those of others. In all of this there is abundant opportunity to be productive, helpful, and great-hearted. In the Master Gardener's hands, even my most humble endeavors become fruitful beyond my wildest dreams.

The third way to clear the weeds of worry from our lives is best summed up in the simple little rhyme: "I'll give God my best; He will do the rest!"

Whatever life gives us opportunity to do, let us do it well. Let us do it to the best of our ability, then leave the results with Christ.

It is not for us to decide or determine what the net result of our living will be. It is God who keeps the eternal accounts. Only He can ascertain that which is of consequence in His economy.

Yet we rejoice over each day we can live for Him. We give hearty and humble thanks for His abundant and gracious care, living in a constant "attitude of gratitude." To live this way is to live out in the open sunlight of His presence; it is to live in honest dignity and strength; it is to live in serene simplicity; it is to live above the clutter and complications of a complex society that would crowd and choke out our fruitfulness for God.

## 2. The Deceitfulness of Wealth

Some Christians have a distinct misunderstanding about wealth. Wealth in itself is not wrong. Riches are not necessarily evil. Affluence is not always a sin. Immense finances are not invariably wicked.

If so, then God would certainly never have bestowed wealth on men like Abraham, Joseph, Solomon, Job or Hezekiah . . . not to mention some modern-day heroes of the faith.

The difficulty lies in our attitude toward wealth. How is it dispensed? For what purposes is it accumulated? To what ends is it dedicated?

For most people the dilemma is the deceitfulness of riches. Riches have the capacity to distort our thinking; riches may blind us to eternal values; riches also have the insidious ability to dominate our desires.

By its very nature wealth leads us to put our trust in it rather than in the One who gave us the ability to accumulate it. Riches have a subtle way of suggesting to us that they themselves can provide security and serenity. In very truth they do just the opposite.

I have found that very often the richest and most wealthy people are also among the least secure and serene. They fret endlessly over the possibility of losing their wealth. This leads to endless worry, anxiety, and discontent.

Many very wealthy people, if not preoccupied with losing their wealth, are equally exercised about increasing it. It is not enough to own one car—we need two! One home is not enough. We need a summer house as well. It is not enough to have one million dollars. Two or even three are better. So there really is no end to the continuous scramble.

Jesus knew all about this. He told parables to point out the folly of pursuing the pot of gold at the end of the rainbow. It was a pointless, pathetic, fruitless pursuit. Remember the rich farmer who determined to build ever larger and better barns to hold his bumper crops? He ended up a pauper who had never established any credit with God. He had no eternal crop of lasting value in God's economy. All his frantic efforts had terminated in fruitlessness as far as God was concerned. He was a fool who had been deceived by his own insatiable desire for wealth. His had been a weedy life, lost in the jungle growth of "getting, getting, getting."

The world's philosophy is "What can I get out of life?" In blazing contrast Christ comes along with the clear, clean, cutting command: "Give what you can to your generation!"

To follow the one is to become entangled in the undergrowth of selfish, self-centered living. To follow Christ is to have the ground of our lives cleared of the constricting weeds that would wrap themselves around us in our pursuit of wealth for its own sake.

Obviously we cannot devote our days to nothing but making money and at the same time devote them to serving God.

The question comes down to this: "Is wealth my master or is Christ?" Who controls what?

For the child of God there is only one way to go in this area. Any riches that come to me are a trust from the Lord. They are not mine to invest, use or squander recklessly. I have no right ever to claim that I am a self-made person. That is colossal conceit and an affront to God. Every capacity, ability to think, strength to work, and means to accumulate wealth comes from Him as a gift. Therefore in humility and simplicity I assume stewardship for all that He entrusts to me. I use it sparingly and wisely to meet my own needs, generously and graciously to minister to the needs of others.

To handle wealth this way is to be a fruitful garden for God. To use it any other way is to allow my outlook, thinking, and behavior to be choked up with the crass commercialism of a godless society. Ultimately in so doing I shall lose my own soul and there will be no fruit for the Great Good Gardener.

In passing let it be said, especially for young people, that if God finds you to be trustworthy in small things at first, He will quickly entrust you with greater riches. Few are the men and women to whom God can give great wealth. It too often goes to their heads. They don't know how to handle it. But those who do can use riches and wealth in mighty ways to produce abundant fruit for the Lord.

It is they who clothe the naked, feed the hungry, heal the sick, educate the illiterate, bring the good news to the lost, cheer the weary, and heal the hurts of a sick and suffering world.

"In as much as ye have done it unto one of the least of these my brethren, ye have done it unto me" (Matt. 25:40).

## 3. The Magnetism of Materialism

Jesus put it bluntly: "The lusts of other things entering in, choke the word, and it becometh unfruitful" (Mark 4:19).

As with wealth so with *things*—many of them in themselves are neither wrong nor wicked. It is the desire for and determined drive to attain wealth which so often divert us from the more important eternal, divine values in life.

We settle for second best.

We are occupied with tinsel while we could be reaching for the stars.

Having grown up overseas in a frugal family and a humble home, I was trained to live in a rather spartan manner. I have yet to adapt myself to the affluence and luxury of North America. All during my formative years I lived among Africans who existed on very little. Their possessions were minimal, their wants remarkably few, and yet their contentment, good will and gay laughter were contagious. Amidst their simplicity and what we in the West would consider stern austerity, I learned first-hand the very basic truth of our Lord's remarks in this area: "Take heed, and beware of covetousness; for a man's life consisteth not in the abundance of the things which he possesseth" (Luke 12:15).

Yet everything in our culture cries out against this concept. Western civilization is based no longer upon the great verities in the Word of God. It simply is not true to say now "We trust in God." Rather our whole society has shifted its weight and reliance upon the twin pillars of the productivity of its industry and the purchasing power of its people.

This is why we face imminent disaster.

Never in human history has any civilization used its mind, strength, and genius to invent, manufacture, and market such a multiplicity of *things*. I am basically a person of simple wants. The array of gadgets, gimmicks, and gaudy displays in our large stores quite literally frightens me. Such a plethora of extravagance makes me uneasy. The endless array of food, clothing, furniture, hardware, textiles, and other items that flood from our factories leave me ill at ease. All I want is to get outside the stores into the sunshine and fresh air. I don't need ten thousand different items to lend dignity to my life or happiness to my home.

But our culture is not content to leave me alone in my simple lifestyle. Day and night the mass media, magazines, newspapers, books, billboards, and flyers crammed into my bulging mail box scream at me to buy this, strive for that, acquire something here, come to possess something there. Relentlessly pressure is applied, both in bold, blatant ways and in smooth, subtle, sophisticated sales pitches to cause me to purchase more than I really need, all much beyond my means.

Those born and raised in this culture are of course completely conditioned to it. They accept this vaunted way of life, built around things, to be the best in the world.

Combined with all of this is the entire credit system. It enables a person, with nothing more than his name on a piece of paper, to purchase almost anything he or she may desire. From boots to Buicks you can buy what your heart desires even if it does plunge you so deep in debt that it may take you twenty years to recover.

The net result of all this *in-put* into our lives is that most of us are irrevocably preoccupied with the magnetism of materialism. We are not only totally mesmerized by the attraction of things, we are snared and engulfed in the difficulties of discharging our debts to pay for them. As if that were not enough we later discover that they contribute virtually nothing to the sum total of human happiness, but more often turn out to be an absolute headache. We do not possess them, they possess us. We are enslaved and trapped into the treadmill of an economy based on appalling waste and obsolescence.

Our Lord said emphatically that it was this sort of *in-put* that would choke out His good Word in the gentle garden of our lives.

Against the garrulous demands of our consumer-oriented society, God's Word sometimes seems absurd. The world urges us to "get, get, get." Christ comes along and says, "Give, give, give." The world says happiness lies in everything from sex to spaghetti. Christ comes along and says our serenity is in knowing Him. The world says make a big splash and show your success by your possessions—impress people. Christ comes along and says that the greatest amongst us is the one who is willing and ready to be a servant.

Who has truth? Where is the answer? Can we really be fruitful and productive for God amid all the pressures put upon us? Or are we going to let the insidious ideologies, the crass concepts of commercialism invade our lives like weed seeds blown into a carefully cultivated piece of ground? Are we going to permit the false philosophies of a humanistic society to choke out the crop of eternal values which God by His Spirit wishes to produce in our experience?

Where is my heart? In things or in Christ?

Where are my affections? On possessions or on God?

Where are my priorities? In covetousness or in cooperation with the compelling overtures of God's Gracious Spirit?

To what refrains does my soul respond? To the clamor of my contemporary world or to the call of Christ the Good Gardener?

I know of only two ways in which we can be turned away from the tyranny of our times, the vicious, victimizing obsession with *things*. Here they are. They will clear the ground of our lives from the weeds of human deception quicker than anything else.

1) God made man for *Himself*, to be His child. He created us with the incredible capacity not only to commune with Him, but to know Him intimately—to be His companions, conformed to His very character.

Anyone who devotes his life, time, and attention to any lesser thing, no matter how grand or noble or glamorous, has missed the mark and the whole purpose of living.

To allow myself to be encumbered and enslaved by things is to have the whole ground of my being cluttered and choked with transient values—whereas I could be producing fruit of eternal duration and consequences. A poor exchange indeed.

2) It is only as I respond promptly and positively to the claims of Christ upon my life and character that I will discover He alone has truth. He alone holds the secret of serenity—strength and stability in a shaky society.

It is in the face of the expulsive power of this new found affection for Him that the attraction and magnetism of materialism will wane. Then the ground of my garden will be free of weeds to allow Him to produce therein His own beautiful fruit.

# 4
# Productive People,
# Good Ground

IN BOLD AND dramatic contrast to the three types of unfruitful, nonproductive soils, Jesus depicted a piece of good ground. He said that when good seed was sown on good soil there could be a flourishing garden full of fruit.

In some instances the returns would be thirty, sixty or even one hundred times that which was originally planted. This was genuine productivity and it was the sort of return the gardener fully expected from his labor on the land.

It is important to recognize the basic fact that rocky soils, weed-infested ground, and land lost to pathways were considered *nonproductive*. They were simply incapable of growing a crop in their natural condition. It was not a question of being somewhat or partially fruitful. There was *nothing*. It was lost ground. There was no crop.

Only the painstaking labor and loving care of a diligent owner could alter their condition. It required tremendous toil with teams and tools to break up hard ground; to clear stony soil; to cultivate and clean up weed-choked land.

The hardened clay clods, set like cement under passing feet, had to be pulverized with plows and harrows and hoes. The rock-riddled ground had to be cleared, the stones carted away to make room for the crop. The roots and stumps of thorny growth had to be torn from the soil and the weed growth piled and burned to fit the garden for the seed. It all required a tremendous amount of toil to turn a piece of untamed, untilled land into good ground for a garden. *Even the best of soil must first be broken before it can become beautiful.*

Only yesterday afternoon, in the mellow warmth of a late September afternoon, I began to prepare a piece of garden soil on a wild, untamed chunk of virgin land that has never grown anything but wild brambles and the hated knapweed. No shovel had ever penetrated this ground before. And as I worked the sweat streamed from my back.

The labor I was engaged in was a labor of love. I love the soil. I am a man close to the land. One of the great delights of my long and adventurous life has been to take marginal soils, whether in great sweeping acreages on large ranches or on little garden plots, and bring them into a state of maximum productivity. This demands hard work and skill.

But it is deeply rewarding and tremendously exciting.

Yesterday the piece of ground on which I began work was probably the least promising corner of my whole property that lies beside a lovely lake. It was choked with weeds. Gnarled granite boulders jutted up here and there through its surface soil. It was riddled with the tangled roots of old wild rose bushes and tough greasewood that had grown there unchecked. For untold years it had been tramped hard where people had hiked across it.

In spite of all these defects and disadvantages I began to dig. I dug with joy and hope. I dug with a song in my spirit, for I could see beyond the boulders, the weeds, the roots, and the hard crusted ground. I could see a garden flourishing there the following spring.

The perspiration poured from me into the warm autumn sun. My muscles heaved and strained as I turned the tough sod. It took tremendous tugs to tear some of the wild roots from the ground. Soon I had a large pile of them ready to burn. Again and again my shovel struck rock. From this small patch of ground I hauled away wheelbarrow loads of stones. Mounds of accumulated debris had to be dug away.

When I was through for the day I smiled. For a good piece of ground, carefully husbanded, lay smooth and dark and soft and clean ready to be sown next spring. There would burst from this warm earth a rich array of green plants that would produce basketfuls of fruit and vegetables next summer.

There would be more than enough bounty to feed ourselves and our friends.

This is what God, the Great, Good Gardener has to do in our lives. We are not naturally "good ground." Beyond our hardness and perverseness He sees the potential locked up in our stony souls. He works on us in hope and love.

None of us is too tough for Him to tackle. In spite of our perverseness, pride, and pollution He can transform us from a wasteland to a well-watered garden. We should want it that way. It does not come easily. It does not happen in a single day. The digging, the clearing, the cultivation may seem to us to be devastating; the disciplining of our souls may seem severe. Yet afterwards it produces the peaceable fruits of His own planting (see Heb. 12:10, 11).

Too many of us as Christians are content to remain wild, waste land. We much prefer to stay untouched by God's good hand. In fact we are frightened of having our little lives turned over by the deep work of His convicting Spirit. We don't want the shearing, cutting, powerful thrust of His Word to lay us open to the sunlight of His own presence. We prefer to remain weedy ground and stony soil—or pathetic pathway people.

We delude ourselves into thinking that out of our old unchanged characters and dispositions somehow a good crop is coming forth. It simply cannot be. You simply do not gather grapes from a thistle patch nor figs from wild brambles. And the good gardener does not even come there looking for fruit. It is strictly a *no-crop* condition. It is a total loss to both ourselves and God.

Our Lord was very specific in describing the spiritual aspects of productive people. Here they are stated in His own words.

1) They are people who bear His Word and all that it implies.

2) They are people who receive and accept that Word.

3) They are people whose lives because of that Word produce the fruit of God's Gracious Spirit in their characters, conduct, and conversation.

This being the case we should carefully examine each of these aspects to understand exactly what Christ meant. The first is *hearing the Word*.

During the days of His earthly sojourn among men, one of the greatest distresses to our Lord was this question of people "hearing" His Word. Over and over He reiterated the fact that "Ears ye have but ye hear not." Or couching the same sentiment in another way He would insist that "hearing" had to be linked with "doing." It was not enough merely to be exposed to truth. There simply had to be a positive response on the part of the hearer.

There are three definite, deliberate steps involved in "hearing" God's Word in order for it to become effective and fruitful. Here they are:

1) *I must recognize it is God who is speaking.* Unless His Word is held in great respect as being of divine content I will simply equate it with other men's words.

Only when I reach the point where I solemnly place great store upon what He says will it ever become a powerful force in my life.

Only when I really take Him seriously will His Word be made Spirit and life (supernatural life) to me.

Only when I recognize that what I am hearing is in fact and in truth divine revelation designed by deity for my own good, will I hear it as a word from above.

God has chosen to articulate Himself to me as a man in four ways: Through the natural created universe around me; through His Word expressed by inspired men who reported it in human language I can read and understand; through the person of Jesus Christ, the Word made flesh, exemplified in human form; through those other humble men and women in whom He deigns to reside by His own Gracious Spirit.

He may speak to me deliberately and distinctly through any one or all of these ways. It is my responsibility then to recognize: "O God, You are communicating with me. I will listen. I do recognize Your voice communing with me."

2) Secondly, to hear His Word implies essentially that *I must respond to it in a positive way.*

In other words I must alert myself to act on it.

I must set aside whatever else preoccupies my thoughts and give my undivided attention to the Lord.

It is not good enough to "half listen" to God. He demands my total concentration on what He is conveying to me. He knows that anything less will leave me half-hearted.

Unless this happens the seed of that Word is simply snatched away by the birds. I don't really believe it. It has fallen on stony soil. Or I am too caught up with other concerns, so it is smothered out.

3) The third step in "hearing" God speak implies that promptly and swiftly *I shall run to do what He requests.*

My positive response results in immediate action on my part. His will is done. His wishes are carried out His desires are complied with happily. His commands are executed without delay or debate.

In short I simply do what He asks me to do.

This is faith in action—the faith of obedience.

This is the gateway into the good ground of God's garden.

This is to "hear" the Word and have it come alive.

This is to have Him implant the good seed of His good intentions for me in the good, warm, open, prepared soil of my responsive soul.

The seed will germinate. The young plants will prosper and grow vigorously. There will be fruit production of His choosing—a harvest that delights Him and refreshes others.

The second striking characteristic of good ground, according to Jesus, was that *it received the word.*

The word "receive" is one of the terms we glibly bandy about in Christian circles without stopping to discover what it really means. We speak of "receiving" Christ, "receiving" the gifts of the Spirit, "receiving" forgiveness. In just the same way we talk freely about "accepting" Christ or "accepting" our salvation without really understanding its full implications and responsibilities.

All too often to "receive" or "accept" are merely thought of in terms of taking from the hand of another that which is offered as a gift.

But to receive or accept in a spiritual sense goes far beyond this limited view.

First of all it means that I must be open, receptive, and amenable to God and His Word.

There cannot be either reluctance or resistance on my part.

It implies that my mind, emotions, disposition, and spirit are open—that I am indeed friable soil prepared by the deep, diligent *in-working* of God's Spirit, ready to receive and accept the seed of His Word introduced to me.

If I am a person with a closed mind, with strong personal prejudices, with deep difficult doubts, with bigoted presuppositions about eternal verities, quite obviously I am not ready to receive divine truth. His Word in me will come to nothing. It will be wasted on the birds of unbelief, on rocky resentment, and on the weeds of worldliness.

So to receive God's Word means I must welcome it. I must reach out to take and accept it eagerly—ready to literally assimilate and incorporate it into the very soil of my daily experience.

It is not some peculiar philosophy relegated to religious ritual once or twice a week. Rather, that viable, vital word is something that must spring to life as it germinates in the good soil of my daily experiences with Christ.

The whole idea of "receiving" God's Word is also associated with my total availability to it. The whole ground of my life needs to be reachable.

In a good garden there are no spots still littered with stones. There are no odd corners cluttered and choked out with weeds. There are no beaten paths where nothing at all can grow. All the ground has to be tilled. All the soil must finally be fitted for fruitfulness.

It will take time to do this. But it must be done. The Spirit of God is very persistent. The Good Gardener must have full management. Christ comes to take over every area made arable.

The extent to which a piece of good ground has received and responded to good sowing is eventually demonstrated by how little soil shows. The entire area planted will be taken over, covered and smothered in a luxuriance of green growth. The onlooker will see, not the soil, but the bountiful produce on it.

So with our lives. If in truth we have received the good Word, and the very life of Christ flourishes, it is the fruitage of His character, the fragrance of His conduct that will be evident to those around us.

It is proper and appropriate in a book of this sort to pause here briefly and explain in simple language exactly what it means to receive Christ. For He was and is "The Word Incarnate" i.e. "The Word of God very God made manifest, expressed visibly and audibly in human form."

The beloved, aged John, writing in the twilight of his life declared emphatically: "He came unto his own, and his own received him not. But as many as received him, to them gave he power to become the Sons of God . . ." (John 1:11,12).

From the cataclysmic point in human history when Adam the federal head of the human family flatly refused to comply with God's best intentions for him, all men have been contaminated with self-will that leads to sin. In spite of the pride, perverseness, and pollution of people that results from sin and selfish self-centeredness God has come to seek and to save and to reconcile wayward lost men and women to Himself.

Because man's best efforts to reclaim and restore himself in the presence of an incredibly holy, righteous, and loving God fall far short, he is incapable of his own redemption. God Himself had to intervene on our behalf. He chose to become the supreme Substitute, who alone could atone for our misconduct and expiate for our sins.

This He did in the person of His own Son, Jesus Christ, the Savior of the world. He is *the Word, the very visible expression of the invisible God.* This "God in the flesh" came to live, move, serve, and die amongst us—to be resurrected and return to His former glory.

The "perfect doing" and the "perfect dying" of God in Christ, because it was that of the *Infinite One Himself,* suffices for all men of all time, be there billions upon billions of human beings.

The good news of our salvation, our forgiveness, our acceptance with God is that He Himself, in Christ, has done all that is necessary to deliver us from the dilemma of our sins and self-will. Through His shed blood, broken body, and complete sacrifice on our behalf He has paid the price for our perverseness, pride, and pollution. It matters not in what area of our lives we may have sinned.

At Calvary He who was God, very God died for us *physically* to atone for sins done in the flesh; He died morally, being made sin for us who knew no sin, in order that we might be made right with His righteousness *morally;* He died *spiritually* in total separation from His Father, which was to taste the awfulness of hell itself, to atone for our spiritual wrongdoing and heal our separation from a loving God.

It is on the basis of this titanic transaction, beyond the capacity of any man to fully plumb, that we are invited to *receive Him as divine royalty. We are urged to accept Him as the only way of reconciling ourselves to a loving God. We receive Him as our Savior.*

This is the supreme objective work of God done on our behalf for our justification in His presence. He has acted for us in history. He asks us to receive, to welcome, to take to ourselves, to believe in and trust this Living Christ who has given Himself to us through His death that we might live through His righteousness. Through His generosity there is *imputed* (credited to our account) His righteousness.

Yet God does not leave it at that. He actually comes now, in the present moment, and invites us to also *receive Him as divine royalty by His Spirit.* He God, very God in Christ, by His Gracious Spirit approaches us asking for the privilege to actually enter our lives as a Royal Resident.

"Behold, I stand at the door, and knock: if any man *hear* my voice, and open the door, I will come in to him, and will sup with him (share life with him), and he with me" (Rev. 3:20).

The person who so receives, accepts or invites Christ by His Spirit into his life, must of necessity also recognize Him as *Lord of his life, and receive Him as Sovereign.*

It is the Sovereign Spirit of the living God resident in our lives who does His supreme subjective work of remaking us. It is He who renews and re-creates us. This is the whole basis of our rebirth and sanctification before God. It is His joy and delight to conform us to Christ. He, the Gracious Gardener, does the deep work to produce and reproduce within our lives the fruits and attributes of His own character.

It was to this profound process that our Lord referred when He said that the third aspect of good ground was, *it brings forth fruit.*

That is to say there is reproduction. God actually duplicates in human character the attributes of His own person. For example, He is known as the God of all mercy. Therefore it follows that in due time mercy will become a hallmark of the man or woman in whom He resides and is at work.

We are told quite emphatically, for instance, that the good seed of the very love (selflessness) of God is shed abroad (scattered throughout) our hearts by the Holy Spirit who is given to us (see Rom. 5:5). Therefore it is proper and legitimate for us to look for that sort of selfless, self-giving to spring up and become apparent in the Christian's life.

It is important to note, too, that God Himself comes looking for that love to be an integral part of our character. As was stated emphatically earlier in this book the chief criteria by which either God or men can conclude whether or not we truly are Christians is by our fruits. The basis upon which we can obtain empirical evidence that a person truly believes in Christ and has received Him both as Savior and Lord is by the fruit of God's own character reproduced in that life. There simply has to be something of the likeness of Christ apparent as proof positive that God is actually at work within.

A skeptical society so often charges the church with hypocrisy for this very reason. They look for attributes of character and attitudes of behavior that are Godlike in those who claim to be Christians. If these are lacking they quite naturally and legitimately insist the churchgoer is a phony and a fake.

This is why our Lord was so devastating in His denunciation of the scribes, Pharisees, and Sadducees of His day. They pretended to be so pious. Yet within they were rotten with corruption, greed, and pride. Their lives were a pretense. They were not good ground. There were no fruits of godliness. Jesus declared emphatically to Nicodemus, the pious Pharisee: "You simply have to be born again—re-made and re-worked."

In Part II of this book each of the fruits of God's own character will be examined carefully. We will see how each is expressed in His conduct toward us, and we will see its effect in our own lives—in our relationship to others as well as back to God Himself. And we will study the means and methods God employs to produce each fruit in our lives.

But before we do that it is essential to emphasize here that the one great, essential ingredient for good soil to be productive under God's good hand is obedience or responsiveness. In our permissive, rather lawless and undisciplined society it is not popular to discuss obedience. Most people prefer to do their own thing, live their own lives, go their own way.

This is selfish self-centeredness at its worst.

Such an attitude is absolutely fatal to fruitfulness.

It is the sure recipe for barrenness, and its end result is desolation and despair.

Note that God's Gracious Spirit is given only to those who obey (Acts 5:32). He will not enter nor reside where there is rebellion or resentment against His Royal Presence. He who is sovereign seeks for, expects, and counts on our complete cooperation and compliance with His commands in all areas of our lives.

If we truly love Christ and love God we will not only endeavor, but also deeply desire to carry out His wishes and will for us. Read John 14 and 15 to verify this.

Five minutes of implicit obedience to God at any point will generate more fruits of right living in our experience than five years of theological or doctrinal discussion that end only in dilly-dallying with the truth.

As God by His Spirit reveals new areas of my life into which He wishes to move and work, my responsibility is to allow Him to have His way without resistance or hindrance. As He steadily and surely takes over more and more ground in my daily experience the crop yield will gradually increase from 30- to 60- to 100-fold.

The more good ground of obedient behavior He encounters and cultivates the greater the productivity. There can be a bountiful harvest of divine fruit because of the Good Gardener's great skill and my simple, humble, hearty response to His work within.

# Part Two
## *The Nine Facets of God's Love*

# 5
# Love—
# the Life of God

So MUCH HAS been written about the love of God that one almost hesitates to discuss the subject again. Some of God's great and noble saints have applied themselves so diligently to a study of this concept that it would seem all that can be said has already been reported for us. Amongst these writings perhaps the most winsome and powerful is Henry Drummond's *The Greatest Thing in the World*.

Any person who will earnestly, prayerfully read that essay once a week, every week, for three months is bound to have the entire fabric of his/her character colored and changed by God's Gracious Spirit.

### *Love—the First Fruit*

Notwithstanding all that has already been preached and published about God's love it must be examined here. It is the first and foremost of the fruits of God's Spirit. It is much, much more than merely "one of the fruits." In reality it is the very basic, essential life of the living Christ which expresses itself in all the nine fruits enumerated both in Galatians 5:22, 23 and 1 Corinthians 13:1–7.

The love of God is the very life of God.

That life, if allowed to grow freely in the good ground of the well prepared soil of our souls, will flourish and fructify in various ways. It will not always express itself in exactly the same manner or to the same degree. Each of us differs in our display of divine life. Yet the evidence of deity *within* is demonstrated irrevocably by supernatural fruit *without*.

Such fruit can and does come only from above.

It is not something which we can counterfeit.

The very life of God, epitomized in the love of God, originates only and always with Him.

Like good seed introduced into good garden soil, it must come from a source outside the garden. It does not, nor can it ever spring from the soil of our own souls and spirits spontaneously.

There may be theologians, scholars, and teachers who would try to tell us that there is inherent good in man which if properly tended and cultivated can be gradually improved so that it ultimately becomes divine. This may strongly appeal to our human pride. It may pander to our self-centered preoccupation with self-improvement. But it is not the teaching of God's Word. Nor is it endorsed by our Lord.

Throughout the Scriptures, the Spirit of God reiterates again and again that our human nature is not righteous—that we are not normally good people who can at will, if we so choose, produce good fruit.

The picture presented to us in unmistakable language is that there must be the divine life of the living God implanted in our spirits. The very seed of the life of Christ sown in us by the Spirit of God can germinate in the ground of our being to mature into magnificent fruitage if we permit it to happen.

*"It is the spirit that quickeneth; the flesh (my human nature) profiteth nothing: the words that I speak unto you, they are spirit and they are life"* (John 6:63).

As this good seed from the Spirit of God germinates in the garden of my life it will begin to flourish and mature. Ripened fruit will eventually emerge. In some lives this will produce fruit thirty, sixty, and even a hundred times the amount originally planted.

### Love Lies at the Root

That amazing love of God will have been reproduced supernaturally, through divine diligence, in a human being. God Himself looks upon the toil and travail of His own soul and is satisfied. He has gotten Himself a crop. The worldling looks on and must admit to himself: "This one is a child of God! He is different—distinctly and decisively."

It must be emphasized here that I have the love of God only to the extent that I have God Himself. God does not dispense the fruits of His Spirit apart from Himself!

To put it another way: I only have the love of God to the degree that God lives His life in and through me. God does not drop neat, glittering, giftwrapped packages of His sweet fruit into my life. We may pray for that to happen, and we may think it can. It never does. We are deluded if we think it will. When we ask God to give us the precious fruits of His own Spirit, these are bestowed always and only through the increased presence of His own person.

The more I have Christ the more I have His love.

The more I have God the more I have His goodness.

The more I have the Holy Spirit the more I have His wholeness.

And this total righteousness, wholesomeness, gracious goodness of the life of God finds full expression to one degree or another in all the nine facets of fruitfulness listed by the apostle Paul in Galatians 5:22 and 23.

Let me illustrate to point out exactly and clearly what is implied by the foregoing.

A head of wheat, barley or oats may contain in itself nine individual, separate, and distinct kernels of grain. Each kernel differs from the others in its own particular shape, size, and content. Yet all nine kernels are from the same source. They are all either wheat, oats, or barley depending upon the plant that produced them. One may be full and round and plump, another may be somewhat shrunken or shriveled. Still they are all either oats or wheat or barley because they were collectively borne upon the same stalk and came from the same seed.

A similar illustration can be given from a cluster of grapes. If the cluster contains nine individual fruits, they will each be the same sort of fruit, though they may differ slightly in size, shape, and taste. One grape in the cluster may be fully ripened, full of sweet juice, pleasing to the eye and delectable to taste. But in the same cluster there may also be several grapes which are somewhat less ripe, rather green, still sour or perhaps even shrunken and shriveled. Still they are all the same grapes growing on a single stem from the same vine.

So it is with the life of God, the love of God that we may say grows from the single stalk of the life of the Spirit of God in us. The individual grape of joy may be very fully matured in my life, but at the same time that of patience may be decidedly small, sour, and shrunken.

With this thought then in the background of our understanding we can look at the love of God and see it in practical terms that remove it from the realm of theory, theology, or ivory tower teaching. We will see this life of God portrayed for us in practical, everyday realities that produce fruits of wholesome (holy), right (righteous) living.

### Love Is Selflessness

To begin with it is imperative to point out here that the "love of God" referred to so freely, especially in the New Testament, is *selflessness:*

> It is *self-giving.*
> It is *self-sharing.*
> It is *self-sacrificing.*
> It is *self-losing.*
> It is *self-abandonment.*
> It is *self-serving others.*

This kind of love found its supreme and most sublime expression in the life and death of our Lord Jesus Christ. He was the visible expression to our humanity of the Invisible God. He was the love of God demonstrated indelibly in the perfect doing and perfect dying of deity. His transcendent life revealed the true nature of God. There simply was no greater means by which He could manifest His own character.

The love of God was shown to be one with the life of God. In no way could the one be separated from the other. They are one and the same.

This is why the apostle John without apology or hesitation declared flatly: "... *God Is Love*" (1 John 4:8).

This caliber and kind of love is not to be confused with erotic love. Nor is it to be equated with filial love. Both of the latter also have their origin with God. It was He who initiated them as part and parcel of the magnificent interrelationships which can make family life so thrilling and satisfying.

But the love of God, so-called *agape* love in the Greek, is essentially selflessness finding form in nine distinct facets. For purposes of simplicity and clarity here are those nine fruits all taken from the same cluster, or those nine kernels all drawn from the same head:

GALATIANS 5:22, 23                    1 CORINTHIANS 13:1–7

| 1. *Love* | Does not seek her own, is not selfish or self-centered. |
| 2. *Joy* | Love does not rejoice in iniquity but rather rejoices in the truth. |
| 3. *Peace* | Love is not easily provoked, but is serene and stable. |
| 4. *Longsuffering* | Love suffers long, perseveres, is patient. |
| 5. *Kindness (gentleness)* | Love is merciful, thoughtful, and concerned; it envies not. |
| 6. *Goodness* | Love is great, gracious, and generous; it is kind and good. |
| 7. *Faithfulness* | Love thinks no evil but has faith in God and others. |
| 8. *Meekness* | Love is humble and gentle, does not vaunt itself. |
| 9. *Temperance* | Love is disciplined and controlled, does not behave unbecomingly. |

Even a cursory glance at the content of God's love discloses that here we are face to face with a powerful, potent life principle. We are dealing with a divine dimension of living, a radical lifestyle.

God grant that within us there might be generated an enormous, overwhelming, irresistible desire to become like Him who is *love* . . . to have reproduced in us the fruit of His life.

## Love Is the Very Life of God

If we pause momentarily to reflect on the practical out-working of such love in our everyday world it may well be the first seed with a spiritual germ to be dropped into the soil of our souls. Here I quote, without apology, from my book *Rabboni*.

"In all the enterprises which engaged this tremendous triumvirate, there are perfect coordination of concept and ultimate unity of purpose in their planning. Unlike human endeavors, it was never marked by discord. Friction was unknown simply because there was no selfish self-interest present. Between God the Father, God the Son Jesus Christ, and God the Holy Spirit there flowed love in its most sublime form. In fact, this love was of such purity that it constituted the very basis of their beings. It was the essence of their characters.

"We earthmen can barely conceive of a relationship so sublime that it contains no trace of self-assertion, no ulterior motive nor self-gratification. But that is the secret to the strength of God. Here was demonstrated the irresistible force of utter selflessness. In the total giving of each to the other, in profound CARING for each other, lay the love of all eternity. This was love at its loftiest level. This was love at its highest source. This was love, the primal source of all energy.

"Just as there is stored within an atom enormous power because of the interaction between neutrons, protons, and electrons, likewise there was inherent unlimited energy in the Godhead because of the interrelationship between Father, Son, and Spirit. And the essence of this energy was love.

"In that outer world love was the moving force behind every action. Love was the energizing influence at work in every enterprise. Love was the very fiber woven into every aspect of Christ's life. It was in fact the basic raw material used ultimately to fashion and form all subsequent matter.

"To the reader this may all seem a bit obscure, a bit beyond belief. But if we pause to find parallels upon our planet, earth, we may soon see the picture in practical terms. What is the most irresistible force upon the earth? LOVE! What pulverizes strong prejudice and builds enduring allegiance? LOVE! What binds men together in indestructible devotion? LOVE!

"What underlies all generous and magnanimous actions? LOVE! What is the source of strength for men and women who gladly serve and die for one another? LOVE! What energizes the loftiest and most noble enterprise of human hearts and minds? LOVE! If this be true of selfish mortal men, then how much more is it the very life of God—and this is the life of Christ."

Obviously such love is not insipid and sentimental. It is strong as steel; tough as tungsten; enduring as a diamond. It is the essence of the eternal.

This love of God is nothing less than the life of God poured out lavishly and constantly. It is what energizes the cosmos. And only when we are brought into full harmony with its own on-going purposes can we sense and know that at last we too are caught up in the grand will of God. Only then do we discover the delight of moving strongly and surely in the supreme designs of God. Then the most minute details of life bear enormous meaning and purpose.

### My Own Experience

You may well wonder how to reach a point where you too can come to receive this love—how you can open your life to allow this new divine quickening of a higher life to enter the soil of your own soul. Perhaps my own experience will help someone to understand a little better.

As my fortieth year of life drew to a close, there crept over my spirit an acute awareness that there was something significant lacking. It was not in the realm of material or moral values. I had a beautiful wife whom I loved deeply. I had wholesome, alert, fine children. The business endeavors in which my strength and energy had been invested were remarkably successful. I had gained financial independence and security. Every aim and ambition set for myself as a young man had been achieved and even surpassed.

But in spite of such apparent success, deep within my spirit was the inescapable conviction that I was missing the mark. The main purpose for which I had been placed upon the planet was being bypassed. I simply was not moving strongly with the stream of God's best intentions for me.

There then began a desperate search to discover what the dilemma was. Where was the difficulty? Perhaps because of my very formidable self-will, my determined drives, or even the slowness of my stony soul I could not seem to see that I had lived pretty much for selfish, self-centered purposes. They had dominated my days.

The malaise of my life came from a lack of love—God's love— a lack of selflessness and self-giving to Him and to others. But once I saw this great, spiritual vacuum within, virtually void of the life of God—the love of Christ—an insatiable, overwhelming, all-consuming desire was generated to have His Spirit sweep into my soul. He alone could satisfy that fierce yearning for fruitfulness and productivity.

The crisis came one mellow autumn day in the foothills of the Rockies. Alone, in anguish of spirit I went to hike along the high cliffs bordering a deep coulee. Down in its depths ran a crystal clear stream of ice-cold water. It flowed from the glaciers and ice fields of the snow-mantled mountains shining in the west.

"O God," I cried out from the depths of my being, "come flooding into my spirit; into my soul; into my entire body and being. O Christ, come in like these snow-fed waters from the high country stream down into this valley. O Spirit of the Living God, pour into this parched and barren soil of mine. Shed abroad in me the very life of God—the love of Christ. Fit me to be good ground in which the seed of your good Word can take root and flourish and prosper."

It was a heart cry of utter desperation. For five full hours I tramped up and down that lonely canyon trail in awesome anguish of soul. If ever a man hungered and thirsted after righteousness—the right life of God—I did that day.

The gentle, gracious, yet galvanizing response of God's Gracious Spirit to my cries came as a surprise: "If you will just comply with *My* wishes; carry out *My* commands; cooperate with *My* desires I will give Myself to you in abundant measure. *I give Myself—My life— My love—My Spirit* wholeheartedly to those who obey *Me.*"

It meant my priorities in life suddenly had to be reversed. Life was no longer to be lived for *myself*, but for *Him* and *His*. It was the beginning of a brand new relationship with God. As I complied with His wishes in everyday details, His life and His love flooded in to produce eternal, enduring fruit.

Looking back over the intervening years I marvel at the generosity of God. He took a barren life and in His own gracious way made it bountiful.

He will do it for anyone who will seriously and sincerely open themselves, becoming available to His Presence.

# 6
# Joy in the
# Christian's Life

IN THE GRAND and deeply moving prophecy of the ancient prophet Isaiah, it was foretold that when Christ came He would impart to His people *"the oil of joy"* for mourning (Isa. 61:3). Joy has ever been one of the most significant hallmarks of God's people. It is a unique quality of character often confused with happiness.

Joy and happiness are not the same.

Each springs from a totally different source.

One comes from the world around me. The other originates directly with the Spirit of the Living God.

Happiness is conditioned by and often dependent upon what is "happening" to me. It is irrevocably bound up either with the behavior of other people, the sequence of events in my life, or the circumstances in which I find myself.

If these are going well in one way or another I am said to be "happy." If, on the other hand, my circumstances are adverse I am described as "unhappy."

For the most part "happy" or "happiness" are words that belong very much to the world. They are seldom used in Scripture (about six times in the New Testament, perhaps sixteen in the Old). And when they are employed it is generally in the traditional Anglo-Saxon meaning of being well-favored or very fortunate. An example is Psalm 144:15b ". . . *Happy* (fortunate—well-favored) is that people, whose God is the Lord."

### The Nature of True Joy

*Joy*, on the other hand, appears in a variety of forms such as "joyful" or "rejoice" (about eight times more often than does happiness). It throbs throughout the Scriptures as a profound, compelling quality of life that surmounts and transcends the events and disasters which may dog God's people. Joy is a divine dimension of living not shackled by circumstances.

This joy springs from the presence of God in a person's life. It is frequently referred to as "the joy of the Lord," or "joy in the Holy Spirit." It is in no way dependent either upon people around me, the course of events in my experience, or the circumstances in which I find myself, be they ever so calamitous or fortunate.

Joy is one of the grand attributes of God Himself. It is an integral part of His character. Joy runs like a sparkling stream of great good-will through His makeup. Known as the God of all joy, He rejoices in all His own accomplishments. He is joyful in His own delectable character.

When we discover for ourselves that God our Father really is like this it endears Him to us in a delightful way. He is not an august, austere, awesome judge standing aloof and apart from us in the agony of our human anguish. He is the one who yearns over us, longs for us, searches for us, and when we are found enfolds us to Himself with inexpressible joy.

He is the Good Gardener who toils over us and tends us with constant care. Patiently he waits for the full fruitage. He finds joy in the planting He has done, and He waits eagerly for a crop. With great joy He gathers the harvest.

There is deep delight in all He does.

There is enthusiasm in everything He undertakes.

There is sweet satisfaction in all His enterprises.

His life, vitality, enthusiasm, and energy are transmitted directly to me by His Spirit who resides within.

It is His knowledge of me, His careful husbanding of the ground of my being, His concern for my welfare, His cultivation of my character, His constant presence in the garden of my little life— that guarantees my joy. For little by little I come to discover that He is totally trustworthy. I learn that no matter how unpredictable people may prove, or how exasperating events may be, or how crushing circumstances may seem, He is still there (here), utterly reliable.

Because of His total integrity and absolute honesty and constant love expressed to me as His person I am charged with joy.

## The Joy-Love Connection

This is what Paul means in writing about love in 1 Corinthians 13. He declares without hesitation,

*"Love rejoices in the truth."*

It is the love of God, the life of God grounded and founded upon His own infallible character. He simply cannot betray either Himself or those in His care. He is bound to bring the best out of any life under His care. It simply cannot be otherwise. And therein lies our joy.

He does all things well.

He is able to do abundantly more than we can ask or even imagine.

He can bring good out of what to us seems evil.

He can take our desolate wilderness lives and turn them into a glorious garden.

He finds joy in such a labor of love.

And it is in the process of pouring His very own life into us that there springs up from the stony, weedy, hard-packed pathway soil of my soul joy: The joy of *knowing He is at work in me and I am under His care.*

Slowly but surely the seed of His good Word germinates in the ground of my life. There emerges from the bareness of my soul a new life with new values, new standards, new concepts based upon *truth*, upon the *verities* of God in Christ.

What before may have seemed folly and foolishness to my worldly-wise mind suddenly begins to make sense. Spiritual insights imparted and implanted in my spirit by God's Gracious Spirit take root and mature. Joy, enormous joy in God, in having found truth, in discovering the true dimension of deeply satisfying life sweeps into my spirit expelling the skepticism and cynicism of my former life.

Perhaps this is the point to pause and explain why people do become such skeptics apart from God. Some of us don't really understand why, in spite of humanity's desperate quest for happiness, most men and women still lack genuine joy. A person may have succeeded in every area of life and still feel he/she has missed the mark. Such a person hasn't found joy . . . that enduring quality that far transcends transient happiness.

## Joy vs. Happiness

Happiness is extremely vulnerable. It is insecure and unsure. At best it is established on unreliable, unpredictable ground.

Happiness wrapped up in people can be torn and tortured. Even our dearest family members, friends or business associates can play us false. Sometimes those who once were fond of each other come to hate and despise one another. Trust turns to distrust.

Happiness centered in wealth or possessions or property is extremely hazardous. Everything (except God) is subject to change and the fluctuations of fad and fashion. The inexorable forces of decay, deterioration, devaluation, and depreciation are everywhere at work in the world. A person expends his time, strength, and thought to amass possessions only to see them fade before his eyes.

Often instead of owning what they have labored to accumulate, they discover that they in turn are "owned" by their possessions. Such people have become enslaved. They are worn and weary wondering if they will lose what they have won.

Happiness based merely on buoyant good health is a delusion. Time takes its toll even amongst the most handsome of men and beautiful of women. Vigor wanes; beauty fades; reflexes slow down; eyes grow dim; hearing fails; teeth fall out; memory falters; and body vitality diminishes.

Happiness grounded in a successful career or outstanding social achievement is invariably short-lived. Soon another new star rises on the horizon to eclipse one's finest accomplishments. Records are broken and fall every year. Names and faces once famous are quickly forgotten to fade into the mists of oblivion.

So the list could go on. The sum total of human enterprise and initiative is like mist that disappears with the sun. It comes eventually to a mere shadow—a mocking memory. The owner is left with lingering skepticism and bitter disillusionment. Subconsciously he feels cheated and double-crossed.

In vain the worldling turns desperately and despairingly to drink from any broken cistern or muddied water that he thinks might slake his thirst for joy. But all disappoints him. For only in God Himself can the source of joy be found.

### Surprised by Joy

In brilliant, blazing contrast the person who permits God in Christ, by His Spirit, to come sweeping into his spirit, is overwhelmingly surprised by joy. The sweet, gracious, generous Spirit of the Lord enlivens him. The very mainspring of life is touched. The quickening influence of the Divine Presence permeates the entire person. A diametrically new, dynamic dimension of living pervades the life so that the whole of the soul (mind, emotions, will) as well as the body (physical makeup) come alive to the Gracious Spirit of the risen Christ now resident within.

This is to know the government of God in my life, to actually experience the control of Christ in my conduct and conversation. It is to sense the sovereignty of the Spirit of God bringing order out of confusion, direction out of despair, and joy out of despondency.

Millions of men and women across the centuries attest to this transformation in their lives. It is what is meant by Paul in Romans 14:17, "The kingdom of God is not meat and drink: but righteousness and peace and *joy in the Holy Ghost*" (italics mine). God is here! He is alive! He is in charge!

This was the irresistible dynamic of the early church. It is still the experience of anyone who truly allows God to enter the garden of his/her life. Enthusiasm and deep delight pervades such a person. There is direction in his/her endeavors no matter how mundane or menial. There is purpose and profound meaning to the minutiae of life. A piece of common clay of ordinary humanity has come under the hand of the Divine Husbandman. And the fruit of joy springs from the soil of that soul.

This joy is not that of selfish self-interest in who I am. Rather it is the joy of *knowing God* at last and realizing that *He knows me*. It lies in the serene surprise of how generous and joyful is His presence.

### The Joy of Forgiveness

Combined with this comes the sweet consolation and exquisite joy of knowing that because of His gracious redemption my sins are forgiven, the guilt is gone, and I am accepted into His family.

In a profoundly purifying way His Spirit sweeps through my being to assure me that I am right with God and He with me. I am made right with others and they are made right with me. A deep, settled assurance that all is well even between me and myself descends upon my spirit. This is to have and know the joy of the Lord. It becomes a formidable force in the very fabric of my life. It is literally a great light illuminating the whole of my interior, dispelling the darkness and despair that formerly dominated my deepest desires.

All of this is so because *He is here.*
Christ has come.
His Spirit is in residence.
God is in the garden on my life.

### Counterfeit Joy

Out of a sense of solemn responsibility to the reader I must state here that there is such a thing as counterfeit joy. It is one of the calamities of Christendom that often people will pursue pleasant sensations believing implicitly that the gratification of sensual desire is to know the joy of the Lord. This is a dreadful delusion that frequently leads the victim to even deeper despair and dismay.

It is perfectly possible to produce the illusion of joy in crowds by the use of emotional mood music, "soul" songs, so called; syncopated rhythms; a swinging "beat"; all can generate deep emotional responses assumed to be joy.

The same is true of sensationalism in preaching—the use of sentimental stories or overdramatization of a person's delivery. Reliance is placed upon sensuality rather than upon the Spirit of God to convict, enlighten, and convert the soul.

Likewise in "sharing" sessions where undue emphasis is placed upon physical contact between persons—where people are encouraged to indulge in hugging, kissing, laughing or crying together there lurks the danger of being deceived by counterfeit joy.

What the victim is experiencing is happiness, either from the music, the manipulated message, or the mood of his associates. Relying upon the people or events around him, He is not experiencing the joy of God's gentle Spirit at work in his spirit.

Counterfeit joy is a passing, titillating, unpredictable sensation that temporarily transcends the despondency of the moment. To seek it is to drink from a sensual source that ever leaves the thirsting, questing spirit unsatisfied, often disillusioned and in subsequent despair.

To know the true joy of the Lord, present always in profound, quiet, still, inner power, because of His presence within, is to have the capacity to triumphantly transcend all the turmoil of our times in strength.

## The Source of Joy

It may be asked, how does one get this strong joy? It comes only with Him who Himself is the God of all joy. The extent to which He occupies the ground of my whole being, that is the extent to which I have His joy.

If Christ controls and has His way in my career, business, hobbies, home, friendships, service, and interests, whatever they be, there I will also experience His joy.

It is quite literally impossible to be at variance with God in any area of life and there find joy. Joy is part and parcel of harmony with Him in my activities. The instant I comply with His wishes, His joy energizes my being. The moment I disagree with His desires joy fades, and faith falters.

As Christ comes into our affairs His desire is that our attention and interest be refocused on Him. It is He who is at work within us both to will and do of His own good pleasure (Phil 2:13). Too often we are preoccupied with the process of fruit production rather than the Good Gardener who is responsible for the fruitage. Too often we are looking for joy when we should just be looking away to Jesus Christ. Our joy is in Him. Our strength is in His ability to produce the joy.

As He moves over the ground of my life, cultivating, tending, loving every corner of it, He will be at work asking me to respond. If in simple obedience I will comply by giving myself away, losing myself for others, there will spring to life the joy of His Spirit in my spirit.

*"It is God, not we, who made the garden grow in your hearts" (1 Cor. 3:6, LB).*

# 7
# Peace and
# Peacemakers

IN THE WORLD around, amongst all men, Christian and non-Christian, peace is regarded as one of the supreme attainments. In the tumultuous history of the twentieth century perhaps no other single subject has occupied more prominence in the hopes, dreams, and aspirations of mankind. Peace is ever upon peoples' minds and lips. It is the profound longing of uncounted millions. Peace is the prize sought for in the depths of the human soul, yet the attribute so often absent.

Why? Why is it so ardently desired yet so seldom discovered?

Why are the Scriptures so true when they declare that men shall cry: "Peace, peace, when there is no peace!" (Jer. 6:14; 8:11).

Why do so few ever find the path to peace?

## The Nature of Peace

The answer lies largely in our basic human misunderstanding of what peace is and how it is produced.

Our Lord, while living here amongst us, placed such a remarkable priority upon peace that He made the amazing statement: "Blessed are the peacemakers (i.e. those who produce peace): for they shall be called the children of God" (Matt. 5:9).

It is appropriate, therefore, to discover what peace really is. As long as we labor under a delusion as to its true character and identity it will ever elude us.

First of all, peace is not just passivity. It is not merely stagnation. It is not sterility. It is not a negative attitude of non-involvement.

The production of peace calls for powerful and a most pronounced action on the part of the peacemaker. The path of peace which God's Word instructs us to pursue is not strewn softly with rose petals. Rather it is a tough trail tramped out with humble heart and lowly spirit despite its rough rocks of adversity.

Peace is the selfless, self-giving, self-losing, self-forgetting, self-sacrificing love of God in repose despite all the adverse reverses of life. It is love standing serene, strong, and stable in spite of every insult, every antagonism, every hate.

Peace is the spirit and soul of persons so imbued with the presence of God's Gracious Spirit that they are not easily provoked: They are not "touchy." They are not irritable or easily enraged. Their pride is not readily pricked. They do not live like a bristling porcupine with all its quills extended in agitated self-defense.

Peace is actually the exact opposite. It is the quiet, potent, gracious attitude of serenity and good-will that comes to meet the onslaught of others with good cheer, equanimity, and strong repose.

To see and understand this quality of life at its best we simply must turn away from our contemporaries and look at Christ . . . God very God.

### The God of All Peace

He is known as the God of all peace. He alone is the source and supplier of peace. Active in our attitudes and actions, he alone can produce this quality of life in our everyday experiences.

All through human history God has approached men in peace. Always He has come amongst us with good-will. This was dramatized in the incredible declaration of the angels on the night of His advent: "On earth, peace good will toward men" (Luke 2:14)!

This has ever been God's generous, magnanimous approach to humanity, despite man's most despicable hatred and opposition to His overtures of good will. It matters not where God's Spirit finds a man or woman, His approach is always in peace. It matters not how deep the sin, how dark the stain, how set the soul in selfishness—Christ comes to us in peace.

He has our redemption in view and our ultimate renewal in mind. He has our restoration to His family as the supreme goal of His own goodness. He comes to us with arms outstretched, with brimming eyes that have looked upon us with longing, with His Spirit spilling over with good will.

> Behold, I will bring it health and cure, and I will cure them, and will reveal unto them the abundance of peace and truth.
>
> And I will cause the captivity of Judah and the captivity of Israel to return, and will build them, as at the first.
>
> And I will cleanse them from all their iniquity, whereby they have sinned against me; and I will pardon all their iniquities, whereby they have sinned, and whereby they have transgressed against me.
>
> And it shall be to me a name of joy, a praise and an honour before all the nations of the earth, which shall hear all the good that I do unto them: and they shall fear and tremble for all the prosperity and for all the goodness that I procure unto it (Jer. 33:6–9).

This is the true nature and character of God revealed in His dealing with difficult and disagreeable people.

### Jesus, the Man of Peace

Even when here amongst us as a man He came in peace. It was the impact of this peace that touched and transformed people as tough as tax collectors, prostitutes, and cursing fishermen. It was the incredible impact of this peace that turned James and John, the flaming, flashing "sons of thunder," into beloved apostles of love. It was the impulse of this peace, this love in action, that made Christ cry out in the midst of His own crushing agony, "Father, forgive them, for they know not what they do!" (Luke 23:34).

He was at peace with His enemies.

They were at war with Him.

He Himself, to explain this enigma, had stated clearly on one occasion: "I came not to send peace, but a sword" (Matt. 10:34). For in His very coming people were polarized. Those whose spirits responded positively to the overtures of His divine love and peace would be passionately fond of Him. Those repelled by His truth and integrity would hate with appalling venom, determined to destroy Him.

It is ever thus. God does not change. Christ does not alter His approach to men. The Gracious Spirit comes always in peace to convict, correct, and convert men. The human response to that coming determines whether in fact men enjoy peace or remain engulfed in terrible hostility.

### The Source of Peace

If the life is opened to receive the divine presence of the risen Christ, He comes in, speaking peace—just as He came again and again to His distraught disciples after His resurrection, saying. *"Peace be unto you!"*

He comes into our lives there to shed abroad a new love, His own life, that expresses itself in peace. When He enters my experience; when He penetrates my personality; when He becomes Sovereign in my spirit, I in turn become a person of peace. It is then that I begin to know what it means to be at peace with God, at peace with others, at peace with myself.

Increasingly as He is given control of my life the entire complexion of my character, conduct, and conversation alters. I discover that He can change me dramatically. Peace, good will, good cheer, and serenity replace animosity, bitterness, hostility, belligerence, jealousy, bad temper, quarreling, and rivalry.

In passing it should be pointed out that these latter attitudes are those listed specifically in Galatians 5:19, 20 as being indicators of the old, unchanged life. People who express such emotions and give vent to such feelings and attitudes are not "peacemakers"—rather they are "problem producers."

Such people produce enormous pain for both themselves and others. They alienate friends, family, and associates, building formidable barriers of ill will between themselves and others. They injure, wound, and grieve those around them. Often their dearest friends and family suffer most because of the despair, darkness, and dismay generated by their anger.

This anger aroused, inflamed, and vented upon others is the exact opposite of peace. Instead of being selfless love it is self-centeredness, self-preoccupation inflamed and aroused in self-defense and self-assertion.

### Peace Produces Healing

On the other hand, the peace of God, which is self-sacrificing and self-foregoing, produces healing. It comes to bind up the wounds; to pour in the oil of consolation; to bring repose and quietness; to still the troubled soul; to speak peace to stormy spirits. This peace comes only from Christ. It is one of the genuine, indisputable marks of God's presence in a person's life.

By the same measure it may be said with equal force that if peace is absent from a person's life it is apparent that Christ really has not come in. It is a delusion to believe or think one is a Christian whose life is marked by constant battling, bitterness or belligerence.

Paul put it forcefully when he stated that "They which do such things *shall not inherit the kingdom of God*" (Gal. 5:21, italics mine).

This should, of course, be obvious to anyone who thinks seriously about the subject. "For the kingdom of God is not meat and drink but righteousness and peace and joy in the Holy Ghost" (Rom. 14:17).

Lest the reader be confused it is important to point out here that the in-coming of Christ does not mean I shall have no enemies in life. It does not mean I am ushered into a utopia where all is at peace, where life becomes a gentle millpond of perfection. We simply are not given any such guarantee anywhere in God's Word. On the contrary, we are advised solemnly that God's people must be prepared to endure afflictions, to face hostility from others, to undergo tribulation, and to be hated by an adverse world.

For years, as a young man, I labored under the false assumption that if I was just gracious enough and good enough everyone would love me. In part this delusion came from false teaching. The unvarnished truth is that even God, the God of all peace, when He came to live amongst us as the perfect person was despised and rejected of men. He stated emphatically to His little band of would be followers just before His death, "If the world hate you, ye know that it hated me before it hated you" (John 15:18).

Where then, it may be asked, does peace come into the picture here? It is a legitimate question that deserves an honest answer.

That answer is best summed up in the statement made by Solomon in Proverbs 16:7, "When a man's ways please the Lord, he maketh even his enemies to be at peace with him."

## It Takes Two to Quarrel

There is no guarantee that I shall not have enemies. I will. They are those polarized by the powerful presence of the Gracious Spirit of God in my life. But even they, like the tough Roman centurion who was charged with crucifying Christ, will admit, "Truly this was (a peacemaker) the Son of God" (Matt. 27:54).

The point we must see here is very important. It takes two to quarrel. If one of the two exudes good will, comes with good cheer, gives of himself in selfless love, that one is at peace. The other may still despise, hate, and abuse the first, but he remains the one with the problem, the one with the inner darkness and despair.

*As God's people of peace we need not be victimized by our detractors. We can be at peace with them, as Christ was, even if they are at odds with us.*

God calls us to be "big" people, strong people, serene people, steady, solid people of His caliber. We are not to be dragged down into the ditch of destructive hatreds, animosities, and mudslinging.

There is a quaint but powerful old proverb, "He who throws dirt only loses ground!" And how true that is in the garden of our lives. There are bound to be some storms of stress and strain that break around me but if the good crop of God's peaceful nature is growing luxuriantly in the ground of my being the soil of my soul will not be eroded or blown away in the downpour of hatred or winds of adversity that beat upon me.

### *Steps to Peace*

Perhaps the most helpful thing one can do here is to explain, in very simple terms, exactly how the peace of God can become one of the most notable products of my life. There are three important steps to be taken.

1) There must be a willingness to face myself squarely. If I am an individual who fights, quarrels, finds fault, and produces problems for both myself and others, it must be admitted. In fact I must come to the solemn and very sobering conclusion that hatred, belligerence, and animosity spring directly from my selfish, self-centered old nature.

This is not a question of indulging in morbid introspection. It is a matter of getting serious with God and myself about my behavior. I must come to hate my hatred!

It is utterly pointless to put up a smoke screen of childish excuses such as: "I can't help it, I'm born with a bad temper," or "I'm just an honest person and say what I think, let the chips fall where they may," or "It's all their fault, they are wrong, they give me good reason to be mad." And a hundred others like them. This is not the path to peace but of terrible peril.

Instead let me cry out in absolute earnestness, "O God, in Christ change me. Come in by Your Gracious Spirit. Let the sweet seed of Your good Word be implanted in the stony ground of my hatred-hardened heart. Let there spring up in my soul, my mind, my emotions, my will the ability to love as You love, to give myself in peace to others as You give Yourself to me."

2) If this prayer is uttered in absolute sincerity some startling things will take place. God in turn will take me seriously. He will

waste no time getting to the point of dealing with my dreadful, selfish, self-centered pride. This is the root cause of hatred, ill will, and jealous animosity.

The weeds of self-assertion, self-agrandizement, self-serving, self-importance, self-assurance must go. All the old worldly concepts of personal grandeur and greatness which so readily invade our thinking will have to be plowed under by the deep in-working of the Good Gardener. It is not a painless process. It is devastating to my inflated ego and bloated self-image.

This personal pride can find expression in a hundred ways, most of them apparently legitimate. Wherever I am proud, that is where I am also provocatively touchy. Wherever I congratulate myself, there I am terribly sensitive to hurt. So God will have to cut down these competing weeds. He has remarkable ways of humbling me in a hurry. He can allow the blight of events to touch my health, my home, my family, my friends, my career, my finances, my achievements, and bring them all down to dust.

But it is the humbled person, the lowly person, who finally finds rest and repose. He is no longer on a pedestal from which he can be knocked to the ground. He has come to practical terms and a realistic relationship with God, with others, with himself.

3) As this process goes on in our lives there is often a tendency for us to ask God to relent. There comes a time when we are tempted to ask Him to stop the plowing, to stop clearing the land, to quit the deep cultivation of our characters. Let us not do so. It is for our good and for fruit.

Peace comes as pride goes.

Peace will replace arrogance.

Peace will grow where animosity formerly flourished.

The person of humbled heart and contrite spirit in the care of a loving Husbandman is a person of peace. Our lives can be like a well-watered garden of Eden. They need not be bloody battlegrounds of bitterness. The world without may be at war all around us. But within, His presence, His life, His Spirit produces peace making me a peacemaker.

# 8
# Patience

THE WORD "PATIENCE" as it is used in the New Testament, really has no true equivalent in the English language. Certainly it does not mean merely being placid and phlegmatic as so many people assume.

Patience is the powerful capacity of selfless love to suffer long under adversity. It is that noble ability to bear with either difficult people or adverse circumstances without breaking down. This implies that one has a certain degree of tolerance for the intolerable. It is a generous willingness to try to understand the awkward people or disturbing events that our Father allows to enter our lives.

Over and beyond all of these, patience is that powerful attribute that enables a man or woman to remain steadfast under strain, not just standing still but pressing on. Patience is the potent perseverance that produces positive results even under opposition and suffering. It is love, gracious, self-giving, pressing on, enduring hardship, because of the benefit it may bring to others. It is a quiet willingness to wait, alert and watchful for the right moment to make the appropriate move.

### What Patience Is Not

Patience is not being phlegmatic or lethargic. It is not indolence or indifference. It is not that fatalistic attitude toward life which sits back, twiddles its thumbs, and hums: "Whatever will be, will be. . . ."

There is nothing weak, insipid or flaccid about it. It is a force of enormous power and influence—that one of God's attributes which, when exhibited in the life of His person, startles and astounds us.

So often we human beings, rather than exercising patience, prefer to opt out of adversity. Endeavoring to escape from difficult situations, we try to avoid and cut ourselves off from awkward people. We kick over the traces, shake off the harness, and break up anything that might bind us into suffering.

Yet the patience of God spoken of in the New Testament is just the opposite. It is really a picture of a beast of burden remaining steadily under control. It is an ox yoked to a plow breaking up the stiff soil of its owner's field. No matter whether the plow runs into rocks, stumps or heavy sod, the patient beast just pushes on steadily. Regardless of summer sun, the annoyance of flies or chilling winds the strong beast goes on breaking ground for its master.

The patience of the New Testament writers is that of a small donkey bearing enormous burdens of firewood, sacks of grain or other produce for its owner. Year in, year out, surely, steadily, safely it transports loads of goods from place to place in quiet compliance with its master's wishes.

This patience is a camel or colt or bullock harnessed to a circular treadmill. There hour after hour, day upon day it moves steadily lifting water to irrigate some little parched plot of ground. Or it may be thrashing out wheat to feed a hungry village. It is all part and parcel of achieving worthy ends through suffering service.

### Christ—A Picture of Patience

This quality of character was beautifully displayed for us in the life of our Lord. He, the Christ, came amongst us as the Suffering Servant. He came, not to be ministered to, but to minister (serve). And the gracious perseverance with which He endured every adversity as well as the abuse of evil men for our sakes and our salvation stirs our souls.

Were it not for the longsuffering patience of our God in dealing with us difficult human beings, where would we be? Long ago the human race would have perished because of perverseness, pride, and the pollution of our characters. But for the patient longsuffering of a Gracious God men could not for a moment stand in His impeccable and wholly righteous presence.

Only as we come to see and appreciate this fact will we bow humbly before Him and beg His pardon. It is only the patient willingness of a generous Father to put up with us, to understand us, and to persevere with us that gives us great hope and good cheer.

Looking back over my own life I tremble to think where I would be but for the loving patience of the Lord in dealing with me. How unrelentingly His Gracious Spirit pursued me down the tangled, twisted trails of my own selfish choosing. How He put up with my pride and perverseness as a self-assured person.

Just reflecting quietly upon this incredible attribute of Christ's loving concern for me crumbles my pride and stills me before Him.

This is the love of God in action—the quiet, strong, persevering determination of divinity to do me nothing but great good. For years and years God's Gracious Spirit came seeking and searching for my soul in good will. Despite my stubbornness, folly, waywardness and confusion He never relented. He never grew weary.

Ultimately it was His patience which prevailed. His perseverance pulverized my resistance. It dawned one day upon my dull and sin-stained spirit that He really cared, and cared deeply for this empty shell of a man, whose life He longed to fill and revive with His own abundant life.

It is this quality in the character of God to which I here refer. And it is an attribute of His own enormous love which He eagerly wants to share with His people. In fact, this is one of the fruits of His own Gracious Spirit which He endeavors to cultivate with care in our lives, if we will allow Him to do so. He comes to the garden of His own looking for it. Sometimes it can scarcely be found.

This is doubly strange when one stops to consider how patient He has been with us. Jesus told a story to illustrate this point. It is related in Matthew 18:21–33. One man who had an enormous debt asked his creditor to be patient with him until he paid. Yet he in turn went out and demanded immediate settlement from one who owed him a mere pittance.

Many of us are like that. This is not the love of God.

We tend to chop people down. By nature we are demanding and harsh. We want our pound of flesh from the next person; we will not put up with poor performance on the part of others. We want almost instant results, and we will not give others the benefit of the doubt or wait to see what God can do in their lives. We will not prevail in prayer for them.

In the case of adversity or difficult circumstances we want "out." Looking for the nearest exit, we duck and dodge to free ourselves from any unpleasant situation. We even pray earnestly to be delivered from every difficult or demanding experience.

All of this is the opposite of love in action. Love means I will push on in spite of obstacles. Love means being willing to suffer and endure the slings and stones of life. And love perseveres against formidable odds, just simply "keeping on."

When even a small glimmer of this grace takes root in our lives by the in-working of God's own Spirit some astonishing things happen, both to us and others.

## The Effect of Patience

Perhaps the most amazing thing is the manner in which our conduct generates hope and optimism in those around us. Even the most difficult people, drowned in despair, lost in their own selfish self-centeredness, will gain hope when they find someone who will be patient and persevere with them—who will pray for them unceasingly.

The very fact that someone cares enough to keep coming back again and again will begin to convince them that all is not wrong in the world.

Patience in God's people is one of the surest signs whereby even a non-Christian can discern and discover something of the nature of God. This attitude will pulverize the nonbeliever's prejudice more surely than almost any other Christian virtue. It will encourage him, reassure him, and convince him that there is more to Christianity than mere theory.

## The Benefits of Patience

For the child of God the development of patience has two enormous benefits. First it produces within his own character tremendous strength and endurance. A better word to use is "toughness"—not tough in the sense of being rough or rowdy, but rather tough in one's ability to endure hard people and hard situations with serenity and stability.

Secondly as we are patient under adversity we discover the great faithfulness of our God to us in every situation. Little by little we learn the practical truth of that great statement made by Paul in Philippians 2:13, *"It is God who worketh in you both to will and to do of his good pleasure."*

## Patience Is a Learning Experience

This fruit of God's Spirit is not something we pray for, expecting God to drop it down into our little lives like a neatly wrapped gift package. If we pray earnestly for the gift of this special grace, God will arrange for such people and circumstances to enter our experience that only the presence and exercise of His patience will enable us to cope at all. Thus we will learn to practice patience in the fierce furnace of affliction.

We will quickly find out that we do not go through life fighting the people or problems put in our path—we do not quarrel and complain with our lot in life. Nor do we try to slip out of every sticky situation. We are not those who look for just the soft spot and the comfy corner.

Instead we face whatever arrangements God our Father makes for us as His proper and appropriate provision for us. We accept these as the great, good mills of God that will grind us into fine flour to feed His hungry people. We recognize our trials as the winepress of God's own creation in which our lives can be so compressed that there will flow from us refreshment for the weary, thirsty world around us.

In such acceptance there lies peace, but also beyond that there also emerges patience. Not a grudging, shriveled sort of sour stoicism, but a cheerful delight in the divine work of the Master Gardener in my life. The deep spading and the heavy plowing of God's Spirit in my soul are what eventually will produce the rich fruit of His own patience in my character. It can come no other way.

In all of this as I continually remind myself that He, God very God, is dealing with me in patience and perseverance, I will lift up my heart and spirit to rejoice. I will rest in the sure confidence and quiet knowledge that He does all things well, both for my sake and His own.

It is when the actual awareness of Christ Himself in our lives steals over our spirits that we become still before Him. We sense that His gracious Spirit can and is conveying to our characters both the peace of God in adversity and the patience of God in tough situations.

This is to know something of Christlike contentment. We are not bent on battling and battering our way through the thickets and obstacles of life. We stand strong and sturdy, serene in the quiet assurance that "All things can and do work out for good to those who love God, who are called to be His contented people amid a very complex and conflicting culture" (Rom. 8:28, paraphrased).

It is God who empowers us to face the fever of living with good cheer and gracious optimism. For He is with us both in our joys and in our extremities. So all is well. We can be at peace and we can also be patient. This is good news for all of us.

# 9
# Kindness—
# Love Showing
# Mercy

THOSE READERS FAMILIAR with the authorized version (King James translation) of the New Testament will wonder why kindness is here listed as the fifth fruit. I use the word kindness simply because it is employed by all the modern translations. The latter then use "gentleness" for the word "meekness" which is the eighth fruit. To avoid confusion the word kindness is used here in all of its simplicity and grandeur.

Of all the fruits of God's Gracious Spirit this is perhaps the one with which most of us are somewhat familiar. We have had this facet of love expressed to us in wondrous ways. In turn there have been times when in our own best moments we, too, have shown great kindness to others. This healing, compassionate, merciful virtue that ebbs and flows amongst us is sometimes called "the milk of human kindness."

Kindness is invariably associated with mercy. It is impossible to be kind without being merciful. Likewise to be merciful is to be kind. It implies that there is a deep and genuine concern for another. This concern is one of compassion and mercy. We are moved to be kind because we care. Caring is the essence of God's selfless love expressed to another.

Kindness is also bound up tightly with honesty and respect. It embraces the whole ideal of dealing with another person in deep integrity. Because I regard and respect others as individuals, regardless of their culture, creed, color or social standing, I treat them in a kindly manner. I endeavor to be helpful and understanding because of a genuine interest in them.

Surprisingly enough human beings are exceedingly sensitive in this area of personal relationships. They can detect in an instant if one is acting in either a patronizing or condescending way. True kindness is not tainted or tarnished with haughtiness. It is leveling with others in love, reaching out to help where it hurts.

## The Cost of Kindness

This facet of love is bound to cost a great deal. Kindness is more than running a bluff on beleaguered people. It is more than pretending to be concerned by their condition. True kindness goes beyond the play acting of simulated sighs and crocodile tears. It is getting involved with the personal sorrows and strains of other lives to the point where it may well cost me pain—real pain—and some serious inconvenience.

The truly kind person is one who does not flinch at the cost of extending kindness. He forgets his own personal preferences to proffer help and healing to another. At the price of inconvenience, labor, and personal privation he goes out quietly and without fanfare to bring pleasure to another. Sensitive to the sorrow and suffering of a struggling society, he undertakes to do what he can to alleviate this suffering. He tries to make the world a better and brighter place for those enmeshed in its pain and pathos.

This is the quality of kindness that characterizes God our Father. He *does* care. He *does* suffer for us. Our Heavenly Father does come to us in absolute honesty and openness. He lays down His life for us, and He expends Himself without hesitation to enrich us. He identifies Himself with us in our dilemma. Utterly merciful, totally compassionate, incredibly self-giving, He has our welfare and well-being ever in mind—always.

In his second letter to the church of Corinth Paul put it this way: "For ye know the grace of our Lord Jesus Christ, that though he was rich, yet for your sakes he became poor, that ye through his poverty might be rich" (2 Cor. 8:9).

## God's Great Kindness

Throughout the Scriptures the great theme of God's unrelenting kindness throbs like a powerful heartbeat. "His merciful kindness is great toward us . . ." (Ps. 117:2), is a refrain that never dies. It is repeated scores of times as a reminder that the mercy, compassion, and kindness of God flow to us freely, abundantly in refreshing rivers every day.

The kindness of God has drawn me to Him with bonds of love stronger than steel. The mercy of my Lord has endeared me to Him with enormous gratitude and thanksgiving. The generous compassion and intimate care of His Gracious Spirit are an enriching refreshment, new every day!

It is extremely difficult to convey on paper in human language, the incredible kindness of my Father, God. It seems to me that whoever attempts to do this always falls far short. This is a dimension of divine generosity that transcends our human capabilities to convey to one another. It can be experienced but it cannot be explained.

It is the kindness of God, expressed in Christ and revealed to us by His Spirit that supplies my salvation. His kindness makes provision for my pardon from sins and selfishness at the cost of His own laid down life. It is His kindness that forgives my faults and accepts me into His family as His dearly beloved child. His kindness enables me to stand acquitted of my wrongdoing, justified freely in His presence. God's kindness removes my guilt and I am at one with Him and others in peace. It is the kindness of God that enables Him to share Himself with me in the inner sanctuary of my spirit, soul, and body. His kindness enables me to be re-made, refashioned, re-formed gently into His likeness. His kindness gives enormous meaning and dignity to this life and endless delight in the life yet to come.

It is the constant, enduring, unchanging kindness of God that gives me every reason to rejoice and revel in life . . . all of life . . . this one and the next.

"Every good gift and every perfect gift is from above, and cometh down from the Father of lights, with whom is no variableness, neither shadow of turning" (James 1:17).

It is the kindness of God that enriches and energizes me not only spiritually but also morally and physically. I am surrounded on every side by the full-orbed environment of His overwhelming kindness. It comes flowing to me in a thousand forms from the fountainhead of His own love. All that I have and experience is an expression of His kindness.

And wonder of wonders—marvel of marvels—all of this in spite of my awkwardness, my waywardness, my stubbornness, my perverseness. Nothing so pulverizes my pride and humbles my hard heart before Him.

Strange as it may seem, many people do not wish to either acknowledge or receive the kindness of God. In their arrogance and supposed self-sufficiency they naively and foolishly assume they are self-made individuals. They proudly proclaim their personal independence. Afraid somehow that they might be brought under obligation to Him, they don't want to be the recipients of God's kindness. They don't want the Divine Gardener interfering in the ground of their lives. So He who has bestowed on them life itself is kept at bay, or so they suppose. Little do they realize how they impoverish both themselves and Him.

## A New Kind of Kindness

If, on the other hand, He is allowed to enter fully and freely into their experience some astonishing results will be produced. Perhaps the most pronounced will be the manner in which a new kind of kindness is generated.

I say this with great care, because kindness is not the exclusive fruit of Christian character. Some of the most moving kindness ever shown me came from total strangers, who, in some cases, were not Christians at all.

There is, however, one startling difference, and our Lord dealt with it in His majestic Sermon on the Mount in Matthew 5:43–18.

He points out that even pagans love those who love them, are courteous to those who can return the compliment, and extend kindness where kindness can be reciprocated.

But His advice to us is that our kindness should be of such a quality that we can even love our enemies, bless those that curse us, do good to those that hate us, pray for those who despise and persecute us. In so doing we demonstrate that we truly are His people.

Just as He bestows His good gifts on the godly and ungodly, and pours out His benefits on both believer and nonbeliever, He asks us to do likewise.

To live this way calls for courage. It means that some of those to whom we extend kindness will turn around and kick us in the teeth. It means that we will often be snubbed or scorned, and that our best intentions will sometimes be misunderstood and misconstrued.

When the good seed of God's own life germinates and takes root in the soil of our souls we give up our little games of playing tit-for-tat with others. No longer do we show love to get love back. No longer are we kind in order to be complimented and thought well of. We no longer give for what we can get. Those days are done—those tactics are terminated. Selfish self-satisfaction is no longer the mainspring of our actions.

### The Gracious Side of Kindness

When God by His Gracious Spirit begins to produce the fruit of kindness in the garden of my character its thrust comes from the gracious generosity of His own goodness. He is kind because He cannot be otherwise. It is His essential nature. And likewise that becomes an integral part of my new nature bestowed by Him. It becomes part and parcel of my conduct, my character and conversation to just simply be kind—not for what I can get out of it, but because of what I can do for another.

It is sheer folly to extend kindness to others expecting that those same people will reciprocate. Often they will not show any appreciation at all. So unless our kindness is of divine origin we will end up deluded and discouraged. Rather, we should leave the results entirely in God's hands. It will surprise us to find that love, affection, appreciation, and kindness are bound to be returned to us, but often from totally unexpected sources and frequently from strangers to whom we never showed kindness in the first place.

God makes very sure that the principle of sowing and reaping never falters. And on the basis of His commitments to us we may be perfectly certain that any act or deed of kindness we show in mercy and compassion to another, will eventually be returned to us in rich and abundant compensation. We harvest what is planted. And when seeds of kindness are sown prayerfully in the garden plot of our lives we may be sure there will be a bountiful harvest of blessings for both us and others. Life can become exceedingly rich in benefits this way.

## Kindness Embraces All of Life

Our kindness should be of such a caliber that it embraces all of life. It should enfold the pets in our care and the livestock on our farms. The shrubs, trees, grass, and flowers in our gardens—the forests, lakes, wildlife, and resources of the earth entrusted to our care—all should be treated with kindness. God in Christ by His Spirit is the Creator and supreme Conservationist. We are made in His likeness so we should do likewise.

Those who live with an active attitude of kindness, compassion, mercy, and concern for all of life are essentially persons of great inner light. There is a radiance and effulgence of enthusiasm and well-being about them. Warmth, affection, and good cheer emanate from them. It is the life and love of God apparent. This kindness dispels darkness, lifts loads, speaks peace, and inspires the downhearted.

Perhaps no other fruit of the Spirit has such far-reaching effects. It comes without display or ostentation, performing its sublime service almost in secret to slip away unseen. Yet its benefits remain to do their divine work in a weary old world.

I am ever reminded of the gentle and kindly David Livingstone. His tremendous foot safaris took him for thousands of miles through unmapped territory amongst strange and savage tribes. Yet wherever his footprints were left behind, there remained the legacy of the love of Christ expressed in his simple, humble kindness to the natives. Long after he was dead and gone to his "heavenly home," he was remembered in the dark continent as "the kind doctor." What greater accolade could any man earn?

## Counterfeit Kindness

Before considering just how such kindness is produced in our characters one point should be made clear here about counterfeit kindness. Kindness and mercy are not an insipid, soft, sentimental indulgence. Nor is it tolerance of wrongs and evil in others.

For example, it is not kindness for a parent to allow a child to do wrong deliberately. It costs something to correct the misbehavior, both for parent and child. To overlook the wrong, to brush it aside, to sweep it under the carpet is not kindness. It is a distinct disservice.

It costs something to care.

There is suffering involved.

It is the kind physician who lances the boil, drains off the poison, cleanses the wound, and so restores the patient.

It is the charlatan who simply spreads salve over the sore while the ulcer does its deadly work beneath the surface.

So kindness entails courage, integrity, and selflessness.

The rather remarkable thing about this sort of kindness is that God puts an enormous priority upon it in His Word. Throughout the Scriptures we are told again and again that He looks for and expects kindness to be a hallmark of His people. It is one fruit that simply must be flourishing in the garden of our lives.

How then is it cultivated?

How does one set about encouraging this crop to take root and grow vigorously?

First of all we simply must recognize its importance—to God, to others, to ourselves. Much of God's good work in the world is achieved through mercy and compassion.

## Kindness Is Caring

As His people we hold in our hands the happiness of others. The sense of self-worth, dignity, and personal esteem so essential to human well-being depends in large measure upon the kindness they receive from others.

We have it within our grasp to enrich the lives of our contemporaries by caring for them in a personal, meaningful, Christlike manner.

To do this takes time, lots of time. It cannot be done in a passing, flippant way. It is time-consuming (that is it uses up time we might otherwise spend on ourselves) to visit people, to make personal calls, to do little favors, to listen to the heart longings of others, to run errands for them, to help out with their work, to bear some of their burdens, to pray for them, to share their joys and sorrows, to write them letters, to give of our time and strength and means to them—to think of ways to brighten and cheer their lives.

Most of us are so terribly, terribly busy. It seems so often the ancient art of merely sitting quietly sharing an hour or two with another in gentle conversation has almost been lost.

Just last evening we invited an aged couple, ripe and mellow and sweet with long years of tough service for Christ, to share an evening with us in our little cottage. After a delicious dinner prepared with love and care by my wife we sat around a crackling fire of old fir knots that I had gathered from the hills in the afternoon.

The cheerful crackle of wood, the gentle warmth, the mellow mood of the room decorated with branches of scarlet sumac brought floods of peace and pleasure to the old people. In retrospect the elderly gentleman, his face aglow, reminisced about his boyhood on a Pennsylvania farm where he too used to go to the hills to gather pine knots for special festive occasions.

As the evening hours slipped away we shared books, pictures, art, and hearty laughs. Then my wife, who is only just learning the organ, offered to play for them. It set their spirits singing. To my amazement in a few minutes the elderly lady herself was seated at the instrument playing the organ for the first time in her life. This winter when we are away, our organ will be in their home to bring them hours of deep delight.

As they went out the door to go home, they were two people who for that evening had recaptured the joy of youth. Their eyes sparkled with gaiety and there was a lively vigor in their steps.

Kindness need not be anything grandiose or complicated. But it does take time and thought and love.

The second powerful, sure way to promote its production in our lives is to remind ourselves often of the great kindness of God to us.

It is my personal, unshakable conviction that when the Word of God instructs us clearly to spend time in communion with Christ, meditating upon His commands, it is primarily in connection with His mercy, compassion, and kindness to us. Anyone who reflects frequently on this will live and move in an atmosphere and attitude of humble gratitude to God. There will spring up constantly within the spirit a sublime sense of upwelling thanks and love for all the benefits bestowed by a loving Lord, the Gardener of his little life.

Under the compulsion and constraint of this love—this life of Christ poured into his own experience—he will go out gently to show kindness in a harassed and jaded old world.

Wherever he walks there will be left behind a legacy of love. For goodness and mercy will follow him all the days of his life.

# 10
# Goodness
# Grace and Generosity

GOODNESS MIGHT APPEAR to be the most obvious fruit of God's Gracious Spirit. It is, however, also one of the most maligned and misunderstood.

In the original Anglo-Saxon, the very word "good" carried the same connotation as "God." In fact, God was considered good. And good, in turn, was regarded as belonging essentially to God. It was just as valid to say "God is good" as it was to say "God is love."

Naturally from this it follows that "Love is good" in the same way that good is a facet of love being expressed. Goodness of this sort comes from God. He puts tremendous emphasis upon it. He extols it. When He was here amongst us it was reported in disarming simplicity that "He went about doing good."

The impact of that goodness moving with waves of irresistible impetus has swept across the centuries to encircle the globe, so that even today the goodness of Christ strikes us with enormous and far-reaching power. This goodness startles and astonishes us. It also stirs our sin-weary souls to their depths.

### The World's Attitude toward Goodness

Yet in direct antithesis to the goodness of God the world often deprecates goodness. If they wish to belittle or deride one who seeks to serve God they call him a "do-gooder." The term "goody-goody" is one of the most malicious and hurtful that children hurl at one another. In the jargon of the world goodness is something insipid, weak, laughable, and to be despised.

In fact when our Lord was amongst us, even His good was evil spoken of by His antagonists. This is simply because good and evil are mutually exclusive. The goodness of God and the evil of the enemy are irresistibly opposed. The unrelenting antagonism between the two is the explanation for the chaos and unending carnage that characterizes human history. May I remind the reader, whoever you may be, that ultimately the goodness of God will prevail over evil. Love will overcome despair. Light will dispel darkness. Life will supplant death.

If this does not happen in the daily experience of your life here and now, ultimately it is bound to take place in the purposes of a good and loving God. It is He who has come amongst us as the Savior, to make this possible.

> For God caused Christ, who himself knew nothing of sin, actually to be sin for our sakes, so that in Christ we might be made good with the goodness of God (2 Cor. 5:23, Phillips).

The cost of accomplishing this was so enormous that quite obviously goodness is a quality of God's character that most of us do not appreciate or value sufficiently. How often do we stand back in awe, overwhelmed, humbled, broken before Him because of His goodness? How often do we deliberately, determinedly, decisively beseech God to impart His goodness to us? How many of us really long above everything else to be made good with the goodness of God?

People will pray for love or joy, peace, patience, or kindness but seldom does one hear a heartrending cry coming from the depths of a sin-shattered, sin-stained, sin-sick soul—"O God, I just want to be made good!"

### The True Nature of Goodness

The goodness of God is not some soft, spineless, sentimental indulgence of sensuality. It is not some passing mood of the moment that makes one "feel so good." It is not an emotional "high" in which reality fades away into some rosy glow of mystical magic.

Goodness is the rugged reality of God Himself coming to grips with the awfulness of sin. Goodness is that invincible power of God's own person overcoming evil. The goodness of God is the greatness of His love that dispels our despair and brings His life out of our death. The goodness of God is His generosity and graciousness in giving us Himself by His own Gracious Spirit. It is the enormous energy of His light and life extinguishing the evil in and around me.

This goodness is the pulsing, powerful performance of right in the midst of wrong all around us.

The truly great person is also a good person. And the really good person is always great. He is an individual of lofty ideals, noble purposes, strong character, reliable conduct, and trustworthy integrity. This is a tall order indeed. Few can claim all these credentials. Yet they were the most apparent, most obvious attributes of our Lord Jesus Christ.

This is why He was either so dearly loved or intensely hated. It was the goodness of God in His life that drew the common people like an irresistible magnet. But by the same dimension of divine goodness the superficially pious frauds were repelled. His goodness polarized people like steel filings in an electromagnetic field. They were either for or against Him.

The same will be true for anyone who truly follows Him. The Spirit of God moving strongly and energetically in anyone's experience polarizes those around him. Either they will be attracted or repelled by the goodness of God evident in the life.

### God's Goodness and His Grace

This inherent goodness of God always moves hand in hand with the graciousness of God. In fact, we might say it is His grace which combined with His holiness (goodness, wholesomeness) makes it possible for us to be drawn to Him gently. His goodness is tempered by His grace. His goodness makes Him approachable.

It is the "good" Lord who is also so gracious to us. He draws near to us with infinite concern and compassion. Our Lord cares so deeply. He does not keep us at arm's length because of His unsullied goodness. Rather He comes running toward us, ready to throw His great, strong, warm arms of love around our sin-weary souls because of His gracious goodness.

He does not fawn upon us, nor does He flatter us. He does not indulge in flim-flam. He sees us in our sin and knows we are stained. Still he comes to grips with our sickened spirits.

As with the prodigal boy back from the pig-sty, there is a gold ring to go on the soil-stained hand; there is a white robe to clothe the sweat-stained body; there are fresh sandals for the dung-stained feet; there are kisses for the tear-stained cheeks.

Oh, the goodness of our God!

Oh, the graciousness of our Lord!

Oh, the generosity of our Christ!

These are the qualities of life exemplified by the goodness of God. They are what we mean when we say "God is good!"


## Goodness Costs!

It costs a great deal to be good!

The price at which it comes is very high.

A great part of that price is personal privation.

It takes a lot to be good and gracious and generous in a world where the mainstream of human thinking moves in the opposite direction.

Generosity that is so much a part of goodness is essentially a willingness to share what one has with another. This reaches out to embrace all of my life, not just my means. Generosity is much more than merely sending a handsome check to a charitable organization. It goes far beyond giving to others out of my surplus and my abundance.

When God, by His gracious Spirit, digs deeply in the soil of my soul He will implant there the new, divine impulse to be truly generous, truly self-giving.

This selfless self-sharing will entail more than just my money. He will put His finger upon my time, talents, interests, strength, energies, and capacities to enrich other lives. He will ask me to set aside my own selfish self-interest in order to give to others.

This is essentially what He did when He was here amongst us. There was never any desire for personal or private remuneration. All that He had and was, was poured out with open handed generosity to those whom He encountered. It was with enormous strength, dignity and self-control that He moved amongst men . . . crowds and mobs and multitudes of men and women. Yet ever and always He ministered to them either singly or collectively in goodness, graciousness, and generosity.

All that He had was theirs.

All He possessed was put at their disposal.

In genuine goodness He poured Himself out for people.

## The Effect of Goodness

When the Spirit of God enters our little lives, there to shed abroad His love of which goodness is such an important part, we become changed people. It is the presence of Christ in the garden who alters and re-makes its entire character. We do in truth find that under the impact of His life and activity we are re-created. Fresh fruit— good fruit—grows in the garden.

> Therefore if any man be in Christ,
> he is a new creature (creation):
> old things are passed away:
> behold, all things are become new.
> 2 Cor. 5:17

There are three reasons for this. The first is that the guilt of the past is gone. Cleansed and forgiven by the enormous outpouring of God's own life in Christ, the person so freed from his past is liberated into a new life of positive, powerful goodness.

There is no sense of being bogged down in the morass of one's own wrongdoing. We are no longer polluted by the weeds and worries of our former wretched behavior. The ground of our souls has been cleaned up, set free from the fears and forebodings of our former lifestyle.

The goodness which begins to emerge from the soil of our spirits is not our own but God's. We do not pretend to be pious. There is no longer any pretense or play acting. Instead simple, honest, sincere, genuine goodness becomes a supernatural outgrowth of the life of Christ within. Not forced or artificial, it is the simple expression of the gracious goodness of God's Spirit at work in me.

When this happens we discover that the second great attitude of graciousness toward others becomes apparent. We are not phony people perched up on little pedestals looking down with condescension upon our contemporaries. We are, rather, humble pilgrims on life's path, ready and eager to reach out to touch others struggling along life's tough trail beside us.

Any sense of pride or patronage toward others is gone. We know that but for the goodness of a loving God infinite in His grace toward us, we too might be down in the ditch of despair and degradation.

It is the good person, the gracious soul, the generous heart who helps the downtrodden. It is they who go out into a weary old world to bind up broken hearts, set the prisoners free, tend the sin-sick strangers, lift up the fallen, bring the oil of joy to those who mourn, spread light and cheer where darkness descends, feed the hungry, and share the good news of God's gracious love to the lost.

All of this can be done without show or ostentation. Goodness does not have to be publicized or paraded. It does not need a public relations program. Goodness is its own best advertisement.

The man or woman who expresses the genuine goodness of a gracious God has nothing to fear, nothing to hide, nothing to protect. There is no need to apologize for his or her performance. It comes flowering like a fresh fruit blossom out of the divine life within, finding its final perfection in rich and ripe maturity of character like Christ's.

This caliber of character spontaneously gives rise to the third notable aspect of a re-made life, namely its generosity. These are the people—simple, open, uncomplicated people—who live with open faces, open hearts, and open hands.

In great good will they gladly share whatever they may possess with others. Spontaneously, happily, and with a touch of hilarity they give and give and give. Whatever they may own is simply held in open hands as a trust from their Heavenly Father. It is not theirs to grasp and gloat over greedily. It comes directly as a gift from God to be given away to others in need.

Whatever we may own, whether in large or small measure, when placed gladly in God's great strong hands can be blessed and multiplied a thousand times to enrich countless other lives. If clutched tightly and timidly to our own selfish souls it will shrivel away to a mere whimsy, wasted on oneself.

### Genuine Goodness

It must be said here that the genuine goodness of God is totally distinct from the so-called "good works" done to gain merit.

The one springs directly from the in-dwelling Spirit of God. The other emerges from the selfish self-centeredness of one who seeks to be well spoken of by others. They are poles apart.

This latter self-righteousness is what our Lord deplored so vehemently amongst the haughty scribes, Sadducees and Pharisees. His most devastating denunciations were directed against the phony, pious pretense of these infamous "do-gooders." His most gracious and generous commendation was reserved for the despised Samaritan who showed true goodness to his neighbor.

How then does one become good with the goodness of God? Briefly, there are several simple measures that will produce this fruit.

1) Come to Calvary again. Spend time contemplating the cross. Read prayerfully the accounts of the crucifixion. Meditate quietly over the cost to God, in Christ, of our salvation. In the furnace of His affliction a titanic transaction took place. He was made sin that you and I might be made good with His own goodness. Accept His offer. Thank Him for it. Let Him bestow it on your broken heart. Allow Him to implant it in the stony soil of your soul. I have written of this at great length in my book *Rabboni*.

2) Cry out to Him to literally invade the territory of your little life. Ask Him to become the Good Gardener who will tend and care for your soul. Give Him liberty to love you, enfold you, cultivate you, and share His own life of gracious generosity with you. He will gladly pour Himself out upon you in tender loving care, so you in turn may do so to others.

3) As He lives in you and you in Him, keep the ground of your life clear, clean, and uncluttered. Confess quickly, in genuine sorrow, any sin or selfishness that might endanger His work within. Do not grieve His Gracious Spirit. Allow Him to have His way. Obey promptly, happily, simply, so that there will work out in your day-to-day conduct what he works in hour by hour. See Philippians 2:12–15.

4) Remind yourself *always* that you are the recipient, not the originator, of every gift, possession, and attribute you own. All come from Christ. Be deeply, genuinely grateful for His gracious generosity. In glad-hearted goodness go out to share His largess with a care-worn world. Let the impact of His goodness be passed on through you . . . to touch other seeking souls. *You will be surprised!*

# 11
# Faith and
# Faithfulness
# in Christians

ALONGSIDE OF LOVE itself, faith is the most frequently discussed facet of the Christian life. So much has been said and written about this subject that there is really nothing new or unusual that can be added here.

But it may surprise the reader to discover that faith, rather than being something distinct and apart from love, is in fact an integral part of it. Not only is faith bequeathed to the Christian believer as one of the fulsome fruits of God's own Gracious Spirit, but it is also bestowed as a special gift of God for the achievement of mighty exploits within the family of God (1 Cor. 12:9).

To fully understand faith that comes to us from Christ it is essential to remind ourselves once more that because it is a part of God's love, it is therefore a facet of selflessness. In other words, when faith is exercised in a person's conduct or behavior, selflessness is being demonstrated.

*Faith by its very nature implies that I can see good in another outside myself.*

This "good" may be either in God Himself, who as we discussed in the last chapter is goodness personified, or it may be in others around me.

This seeing, appreciating, and recognizing something of value and worth in another implies that I am reaching out of myself to touch the good in another. It means that I am no longer so self-centered or self-preoccupied that I see good only in myself as though I was the sole proprietor of good.

The simplicity of this concept may seem absurd to the reader. The subconscious response may well be, "Why of course there is bound to be some good in God and in others!" True enough. Why then are so many of us reluctant to respond to that good? Why do we hold back from giving ourselves to that good in glad freedom of spirit?

After all that is what faith is in action.

*Faith is my deliberate and positive response to the good in another to the extent that I will act on his behalf in a personal, powerful way.*

This activity on my part means that I am fully prepared to invest something of myself in another. It means that I am willing to share my life along with all its capacities (time, strength, attention, talents, means, energy, affection, acceptance) with another. It means that I actively, energetically give of my best to another outside of and apart from myself.

To speak of faith in any other way than this is to indulge in mere "believism." It is to play around with pious platitudes that pack no punch at all. This sort of superficial spirituality is actually the great bane of Christianity. Literally hundreds of thousands of people claim they trust in God; they claim to have faith in Christ; they claim to be believers, yet their lives and personal conduct are a denial and travesty of true faith.

The reason for this assertion is the obvious and devastating lack of genuine faith everywhere. When our Lord lived amongst us He was continually looking for this dynamic trust and response to Himself. Whenever He found even the tiniest fragment of faith being exercised in Him He was delighted. Over and over He remarked joyfully that here and there amongst the most unlikely individuals living, viable faith was active.

## The Source of Faith

This faith of God's Gracious Spirit can spring only from the fountain source of God's own generous love shed abroad in our lives.

Having its source in Him, it flows freely to us. It becomes active in our innermost being, then flows out in our self-giving back to Him and others.

This is what the author of the epistle to the Hebrews meant when He declared unequivocally in chapter 12:2, "(We look) unto Jesus the author and finisher of our faith."

This faith is the facet of God's love which finds me giving myself to others in faithfulness, fidelity, and unyielding loyalty. It expresses itself in a constant yet continuous investment of all that I am and own in both God and men. I believe in them to the point where I am prepared to pour my life into them.

Now if we want to see this caliber of conduct in bold relief, we do not look at men or women. We look at God Himself. The faith of God finds its fullest and most sublime expression in His faithfulness to us mortals.

Just as His love, kindness, patience, and goodness emanate from Him in an eternal, unending stream of benevolence to us, so His great faithfulness flows to us undiminished every day. It simply cannot be otherwise because of who He is.

The Word of God abounds with divine declarations about the faithfulness of God. Just as an example in Psalm 36:5–9 inspired by God's Spirit David, the great poet-singer of Israel, exults:

> Thy mercy, O Lord, is in the heavens;
> and thy faithfulness reacheth unto the clouds.
>
> Thy righteousness is like the great mountains;
> Thy judgments are a great deep: O Lord,
> thou preservest man and beast.
>
> How excellent is thy lovingkindness,
> O God! therefore the children of men
> put their trust under the shadow of thy wings.
>
> They shall be abundantly satisfied with
> the fatness of thy house;
>
> And thou shalt make them drink
> of the river of thy pleasures.
>
> For with thee is the fountain of life:
> in thy light shall we see light.

It is legitimate and appropriate to ask, how can God very God, He who is righteous and impeccable in character, deign to have faith in us feeble, frail human beings with all our foibles and follies? How can He who so transcends our tiny mortal lives with the greatness of His eternal goodness be faithful to us? Why does He even bother to bestow Himself and all His benefits upon us? How can He be so gracious, generous, and good to share Himself with unpredictable people who in turn are so often unfaithful—either to Him or one another?

These are indeed sobering and searching questions.

If we take them seriously and ponder them privately in the seclusion of our own spirits they will humble us.

There are two simple answers:

## The Nature of God Himself

The first and foremost is His own inherent righteousness, justice, integrity, and holiness. So wholesome, so good, so selfless is our God that He cannot be anything but faithful. He is that way because that is His very makeup.

If for no other reason, *He must inevitably be faithful (true) to Himself.* He is very truth, hence He cannot act except in utter good faith. This being so it explains why He comes to us in good will, with peace, eager and anxious to pour this same attribute of His own character into our little lives. He yearns to share this self-giving capacity with us selfish, self-centered people. With profound longing He waits to see this fruit of His own Spirit spring to life in us. He waits patiently to see it ripen and mature into active, living faith of obedience that is reciprocated back to Him and out to others.

The reason He is prepared to do all this is not what we may be initially ("There is none that doeth good, no, not one"—Ps. 14:3. "For all have sinned and come short of the glory [character] of God"—Rom. 3:23), *but what we may become. He sees within us the capacity to be conformed to His own character.* He who made us knows that under the impulse of His own Gracious Spirit, and the divine direction of His own living Word we can become His sons and daughters, adopted into His family, maturing into the very likeness of Christ.

This is not theoretical theology. It is not just divine doctrine. It does happen in human hearts and lives. We can be re-born. We can be re-created. We can be made into men and women, whose character, conduct, and conversation are like Christ's (see 2 Cor. 5:15–17).

And because all this is possible He finds joy in being faithful to us. He is confident of what He can achieve and accomplish working in the garden of our little lives. He can tear out the old brambles and briars; He can clear the ground of rocky unbelief; he can break up the hard-packed paths; He can open us up to receive the good seed of His own winsome Word.

This He does with unfailing good will and unending faithfulness. Initially God made man in love, chosen before ever planet earth was formed, to become His own dear children. And though humanity has been blighted and devastated by sin and evil, He alone knew that because of His faithfulness to His own creation, light could drive back the darkness; life could vanquish death; love could dispel despair; and faith (His faith) could displace our unfaithfulness.

All of this stirs my spirit to its depths. It enlivens my confidence in Christ and quickens the response of my soul to His overtures. It generates within the garden of my life a climate and condition conducive to genuine faith. I begin to see that because He is faithful to me, I in turn can be faithful to Him and others. Because He first loved me it is possible in turn for me to love (1 John 4:4–19).

The immediate result of such faith becoming evident is that God Himself is delighted. The Scriptures state unequivocally that without faith it is impossible to please God (Heb. 11:6).

When by the positive response of my whole person I actually determine to do what He asks of me: when in quiet, simple confidence I comply with His will and wishes: when gladly, freely I give myself and what I have to him: when I deliberately invest myself in His enterprises knowing that my life can be spent in no better way, God is delighted. He has found faith. He has a crop of trust, loyalty, and fidelity springing up in the field of my life that He has tilled and tended with such diligence and faithfulness. Are we surprised that He should be ecstatic?

## Faith's Impact on Others

The second great result of faith beginning to flourish in us is the impact it has upon our contemporaries. In spite of the unpredictable character and conduct of people we begin to look for the good in them. In spite of their fickle ways and foolish behavior we begin to believe in them. In spite of their human failures and foibles we start to see them as God our Father does. We look at them the way our Lord looks at them, and begin to see as the Spirit of God sees. His love is being shed abroad in our hearts, so now we can discover and discern the potential locked up in people. Our faith is not in their peculiarities but in their possibilities. With faith we believe and know and are assured that under God they can become great and noble.

Faith active in this way produces miracles in those around us. Such faith puts the best construction on every situation and looks for the silver edge on every dark cloud. It searches for any hint of honor and dignity. It believes that with God, all things are possible. It pushes on, perseveres, remains loyal in spite of reverses and disappointments. Such faith is steadfast in spite of shaking experiences and has its gaze fastened upon Him who is faithful, not upon the chaos and confusion of circumstances around us.

It is in the atmosphere of this confidence in Christ that the faithful person (a person full of faith) quietly carries on living in serenity, strength, and stability. He is not shaken by the stormy events or unpredictable behavior of others around him. Gently, calmly, without fanfare he simply gives and gives and gives himself to God and others. This he does in a hundred unobtrusive little ways wherein his life is poured out, laid out, on behalf of them because he really does "believe in them" and in what God can do.

In his classic essay on God's love, *The Greatest Thing in the World*, Henry Drummond deals with this concept in moving language:

"You will find, if you think for a moment, that the people who influence you are people who believe in you. In an atmosphere of suspicion men shrivel up; but in that atmosphere they expand, and find encouragement and educative fellowship. It is a wonderful thing that here and there in this hard, uncharitable world there should still be left a few rare souls who think no evil. This is the great unworldliness. Love 'thinketh no evil,' imputes no motive, sees the bright side, puts the best construction on every action. What a delightful state of mind to live in! What a stimulus and benediction even to meet with it for a day! To be trusted is to be saved. And if we try to influence or elevate others, we shall soon see that success is in proportion to their belief of our belief in them. For the respect of another is the first restoration of the self-respect a man has lost; our ideal of what he is becomes to him the hope and pattern of what he may become."

This faith moves mountains of inertia and perverseness in other people. It pulverizes prejudices and impossibilities. This faith is the fruit of God's Gracious Spirit that sweetens a sour world. It replaces suspicion and distrust with friendship and hope and good cheer. It makes our friends, family, and casual acquaintances stand tall. It turns the cynic and skeptic from cynicism to salvation.

Sad to say there simply is not much of this faith abroad in the world. In fact it is becoming a rather rare attribute. It matters not where we look for it—in the home, between families, in business, in the church, amongst nations or between individuals. The virtues of deep loyalty, mutual trust, fidelity, and consistent faithfulness, which are all part and parcel of faith in action, are rapidly diminishing in society. It is not the least surprising that our Lord asked the question: "When the Son of man cometh, shall he find faith on the earth?" (Luke 18:8).

Faith is or is not apparent and present to the same degree that selflessness is. It is really that simple. If people are preoccupied with only their own self-centered self-interests then love (the love of God) with its attendant attribute of faith simply does not function.

On the other hand, when faith is active it affects all of life. We see ourselves as stewards entrusted with time, talents, means, and concern to be used on behalf of God and our fellow men. We are entrusted with enormous responsibilities which can benefit and enrich the generation of which we are a part. We are required to be faithful stewards of all that has been put at our disposal for the uplift and encouragement of our contemporaries. It is our privilege and pleasure to give ourselves and share what we have with a world in deep distress. This is all an integral and practical part of living faith in action.

Faith of this caliber comes from God. If we lack it we must ask for it. He urges us to come boldly requesting good gifts from Him (Luke 11:9–13). He does bestow His Gracious Spirit on those who request His presence and are prepared to cooperate wholeheartedly with His commands (Acts 5:32). He will not withhold any good thing from those who seek His faith in sincerity. He is faithful!

As we see this faithfulness demonstrated to us daily in a thousand different ways by a loving Father it will increase and fortify our faith in Him. Likewise it will motivate us to go out and have faith in our fellow pilgrims on life's rocky roads. We will come alongside to help lift their loads, cheer their spirits, and inspire their souls.

Faith of this sort comes from a clear conscience. If our view of God in Christ is clear and uncluttered, our estimation of others is not dimmed or distorted. We see our responsibilities to both God and man clearly. Accordingly we act in good faith. Allowing nothing to come between us and others, we walk in the light as He is in the light, faithful always.

In every situation that arises we count on the vigilant, faithful presence of God Himself to guide and empower us in our decisions and demeanor. He who said, "Lo, I am with you always, even unto the end of the age," will be faithful to Himself, to His Word, and to us.

# 12
# Humility—
# Meekness
# and Gentleness

IN THE ROUGH and tumble of our abrasive twentieth century, humility is scarcely considered a virtue. Such qualities as meekness and gentleness are not the sort that most people seek in order to succeed. We are a fast-moving, masterful, permissive people who from the cradle (if there are still cradles) learn to shove and push and scream and scramble to get ahead—to plant our proud feet on the top of the totem pole.

Fiercely we contend for our rights, believing the strange philosophy that to be big and bold and brazen is best. We subscribe to the idea that since no one else will blow my horn for me, I must blow my own bugle loudly and long. We are completely convinced that unless we make our own mark in the world we will be forgotten in the crush—obliterated from memory by the milling masses around us.

From the hour we begin to take our first feeble, frightened steps as tiny tots we are exhorted to "stand on your own feet." We are urged and encouraged to "make it on your own." We are told to "make your own decisions." We are stimulated to be aggressive, self-assertive, and very self-assured. All of these attributes we are sure will lead to ultimate greatness.

In the face of all this it comes to us as a distinct shock to hear our Lord declare: "Whosoever therefore shall humble himself as this little child, the same is greatest in the kingdom of heaven" (Matt. 18:4).

Somehow in our society humility and greatness are thought to be mutually exclusive. Consequently many Christians are confronted on this point with the necessity of making some sort of mental, emotional or volitional adjustments. Where does truth lie here? Who has the secret of success? Does one adopt the view of contemporary culture or the rather unpalatable proposition of Jesus Christ who stated without hesitation, "Let him who would be greatest amongst you be your servant"?

First Corinthians 13:4, 5 states bluntly that charity (love) "vaunteth not itself, is not puffed up, doth not behave itself unseemly, seeketh not her own."

The selfless, self-effacing character of God's love simply does not permit it to strut and parade itself pompously. It will have no part of such a performance. It is not proud, arrogant, puffed up with its own importance.

## The Essence of Humility

This quality of life that produces genuine humility in the human spirit bestows upon us a truly balanced view of ourselves and others. We see the greatness and goodness in our God and in others around us. Likewise it enables us to see ourselves as we really are. We see our own relative insignificance in the great mass of mankind, yet we also see we are of great worth to Christ who has called us from darkness into the light of His own love. We see ourselves as sinners, yet at the same time those who have been saved from their despair to become the sons of God.

So it is the generosity of our God, the kindness of Christ, the patient perseverance of His Holy Spirit drawing us to Himself that humbles our haughty hearts. It is the depth of Christ's compassion which crumbles the tough crust that accumulates around our self-centered characters. The inflowing impartation of His own gentle, gracious Spirit displaces our own arrogance and self-preoccupation. It leaves us laden with His own fruits of lowliness and gentleness.

There is an old saying among orchardists that "The most heavily laden branches always bow the lowest on the tree." It is likewise true in human conduct.

## Meekness not Weakness

Meek men are not weak men. The meek are gracious, congenial individuals who are easy to get along with. These genial, good-natured souls win friends on every side because they refuse to shove, push, and throw their weight around. They do not win their wars with brutal battles and fierce fights. They win their way into a hundred hearts and homes with the passport of a lowly, loving spirit.

Their unique genius is their gentleness. This quality of life does not come from a position of feeble impotence, but rather from a tremendous inner strength and serenity. Only the strong, stable spirit can afford to be gentle. It is the sublime Spirit of the living God who bestows upon us the capacity to express genuine concern and compassion for others. His selfless self-giving enables us to treat others with courtesy and consideration. This quality is much more than a thin veneer of proper propriety or superficial politeness.

This caliber of humility, meekness, and gentleness comes at great cost. It is not a mere convenience that we use to accommodate our own selfish ends. Rather, it is the epitome of a laid-down life, poured out, laid out, lived out on behalf of others.

## The Meekness of God in Christ

If we are to see this humility, this condescension, this meekness at its best we must look at the life of our Lord. In a few short, stabbing, stunning verses it has been summed up for us in Philippians 2:1–11.

> Look not every man on his own things,
> but every man also on the things of others.
>
> Let this mind be in you,
> which was also in Christ Jesus:
>
> Who, being in the form of God,
> thought it not robbery to be equal with God:

but made himself of no reputation,
and took upon him the form of a servant,
and was made in the likeness of men:

and being found in fashion as a man,
he humbled himself,
and became obedient unto death,
even the death of the cross.

Wherefore God also hath highly exalted him,
and given him a name which is above every name.
(Phil. 2:4–9).

Such enormous condescension and self-giving stills our spirits in His presence. What lengths He went to become identified with us struggling mortals in the morass of our sins! O the depths to which He descended to deliver us from our dilemma of despair! What humiliation He undertook deliberately to rescue and redeem us from the enemy of our souls!

Yes, it costs a great deal to experience and know true humility. For most people its price is prohibitive. They simply will not pay it. There is a real "buyer's resistance" to the cost of gentleness and meekness amongst us.

We simply do not wish to become of "no reputation."

We want no part of playing "the suffering servant."

We refuse to become "doormats" on whom others wipe their feet without compunction.

We are not excited by involvement with the weak and woebegone.

We are not attracted by the "Man of Sorrows." There is nothing glamorous about this One. Like so many others we tend to despise and reject such submissiveness.

The consequence is that in the garden of our lives there springs up a mixed crop of fruit and weeds. On the one hand there are places where pride, self-assertion, arrogance, self-indulgence, and abrasive aggressiveness mark our behavior. These often tend to overwhelm the more gentle fruits of God's Gracious Spirit. They climb all over them, almost choking them out completely.

Unless we keep clearly in view the life and character of Christ we will succumb to the eternal temptation of living like our contemporaries—giving tit for tat, insisting on our rights, demanding our pound of flesh, stepping on anyone who trespasses against us, while all the time pushing for prominence and recognition. This is the world's way. Christ calls us to tread in His footsteps. He tells us to deny ourselves daily (give up our rights to ourselves). He asks us to take up our cross continuously (that which cuts diametrically across my selfish self-interest), crossing out the great "I" in my life to produce peace.

None of this is very appealing.

It goes against the grain of our old nature.

It is not a bit glamorous or romantic.

## The Benefits of Meekness

Yet its fruitage has three fantastic benefits which escape most people. Here they are:

1) Humility is the only seedbed from which faith can spring. The pompous, proud, self-assured soul sees no need for God or others in his/her life. Such people will "make it on their own," they believe naively. They have faith only in themselves. They end up disillusioned, self-centered, lonely, and mocked by their own self-pity.

In brokenness and contrition the humbled person cries out to God for help. He reaches out to Christ for restoration and healing. He exercises faith in another because he knows he must touch someone greater than himself. Similarly he seeks out others he can serve and in his suffering service finds fulfillment and freedom from himself.

2) It is to such souls that God gives Himself gladly, freely. He draws near to those who draw near to Him. He delights to dwell with those of a broken and contrite spirit. "The Lord is nigh unto them that are of a broken (humbled) heart; and saveth such as be of a contrite (meek) spirit" (Ps. 34:18).

The reason for this is so self-evident most of us almost miss it. God, who is selfless love, can only feel at home and be in harmony with the person who is likewise selfless. Here there can be no friction. All is at peace. All is well.

In vivid and shattering contrast we are warned explicitly that God actually resists the proud. He does not just tolerate or indulge arrogant souls. He actually opposes them actively. This is a terrifying truth that should make any self-centered, haughty individual tremble (see James 4:4–10).

How appalling to realize that in our pride we are being diametrically resisted by our selfless, self-giving God. This is inevitable because the two are mutually exclusive and eternally opposed to one another.

What a dreadful discovery to find that instead of going through life being helped by God, we are in fact struggling along "hindered" by Him. Are we surprised we don't succeed?

3) In contrast to this the third amazing reality about humility is the impact it makes upon our fellow men.

It is the genuinely humble, gentle soul who wins friends and draws around him a circle of loving associates. This quality of life draws others as surely as nectar in a blossom attracts bees.

The gentle, genial person is the recipient of affection. People bestow on him their blessings. He is lavished with love and surrounded with compassion. And wherever he goes hearts and homes are flung open with a warm welcome to his winsome presence.

The proud, arrogant, haughty person has few if any friends. He stands upon his little pedestal of pride in grim and gaunt loneliness. Others leave him alone. They ignore him deliberately. If he is so independent let him live his own life; let him go his own way; let him suffer the agony of his own selfishness.

## Humility Is an Everyday Affair

In my wallet I carry a faded, yellow newspaper clipping that has traveled around the world with me for nearly 30 years. It reads: "The old order may change, giving place to new, but there are a few fundamentals that remain with us as time goes by." A reader has sent me an excerpt from a book entitled *Quite a Gentleman,* written 100 years ago.

It stated, "Here's a list of little marks by which we may single out a gentleman from the common crowd: He is particular about trifles, answers his letters promptly, is quick to acknowledge a kindness, thankful for small mercies, never forgets to pay a debt nor to offer an apology that is due. He is punctual, neat, doing everything he undertakes as thoroughly and as heartily as possible."

The reader may well ask, "What has punctuality got to do with being a gentleman?" or "What has answering letters promptly got to do with love and the fruit of God's Spirit called gentleness?"

Let me explain. When all is said and done the fruits of God's Gracious Spirit must find expression in the simple, down-to-earth conduct of our everyday lives. They are not just theory or theology.

The person who is invariably late is demonstrating by his action that he does not care if he inconveniences another. He is saying not in words but in his behavior, "My time is more important than yours! You can wait! Your time can be wasted. It is of no consequence!" Here we see selfish, self-centered pride and arrogance actually being acted out toward another in brazen behavior. This is the antithesis of the love of God.

The person who is irresponsible about replying to letters is equally selfish. The common excuses are a dead giveaway. "I didn't have time. I was too busy. I just didn't get around to it." Note the prominence of I in the picture. In so many words these people are saying, "It doesn't matter to me how long you have to wait. I don't care if you are worried and wonder what is happening. I'm so busy taking care of myself there really is no time to spare for you. I don't really feel responsible for your peace of mind."

Too many of us have the idea that somehow the fruits of God's Spirit are some mystical, magical, superspiritual effulgence that flows into our emotions and minds moving us to be superspiritual people. This is not so.

The fruits of God's Spirit are sown in the soil of my soul and spirit by His Spirit. And what He works in, I must then proceed to work out. What God impresses upon me as being proper and appropriate I have an obligation to carry out. We are not plaster-cast saints.

As people who deliberately decide and determine to do God's will, we set ourselves to comply with His wishes. We set our wills to seek His face—to serve others and to deny ourselves. There is a cost to consider—a price to pay. There is a death to self to endure daily.

If we need stimulation and inspiration to so live a laid-down life we need look in but one direction to find it—to Him who loved us and gave Himself for us.

> Hereby perceive we the love of God, because he laid down his life for us: and we ought to lay down our lives for the brethren (1 John 3:16).

It is a straightforward case of cause and effect, not some complicated formula or technique. In fact, not until the impact of the laid-down life of Christ comes crashing through the crust around our hard, self-centered hearts will humility ever displace our despicable self-preoccupation. Then and only then will the expulsive power of humility's presence displace our selfishness enabling us to go out into a broken, shattered, bleeding, wounded world as suffering servants.

The humility of Christ, the meekness of His Gracious Spirit, the gentleness of our God can only be known, seen, felt, and experienced by a tough world in the lives of God's people. If the society of our twentieth century finds God at all they will have to find Him at work in the garden of His children's lives. It is there His fruits should flourish and abound. It is there they should be readily found.

As we contemplate and meditate over the gracious generosity of God in Christ, humbling Himself on our behalf, it should warm our cold hearts and flood them with the warmth of His love. Out of an enormous, overflowing, spontaneous sense of thanks and gratitude we should be able to go out and live before others in humility and gentleness, serving them in sincerity and genuine simplicity. As the Father sent the Son into the world, so He in turn sends us out to serve a sick society.

This we can do without pomp or pretext. This we can do walking humbly, quietly, gently with our God. It may astound and amaze a skeptical society. After all, it isn't the norm. It won't win applause or accolades. But it may very well win some for the Savior.

This is no soft life to live. But it is the restful way. It is the peaceful way. It is the best way. It is His way!

> Come unto me, all ye that labour
> and are heavy laden, and I will
> give you rest.
>
> Take my yoke upon you, and learn of me;
> for I am meek and lowly in heart:
> and ye shall find rest unto your souls.
>
> For my yoke is easy, and my burden is light
> (Matt. 11:28–30).

# 13
# Self-Control
# (Control of Self):
# Temperance—Moderation

SELF-CONTROL, TEMPERANCE, moderation, self-restraint are all terms used to define the last of the nine fruits of the Spirit listed in Galatians 5:22, 23. To put it in the terminology of 1 Corinthians 13:1–7 the phrases, "Doth not behave itself unseemly," or "Does not act in an inappropriate or unbecoming manner," are used.

This sounds so simple and somewhat dignified, but it is so very, very difficult to do in actual life.

Self-control may be the last facet of God's love in the list, but that certainly does not reduce it to the least important.

No doubt it is true and fair to say that it is one aspect of Christian conduct and character and conversation with which most of us have the greatest difficulty. Of all the fruits which should flourish in the garden of our lives this may well be the one which is the most "spotty," "uneven," and "irregular."

In some situations we behave in a most exemplary and commendable manner. At other times we behave worse than beasts. There are days when we seem to act in decent and dignified ways. On other occasions we can become erupting volcanoes of venom and violent vituperation. If we are earnestly honest with ourselves we discover that there is too often, as James puts it so forcefully, both sweet and saline water springing up from the same inner fountain. Or to use our Lord's metaphor, the ground of our personalities produces both grapes and wild brambles, figs and thistles.

Consistency and credibility are so often not apparent. As the prophet of old put it in such poignant poetry, the good husbandman came to his garden looking for sweet fruit and found instead only wild, sour grapes:

> Now will I sing to my well-beloved a song of my beloved touching his vineyard. My well-beloved hath a vineyard in a very fruitful hill: and he fenced it, and gathered out the stones thereof, and planted it with the choicest vine, and built a tower in the midst of it, and also made a winepress therein: and he looked that it should bring forth grapes, and it brought forth wild grapes (Isa. 5:1, 2).

Such fruit sets one's teeth on edge.

Stating it in rather simple layman's language we would say that instead of being people who do God's will, who speak His words and work His works in the world, we frequently find ourselves outside His control, living out our own strong-willed, wayward ways.

## The Character of Self-Control

What, then, do the Scriptures mean when they speak of self-control? What is true temperance? What is the meaning of genuine moderation in a man's life? Is it possible of production? Can it be cultivated? Or is this one of those fickle fantasies that eludes us in our everyday experiences where we encounter a thousand temptations to cast off all restraint and live life to the hilt?

Before answering these questions one thing must be made clear. This so-called "self-control" is not the worldling's concept of being a stoic. It is not being a stern spartan. The picture here is not the grim, rigid idea of setting the jaw, steeling the will to endure life with cold cynicism. It is not a case of "grin and bear it." Self-control for God's person does not imply that with severe self-discipline I can control my conduct.

No, no, no! The answer does not lie there.

Self-control for the Christian means that my "self," my whole person, my whole being, body, soul, spirit comes under the control of Christ. It means that I am an individual governed by God. My entire life, every aspect of it—whether spiritual, moral or physical—has become subject to the sovereignty of God's Spirit. I am a "man under authority." The running of my affairs, my attitudes, my actions is a right which has been relinquished and turned over to God's Gracious Spirit.

To use the word picture of a garden, the "Good Gardener" has come through the gate. The ground of my entire being is His to do with as He wishes. It is His privilege to produce what He wills in the way He desires without hindrance. He it is who alone has the right to control the crop production. It is He who decides what shall be done in every area of this garden.

## Christ—One in Control

If we wish to see this kind of control at its best we do not look at other human beings. Even the choicest Christians are sometimes speckled birds. The best of men have feet of clay. The sweetest saints can sometimes turn sour.

Instead we look at God Himself. We see Him best in Christ. When He was here amongst us He stated unflinchingly, "He that hath seen me hath seen the Father" (John 14:9).

It was this One who repeatedly asserted that He was completely under divine control. He came, not to do His own will, but His Father's. The words He spoke were not His, but the Father's. The works He carried out were God's own enterprises. Because of this "inner control" He in return was in control of every situation He faced.

Wherever Christ moved, whomever He met, whatever circumstances He encountered, the remarkable aspect of His life was that He was always in control. He was never taken unawares, never caught in a crisis. Jesus was never manipulated, nor was He ever at the mercy of the mob. Even during those desperate, diabolical last hours from the time of His betrayal until His battered body hung on a cruel Roman cross, He moved in quiet strength, enormous dignity, and majestic might. Before the Pharisees, the Sadduccees, the scribes, even Judas His betrayer, the high priests, the Sanhedrin, cunning King Herod, the political opportunist Pilate, the brutal Roman soldiers, the blood-thirsty mobs of Jerusalem, Jesus of Nazareth, the Christ of God, was supremely in control.

And this was because He was God-controlled.

I have written at great length on this theme in *Rabboni*. It will not be elaborated here.

But it must be said with great emphasis that if some of us wonder why our lives are such a tangle; if we wonder why we seem to live in an inner jungle; if the soil of our souls seems to be buried beneath a bramblelike growth of unchecked, uncontrolled wild vines, it is because we have not allowed ourselves to be brought under the control of the Good Gardener.

We simply don't want Him interfering in the grounds of our lives. We prefer to go our own way, to carve out our own careers, to do our own thing, to grow our own sour grapes, to live lost in the briars and brambles of self-determination. In our stupidity we seem to think we can control our own destiny only to discover that our lives are *unmitigated disasters*.

Yet I would pause here momentarily to remind the reader that despite our willful waywardness God does not write us off as a total loss. He does not dismiss us in disgust, nor does He deal with us in a diatribe against our sins. He does not reward us with abuse and malignancy according to our iniquities. Read Psalm 103.

If He did, where would I be?

Rather He comes to me in His own gracious, generous, gentle self-control, offering to move quietly into the turmoil of my soul and there take control. He longs to be given the chance to govern me as God, very God. He is eager to bring order out of the inner chaos of my character. He, the Christ of God, comes to me willing to become my Lord, my Master, my King, who alone can adequately control the untamed territory of my life. He, the Gracious Spirit of the Living God, will gladly enter the ground of my being to there exercise His own superb sovereignty in such a way that His purposes for me as His person are realized.

In all of this there is tremendous hope.

The control of my self is more than mere wishful thinking. It can happen. It can become increasingly the norm for life.

## Controlled by Christ

My whole spirit, its intuition, conscience, and communion with Christ can come steadily under the control of God's own Gracious Spirit. My total personality—mind, emotions and will—can be at Christ's command. My entire body—its appetites, drives, desires, and instincts—can be governed by God. It is possible to live a godly life of moderation and temperance in testing times.

But there is a price to pay.

Inner peace and outer strength come at high cost. Righteousness, rightness in our relationships to God, others, and ourselves is not a "run of the mill" product. It doesn't just come about by happenstance. The manner in which a man is changed from the old, erratic life of wild and untamed behavior to one of stability and serenity is pretty severe.

It means giving up my rights. It goes beyond daydreaming about being a delightful sort of soul. It gets down to the grass roots where I relinquish my self-rule and turn myself over irrevocably to God.

In a book of this sort it is not intended to go into all the ramifications of what such a total relinquishment might entail. Each of us soon discovers those areas in which we have not turned over the territory to God for His absolute control.

But at least I will deal briefly with the soul: i.e. my mind, emotions, will (disposition).

Our minds and imaginations can be monsters. We can allow them to literally monopolize our entire outlook on life. Our thought patterns can become so set against that which is good that even God Himself does not enter our thought life. He is excluded from the reasoning we do or the vain and sometimes vicious imaginations we indulge in. Pride and self-preoccupation are the pompous rulers of our minds. All our days and even some of our dreams are devoted to selfish aims and ambitions. God's Gracious Spirit really has no input into our thinking.

Yet the Word of God makes it clear that our thoughts, minds, and imaginations should and must all be transformed and renewed (Rom. 12:1–3). We are not capable of self-improvement in this way. It is a case of deliberately turning over this terrain in the garden of our lives to God. He is the one who will come in to effect the change. He can alter the direction of our minds.

## A Prayer of Submission

It is proper and appropriate to request verbally and audibly, "O Christ, here I am with my tumultuous thoughts and rampant imagination. I turn them over to You. Take them under Your control. Invade this territory of my being. Lay claim to this chunk of grievous ground. I give it to You for Your government. Manage it. Think Your thoughts through me. Concentrate my interest in Yourself. Center my attention on that which is beautiful, true, worthwhile, and noble! Remake me as you desire!"

This is not a simple, easy petition to make in earnest.

The monster of my mind may well contest such a request.

But if in total, genuine, sincere relinquishment this is done the results are bound to be beautiful. Christ will take control.

It must be said here unequivocally that any area of my being deliberately, sincerely and wholeheartedly turned over to the control of Christ, He will take. This does not mean there will always be sudden and dramatic changes. But it does guarantee that gradually there will be a gentle growth in godliness. The growing of fruit and flowers does not happen in a day. The process is a slow but steady unfolding of the blossom, the formation of the fruit, and at last its beautiful ripening. Luscious purple grapes are not produced in one week nor does a gracious mind mature in a moment.

In the realm of our emotions the need for the Spirit's control is absolutely imperative. Apart from His Gracious Presence our inner feelings can be terrible tyrants. Because of the never-ending ebb and flow of our interrelationship with other human beings the tensions produced by unpredictable people make life a complex maze.

In very truth we simply never know what new and difficult dilemmas a day may bring. We find ourselves interacting with strange people and new circumstances. Our actions and reactions too often are governed not by God but by our own selfish self-interest. We may be entertaining all sorts of abhorrent inner attitudes to protect our pride, position or property. These may or may not find expression in hostility, anger, criticism, bitterness, jealousy, hatred or a score of other more subtle feelings and emotions.

As God's people this sort of performance is not acceptable. In Galatians 5, and even more clearly in Romans 8, we are warned and alerted to the formidable fact that such behavior is in truth the wild, bitter fruit of our old self-life. These are called "the works of the flesh" (Gal. 5:19–21). They are the exact antithesis of the fruits of God's Spirit.

Those who produce such attitudes quite obviously are not under the control of Christ. They are not being governed by God, nor are they subject to the sovereignty, the direction, the leading of His Spirit.

*As Christians we do not live under the tyranny of our temperaments. We live by faith in Christ's capacity to control our tempestuous emotions.*

Just as with our minds, so with our feelings. These must be put at God's disposal definitely and deliberately. A prayer as earnest as that made for the mind is appropriate here:

"O Gracious God, life is too complex, too full of tensions and turmoil for me to cope alone. I so easily lose control of myself. My emotions are prone to such perversion. Like a wild, unchecked growth they soon smother out the good growth of Your planting. Move in mightily and take over my whole temperament. Tame my inner turmoil. Water me with Your presence. Let me know You are here. Do that within me which I cannot do myself. Empower me to love and live and lay down my 'self' as You did when You were walking the dusty trails of this tired old world. May my feelings become a garden of refreshment for Yourself and those who meet me."

### The Christ-Controlled Will

Then there is the realm of my will. This is the central citadel of my disposition. It is where the deep, permanent decisions of my volition are decided. I have written at great length about the will in my book, *A Shepherd Looks at Psalm 23*.

Suffice it to say here that my will is the key area which Christ must come to control if I am to be of any consequence in His economy. It is utterly absurd to assume or suppose that a person who is determined to do his own will can ever please God. Only as our wills are brought into harmony and submission to His will do we discover the secret of divine power and productivity.

One short, stabbing, self-sacrificing sentence sums up this whole subject: "O God, not my will, but Thine be done." There is no more potent prayer.

The person who says this, means it, and has decided he will do God's will, whatever the cost, is delighted to discover: "It is God who worketh in (me) both to will and to do of his good pleasure" (Phil. 2:13). Such a person moves and lives and has his being in Christ.

He knows and experiences genuine self-control. This is the person in whom God's love is shown in magnificent and magnanimous moderation.

What has here been discussed in some detail with respect to the soul, can be applied equally to the realm of our spirits as well as all areas of our bodily life. This the reader, if earnest about his relationship to God and others, can do for himself.

It is a matter of taking a long, hard look at the garden of my life. What is it producing? What kind of crops are coming from it? Is the Master satisfied? Is He getting what He hoped to produce? Have His efforts been in vain or is there a bountiful yield? The yield of eternal fruitage is directly proportional to the degree in which my life is yielded to Him. The more I am available and open the more active He becomes in any given area of my life.

John the Baptist, speaking about his relationship to Christ, put it pungently when he declared boldly: "He (Christ) must increase, but I must decrease" (John 3:30). If we wish to see an increase in the fruits of God's own Spirit in our lives then it can come about only in this way. There is no other formula for fruitage. It is He and only He by His increasing presence within who can guarantee good production in generous proportion.

Lest the reader be discouraged, let it be said here again that fruit production in our Christian experience, just as in an orchard or garden, is not something that goes on with great fanfare, noise or theatrics. From the opening of the first tiny bud under the impulse of spring sunshine, to the perfect ripening of the fully formed fruit beneath late Indian summer skies in fall, the whole process goes on quietly, serenely, and surely. It is the Spirit of God who by His presence within guarantees growth, maturity, and conformity to Christ.

So gently, so gradually does this divine work of the Good Gardener proceed that often we ourselves are unaware of the changes occurring in our characters, our conversation or our conduct. But others around us are aware. They will notice the transformation taking place, and they will be aware of the ripening fruits of the Spirit in our lives. And by this they will know this garden is coming under Christ's control.

This is the ultimate, acid test of one's claim to be a Christian.

*We who were once wilderness can become the garden of God!*

> My life is a garden.
> Your life is a garden.
>
> Is it a waste, untilled and wild?
> Like an untaught, untrained child?
>
> Or is it good soil under the Master's hand?
> Is my soul His own cherished land?
>
> Is it grown thick with thistles and weed?
> Or has it been sown with His good seed?
>
> What is the harvest that comes from this life?
> Goodness and love, or hatred and strife?
>
> O Lord, take this stony ground of mine.
> Make it all, completely Thine!
>
> Only then can it ever yield,
> The pleasant fruits of a godly field.
>                              Amen and Amen.

*On that day the Lord will say of his pleasant vineyard, "I watch over it and water it continually. I guard it night and day so that no one will harm it . . ."*
                              Isaiah 27:2, 3, *Good News Bible*